I0820340

JFK Was Killed by Consensus

Dealey Plaza Was Just the Final Stop

David W. Mantik, MD, PhD

JFK Was Killed by Consensus: Dealey Plaza Was Just The Final Stop

Published by:
Trine Day LLC
PO Box 577
Walterville, OR 97489
1-800-556-2012
www.TrineDay.com
trineday@icloud.com

Library of Congress Control Number: 2025930612

Mantik, David W., JFK Was Killed by Consensus —1st ed.
p. cm.

Epub (ISBN-13) 978-1-63424-508-1
Trade Paper (ISBN-13) 978-1-63424-507-4

1. Kennedy, John F. (John Fitzgerald), 1917-1963. Assassination. 2. Conspiracies History. United States. 3. Oswald, Lee Harvey . 4. Johnson, Lyndon B. 1908-1973. 5. United States History 1961-1969 . I. Mantik, David W. II. Title.

First Edition
10 9 8 7 6 5 4 3 2 1

Mantik's website may be accessed by entering themantikview (https://themantikview.org).

Distribution to the Trade by:
Independent Publishers Group (IPG)
814 North Franklin Street
Chicago, Illinois 60610
312.337.0747
www.ipgbook.com

Publisher's Foreword

Immediately I could see on my clothes, my clothing, I could see on the interior of the car which, as I recall, was a pale blue, brain tissue, which I immediately recognized, and I recall very well, on my trousers there was one chunk of brain tissue as big as almost my thumb, thumbnail, and again I did not see the President at any time either after the first, second, or third shots, but I assumed always that it was HE who was hit and no one else.

I immediately, when I was hit, I said, "Oh, no, no, no." And then I said, "My God, they are going to kill us all." Nellie, when she pulled me over into her lap–

–John B. Connally, Warren Commission Testimony

"Beyond any question, and I'll never change my opinion, the first bullet did not hit me. The second bullet did hit me. The third bullet did not hit me."

–John B. Connally

I will fight anybody that argues with me about those three shots, I do know what happened in that car. Fight me if you want to. ... With John in my arms and still trying to stay down ... I felt something falling all over me.... My eyes saw bloody matter in tiny bits all over the car. Mrs. Kennedy was saying, "Jack! Jack! They have killed my husband! I have his brains in my hand."

– Nellie Connally, *Newsweek*

How many more years will we "debate" who killed John Fitzgerald Kennedy ... and why the deed was done? This particular "who and why" continues to haunt us, delineating many generational zeitgeists, conflicts, and musings of how the world *really* works.

The "lone nut" thesis paraded about, by friend and foe alike, has very pragmatic outcomes: controlling the narrative, minimizing the impact of treasonous actions, and covering up the work of the "guilty" parties.

Where are we after all these years of investigations (independent and governmental), conferences, books, movies, TV shows, electronic forums and social media posts? We have recently had another "data dump" of JFK assassination documents by the federal government. Nothing has happened (so far). There have been no official public pronouncement of who was responsible or of *why*. Leaving us a lingering, festering malaise of conspiratorial sludge filled with both intentional and non-intentional mis and disinformation astrew a semblance of reality.

David W. Mantik, M.D. (who first earned a PhD in physics), brings a scientific sensibility and trained eye to the rigors of historical research. He has lent his expertise to the study of the forensic evidence to great acclaim showing the falsity and sheer arrogance of official government exhibits in his earlier books: *JFK Assassination Paradoxes: Essays And Reviews & JFK's Head Wounds* (2022), *The JFK Assassination Decoded: Criminal Forgery in the Autopsy Photographs and X-rays* (2023), and *The Assassination of John F. Kennedy – The Final Analysis: Forensic Analysis of the JFK Autopsy X-Rays Proves Two Headshots from the Right Front and One from the Rear* (2024) with Jerome Corsi.

With this new book, *JFK Was Killed by Consensus: Dealey Plaza Was Just The Final Stop,* Dr. Mantik has taken on those "who and why" questions with vigor, tenacity and insightful observations. His wry humor and playful prose give the book a personal touch all while delving into very serious matters. With interesting discourses and intriguing sojourns, Dr. Mantik explores and elucidates a coherent exposition beyond simply naming the standard suspects – towards a unified understanding of the crime.

Personally, I enjoy his peeling away the layers of LBJ's foreknowledge (a subject some have sadly dissuaded), and his focus on Major General Ed G. Lansdale, whom I (and others) have posited was the "scriptwriter" for the assassination. Lansdale served with my father during WWII in G2 and then the CIA. Recalling a meeting with Lansdale in 1956 in Vietnam, my mother said, "That's when I stopped *believing* what I read in the newspapers."

TrineDay is honored, privileged and proud to present Dr. Mantik's succinct and groundbreaking exposé of the murder of our 35th president of the United States, an atrocity that has infected our body politic with fear, doubt, trepidation and hopelessness.

The actions of a few affect the many…

Onward to the Utmost of Futures!
Peace,
RA "Kris" Millegan
Publisher
TrineDay
May 31, 2025

Dedication

Meredith M. Mantik

My daughter has been an All-Star soccer player, visual artist, guitarist, vocalist, and pianist – most of these before she became the fourth Phi Beta Kappa scholar in our family. She is now a Hollywood film editor for feature fiction films (e.g., *The Burial*). At the UK's premier film school (NFTS), she won the award for Best Film Editor, and (as sole editor) her student film, *Sweet Maddie Stone,*[1] won the 37th London Film Critics' Circle Award. See sweet maddie stone – Search[2] *and* Meredith Mantik.[3]

Meredith is a graduate of Colorado College, where Sue Woolsey was then the Chair of the Board of Trustees. Concurrently, her husband was James Woolsey, then CIA director under President Bill Clinton. But Bill met less frequently with Jim than he did with Monica (whose father requested that I care for his oncology patients while he assisted Monica during her stressful days in DC).

Meredith's current documentary, *Conspiracyland,* is due for release this year (2025). It is a result of dozens of interviews with JFK researchers around the country. She has also filmed at numerous JFK meetings, especially in Pittsburgh and Dallas, always accompanied by her professional support team. This team has even included her own Colorado College film professor, who joined the team not only because of its focus, but

1 Maddie is not related to either Oliver or Roger or Sharon – nor does she have any known relationship to the Rosetta Stone.

2 https://www.bing.com/search?pglt=427&q=sweet+maddie+-stone&cvid=1a18a925f188451d9a7893dfe34d7843&gs_lcrp=EgRlZGdlKgYIABBFGDky-BggAEEUYOTIGCAEQABhA0gEIOTY0NmowajGoAgCwAgA&FORM=ANNTA1&PC=U531.

3 https://nfts.co.uk/people/meredith-mantik.

also because he highly respects Meredith's film skills. She has taught film courses at her alma mater and has created a documentary about the college for new applicants.

She also has a lengthy video interview with Major Ralph P. Ganis, the author of *The Skorzeny Papers: Evidence for the Plot to Kill JFK* (2018). Because I observed the entire interview, I know that Ralph's comments will be an enlightening supplement to this website: The Skorzeny Connection – The New JFK Show Blog.[4]

Although she was not a radiologist at the tender age of 5, she quickly spotted the (bogus) 6.5 mm, nearly circular, cross section on JFK's AP skull X-ray. (See the image below to appreciate what Meredith had spotted.) This is the same object that was *not seen* – or reported – at the autopsy. Furthermore, the pathologists denied seeing this same object during their subsequent review – shortly before the Clark Panel publicly reported it in 1968. It is still there on the X-ray at the Archives today. So, the pathologists cannot (even sympathetically) be viewed as merely incompetent – they had actually lied. There is a difference. Of course, they had also substituted a stranger's brain for JFK's brain.[5] That requires yet another level of incompetence!

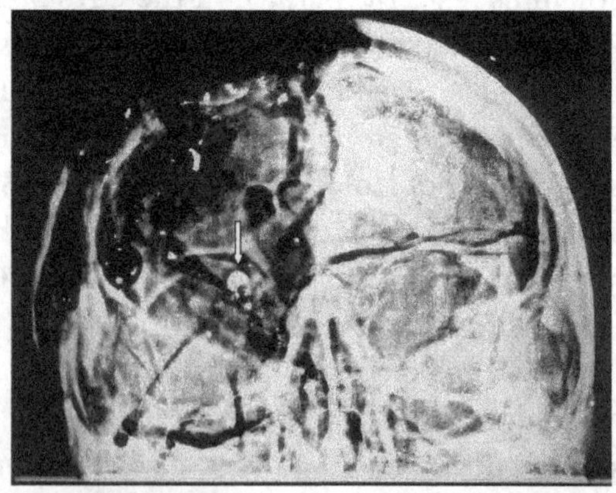

As I leave the JFK scene, Meredith becomes the link between my generation and hers. When the time comes for my eternal rest, I shall quietly depart knowing that the future is in secure hands. Her website is here: About – MEREDITH MANTIK.[6]

4 https://merdist.com/wp/2022/05/08/the-skorzeny-connection/.

5 Based on timelines and brands of film, Douglas Horne first reported this substitution publicly while working for the ARRB. But my myriads of optical density measurements (taken even before that) provide firm quantitative grounds for this unavoidable conclusion.

6 https://www.meredithmantik.com/about/.

Preface

In 1998 (the final year of the Assassination Records Review Board (ARRB)), my daughter was in the fifth grade. I was exercising my parental prerogative by visiting her classroom for a few hours. After a short interlude of routine education, her friend (and frequent playmate) summarized her recent reading for the entire class. To my amazement, with the blessing of the teacher, she enlightened everyone about Lee Oswald – he was the lone assassin! I was stunned. After all, during the preceding several years I had spent eight full days at the National Archives examining all of the JFK artifacts. And we had just published our first book (*Assassination Science*) that same year (1998), which showed indisputable proof that the autopsy photographs and radiographs had been altered. Until that moment, it had not occurred to me that Oswald had the skill to (remotely) manipulate these items while in a Dallas jail cell.

Ironically, Meredith's playmate lived right next door to Frank Sinatra's house, to which I had often escorted her for playdates. Frank's neighbors included Jack Benny, Danny Kaye, and all four Marx brothers. In fact, Barbara (Frank's fourth wife) was still Mrs. Zeppo Marx when she met Sinatra.

Of course Frank was no longer at that house in 1998; because of his increasing senility, he and Barbara had moved to Beverly Hills some years before. Nonetheless, Frank had died that same year (May 14, 1998) of a massive heart attack while at the Cedars Sinai Medical Center.

In 1962, expecting to host JFK, for whom Frank had campaigned vigorously,[7] Sinatra added a four-bedroom, four-bath guesthouse with a private pool and helipad adjacent to the 17th fairway of the mostly Jewish Tamarisk Country Club. But that visit was aborted. RFK quashed it due to Sinatra's alleged mob ties.[8] Citing security issues, JFK instead stayed at Bing Crosby's desert home. Sinatra was deeply wounded. Peter Lawford was later quoted – Sinatra had taken a sledgehammer to the concrete he-

7 In 1960, Frank Sinatra changed the lyrics to his song "High Hopes" to support JFK's presidential campaign. http://bit.ly/2eo9whL #musicMW.

8 Prime Video: Kennedy, Sinatra, and the Mafia, Season 1 (https://www.primevideo.com/detail/Kennedy-Sinatra-and-the-Mafia/0L50VBBAMH0BA15BOTECBSPHBR).

lipad. Nonetheless, Frank had escorted Jackie for JFK's inauguration the year before this; see their photograph here.

Frank had married Ava Gardner in 1951, but then she filed for divorce in 1954. After first visiting Spain in 1951, she moved (in 1955) into a luxury apartment in downtown Madrid and lived there until 1966.[9] In the flat below her lived Otto Skorzeny, Hitler's top commando.[10] (These two did meet; Otto had moved to Madrid in 1952.) Otto also directed a school for assassins there and was a likely collaborator in JFK's execution. But Ava was not one of the students.

In the early to mid-1940s, Gardner became a friend and protégé of businessman and aviator Howard Hughes; their relationship lasted into the 1950s. The Hughes Tool Company, located in Houston, Texas, racked up about $6 billion (sic) in contracts for paramilitary and clandestine warfare hardware.[11] The Pentagon kept 300+ lobbyists active on the Hill. The military offered "*VIP tours, dinners, films, speakers, planes, sporting weekends and other perquisites.... A quarter of Congress held reserve commissions.*"[12]

9 In 1961, Sukarno traveled to the US and wanted to meet Ava Gardner, but she was in Europe, so Marilyn Monroe had to fly in from Canada; she even sang for him – as she later did for JFK (Kinzer, Stephen. *The Brothers: John Foster Dulles, Allen Dulles, and Their Secret World War*, 2013, Kindle 218). Marilyn's singing proved to be an ominous sign for both JFK (1963) and Sukarno (1965).

10 Read Part II for more about Otto.

11 *Deadly Secrets: The CIA-Mafia War Against Castro and the Assassination of JFK* (1981) by Warren Hinckle and William Turner, p. 16.

12 *The March of Folly* (1984) by Barbara Tuchman, p. 334.

Robert Aime Maheu worked both for the FBI and the CIA,[13] but he also worked for years for Howard Hughes (he was dismissed in 1970), so he was ideally situated to facilitate connections. But Maheu never met Hughes face-to-face; they worked solely via memo and telephone. According to Maheu's associate (John Gerrity), these two men met in Vice-President Richard Nixon's office in 1954 at the invitation of the National Security Council. Tricky Dick gave Maheu (and the CIA) permission to use dirty tricks to disrupt a pending agreement between Aristotle Onassis (Jackie's later replacement husband) and Saudi Arabia.[14] So Maheu, well before 11/22/1963, had travelled in elevated circles.

But we have strayed. In 1992, Congress passed The President John F. Kennedy Assassination Records Collection Act. Henry F. Graff was chosen as one of five board members; he had once served as chairman of Columbia's history department.[15] But Henry should have recused himself – his 1988 high school history textbook (which included a "Critical Thinking Skills" section designed for the teachers' edition) had decreed a clear verdict against Oswald (p. 787):

> Meanwhile, Dallas police combed the city to find the President's assassin. Within an hour and a half of the shooting, they arrested Lee Harvey Oswald in a Dallas theater. Oswald, a former marine who had once tried to become a Russian citizen, was taken to the city jail. He denied any knowledge of the shootings, but the evidence against him was overwhelming.

I have never understood how Graff, with his barefaced bias, was ever allowed to serve on the ARRB, but we must leave that mystery to President Bill Clinton, who appointed him. After all, Bill was widely believed to be intelligent and politically astute (until he met Monica). Furthermore, I have never understood why anyone with *"critical thinking skills"* would ever regard Lee as a murderer.[16]

13 Robert Maheu - Wikipedia. In testimony before the Church Committee in 1975, Maheu confirmed his role in the assassination plots against Castro.

14 "Maheu Admits '54 Anti-Onassis Drive" - *The Washington Post.*

15 LBJ had even invited Henry to attend several sessions of his very private Tuesday lunches; he even permitted him to interview its members. "*The resulting account did not erect the monument he* [presumably LBJ] *hoped for*" (Tuchman, p. 323). Graff failed to comment publicly. Nor did he ever comment on his textbook's indictment of Oswald.

16 Ernst Titovets, Oswald's best friend in the USSR, firmly held that same (benign) belief in Lee; see *Oswald: Russian Episode* (2013) by Ernst Titovets and Paola Botan. Ti-

But Clinton was not married to the Warren Commission's conclusion. Just before beginning his first term (January 20, 1993), he made a very strange request to close family friend and lawyer Webster Hubbell: *"If I put you over there in Justice I want you to find the answer to two questions for me: One, who killed JFK? And two, are there UFOs?"*[17]

So, I dedicate this book to future generations of Americans who must, every November, endure the mendacities of the main stream media. My chief hope is that our educational system will eventually teach truth in history, but that would be a major marvel.[18]

---

tovets: *"I hotly protested Oswald's innocence before TV cameras…"* (Titovets, Kindle, 23). How often does the media tell us this every November? And did Graff ever read this book?

17 *Kennedy's Last Stand: Eisenhower, UFOs, MJ-12 & JFK's Assassination* (2013) by Michael E. Salla. Hubbell was once a US Associate Attorney General (1993 to 1994), who proved that this exalted position in Justice was no protection from justice. As part of the Whitewater controversy, Webb pled guilty to one count of wire fraud and one count of failing to disclose a conflict of interest, and so was sentenced to 21 months in prison. Even worse, he never discovered who killed JFK. "Kennedy's confrontation with the CIA & MJ-12": https://exopoliticsjournal.com/vol-3/vol-3-2-Salla.htm.

18 According to a 2013 survey, most "historians" (who actually write the American history textbooks) were still *unaware* (15 years later) of the ARRB! See "The JFK Assassination According to the History Textbooks – Part 1" (https://www.kennedysandking.com/john-f-kennedy-articles/the-jfk-assassination-according-to-the-history-textbooks-part-1).

Contents

Acknowledgments – Bill Simpich

My deepest appreciation goes to Bill Simpich for his long and incisive essay, "State Secret: Wiretapping in Mexico City, Double Agents and the Framing of Lee Oswald."

He emphasizes the critical importance of the "poison pill" (the fake calls from Mexico City) and the concept of piggybacking one operation on top of another. He is undeniably on target.

Introduction

The JFK assassination is no longer a mystery. That lie is now 60 years old and is well past its sell-by date. Any such myth (of a mystery) reeks of the garbage dumps of fraudulent evidence in this case.

–David W. Mantik[1]

If anything in this life is certain, if history has taught us anything, it is that you can kill anyone.

–Michael Corleone[2]

[JFK] died because he lost the support of his peers.

–Indira Gandhi, Prime Minister of India[3]

---

1 *JFK Was Killed by Consensus* (2025), from the Introduction.

2 From the movie, *The Godfather II*. Of course, some doomed characters confronted this truth quite personally: Abel (Cain's brother), Uriah the Hittite (Bathsheba's first husband), Socrates (399 BC), Julius Caesar (44 BC), Jesus of Nazareth (33), Justin Martyr (165), Harold Godwinson (1066), Thomas à Becket (1170), Joan of Arc (1431), Richard III (1485), Ferdinand Magellan (1521), Giordano Bruno (1600), Dr. Joseph Warren (1775), James Cook (1779), Jean-Paul Marat and King Louis XVI and Marie Antoinette (1793), Maximilien Robespierre (1794), Abe Lincoln (1865), George Armstrong Custer (1876), James Garfield and Czar Alexander II (1881), William McKinley (1901), Franz Ferdinand (1914), Czar Nicholas II (1918), Pancho Villa (1923), Huey Long (1935), Leon Trotsky (1940), Reinhard Heydrich (1942), Ernst Röhm (1943), Dietrich Bonhoeffer (1945), Mohandas Gandhi (1948), John Douglas Kinser (1951), Frank Olson (1953), Henry Marshall and Rafael Trujillo and Patrice Lumumba and Dag Hammarskjöld (1961), Marilyn Monroe (1962), Ngô Đình Diệm and Ngô Đình Nhu and Lee Harvey Oswald and JFK (1963), Mary Pinchot Meyer (1964), Dorothy Kilgallen and Malcolm X (1965), Lee Bowers (1966), Che Guevara and Eladio del Valle and Antoine Guerini and Richard Cain (1967), RFK and Martin Luther King, Jr. (1968), René Schneider Chereau (1970), Lucien Sarti (1972), Jimmy Hoffa and Sam Giancana (1975), Orlando Letelier and Johnny Roselli and Richard Welch [no kin to Raquel] (1976), Charles Nicoletti and William Sullivan (1977), Lord Louis Mountbatten (1979), Francis John Nugan (1980), Anwar al-Sadat (1981), Robert Calvi (1982), Benigno Aquino (1983), Indira Gandhi (1984), William F. Buckley (1985), Barry Seal (1986), Rajiv Gandhi (1991), Yitzhak Rabin (1995), William Colby (1996), Saddam Hussein (2006), Benazir Bhutto (2007), Moammar Gadhafi (2011), and Shinzo Abe (2022), as well as many popes including St. Peter (a Jewish pope). [See List of popes who died violently - Wikipedia and Lists of unusual deaths - Wikipedia. James Garfield is one of my favorites; after all, what other president has published an original proof of the Pythagorean Theorem? See Garfield's proof of the Pythagorean theorem - Wikipedia. I once admired Cook's monument while snorkeling with my children at Kealakekua Bay. Robert Calvi, the Vatican banker (aka "the hanging man") is portrayed in the movie, *The Godfather III*. Calvi appears later in this book.]

3 *The Other Oswald: The Story of Lee Harvey Oswald and Robert E. Webster*

Joseph P. Kennedy had made his son fully aware of Dulles's dangerously unsupervised management style.

–David Talbot[4]

It wouldn't make the slightest bit of difference [if Vietnam became communist].

–Robert Strange McNamara (in late January 1966)[5]

Six decades ago, attorney Vincent Salandria made the following (sage) claims:[6]

1. The JFK execution was *ordered* by the highest levels of the national security state.

2. The primary motive for this murder was JFK's persistent search for peaceful coexistence during the Cold War.

3. The machinations of the American power elite were safely whitewashed by subservient government employees and by the indolent – and even compliant – mainstream media.[7] Anyone who invoked even a modicum of common sense (to object) automatically was

---

(2019/2020) by Gary Hill, p. 5. The American media should have wondered who informed Oswald that JFK had lost this critical support. Also see "Assassinations: How Nehru-Gandhis, Kennedys were similar" – *The Week* (https://www.theweek.in/news/world/2018/06/05/rfk-assassination-similarities-nehru-gandhis-kennedys.html).

4 *The Devil's Chessboard: Allen Dulles, the CIA, and the Rise of America's Secret Government* (2015) by David Talbot, p. 373. The CIA's reprieve from (virtually all) accountability had been put into law by the CIA Act of 1949. In retrospect, 1949 was the tipping point – the American experiment with democracy was forever altered that year. Mike Mansfield stated that the agency was *"freed from practically every ordinary form of Congressional check."* No one could be sure whether it was *"staying within the limits established by law"* or exceeding the law to become *"an instrument of policy"* (Kinzer 2013, Kindle, 162). In 1954, Mansfield proposed a bill to create a "watchdog commission" to oversee the CIA, but *Allen Dulles derailed the bill* (Kinzer 2013, Kindle, 163), and so the CIA has been an integral component of our national security state for 76 years (since 1949).

5 *Remembering America* (1988) by Richard Goodwin, p. 453. This conversation occurred in McNamara's office at the Pentagon during a tête-à-tête with Dick Goodwin. It bears re-reading. So does Goodwin's book. As I typed this, and considered McNamara's inadvertent prophecy, I could only smile – at that very moment, my daughter was on honeymoon in Hanoi. We would all love to hear McNamara comment on that.

"No systematic or serious examination of Vietnam's importance to the US was ever undertaken" – Leslie Gelb, the editor of the *Pentagon Papers*, writing a quarter century later (Kinzer 2013, Kindle, 209).

6 *False Mystery* (2004) by Vincent Salandria, p. 152. He reached these conclusions *shortly after* 11/22/1963! I had the pleasure of meeting him once – at a 1998 JFK conference.

7 "The CIA And The Media" – Carl Bernstein (https://www.carlbernstein.com/the-cia-and-the-media-rolling-stone-10-20-1977).

tarred as a "conspiracy theorist;"[8] this label alone supposedly won the argument.

4. *By themselves,* even powerful individuals or secret, rogue factions could not have carried out this public execution. Only the full power of the warfare state could so abort the ballot box of a republic.[9]

This book has reached precisely those same conclusions. There is nothing fundamentally new under the sun.[10] What is new, however, is the overdue recognition of the enormous trash pile of fraudulent data in this case. Virtually all of this compost heap was created within the first week of JFK's execution – virtually all of it by taxpayer-supported public employees. Many of these characters merely acted under orders, not fully recognizing their culpability. But others did understand, some of them only years later.

One of them was the father of Chana Gail Willis. She only told her story publicly last November (2024);[11] she also spoke at Dealey Plaza. Her father,[12] a highly qualified navy photographer, was coerced into shooting a movie film of the motorcade that day. Most likely, this is the film (or actually a copy of it) seen by a handful of civilians; it shows the limousine turn at Houston and Elm, and it shows the "rolling" stop on Elm St. The perspective appears to be from slightly behind Zapruder's site. When Chana took her father to this 1963 site (at the north pergola), he broke down and became "inconsolable."[13] When I shared the above paragraph with Chana on April 3, 2025, she replied via e-mail as follows:

I (Chana Gail Willis) was raised in Dallas most of my life, after quickly arriving on November 4, 1963, from our home at the Jacksonville Naval Air Station in Florida, where my father previously

---

8 Although I have made literally hundreds of measurements at the National Archives directly from the extant JFK autopsy X-rays, I too have been labeled a conspiracy theorist. On the contrary, anyone who knows the English language (or physics), should have called me a *"conspiracy experimentalist."*

9 When once the CIA was terrified that it might be exposed, it hatched plans to admit to three gunman and then to scapegoat its lesser members, e.g., E. Howard Hunt and/or Frank Sturgis (Talbot 2015, pp. 505-506).

10 *Everything Is Predictable: How Bayesian Statistics Explain Our World* (2024) by Tom Chivers.

11 *JFK Magazine*: "Chana Gail Willis: Her Father's Life Story" (July 16, 2017) (https://www.jfkmagazine.org/2023/07/chana-gail-willis-her-fathers-life.html).

12 Freddie Spainhouer Obituary (1923 - 2014) - Dallas, TX - *Dallas Morning News* (https://obits.dallasnews.com/us/obituaries/dallasmorningnews/name/freddie-spainhouer-obituary?id=10754941).

13 My longtime JFK friend, Douglas Mizzer, learned this when he interviewed Chana after her November 2024 talk (e-mail to me from Mizzer, January 25, 2025).

headed up the photo recon in VAP 62 over Cuba. My father, Freddie Philmon Spainhouer, was a highly competent and decorated US Navy Master Chief with expertise in photographic intelligence used during Korea, the height of the Cold War, and Vietnam. Dad was not only ONI, but was CIA and held a NATO cosmic clearance, and he was forced into being involved in Dallas before, during, and after The Big Event, including filming the motorcade that day.

These (involved) people state that the imagery is very graphic and very professional in nature. They stated, *"It shows the Presidential limousine turn at Houston and Elm, and almost roll to a stop on Elm St. as the multiple shots rang out from three locations."* The camera seems to be a little behind Zapruder's location. In 1977, when I was assisting my father in his (City of Dallas, City Hall) Fire Department photo lab where he was ("planted") as DFD Photo Chief, preparing photographic prints of the Dallas Police Department assassination records and evidence files for the House Select Committee on Assassination, we took a lunch break. Coincidentally, my father's photolab was in the sub-basement, underneath the basement where Jack Ruby shot Oswald just 14 years before.

I was 17, and it was the only time I ever remember leaving dad's job for the city at his Main Street photo lab and dad going to Dealey Plaza. We weren't to ask questions or talk about it growing up, much less when we were adults. He stood behind the pergola and the picket fence, gazed over the fence on Elm Street with a glassy stare and couldn't muster a word. Later, I recalled that before dad died in 2014, he said he regretted that I pieced it all together and asked him point blank for the details and confirmation. We talked, and I cried. Then dad asked for my help in getting his last debriefing so he could die in peace. It was extremely difficult for me and my congressman to obtain, but dad finally got his meeting in May and he died in August 2014 at age 91. Dad loved our country, and said, *"We simply … had no choice, or our family would be dead. One guy on my team committed suicide that week when he found out the true mission, another went bonkers. Lee was also on my team, ONI and CIA, and in the end, knew he was being set up, and he too, faced the same threats toward his family.* 'No way out.'"

The reader can choose to believe or disbelieve this personal narrative, but this book provides powerful evidence that someone did shoot a (heretofore unrecognized) movie film from that specific site that day. But this (intelligence-related) individual has never been publicly identified. For our purposes, the name is incidental. In the photograph shown here, taken on 11/22/1963 by Wilma Bond,[14] someone stands at precisely the suspected site. Note the illuminated transparent square near the top of the red ellipse (third from the top); we will focus on this object later. The expurgators simply missed this photograph – and so did Richard Trask.

By the way, think about this. Since we now understand that the CIA knew in advance about their big hit that day, where was their photographer? How could they possibly be so delinquent as to leave their biggest hit go unrecorded? In fact, federal agencies took almost desperate measures to ensure the capture of every single one of 500+ Dealey Plaza photographs. Quite bewilderingly, however, no photograph or movie film was ever ascribed to the CIA. How is that possible? If no CIA photographer

14 wilma bond photographs - Search Images (https://www.bing.com/images/search?view=detailV2&ccid=ZVq2dYQP&id=7551C19B648A8C34F4A6A1F82B017D7806DB3CC9&thid=OIP.ZVq2dYQPAhJAzP5cpSjZNwHaEK&mediaurl=https://1a-1791.com/s/s8/6/J/y/W/0/JyW0n.4Wpjb.jpg&exph=1080&expw=1920&q=wilma+bond+photographs&simid=608055434690111439&form=IRPRST&ck=21F34346638C00C5F1982ECCE8B44B69&selectedindex=4&itb=0&ajaxhist=0&ajaxserp=0&vt=0&sim=11&mid=9C19B0051413007C909C9C19B0051413007C909C&cdnurl=https://th.bing.com/th/id/R.655ab675840f021240ccfe5ca528d937?rik=yTzbBnh9ASv4oQ&pid=ImgRaw&r=0)

was present, someone in the CIA should have been fired for that oversight. But here is what is even more incomprehensible: No one yet has even asked where the CIA was located that day.

Quite stunningly, however, in films taken that day in Dealey Plaza the exact same site (at the north pergola – inside that red ellipse above) has been carefully blacked out – *in six independent films.* It is the same site in each; often *geometric* patches have been inserted. This cannot occur randomly. It had to be deliberate. Furthermore, to this day, no copy of that famous Mary Moorman photograph exists without an opaque (man-made) mask, which obscures that illuminated square cited just above. You can look for one, but you will not find one.[15] These images will soon appear in this book, along with contemporaneous control photographs (without such black patches) *from 11/22/1963.* Someone altered the Moorman photograph – *on 11/22/1963.* My friend, Roy Schaeffer (who still lives), promptly noticed photographic alterations early on the morning of 11/23/1963; he took fresh images off the fax machine at the *Dayton Daily News.*[16] The device for such alteration is displayed later in this book. Roy even owned one and such devices can still be purchased online. Soon after that illicit Moorman alteration, the other five films (but not Bond's film) suffered the same fate. These obviously altered images are all displayed in this book. So, the reader must decide: Do you believe your own eyes – or do you still rely on persistent mainstream media claims that all has been kosher? Who would know best?

But this should surprise no one. From my nine (all day) visits to the National Archives (three decades ago now), we already knew that all three extant skull X-rays were copies. The originals have vanished. We know precisely where and how clever alterations in these three X-rays were created in 1963; I was able to duplicate just such alterations myself. These were designed to criminate Oswald, but when viewed later, these absurd X-ray alterations totally flummoxed the autopsy pathologists – as well as subsequent official "experts." In particular, that fake 6.5 mm cross section (on the frontal X-ray) was not seen by anyone that night – but there it is on the X-ray today at the National Archives. (It was easily identified by my

15 That annoying fingerprint is always there, too, possibly placed by the person who altered the film.

16 From: r_schaeffer@att.net
To: DAVID W MANTIK
Wed, Mar 19, 2025, at 11:30 AM
The proof of the Moorman photo being altered is the black opaque mask I first noticed on 11/23/1963 when taking the fax to engraving at 7:15 am.

5-year-old daughter – in a copy in Lifton's book.) Nor does this physical "metallic" cross section exist anywhere today in the National Archives; furthermore, no such piece of metal has ever been there. Astoundingly, even David Lifton in his best-selling book (*Best Evidence*) totally overlooked this bizarre feature of the skull X-rays. Still worse, Harold Weisberg, the consummate crusty critic of the *Warren Report* (in a personal letter) assured the cynic in me: no X-ray alteration had occurred. So, Lifton had not paid attention, and Weisberg was flatly wrong.

Likewise, the huge, gaping hole at the back of JFK's head could not possibly have been displayed to the public. Such unaltered evidence would have promptly announced – to the entire world – that the fatal head shot had come from the *front*.[17] So, our diligent, well-paid artists had no choice – that hole had to be covered. And so, they did just that – in the autopsy photograph and in the Zapruder film. I am one of the rare individuals who have repeatedly scrutinized the back of JFK's head (at the National Archives) via a stereo viewer. But this has never yielded a 3D image – it was always, and only, 2D. By contrast, all of the other autopsy pairs yielded a 3D image. And yes, I actually had time to examine all of them. Robert Groden agrees with me.

Furthermore, I am one of the rare individuals (along with Sidney Wilkinson) who have seen the *initial* MPI transparencies (of the Zapruder film) at the Sixth Floor Museum. These *first-generation copies* revealed a childish, geometric black patch precisely (and only) over JFK's huge occipital hole. No such mask was visible on the back of John Connally's head. Nor was this mask visible on JFK before the headshot frame.

This list (of fraudulent JFK evidence) could be protracted interminably, especially for the 455 Oswald items. At 7:25 PM on 11/22/1963, LBJ telephoned J. Edgar Hoover, who was at home.[18] Shortly after this, the Dallas Police Department (DPD) was ordered (by Hoover) to surrender these Oswald items to FBI agent Vincent Drain; he then departed with them at 3:10 AM from Carswell AFB (for DC) via a C-130 tanker on 11/23/1963.[19] Quite oddly (perhaps even suspiciously) Drain never testified before the Warren Commission (WC). John Armstrong noted:

17 *"... the president was struck in the right temple by the* [sic] *bullet.... The AP* [Associated Press] *flatly declared that JFK had been shot* 'in the front of the head'" (*The Death of a President* (1967) by William Manchester, p. 354). My forensic analysis at the National Archives (ratified by Michael Chesser, MD) has confirmed these two statements.

18 Manchester, p. 405. Hoover, obviously not concerned about national security, had not met LBJ at the airport.

19 "Vincent Drain, Special Agent, FBI" in *No More Silence* (1998) by Larry Sneed, pp. 249 ff.

> *...Oswald's possessions were* **secretly** [emphasis added] *sent to the FBI on November 23, 1963 ... and then returned to the Dallas Police after numerous items had been altered, modified, substituted, or added to the evidence.*[20]

After arriving at FBI headquarters on 11/23/1963, Drain spoke to Hoover, and then he

> *...watched them do a lot of the experiments such as firing the rifle,*[21] *looking for prints, ballistics markings, hairs, fibers, blood stains....*[22]

After this, Drain left DC for Dallas with some items late on 11/23/1963, and returned them to the DPD just as Oswald was shot (on Sunday, 11/24/1963). That marked the end of the *first* round trip. This trip was secret and had no legal jurisdiction.[23]

On Monday, 11/25/1963 (JFK's funeral), the DPD finally prepared a thorough inventory. They used 4 rolls of film (each 25 feet long) and another roll of 100 feet. Each item was listed on their 25 typewritten pages. In 1999, at the National Archives, John Armstrong meticulously compared items from these two occasions.[24] He found that many items had been added or altered while in DC, e.g., W-2 forms for Oswald. (We can only wonder if Oswald had helpfully deposited these in DC in order to assist the FBI.) But here is what is particularly striking: none of these added items had police initials! So, we can only further wonder why Oswald had aborted his charitable task of assisting the FBI so early (without these initials). Armstrong also noted that some items had been discarded and others had been switched, including the infamous Minox (spy) camera, shown here (82 x 28 x 16 mm).[25]

---

20 Armstrong, John, *Harvey and Lee: How the CIA Framed Oswald* (2003), p. 963. John gifted his monumental 983-page book to me, which I did actually read. Noel Twyman's masterpiece (and treasure house of information) is the only other JFK book that I keep at my bedside. I have read Twyman's book multiple times.

21 This is beyond belief, but there is no reference to an FBI laboratory test (with a cotton swab) of the alleged weapon. So, the FBI has never told us whether the critical weapon was fired earlier that day! See *The Assassination of John F. Kennedy: The Final Analysis* (2024) by David W. Mantik and Jerome Corsi, p. 4.

22 Sneed, p. 250.

23 Bishop, Jim. *The Day Kennedy was Shot: An Uncensored Minute-by-Minute Account of November 22, 1963*, 1968, p. 517.

24 Armstrong, p. 909.

25 For a more detailed (and quite brilliant) discussion of this Minox fiasco, read Carol Hewitt's annihilation of the FBI's fictions in *The Assassinations* (2002), edited by James DiEugenio. The Minox A/III camera was used by George Lazenby in the movie, *On Her Majesty's Secret Service* (1969). Not surprisingly, James Bond innocently held the camera upside down! Even Oswald would have done better than that.

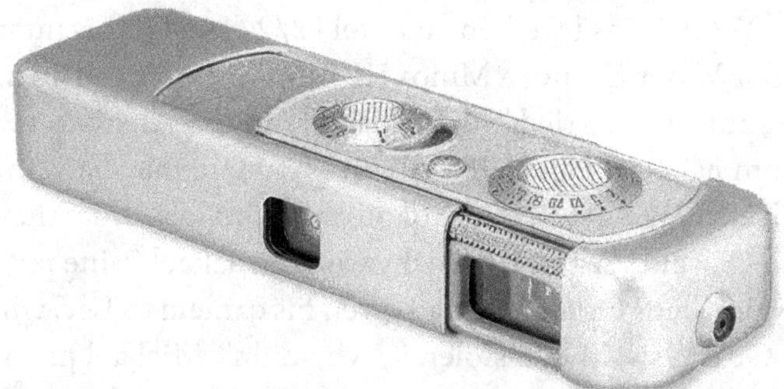

On Wednesday, November 27, Drain left Dallas for DC in his *second round trip* with the Oswald items. This time he had *"4-5 baskets full of that stuff."*[26] When some of these items were later (again) received back in Dallas, Chief Jess Curry noted that many photographic negatives were missing. In fact, on 12/3/1963, Curry wrote that *"…items #164 – 360 inclusive did not record."* In short, in their resolute pursuit of justice, the FBI had lost 3 rolls of film. Actually, 196 continuous frames had been *physically cut* from the original 5 rolls – so this "blunder" required some due diligence.

In most cases, the physical items (even many documents) were *not provided* to the WC; instead, the FBI merely offered photographs. Even worse in many cases, the original evidence was photographed, and then the actual item simply vanished!

At the very least we know that the Minox III (spy) camera was present in the original inventory.[27] The FBI tried *three times* to get the DPD to erase this fundamental fact, but they failed. In their photographic re-creation, the FBI even tried to substitute a Minox light meter; however, they forgot to explain why the light meter required the attached *Minox film*! Moreover, the FBI (in their artlessness) forgot to lose the Minox III camera from Ruth Paine's garage. Today this Archives camera is inoperable and cannot be opened, so its serial number is not known. But the FBI, still trying to evade Oswald's ownership, attempted one more magic act – they attributed a Minox camera to Michael Paine, even though the camera in ques-

26 Sneed, p. 251.

27 Black and white police photograph of objects belonging to Oswald | The Sixth Floor Museum at Dealey Plaza The Sixth Floor Museum at Dealey Plaza (https://www.jfk.org/collections-archive/black-and-white-police-photograph-of-objects-belonging-to-oswald/). Also read "The Spy Camera," in *JFK: First Day Evidence* (1993) by Gary Savage. These photographs and recollections derive from DPD Crime Lab Detective R. W. Livingston. Gary's book also includes an enlightening Chapter XI: "The Acoustic Evidence Disproved." For a high resolution photograph of these Oswald items, see *Cover-up* (1992) by J. Gary Shaw, p. 46.

tion was found *in Oswald's seabag*! Unfortunately for the FBI, that serial number (27259) was listed on an airtel (2/2/1964); this number proves that it was a *Minox II* – not a Minox III. Thus one of the FBI's most critical improvisations miscarried. So, the camera in the Archives today cannot derive from Michael Paine. The Archives camera may have the initials of DPD officers Gus Rose or Richard Stovall, who insist that they found the camera in Oswald's sea bag. But why would Michael Paine put his camera into Oswald's bag? Or if Paine had given his camera to Lee, why would he do that? Or if Oswald had stolen it, why didn't Michael just say so? (He never did.) Malcolm Blunt speculates that the National Archives does not want the public to learn that Oswald actually owned this camera.[28] We can only hope that, someday, the FBI (and the Archives) will explain exactly whose camera they still conceal today.

The bullet hulls (aka "shells" or "spent rounds") found on the Sixth Floor are supposedly the definitive evidence that convicted Oswald. But the story of these hulls is even more preposterous than the Minox story. The evidence is overwhelming – even dispositive – that only *two hulls* were found that day. The third forensic item was an *intact bullet* – not a hull. If this is true, then *only two shots* were fired from this site – and an additional gunman is required. All of the initial documents – and even the photographs – consistently describe only two hulls. Twyman displays both (i.e., documents and photographs) in his monumental book.[29] For several November days, we knew about only two hulls. The third hull only arrived days later, *after Oswald was dead*. J. Gary Shaw displays in electrifying clarity the two contradictory documents – the original police report (2 hulls) and then the WC Exhibit (CE-2003), which lists 3 hulls.[30] Most curiously however, in the WC document the digit "3" appears altered. For a thoroughly masterful demolition of this FBI myth, read Barry Krusch.[31] Krusch adds this critical information: as of 11/26/1963, only two hulls – not three – were sent to the FBI,[32] as shown here in this summary table.

Notice the odd shape of this digit "3" in the right image, which Krusch scrutinized closely; he concluded that this "3" had been altered. And

28 *The Devil is in the Details* (2020) by Malcolm Blunt with Alan Dale.

29 *Bloody Treason: The Assassination of John F. Kennedy* (1997) by Noel Twyman, pp. 110-116.

30 Shaw, pp. 159-160.

31 *Impossible: The Case Against Lee Harvey Oswald*, Volume One (2012) by Barry Krusch.

32 Krusch, Kindle, 237. A photograph (CE-738) of these two hulls en route to the FBI also appears in *Retired Dallas police chief, Jesse Curry reveals his personal JFK assassination file* (1969) by Jesse Curry, p. 88.

here is the re-created – but undated – (cropped by me) photograph of the Sixth Floor (no identifiable first-day photograph exists):

6.5 spent rounds (2)	6.5 spent rounds (3)
The line on the original Oswald evidence sheet as it appears on the record from the Dallas Police Department.	*The line as it appears in Warren Commission Exhibit 2003.*

Notice that A displays an intact bullet – not a hull. B and C are obviously hulls. (C is not shown here, but see Twyman or Krusch for the full photograph.) So this photograph agrees with the documents: *two hulls and one intact bullet.* But there is an even more serious problem with one of these two hulls (CE-543) – it was seriously dented, so this hull could not be linked to a successfully fired bullet.[33] So, that leaves only *one* viable hull.

As expected of an inveterate prosecutor, Vincent Bugliosi[34] claimed that he could untangle this Gordian knot. He agreed with Police Captain Will Fritz, who claimed to have tossed one hull into his desk drawer on 11/22/1963. Fritz maintained this preposterous caprice even though such an action disagreed brutally with both the documents and the photographs. Furthermore, such absolute secrecy violated any reasonable concept of police protocol. And Fritz never said (or wrote) a word about it *until days later* – not even to the FBI! In fact, if Fritz had not fortuitously recalled this hull in his desk drawer, the case

33 *Mortal Error: The Shot that Killed JFK* (1992) by Bonar Menninger, p. 114. Howard Donahue is the only person who was able to exceed Oswald's supposed marksmanship. Howard was also an expert on firearms and ballistics; I once visited Howard and his wife at their Maryland home. He was quite adamant in his verdict: the dented shell *could not be linked* to a bullet fired that day. But the WC "experts" disagreed with Howard. Unfortunately, the WC offered no reasonable argument for their naïve conclusion.

34 Except for the notable exception of the acoustic evidence, Vince and I disagreed about almost everything in this JFK case – although he always dodged *all* of my most serious arguments. Nonetheless, he once sent me an album of Italian love songs! On the other hand, we agreed about conspiracy in the RFK case. And RFK, Jr. agrees with me about both cases.

for the lone gunman would promptly have vaporized (two hulls were not enough) – and a conspiracy was inevitable. So, Fritz's fortuitous memory saved the day and thus he became an accessory in Oswald's murder.

To appreciate just how bizarre Fritz's actions were, recall this: the official Crime Scene Search (CSS) form of 11/22/1963 was time-stamped between 1:30 and 2:15 PM. Furthermore, the names of the three officers who (*together*) submitted the evidence of *two hulls* included – guess who – "Captain Fritz"! He did *not* add a note to clarify that a third hull was in his own drawer. So, we can only wonder if Fritz meant to imply that he had covertly palmed one of the hulls – literally within minutes of their discovery – and secreted it in his pocket without telling his two colleagues. On the other hand, if common sense is relevant, another option emerges: Fritz had no third hull to confiscate. At least, his two fellow signatories (on that CSS form) surely did not know about a third hull, so Fritz must have been a master of legerdemain. Furthermore, notice that the above Sixth Floor photograph was a *re-construction;* it was almost certainly taken after 11/22/1963. So, are we seriously to believe – at this rather late date (i.e., several days later) – that these photographers still did not know about Fritz's hidden hull? To return to reality, Krusch argues definitively, over many, many pages (with even more data), that Fritz was desperately hapless here – he could not possibly have put that third hull into his desk drawer – or, for that matter, anywhere else either. And Bugliosi was merely spinning fairy tales. That hull simply did not exist. Krusch concludes that the third hull was later illicitly inserted into evidence (after it became a *sine qua non* for the WC case) – likely by the ever-present Vincent Drain (a very good friend of J. Edgar Hoover and also of "Deke" DeLoach).[35] John Armstrong concurs. So do I.

So, now if anyone wants to debate me about the case for conspiracy, I only smile. There can be no debate. Astoundingly, the media, but especially the national security state, would like nothing better than to promote

35 DeLoach was associate deputy director of the FBI. That first weekend, Deke saw a version of the Zapruder home movie in which JFK went forward, i.e., *no head snap*. Dan Rather had the same experience that weekend. William Reymond (from Paris) also saw an alternate version (probably derived from French intelligence), in which Reymond saw the limousine stop: Rich DellaRosa and the "other" film of the assassination - JFK Assassination Debate - The Education Forum (https://educationforum.ipbhost.com/topic/30444-rich-delarosa-and-the-"other"-film-of-the-assassination/). Also see "Rich Dellarosa: The Other Zapruder Film" - Black Op Radio 2-26-09 (https://www.youtube.com/watch?v=wRhcQI4tFTI). But Drain is even more ill-omened than he appears. On 11/21/1963, he and Frank M. Brandstetter portentously discussed the bubbletop on JFK's limousine; read more about "Brandy" in Part II.

such ill-advised discussions. From such digressions, listeners walk away confused, and they conclude that *"we will never know."* Today that is deliberately false and misleading. It is even absurd. It would be like turning the lectern over to a flat earther – Kyrie Irving, anyone?[36] Or like proclaiming that rocks cannot fall from the heavens.[37] Or for a medical specialist like me, it would be like my (imaginary) belief in the four humors of medicine.[38] But this is no longer 1963, when all of these forgeries were still concealed and the public (I among them) actually trusted the state. But that day passed us by long ago (although some folks missed it) – because the truth (now nearly the *full* truth) has bolted into public view.[39]

Nonetheless, some of my valiant colleagues still (in early 2025) eagerly anticipate Trump's new records' release. I will be pleased to see them, too. But, for me now, we are only missing a handful of puzzle pieces in a picture of 1000 parts. Not much is still unaccounted for in our reconstruction of the JFK assassination.[40] Of course, if these new releases contain an

36 Kyrie Irving says the Earth is undeniably flat: 'This is not even a conspiracy theory' - CBSSports.com (https://www.cbssports.com/nba/news/kyrie-irving-says-the-earth-is-undeniably-flat-this-is-not-even-a-conspiracy-theory/).

37 Raining Stones and Other Bizarre Objects Falling from the Sky - Historic Mysteries (https://www.historicmysteries.com/unexplained-mysteries/raining-stones/33683/).

38 Humorism - Wikipedia.

39 While seeing patients at Loma Linda University, one of my lovely head and neck patients (a former high school teacher) reminded me of Bryant (not Kobe, but rather William Cullen – in 1837). Well did she recall 11/22/1963 – it was her birthday!

Truth, crushed to earth, shall rise again;
`The eternal years of God are hers;
But Error wounded, writhes in pain,
And dies among his worshippers.
–"The Battle-Field," Stanza 9

40 Examples of still-missing items include the 1963 itineraries (especially during July–November) of these characters: Charles Willoughby, Ed Lansdale, Bill Harvey, David Morales, Allen Dulles, Howard Burris, William C. Bishop, and Felipe Vidal Santiago. Especially interesting would be joint trips by the latter two. And quite disquieting would be the discovery of Spainhouer's order to film Dealey Plaza that day – or any intelligence-related communication with him.

This list of missing autopsy items was assembled by Douglas Horne on March 29, 2025.

Missing skull X-Rays: Two oblique views showing damage to the right rear – and all three originals of the extant skull X-rays now in the Archives. (The three extant skull X-rays are all copies, not originals.)

Missing bone fragments: Harper and Burris (not Howard).

Missing bullet fragments: Dennis David prepared a receipt for four large bullet fragments.

Missing autopsy photographs: (1) large bruise atop the right lung inside the empty chest cavity, (2) entrance wound in lower right skull viewed from outside with scalp reflected, (3) entrance wound in the lower right skull viewed from inside the empty skull, (4) back of head showing exit wound in mid-skull taken *after* embalming and reconstruction, (5) negatives from B&W film pack showing metal probes in the body, (6) B&W prints showing the large exit defect in the rear skull, (7) B&W prints showing bullet entry order for Chana's father to take a movie film in Dealey Plaza, I would be delighted. But no order to carry out the execution will ever appear. Even a hint of complicity between members of this power elite is not likely to exist anymore (if it ever did). But this no longer matters much – we now know who they were.[41] Just continue reading this book.

The most obvious suspect is McGeorge Bundy.[42] Even his former JFK colleagues often viewed him as a traitor. David Talbot actually called him *"Dulles's mole in the White House."*[43] A timeline in this book details Mac's

---

wound high in the right forehead above the right eye.

41 *"The general rule in psychiatry is: if you think you've found a theory that explains everything, diagnose yourself with mania and check yourself into the hospital."* – Scott Alexander (Book Review: Surfing Uncertainty | Slate Star Codex) (https://slatestarcodex.com/2017/09/05/book-review-surfing-uncertainty/). Of course, since I often visit the hospital very day (to see patients), this comment makes little sense to me. Besides, who would believe a psychiatrist?

42 After McGeorge's epiphany on 11/22/1963, the DRE quickly moved into action (using information apparently unknown to Bundy). *"DRE-associated individuals were already aware the night of the assassination that Oswald had been in Mexico, and were prepared to offer witnesses who would support the idea that he had threatened JFK, and/or support the idea that he was a potential assassin"* (Hancock 2025, Kindle, 346). Unfortunately, these DRE sources had not spoken to Ernst Titovets, Oswald's closest friend in the USSR; Ernst bluntly disagreed with these DRE liars. Since no one else, not even Bundy, knew (on 11/22/1963) about the Mexican affair, we can only wonder if David Phillips (or George Joannides) had secretly advised the DRE of Oswald's "guilt." Amazingly, the DRE campaign against Oswald had begun well *before* his Mexico visit, i.e., in August 1963. This had included letters (from the DRE) to Congress and warnings to Cuban exile groups and even to local journalists in Miami (Hancock 2025, Kindle, 24). Hancock emphasizes that *"...it is virtually inconceivable to think that CIA officers at the Miami station were not aware of Lee Harvey Oswald as of August 1963...."* (Hancock 2025, 229). Also recall that the Oswald watch had been placed on August 13, 1963 – after his arrest in New Orleans. Then think about this: Even into the 21st century, the CIA went to court to protect records about the DRE-Joannides connection – so this was no trivial matter to the CIA (Hancock 2025, 225).

43 *The Devil's Chessboard* (2015), p. 407. Talbot also notes that the two Bundy brothers were solid members of Allen Dulles's inner circle. Furthermore, McGeorge had worked with Allen on the Council on Foreign Relations – and on the Dewey presidential campaign (p. 219). Mac actually used his position as a Harvard dean to recruit for the CIA! In fact, one of his former students was deeply involved in the Lumumba caper. This was Lawrence Devlin, the Congo CIA station chief (Talbot 2015, pp. 373, 382). If he had only known, JFK would have been deeply distressed by the devious deeds in the Congo by his fellow Harvard alumnus. About Devlin, also see *The Dark Side of Camelot* (1997) by Seymour Hersh, p. 191. For the CIA infestation of hundreds of professors at over a hundred campuses, read *The CIA and the Cult of Intelligence* (1974) by Victor Marchetti, pp. 76, 226. Ellen Schrecker specifically cited Mac's collaboration with the national security state: *"In 1977, Columbia sociologist and historian Sigmund Diamond revealed that in 1954 the then-dean of Harvard, McGeorge Bundy, deprived him* [Diamond] *of a job because he* [Diamond] *refused to name names to the FBI"* (*No Ivory Tower: McCarthyism and the Universities* (1986) by Ellen W. Schrecker): Academic Freedom and the Cold War on JSTOR (https://www.jstor.org/stable/4638328).

prompt and frequent encounters with LBJ after 11/22/1963 – he is the favorite son. But even during the flight from Dallas that day, LBJ was frequently on the telephone with him.[44] (Secretary of State Dean Rusk was still flying home over the Pacific – he arrived in DC at 12:35 AM local time on 11/23/1963.) In view of a supposedly looming nuclear holocaust, the Secretary of Defense (McNamara) remained oddly absent. He did *voluntarily* greet LBJ at Andrews AFB that night, but LBJ merely asked if there was anything new.[45] Moreover – *mirabile dictu* – the DEFCON barometer barely budged that weekend,[46] but LBJ seemed not to notice. Furthermore, as documented here, McGeorge was ubiquitous in those critical days after 11/22/1963 – even after Rusk had returned. But McNamara, too, was mostly absent; in view of the supposedly imminent nuclear holocaust (as proclaimed by LBJ), this is incomprehensible. Review the timeline later in this book.[47]

Even William Walton (a close Kennedy family friend) said that, on 11/23/1963 with the US government completely paralyzed, McGeorge Bundy was the *de facto* head of government.[48]

JFK once said, *"You just can't beat brains."*[49] At Harvard, after his promotion to full professor in 1953, Mac Bundy (without a PhD – or a previous academic course in government) was appointed Dean of Harvard's Faculty of Arts and Sciences.[50] As of 2019, he was still the youngest ever (in Har-

44 *The Day Kennedy was Shot* (1968) by Jim Bishop, p. 354. I have just renewed my acquaintance with this book; the errors (especially about the autopsy) are beyond belief. Jim gets very little right. There should be a law against such incompetence. In any case, here is the pertinent quotation from Bishop (p. 354): *"It seemed that he* [LBJ] *was phoning McGeorge Bundy in the White House Situation Room every few minutes* [when he (LBJ) wasn't usurping the presidential bedroom from Jackie], p. 386. *Bundy was in the basement amidst all of the "instantaneous" sources of information from around the world."*

45 *"The President [LBJ] turned to the Secretary of Defense:* 'Any important matters pending?'" (Manchester, p. 402.)

46 *Someone Would Have Talked* (2006) by Larry Hancock, p. 304.

47 A nearly comprehensive chronology is located inside the front cover of Manchester's book. Another chronology is in Fonzi's book, p. 421.

48 For Walton, see (6) November 30, 1963: RFK and Jackie Say JFK Was 'Felled by Domestic Opponents' (https://jfkfacts.substack.com/p/november-30-1963-rfk-and-jackie-blame). For Bundy's role, see Peter Kross, Kindle, 4726.

49 "The very expensive education of McGeorge Bundy" by David Halberstam in *Harper's*, July 1969, p. 22. (The title is slyly ironic.) McGeorge had a perfect score on his Yale entrance exam. Like George H. W. Bush (also a Republican), McGeorge was a member of Skull and Bones.

50 Mac was to supervise 288 full professors and 20 laboratories. Although Halberstam agreed that Mac would become the perfect dean, he feared that Mac's arrogance and hubris (in political office) might be very dangerous (*The Best and Brightest* (1972) by David Halberstam, p. 59). In fact, Walter Lippman later concluded that Mac's White House experience had *"coarsened his mind"* (*The Color of Truth: McGeorge Bundy*

vard's history – at age 34) with a decanal appointment. So, McGeorge surely had brains – undoubtedly one of the highest IQs in DC. And he knew it; when someone cited Ormsley-Gore (a British diplomat)[51] as brilliant, Mac took offense. As Mac managed the Situation Room on 11/22/1963, Manchester praised him as *"…the most precise man in government…."*[52]

But here is the clincher: the first person to publicly indict Oswald was McGeorge Bundy. This unexpected conclusion was confirmed by Theodore White in his 1964 book; the presidential party on AF-1 *"…learned that there was no conspiracy, learned the identity of Oswald and his arrest…."*[53] On that Friday afternoon, while in the White House basement (Mac had promptly left the Pentagon for the Situation Room), when not on the telephone with LBJ, Mac was advising the passengers from both Dallas and from Hawaii of his verdict: the assassin was Lee Harvey Oswald. *This was the very first official announcement of Lee's guilt.* During this same time, George Ball had asked for Oswald's file; the dossier arrived – it was *"thick."*[54] So, in disagreement with the authentic same-day evidence in Dallas,[55] and surely oblivious to this "thick" file, this very brilliant

and *William Bundy: Brothers in Arms* (2017) by Kai Bird, Kindle, 348). Of course, Halberstam's book title was meant to be satirical. But Dick Goodwin was more forthcoming: [McNamara, Mac Bundy, Dean Rusk, and Walt Rostow] –*"they were neither the best nor the brightest"* (Goodwin, p. 386). Barbara Tuchman emphasizes that none of these political newcomers had ever held elective office, but that *"power and status exhilarated these men"* (Tuchman, p. 286). In my opinion, that perfectly characterizes Mac Bundy. Regarding Cuba, Mac (much later) confessed: "The Brigade's My Fault," in the op-ed section of the *New York Times*, October 23, 1979. Nonetheless, JFK never fired him.

51 William George Arthur Ormsley-Gore, a veteran of the British Arab Bureau (where Sir Mark Sykes and T. E. Lawrence had also served) will reappear in my next book (*Evil is Eternal*); Ormsley-Gore helped to implement the Balfour Declaration.

52 Manchester, p. 403.

53 *The Making of the President 1964* (1966) by Theodore White, p. 33. White specifically confirmed that the message had come from the Situation Room. In 1993, this was also endorsed by Robert Manning, who was JFK's Assistant Secretary of State for Public Affairs (*Let Us Begin Anew, An Oral History of the Kennedy Presidency* (1993) by Deborah H. Strober). This announcement was also heard onboard their Pacific plane by cabinet members returning from Hawaii; see *With Kennedy* (1969) by Pierre Salinger, p. 10. This incriminating evidence was too hot to persist: the tapes have disappeared (likely as ordered by McGeorge), and so has Salinger's transcript. See further critical comments by Douglas Horne about these essential missing items (Salandria, p. 201).

54 Manchester, p. 365. On April 2, 2025, to The House Task Force, Jeff Morley described the 1963 Oswald file as 185 pages thick. In November 1963, this information was held in the second floor office of counterintelligence chief James Angleton, at CIA headquarters: Morley-Written-Testimony.pdf (https://oversight.house.gov/wp-content/uploads/2025/04/Morley-Written-Testimony.pdf). On June 4, 2025, Jeff Morley updated the CIA's Oswald file: "Before JFK's Murder the CIA Compiled a 194-Page Dossier on Lee Harvey Oswald" (https://jfkfacts.substack.com/p/updated-the-cia-compiled-a-194-page).

55 Meanwhile in Dallas, the DA (Henry Wade) had stated, *"…preliminary reports indicated more than one person was involved in the shooting…the electric chair is too good*

man immediately knew that Lee had done it. In fact, Lee was not officially charged with this crime *until the next day* (at 1:30 AM Dallas time),[56] so Dallas should simply have left everything to Mac Bundy. After all, much time and expense could have been saved. Perhaps we could even have skipped the Warren Commission con job, and thereby saved our taxpayers millions of unnecessary dollars. The cost of this travesty, and of the other JFK (mis)investigations, is reviewed later in this book.

McGeorge had been JFK's national security advisor. At the Oahu conference *during that very week*, McGeorge had signed the very first draft of NSAM-273. While there, he had (supposedly) represented JFK's pacific views (as opposed to the opposite views of the military), as well as JFK's plans for withdrawing 1000 troops from Vietnam that year. (This NSAM is summarized in some detail later in this book.) But Mac was a true hard-liner; did JFK not know this? Well yes, he did. JFK and Mac had known one another since their days together in the Dexter Lower School and they had socialized in Boston, often at the home of Arthur Schlesinger, Jr. In fact, JFK had described Bundy as *"Harvard's own Lyndon Johnson, Mac Bundy."*[57] Despite this, however, *"They knew and liked each other far more than they would later let on…."*[58]

While at Harvard, this Bundy (not his brother Bill) had been a disciple of Richard Bissell. Bundy and Bissell had worked together as *chief planners* for the Bay of Pigs, after which Bissell (*but not Mac*) was fired. Even way back in 1948, Bundy and Bissell (and even E. Howard Hunt) had worked together (on the Marshall Plan – which generously supported the CIA); Allen Dulles was also a member of that group. Furthermore, in 1948 Bundy had campaigned (under the direct supervision of Allen Dulles) for two *Republicans* (Tom Dewey and *Earl Warren*); in fact, he was a speechwriter specializing in foreign policy issues. After Dewey's fully anticipated win (over Truman), Mac had expected a senior post in Dewey's administration. As for that ill-fated Cuban invasion, of course, Mac and Bissell had worked hand-in-glove with CIA deputy director, Charles P. Cabell (thereafter fired by JFK), the brother of Earle Cabell, who was the 1963 mayor of Dallas. These "patriotic" Cabells were descended from Pocahontas, so this was a true-blue American conspiracy.[59]

---

for the shooters" [plural]. This statement appeared on 11/23/1963 in the *Dallas Morning News*. But Henry Wade (an old friend of LBJ – see their bear hug in this book) was soon severely drilled about his exam failure – he had missed the (political) target.

56 Lee had been charged with the Tippit murder at 7:10 PM on 11/22/1963.

57 Bird, Kindle, 187.

58 Ibid.

59 Charles P. Cabell - Wikipedia

The House Select Committee on Assassinations (HSCA) during 1976-1979 was mostly a charade.[60] Just as it was wrapping up, G. Robert Blakey focused on the red herrings in the acoustic data[61] and then announced the HSCA verdict of a "probable conspiracy." But the HSCA never officially named their suspects! Of course, Blakey (an expert on the Mafia) knew who had done it, so he proclaimed his discovery in his subsequent book.[62] But Blakey, who had servilely accepted whatever the CIA told him (despite the protests of his students), is now fatally remorseful for his naïvety. Although he once stated that he had achieved full cooperation from the CIA, he now is furious (chiefly at himself) for ever trusting them. This deadly outcome was, of course, triggered by the deceit of George Joannides (Jeff Morley's *bête noire*), who was the CIA's liaison to the HSCA. Blakey later learned about George's 1963 role with his personal anti-Castro Cubans (the DRE),[63] but that is another story. Jeff Morley (a modern American hero) tells it exceptionally well.[64]

Blakey had once announced that neutron activation analysis was the "linchpin" of the case for the Magic Bullet. (Instead, he should have cited LBJ as the linchpin.) But that linchpin has long since fully fractured, so Bob has had to trash it. So have the US courts of law. But Blakey attended

---

60 Consistent with this inattention, the name of David Phillips is not cited in the HSCA report. It appears only in a volume of appendices (*The Last Investigation* (2013) by Gaeton Fonzi, p. 267). Blakey was so dedicated to the task that he returned $425,000 of the first year HSCA funding to the US treasury! (Fonzi, p. 229.) In one more HSCA oversight, Robert Tanenbaum, Deputy Chief Council of the HSCA, saw a now-disappeared film (taken by David Ferrie at an anti-Castro training camp just north of Lake Pontchartrain) in which these specific characters appeared: Guy Banister, David Phillips, Lee Harvey Oswald, and Antonio Veciana. The source for the story about this film is *The Other Oswald* by Gary Hill, pp. 180-181. Hopsicker (p. 130) also provides a thought-provoking perspective on this lost film. Beguilingly, Tanenbaum confirmed privately to me that Dan Rather had confessed to him: *"We really blew it on the Kennedy assassination."* My daughter and I had the pleasure of a private visit with Tanenbaum at his home in Beverly Hills, where he had once been the mayor. While there, Bob gifted us with several of his novels – and regaled us about his basketball encounters with another Bob – Cousy of the Celtics. (Tanenbaum is very tall and had attended Berkeley on a basketball scholarship.)

61 See my website, where I discuss the misleading acoustic data over zillions of pages: The Mantik View - Articles and Research on the JFK Assassination by David W. Mantik, M.D., Ph.D. (https://themantikview.org). Even Pat Speer now agrees with me that this acoustic data is quite irrelevant. But this data is complex, so we should not be too harsh on our treasured colleagues who distrust the *Warren Report*, but who nonetheless ingenuously admire these tasty red herrings.

62 *The Fatal Hour: The Assassination of President Kennedy by Organized Crime* (1993) by G. Robert Blakey.

63 George Joannides - Wikipedia

64 *Our Man in Mexico: Winston Scott and the Hidden History of the CIA* (2008) by Jefferson Morley.

the 2014 conference in Bethesda,[65] where Veciana publicly admitted that David Phillips was Maurice Bishop. While there, I had the chance *publicly* to pin Bob down, so I asked him: *"Do you still accept the single bullet theory?"* To my utter amazement, he admitted that he did! And he still believes that the Mafia masterminded the hit, and that Lee shot JFK! He thinks the CIA is still hiding *something* about JFK, but probably nothing important. If only I had another chance, I would ask him this: *Why, after six decades, has the CIA so persistently and relentlessly covered up for the Mafia?* I have no idea what he would say. *And, by the way, Bob, do tell us why the Mafia hired Lee – was he truly the best they could afford?* One final comment about Blakey – his hat is no longer snow white. Despite being an esteemed and long-serving (Catholic)[66] Notre Dame professor, he has been cited for an ethics violation.[67] It would have been interesting to ask Allen Dulles (or Cord Meyer) to comment on this.

The Assassination Records Review Board (ARRB) came next, during 1994-1998. By comparison to its antecedents, it was a miraculous revelation. Nonetheless, without full cooperation from the federal agencies (especially the Secret Service), the investigation still fell short. This was nowhere more apparent than in the medical evidence. Well before they closed shop, I sent a list of twenty medical questions to the chairman Jack Tunheim (whom I had met in DC). I was curious about the board's medical competence. These questions were to be delivered to each board member; Jack said he would distribute these and then return their answers to me. Unfortunately, no answers were ever received from anyone, not even from Jack. Douglas Horne (a full-time employee of the ARRB) reports that each and every board member was blissfully ignorant of the

65 The AARC Conference at the Bethesda Hyatt - JFK Assassination Debate - The Education Forum (https://educationforum.ipbhost.com/topic/21379-the-aarc-conference-at-the-bethesda-hyatt/).

66 I would pay a high admission price to hear Blakey discuss these JFK issues with his fellow Catholic, James Jesus Angleton. We might even invite a third Catholic (James J. Humes) to chime in. To really boil this pot though, we could toss in fellow Catholics JFK, RFK, James Rowley, and John McCone. The latter three believed in conspiracy, so they would likely blow the lid off of this pot (or plot). We cannot know what JFK believed about 11/22/1963, but he had told Paul B. Fay, Jr. (his friend of 21 years, beginning in the Pacific Theater) that he might be killed by the national security state (*The Pleasure of his Company* (1966), p. 190). This 1962 conversation had been triggered by *Seven Days in May* (1962) by Fletcher Knebel and Charles W. Bailey II. JFK had just read this novel, which was soon turned into a movie, for which JFK accommodatingly loaned the White House to the producers, so it could be used as a set.

67 "Emeritus Law Professor Sanctioned Over The Disclosure Of Documents" – Above the Law (https://abovethelaw.com/2015/12/emeritus-law-professor-sanctioned-over-the-disclosure-of-documents/).

medical evidence. Nonetheless, Anna Kasten Nelson (an obtuse board member) knew better – while knowing zero about the medical evidence, she insisted that no "smoking guns" existed anywhere in the new ARRB evidence.[68] With such remarkable ESP, we could simply have dispensed with any actual research. Henry Graff was no better. His widely used American history textbook then still proclaimed Oswald's guilt! But no one has ever explained why such an obviously biased historian was ever appointed to the board. We should ask Bill Clinton.

It is now almost 30 years since we said goodbye to the ARRB. (Their final report was dated September 30, 1998.) But records – even odd varieties – of new evidence still keep popping up, e.g., the curious recent resurrection of the memory of Secret Service agent Paul Landis. (His ominous, but unbelievably delayed, recollections are discussed in detail in my previous work.) If I may, I would cite my own work on evidence destruction – the trashing of the limousine windshield at the Ford plant in Dearborn on the day of JFK's funeral. Thanks to my University of Michigan Medical School roommate (Duane Harrison, MD), we know that his father witnessed the through-and-through hole in the windshield that day – to his father's everlasting dismay. Of course, we already knew much earlier that this hole (a perforation) was due to a *frontal shot*; this information came from a Ford plant supervisor – George Whitaker. This is all discussed in great detail in my earlier books and shall not be reviewed here. We have other fish (actually villains) to fry here.

But here is what should interest the casual student of this case. Almost whenever some bit of new evidence arrives, it is consistent with conspiracy. Almost never does it support the absurdity of the lone gunman. So, it is now time to end this introduction and promptly resume the authentic history of this most famous murder in history. Well, I concede – the crucifixion of Jesus of Nazareth is still number one.[69] Lots more religious structures remind us of Jesus today than do JFK's remembrances in airports, freeways, schools and museums. In any case, let us next recall some unadulterated history.

DAVID W. MANTIK, MD, PhD
Rancho Mirage, California
Lincoln's Birthday 2025

68 By that time, thanks to Douglas Horne, the ARRB had my optical density measurements and my full analysis of the fraudulent alterations in the JFK X-rays. Anna died in 2012, but she never tried to contact me. I do not believe she ever heard of me.

69 Ironically, just today I purchased two tickets for one of my favorite musicals, *Jesus Christ Superstar*.

Part I: The Mechanics

Into the Heart of Darkness – with Bill Harvey and David Morales[70]

Of all tyrannies, the one that is invoked for the good of its victims[71] is the most oppressive. Those so-called humanitarians who torment us for our own good merely assuage their own consciences. To be cured against one's wishes is to be treated as an imbecile or a domesticated animal.

–Paraphrased from C. S. Lewis

Neither James Jesus Angleton nor Richard Helms nor Cord Meyer *actively* played primary roles in the JFK assassination.[72] In fact, for several years after 11/22/1963, Angleton (1917-1987) was convinced that the Soviets had controlled Oswald. (Richard Helms made the same claim – see Part II in this book.) Even during 1975-1976, during three long interviews with him, Dick Russell reported[73] that Jim was still pushing for Soviet-Cuban involvement. On the other hand, if Angleton truly believed in a Soviet conspiracy, why did he (and Helms, too) get so tied up in knots about the Golitsyn-Nosenko debate?[74]

70 Part I is a summary (and expansion) of my associated PowerPoint presentation for CAPA on November 24, 2024, as given via ZOOM. The PowerPoint will be posted at my website: The Mantik View - Articles and Research on the JFK Assassination by David W. Mantik, M.D., Ph. D. (https://themantikview.org).

71 The plotters of the JFK assassination assumed that they knew what was best for the US. So also did the Athenians know what was best for their city when they voted to kill Socrates. The Sanhedrin also flaunted their self-righteous arrogance when they turned Jesus over to the Roman authorities. Too much "knowledge" is deadly. Quote by C.S. Lewis: "Of all tyrannies, a tyranny sincerely exercised…" | Goodreads

72 Ed Lansdale and David Phillips are likely exceptions; see Part II. Allen Dulles is also a suspect. Desmond FitzGerald, on the other hand, while watching Oswald shot on TV, began to cry. He turned to his wife and exclaimed, *"Now we'll never know"* (*The Very Best Men: Four Who Dared: The Early Years of the CIA* (2006) by Evan Thomas, p. 324).

73 *The Man Who Knew Too Much* (1992) by Dick Russell, p. 198. Perhaps Angleton (and LBJ, too) had missed the mysteriously quiet DEFCON level during November 22-23, 1963. Furthermore, the Joint Chiefs were in a meeting at the time; after they were informed of the assassination, they did not promptly disperse to their command centers. They just stayed in their meeting! (See *Someone Would Have Talked* (2006) by Larry Hancock, p. 304.)

74 "KGB agent defected, then was imprisoned three years by the U.S." - *Los An-*

Yuri Nosenko[75] (who defected to the US in February 1964) claimed that he had been Oswald's case officer, but he also claimed that the KGB had nothing to do with Oswald in the USSR. On the other hand, Anatoliy Golitsyn (who defected to the US in December 1961) claimed that Nosenko was primarily a provocateur.[76] After all, if the CIA had simply accepted that the Soviets were innocent (per Nosenko), those debates were, at least partly, a tempest in a teapot, but Angleton did not trust Nosenko; it was Golitsyn who was his protégé.

In May 1962, Tennant "Pete" Bagley had made first contact with Nosenko in Geneva, Switzerland. In 2007, long after Angleton had kept Yuri in sub-human conditions for years, Pete insisted that Yuri had *not* been a "good faith" defector. Contrary to Angleton's paranoia, and in disagreement with Bagley, the CIA has since (mostly based on a rather long report by Bruce Solie) certified Nosenko as a genuine defector.[77]

To support Pete's dissent, listen to John Newman: *"Nosenko was not a bona fide defector when he was dispatched to the US in 1964. He was a provocateur in 1962 and a false defector in 1964."*[78]

Malcolm Blunt concurs: Bagley *"found that Yuri Nosenko was a false defector."*[79] Bagley also notes that Bruce Solie (Newman's mole) protected Nosenko and – *mirabile dictu* – Solie and Nosenko married sisters! In fact, Solie was best man at Nosenko's wedding.[80] To add even more fuel to this farce, in May 1962, when Bagley first encountered Yuri, Bruce Solie was hiding in the adjacent room, passing questions to Bagley (for him to ask).[81]

If Angleton had believed Nosenko from the beginning (as the CIA now declares he should have), he would then have known that there was no Oswald-KGB connection. So, every November, do the media ask the CIA about its belief in Nosenko as a genuine defector?

---

geles Times. For more on the CIA and Nosenko, see *Cold Warrior: James Jesus Angleton* (1991) by Tom Mangold, pp. 151 ff.

75 *"Richard Helms, realizing that Nosenko was probably a false defector, convinced Earl Warren to not allow Nosenko to testify to the Warren Commission, which at that time was investigating the assassination. Nosenko did, however, testify to the HSCA in 1978, but the members of the commission found him to be uncredible:"* Yuri Nosenko - Wikipedia.

76 Click on the "printed version:" JAMES J. ANGLETON, ANATOLIY GOLITSYN, AND THE "MONSTER PLOT": THEIR IMPACT ON CIA PERSONNEL AND OPERATIONS (https://www.cia.gov/readingroom/print/2070863).

77 *Spy Wars: Moles, Mysteries, and Deadly Games* (2007) by Tennant Bagley, pp. 264, 283.

78 *Uncovering Popov's Mole: The Assassination of President Kennedy* (2022) by John M. Newman, p. 369.

79 *The Devil is in the Details* (2020) by Alan Dale with Malcolm Blunt, p. 340.

80 Ibid., p. 57.

81 Ibid., pp. 56, 394. This is amazing, but Bagley omits Solie from this scenario in his book, *Spy Wars*!

On the other hand, Angleton, with his rejection of Nosenko, would seem to have left the door open to Oswald's possible guilt. In fact, the opposite is the case – Jim persistently refused to believe that a single gunman could have done this. Instead, for years he favored the Soviet connection. Even as late as 1987, Ray Rocca, Jim's longtime assistant, said this (about Angleton's *disbelief* in the lone assassin): *"He hung onto it and would not let go of it."* For Angleton, his nagging belief that the KGB had murdered JFK had become an obsession.[82] So Angleton never accepted the Warren Commission (WC) conclusion that Oswald was the lone gunman!

So, we might ask this: why did Bill Harvey not tell Jim the truth about 11/22/1963 (i.e., that 11/22/1963 was Bill's own operation)?[83] After all, these two were friends until death separated them. In fact, Harvey had written a letter to Angleton (dated June 3, 1976); Bill died on June 9, 1976. CG (Bill's wife) added, *"We were all good friends right up to Bill's death."*[84]

There may an answer to this. As Bayard Stockton summarizes: *"He [Bill] intensely disliked the possibility that his history could be documented…."*[85] His refusal ever to respond David Martin's telephone calls is consistent with this. So is the remarkable paucity of photographs of him, as I discovered while writing this book. But this is exactly the quality that served him well on 11/22/1963.

McNamara was certain that Dulles and Helms were not involved in the JFK plot. Fletcher Prouty agreed, saying that he knew both of them as friends, and in no way could they do this.[86] But see a subsequent footnote about McNamara's different take on LBJ and William Harvey. As for David Phillips, only at the end of his life did he concede that rogue CIA men (certainly not women) had been involved.

If Angleton was truly duped to believe so persistently that the JFK assassination was a Soviet plot, then what shall we conclude about An-

---

82 *The Secret History of the CIA* (2001) by Joseph J. Trento, p. 282. I wonder if Angleton was ever directly asked if he accepted the *Warren Report*; I do not know the answer to this. We'd like to ask Harvey the same question. Intriguingly, many suspicious characters claimed to have been in Dealey Plaza that day. Someone should compile a list. Dan Hardway (for the HSCA) noted that Harvey traveled a lot during the months before 11/22/1963, but when Dan asked the CIA for Harvey's travel vouchers, they blocked him. By the way, do the media ever ask the CIA why Angleton never accepted the lone gunman scenario?

83 In an e-mail to John Simkin (Thurs, Apr 17 at 7:25 AM), David Kaiser said, *"The more I learned about the Agency – and I spent many hours on agency documents at NARA – the more I came to think that* [italics in the original] ***agents keep a great many secrets from each other there****. The FBI is very different in that respect."*

84 *Flawed Patriot* (2006) by Bayard Stockton, pp. 303-305.

85 Ibid., 243.

86 *Bloody Treason* (1997) by Noel Twyman, pp. 537-538.

gleton? Ironically, he himself seems more related to a mole than anyone has suspected. After all, North American moles ("scalopus aquaticus") are colorblind (Angleton could not distinguish friend from foe) and nearsighted (his suspicions mainly targeted his own turf at the CIA). As further support for Angleton as a victim, he told Joseph J. Trento, *"What I'm trying to tell you is, some very odd things were going on that were out of our control."*[87] In addition, Angleton was quite distraught when he learned that an internal KGB study concluded that the perpetrators (note the plural form) had been "right wing."

Scalopus aquaticus

However, if either David Phillips (1922-1988) or Edward Lansdale (1908-1987)[88] or Joseph Milteer or Jack Ruby had been in Dealey Pla-

87 Russell 1992, p. 475. Angleton did not know about the piggyback operation that David Phillips had devised in Mexico City. This clever scheme was imposed on a pre-existing molehunt that Angleton surely knew about. But Jim did not know who had instigated the fake telephone calls in Mexico City. Even more amazing, most likely he did not (at least at first) grasp *why* these were done. For more, see Part II.

88 Lansdale had been a psychological warfare specialist under Charles Willoughby during WW II. Also recall that Lansdale and Harvey had worked together in Operation Mongoose. Another intriguing character, Colonel William C. Bishop, had also served under MacArthur's intelligence chief, Charles Willoughby. So, both Lansdale and Bishop served under Willoughby.

Operation Mongoose included terrorist attacks against Cuban civilians as well as covert operations by the CIA. It was officially authorized on November 30, 1961, by JFK. It was run out of JMWAVE, a secret CIA station on the campus of the University of Miami. The concept was triggered by the failure at the Bay of Pigs. Although it is sometimes equated with assassinations, that was not officially part of its charter, but many individual plans were devised by the CIA to assassinate Fidel Castro. However, none were successful (Operation Mongoose - Wikipedia).

Although it is still sometimes debated, most students today do not believe that JFK (or RFK) approved any assassination plots against Castro. (Apparently John McCone, as a Catholic CIA director, was deliberately shielded from these dark arts, but JFK was also a Catholic.) But Bob McNamara felt otherwise. In the middle of May (apparently 1961), Dick Goodwin attended a meeting of 20 individuals at the State Department. After an hour, Bob arose, put his hand on Dick's shoulder and said, *"The only thing to do is to eliminate Castro."* Then the CIA representative looked toward Bob and said, *"You mean Executive Action?"* McNamara nodded, then looking at me [Dick] he said: *"I mean it Dick, it's the only way"* (Goodwin, p. 189). [In Part II of this book, we will see that Ike favored the assassination of Lumumba, so McNamara and Ike had learned ethics from the same manual.]

Executive Action (1973) was written by Donald Freed and Mark Lane. The movie script za that day (as some believe),[89] then something does seem "rotten in Denmark." Some observers see Lansdale in the photograph of the three tramps (see more in Part II). Phillips's nephew claimed that Dave told his brother Jim (the nephew's father) that he was in Dealey Plaza that day. As further emphasis, Phillips was known as a propaganda and "psy op" specialist. In any case, by the end of his life (of routinely lying), Phillips had named rogue CIA agents as primary culprits, so he passed his final exam – but without admitting to his own role. (More discussion about David follows in Part II.)

But who lifted the FBI "watch" on Oswald? The watch had been placed on August 13, 1963 – after his arrest in New Orleans. Then on October 9, 1963,[90] FBI agent Marvin Gheesling lifted the watch, perhaps based on his belief the Lee had cooperated with the FBI in New Orleans (after his leafleting demonstration) – or maybe the watch was lifted because Oswald's name was pending further use in a molehunt, possibly (this time) related to the Mexico City affair.[91] In any case, Hoover punished Gheesling afterwards, but no one ever dared to punish Hoover.

But J. Edgar Hoover (1895-1972) was a hypocrite – in fact, he knew a great deal about Oswald.[92] Recall his 1960 letter, noting two Oswalds in

---

was written by Dalton Trumbo: executive action movie 1973 - Search.

89 "Familiar Faces in Dealey Plaza" (https://www.memresearch.org/econ/faces/familiar_faces.htm).

90 Remarkably, this was the *same day* that Phillips completed his nine-day trip to DC and Miami. By October 9, 1963, he had returned to hjs post in Mexico City. Did he truly not know that the watch had been lifted that same day?

91 Ann Egerter had used one of several "marked cards" (e.g., Lee Henry Oswald – deliberately misnamed) to facilitate a molehunt: "THE JFK CASE: THE TWELVE WHO BUILT THE OSWALD LEGEND" (Part 3: Counterintelligence Goes Mole Hunting with Oswald's File) - ASSASSINATION ARCHIVES (https://www.opednews.com/populum/page.php?f=THE-JFK-CASE-THE-TWELVE-W-by-Bill-Simpich-101205-794.html#google_vignette).

A memo from Win Scott to the U.S. Ambassador in Mexico City (10/16/1963) cites "Lee *Henry* Oswald": http://www.aarclibrary.org/publib/jfk/fbi/...10418_0002a.htm.

92 Oswald's mother, Marguerite, also knew a lot of characters: Bobby Baker (and his mistress), Fred Korth (Navy secretary), Forrest Sorrels (SS), Mike Howard (SS), Joseph Schott (FBI), Amon Carter (publisher). She knew about Billie Sol Estes and she claimed that Ruby was a paid assassin ("An outsider's look at the insufferable Leon Jaworski" in *Garrison: The*

Mexico.[93] After all, Eugene Dinkin and Joseph Milteer had informed him about the pending JFK plot. Furthermore, so had Richard Nagell, as exhaustively documented by Dick Russell.[94] So, if Hoover knew all of this, why didn't he tell Gheesling to lift the watch? Moreover, CIA officers should also have known that the watch had been lifted. According to Dick Russell, through CIA channels (posted August 27, 1963), Richard Case Nagell had advised Desmond FitzGerald (CIA Special Affairs Staff) of the Dallas plot. This is difficult to deny – because the FitzGerald-Nagell relationship had begun way back in Tokyo. Moreover, based solely on the bewildering – and highly suspicious (to CIA headquarters) Mexico City affair – why didn't the CIA tell the FBI to restore the watch on Oswald? After all, we now know (from Anne Goodpasture[95]) that the CIA had a "keen" and abiding interest in Oswald. Did they have temporary amnesia?[96]

Top (L-R): Richard Helms, Anne Goodpasture, Ann Egerter, Allen Dulles, Jane Roman. **Bottom (L-R)**: Bill Harvey (with wife CG), Silvia Odio, Cord Meyer, Ed Lansdale, Bruce Solie.

Journal of History and Deep Politics by Edgar F. Tatro, Issue #010, June 2022, pp. 76-156).

93 *"Since there is a possibility that an imposter is using Oswald's birth certificate…."* Hoover letter: FBI file NO. 105-82555, addressed to the Office of Security, Department of State. See Appendix I-C.

94 Russell 1992. *"Richard Case Nagell is considered by many to be the most important witness in the JFK assassination, and for reasons that follow, I am inclined to agree"* (Twyman, p. 605).

95 According to Ed Lopez (HSCA staff), she should indeed have been put out to pasture. In fact, Ed said that she belonged in jail. She worked in Staff D, and had answered for years to Harvey. Based in Mexico City, she served as the specific CIA case officer for Mexico City events.

96 See Bill Simpich: "THE JFK CASE: THE TWELVE WHO BUILT THE OSWALD LEGEND (Part 5: The Double Dangle)" - ASSASSINATION ARCHIVES (https://aarclibrary.org/the-jfk-case-the-twelve-who-built-the-oswald-legend-part-5-the-double-dangle/).

Also see "(6) Before JFK's Assassination, the CIA Had Compiled a 181-Page Dossier on Lee Harvey Oswald" (https://jfkfacts.substack.com/p/before-jfks-death-the-cia-compiled).

John Newman argues[97] that it was Bruce Solie (not Angleton) who presented Oswald as a dangle to the Soviets (in a molehunt). But, according to Newman, this was more of a fake molehunt. (In any case, Oswald would have been oblivious to a molehunt of any color.) Recall that Angleton had been totally duped – over many years – by Kim Philby. So, if Newman is right, Solie would be strike two against Angleton. Finally, if my insinuations here are correct, Angleton also missed the crucial role of Harvey in the JFK murder. That would be strike three on Jim.[98]

Top (L-R): Curtis LeMay, George Joannides, Sam Giancana, Santo Trafficante, Jr., Jack Crichton. Bottom (L-R): Dick Russell, John Newman, David Talbot, Noel Twyman, Ted Shackley.

William King Harvey (1915-1976)

Bill Harvey meets all of the requirements for the primary mastermind for the Dealey Plaza events. He had a nearly flawless photographic memory. He was brilliant, amoral, highly secretive, independent of authority, full of hatred for JFK (with a "purple passion" loathing for RFK), yet he was exceedingly sensitive to security – despite his astonishing alcohol intake. Even during the House Select Committee on Assassinations

97 *Uncovering Popov's Mole: The Assassination of President Kennedy, Volume IV* (2022) by John Newman.

98 Angleton's reputation as a "Whiz Kid" has prevented many from glimpsing his shortcomings (see *In Banks We Trust–Bankers and Their Close Associates: the CIA, the Mafia, Drug-traders, Dictators, Politicians, and the Vatican* (1984) by Penny Lernoux, p. 190). Furthermore, John Newman has insightfully noted, *"But Angleton did not have the skill required to match wits with Philby"* (Newman 2022, p. 317). Anthony Cave Brown concurs. *"He* [Angleton] *did not have the highly disciplined classical mind of Philby; and that was why Philby was able to make mincemeat of him, even on his home ground"* (*Treason in the Blood: H. St. John Philby, Kim Philby, and the Spy Case of the Century* (1994) by Anthony Cave Brown, p. 394).

(HSCA), Ed Lopez wrote that Harvey was a possible suspect.[99] Furthermore, his friends report that he never recovered from his demotion (in essence, he was fired) after the Cuban Missile Crisis. His next (and penultimate) stop was as CIA station chief in Rome, which was a clear downgrade. Furthermore, his behavior while in Rome confirmed that he had earned this relegation.[100] Ironically though, in his new position in Rome (beginning in late June 1963), although it was a punishment (and he was deeply humiliated), he now had easy access to Corsican hit men. Furthermore, throughout all of 1963, Harvey still had global access to all CIA files. His travel records for that summer would be enlightening, but the CIA persistently refuses to release them. Six decades later, is this truly a national security issue? In any case, Harvey's deputy, F. Mark Wyatt had bumped into Harvey on a plane to Dallas, probably in early November 1963. Harvey explained, *"I'm here to see what's happening."* Dan Hardway said, *"I wouldn't be surprised to learn Harvey was in Dallas [sometime] in November 1963."*[101]

Even while in Rome, Harvey saw nothing wrong with violating the law. He saw murder as a legitimate political tool. Wyatt was stunned one day, when Harvey proposed hiring Mafia hit men to kill Italian communists.[102]

After Harvey died, his Indiana house experienced two burglary attempts. His wife (CG) claimed that "they" were after his papers. This reeks of a CIA attempt to recover assassination-related documents.

Harvey's biographer, Bayard Stockton,[103] intimates even more about Bill's psychological profile. He describes Harvey as a closed book, always covering his trail.[104] And Harvey warned his wife never to talk.[105] (She

---

99 Noel Twyman once asked Robert McNamara about Harvey. McNamara admitted that he knew Harvey. When Twyman further asked if McNamara could picture Harvey as a JFK assassin or even possibly as the mastermind. McNamara conceded that possibility. Twyman persisted and asked McNamara if LBJ might have known in advance. McNamara also granted that possibility, but added that he did not believe it (Twyman, pp. 500-502).

100 Before Harvey was sacked from his position in Rome, he had pursued alcohol and women (except for his wife) quite relentlessly. The CIA station even suspected that he had found time to impregnate a secretary (Talbot 2015, p. 474).

101 *The Devil's Chessboard* (2015) by David Talbot, p. 477.

102 Ibid., p. 475.

103 Stockton, p. 243.

104 Anyone who has tried to locate good photographs of Harvey will sympathize with me. In book after book, the same limited number of (low quality) Harvey photographs appear. I tried diligently to be original, but I fell short. Harvey really did mean to be elusive.

105 David Martin recalled perhaps a hundred conversations with Angleton (until 1978), but he never got even one with Harvey. Whenever he called Harvey, Bill just hung

burned his papers after his death.) And, despite the CIA's irritation about his unrelenting bond with Mafia man, Johnny Roselli, he would never quit that alliance. This defiance was a genuine challenge to CIA hierarchy. In fact, because of it, the CIA put Harvey under suspicion and he became aware that Helms no longer trusted him. In fact, both the FBI and the CIA considered him a "potential time bomb."[106] Hoover, too, had never forgiven him (Bill had first been an FBI agent) for not being a team player.[107] We therefore conclude that Harvey clearly – and persistently (over many decades) – was a lone ranger, a role that was not relished by his superiors. This trait (autonomy) on the other hand, further marks him as ideal for the role of mastermind for the on-site operation of 11/22/1963.[108]

Chief Suspect #1: William King Harvey (1915-1976)

- Law degree from Indiana University (1937)
- An Indiana hick, he joined the FBI (Dec 1940), known then for its blue-collar employees.
- Resigned from the FBI in 1947
- Promptly joined the nascent CIA in 1947

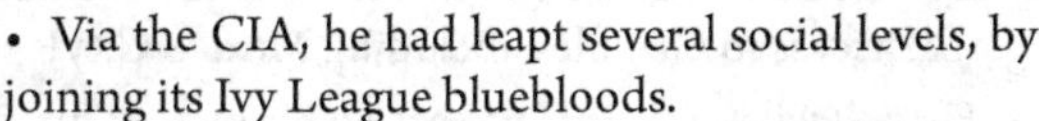

- Via the CIA, he had leapt several social levels, by joining its Ivy League bluebloods.

  To wit: while Angleton grew orchids, tied fishing flies and created gold cufflinks, Harvey collected guns and drank martinis.

- 3+ ppd of Camels or Chesterfields
- 2 martinis before lunch, plus many during and after
- Most proficient imbiber in the entire US government
- Best friend of Johnny Roselli (Mafia)
- Knew Ian Fleming (JFK's favorite author)
- "Extremely intelligent" – biographer Bayard Stockton
- Supervised BOB (The Berlin Tunnel)
- Operation Mongoose (with Lansdale in 1962) & Task Force W (200 officers)
- CIA Station Chief in Rome (June 1963-)
- Most likely, his CIA superiors & colleagues were unaware of his role in the JFK hit.
- Nailed Soviet master spy Kim Philby in a memo of June 13, 1951. Philby had duped Angleton for years.

Philby USSR Stamp

---

up. However, Martin reports one brief conversation with Mrs. Harvey after Bill died (*Wilderness of Mirrors* (1980) by David C. Martin, pp. xii-xiii).

106 Stockton, pp. 245, 253-255.

107 Ibid,, p. 245.

108 Harvey did not hold authority figures in awe (e.g., Hoover, who never forgave him). At the CIA, he detested both of his bosses, Richard Helms and Desmond FitzGerald.

Traits of a Mastermind: Bill Harvey

- His psychological profile (as an outsider), his amorality, his known hatred of JFK, his phenomenal memory, his resume (especially in assassinations), his Corsican and Mafia contacts – all of this makes him the ideal mastermind of the JFK assassination.
- Traveled to Dallas from Rome in early November 1963 – per F. Mark Wyatt, his deputy, who saw him on that plane
- Strongly detested both Desmond FitzGerald (his immediate boss) and Richard Helms
- Near photographic memory; his briefings lasted for hours (from memory)
- Directed ZR/RIFLE (for assassinations – inside Staff D) – through 1963 he had global access to CIA files, including Mexico City!
- He was willing and able to act on his own. Witness his deliberate defiance of JFK's order – the 60-person commando raids into Cuba during the missile crisis – which got him demoted. But he always maintained high security.
- He never quite fit in at CIA; by his actions and his attitude, he often deliberately announced his rebellious demeanor. He felt superior to most other CIA officers (probably with good reason).
- He had little good to say about other CIA officers such as Bissell (who directed the Bay of Pigs operation).
- In October 1960, he made a recruiting trip to Europe – to vet potential criminal accomplices.
- From childhood he was taught to be a Shakespeare scholar – by his mother, an English professor. They often traded Shakespeare quotes. From these tragic tales, he was thereby early immersed in deception.
- He was reported to be a prodigious womanizer, which requires some degree of deception!
- Noel Twyman asked Robert McNamara if he could picture Harvey as the mastermind of the JFK assassination. His answer: *Yes, it was a possibility* (Twyman, p. 502).

David Sanchez Morales (1925-1978)

Meanwhile, Morales was ideally situated in Miami (as second in command to Ted Shackley, a Harvey devotee). But Morales also spent extended periods of time *during 1963 in Mexico City.* As head of the 150 Spanish-speaking AMOTs,[109] he most likely had interacted directly with the

---

For example, even though Helms was two years older than him, Harvey once called Helms *"the boy diplomat"* (Trento, p. 408). Regarding Harvey's commando raids during the Cuban Missile Crisis, "[Bobby (RFK) said that] *'I checked into it. And nobody knew about it. The CIA didn't. The top officials didn't. We pinned it down to the fellow who was supposed to be in charge* [William K. Harvey]. *He said we planned it because the military wanted it done. I asked the military, and they never heard of it ....'*" (*The JFK Assassination Chokeholds,* Kindle, 98).

109 These were anti-Castro Cuban exiles, trained as intelligence agents, who were overseen by Morales. Most were in Miami, but some were in Mexico City. The CIA paid them. Their organization was sometimes called Operation 40.

AMOTs in Mexico City that summer.[110] Also recall that he had worked together with Harvey over many years, beginning with BOB (in Berlin in 1951). That was *twelve years* before 11/22/1963. The incredibly early death of Morales (at age 52), suspiciously *just after a visit to DC*, has an unpleasant odor about it. This is especially so in view of Didi's (David's nickname)

Chief Suspect #2: David Sanchez Morales (1925 – 1978)

- Drinking buddy of Roselli (often with Rip Robertson)
- "He drank like crazy, but he was bright as hell" – Tom Clines (CIA)
- Was the agency right to be afraid of his honesty? Ruben Carbajal (best friend) *"You're goddamn right … you want the truth, here it is."*
- Worked at BOB – under Harvey
- With Shackley, he led the Phoenix Program in Vietnam*
- *Killed 30,000 – 100,000 Vietnamese (aka Viet Cong)
- Head of Pakse CIA base (for bombing the Ho Chi Minh Trail)
- Assisted David Phillips in the Allende coup (1973)
- Under Shackley (Harvey's disciple), Morales essentially ran the Miami CIA station (for Cuban operations). It was the largest in the world, with 500 employees.
- With help from Félix Rodríguez, they captured Che Guevara
- Right after he died, CIA officials visited his family. *"They were making sure he was dead,"* per a relative.

110 Larry Hancock notes that Jose Sanjenis worked closely with David Morales in 1962 and 1963. Larry adds that new documents from Malcolm Blunt confirm that Jose was in charge of Operation 40; he was the number one exile in the AMOT organization, which was trained and prepared by David Morales. For more on Sanjenís, see Hopsicker, pp. 143 ff; also see Hinckle and Turner, p. 365. Sanjenís is sometimes cited as José Joaquín Sanjenís Perdomo (aliases: "Joaquin Sanjenis" and "Sam Jenis"): "KILL THE MESSENGER: Compelling evidence points to CIA Assassin, Jose Joaquin Sanjenis Perdomo, as Lennon's killer" | RIELPOLITIK (https://rielpolitik.com/2016/12/08/kill-the-messenger-december-8th-1980-an-investigation-into-john-lennons-assassination/). Sanjenís was a doorman at the Dakota Apartments (at 1 West 72nd Street); John Lennon was killed at this same address. José had also worked for the Watergate burglar Frank Sturgis for about ten years.

explanation for his elaborate security system: he was afraid of his "own" people. But we also should recall that he had confessed (to his best friend and to his attorney) about his active role in the JFK murder.

There is yet more about Morales.[111] The CIA never acknowledged that he worked for them – nor is it on his gravestone[112] (in Wilcox, AZ), nor in his retirement notice nor in his obituary.

In fact, after Morales retired, and when Phillips (inattentively) identified him as CIA, Morales threatened a lawsuit. This response strongly suggests that Morales wanted the CIA to forget about him; was he afraid of blowback from the agency? His best friend, Ruben Carbajal, reported that his Pentagon parking spot was equivalent to that of a general. In 1954, Morales and Phillips had debriefed Ike about their success in the Guatemalan coup, so (in some circles at least) Morales was quite famous *nine years* before 11/22/1963. He had also told his friend Ruben that he (personally) had killed a Chilean general. Furthermore, Morales and his close associate (Tony Sforza) told David Talbot that the agency was behind the JFK plot.[113]

Regarding that coup in Guatemala, although Ike was very pleased with it, Diego Rivera (the Mexican artist), was not. This coup (in 1954) so incensed Rivera that he promptly painted this heroic 8 ½ x 15 foot linen canvas, *La Gloriosa Victoria* (*The Glorious Victory*), which reflects Aztec and Mayan artistic traditions. It resides (but is not displayed) in the Pushkin Museum in Moscow. Hundreds of thousands were killed in the civil war that later followed this coup. Incidentally, Allen loved this painting (of course, without my captions) and he presented copies to friends!

---

111 "David Sanchez Morales – The CIA's 'One-Man Gang'" – The New JFK Show Blog (https://merdist.com/wp/2020/12/08/david-sanchez-morales-the-one-man-gang/).

112 "David Morales' Grave – TangoDown63" (https://tangodown63.com/morales-david-sanchez/).

113 *Brothers* (2007) by David Talbot, pp. 398-400. Much of this personal information about Morales derives from the work of Talbot. He visited with Ruben "Rocky" Carbajal for hours in Nogales, Arizona. See "DAVID TALBOT: The JFK Assassination at 60: What Did We Know and When Did We Know It?" - ASSASSINATION ARCHIVES (https://aarclibrary.org/david-talbot-the-jfk-assassination-at-60-what-did-we-know-and-when-did-we-know-it/).

But he would likely not be so pleased to learn that Foster's bust has been stashed in a locked room near baggage at Dulles International Airport.

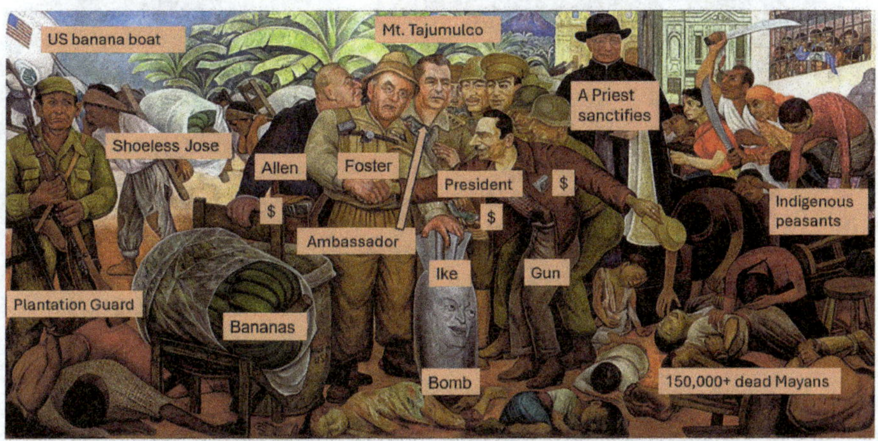

The 1978 death of Morales was oddly timed. Although officially it was a heart attack, in fact he had just returned to Arizona from DC. His death was unexpected (at age 52) – he had had no symptoms of heart disease. Ominously, just shortly before his trip to DC he had been listed as a witness for the HSCA by Gaeton Fonzi. Even after his death the CIA still had not lost interest in Morales; according to a relative, they visited sometime after the funeral, just to be sure he was truly dead![114]

Morales's funeral in remote Wilcox, Arizona also evoked some astonishment. An extended line of high-ranking military brass and well-dressed (and apparently eminent) acquaintances in civvies and sunglasses arrived from far and wide. When he was interred (in Wilcox) the line of mourners extended all the way through town, to the amazement of the locals.[115]

Ruben Carbajal was asked about whether the agency had a right to fear Morales's honesty. *"You're goddamn right,"* he said. *"You ask him a question ... and he got right to the point, no horse-shitting around.... You want the truth, here it is."*[116] Ruben Carbajal told Fonzi his impression of Morales during his final years; David had *"a festering disillusionment and resentment towards the Agency...."*[117] If the CIA understood this, and also knew about David's pending encounter with the HSCA, disaster might well have followed for Morales.

114 At the Baton Rouge funeral home (where Barry Seal lay in the casket) there was an entire line of men in sleek, dark suits. His wife, Debbie Seal, was asked who they were. She said, *"They're with the government. They've come to make sure that he's dead"* (Hopsicker, p. 379).

115 Twyman, p. 449.

116 Talbot, p. 401.

117 *The Last Investigation* (2013) by Gaeton Fonzi, p. 386.

William "Rip" Robertson (1920–1970)

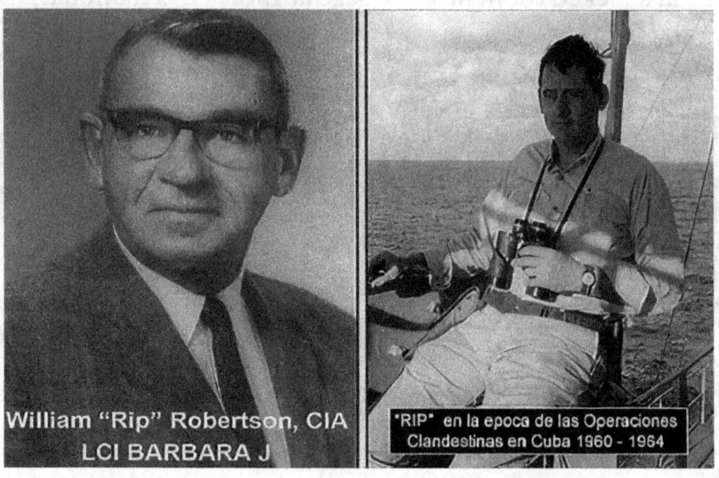

William "Rip" Robertson, CIA
LCI BARBARA J

"RIP" en la epoca de las Operaciones Clandestinas en Cuba 1960 - 1964

Robertson was either trusted by the inner circle, or he was a welcome visitor. He was a decorated WW II veteran. Like Harvey, he had joined the CIA in 1947. He had been an operations officer for the Cuban exiles and he was one of only two CIA operatives with Brigade 2506 at the Bay of Pigs. While on the beach and under fire for several hours, he supervised the brigade. (Morales was also there.) He later led an unsanctioned mission to Cuba during the Missile Crisis – likely under orders from Harvey. He was also on the JM/WAVE staff with Morales. He had provided military support for the Guatemalan coup (after which Morales helped to debrief Ike). He also reported to Morales while on the Bayo mission to Cuba on June 8, 1963.[118] According to Bill Simpich, Rip was a frequent (night long) drinking buddy of both Morales and Roselli. Gung-ho specialists like Rip were known as "cowboys." Ray S. Cline (CIA) said, *"You've got to have cowboys---the only thing is you don't let them make policy. You keep them in the ranch house when you don't have a specific project for them."* During the 1954 coup in Guatemala, Rip escaped from Cline's ranch house. He dispatched a pilot to bomb a Soviet ship, but the pilot instead accidentally sunk a British merchantman! So, the CIA had to reimburse Lloyd's of London with $1.5 million.[119] Rip was then permanently locked into the ranch house.[120] No matter, he is buried in Arlington National Cemetery (where JFK also rests).

118 Operation Tilt (Bayo/Pawley Mission) (https://spartacus-educational.com/JFKtilt.htm)

119 *Deadly Secrets: The CIA-Mafia War Against Castro and the Assassination of JFK* (1981 and 1992) by Warren Hinckle and William Turner, pp. 67-68.

120 Or maybe he eventually escaped. Hopsicker (p. 74) reports that Rip flew again at the Bay of Pigs – after becoming a good buddy of Nicaragua's Anastasio Somoza.

Carl Elmer Jenkins (1926 - ?)[121]

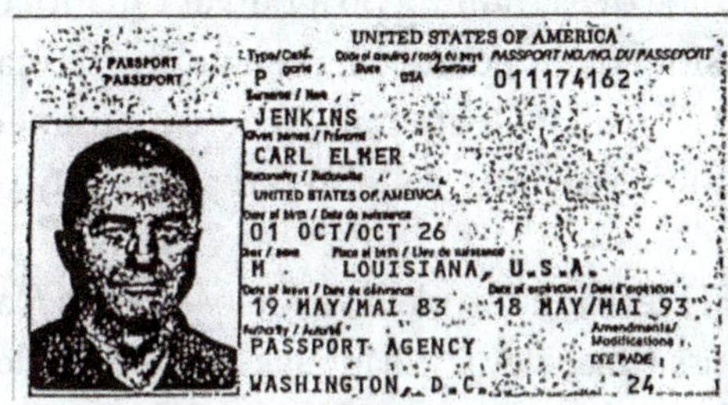
UNITED STATES OF AMERICA
PASSPORT
PASSEPORT
P USA 011174162
JENKINS
CARL ELMER
UNITED STATES OF AMERICA
01 OCT/OCT 26
M LOUISIANA, U.S.A.
19 MAY/MAI 83 18 MAY/MAI 93
PASSPORT AGENCY
WASHINGTON, D.C. 24

Jenkins does not have a Wikipedia page, but he does appear in Wikispooks.[122] The following is adapted from that page.

Jenkins joined the CIA in 1952. He worked with Executive Action, most notably against the government of Jacobo Arbenz Guzman in Guatemala.[123] During this time he worked with William "Rip" Robertson and many suspects in the JFK assassination, including Tracy Barnes, E. Howard Hunt, David Atlee Phillips, and David Sanchez Morales.

On his return to the US from Vietnam he joined the two Davids (Phillips and Morales) at Theodore Shackley's JM/WAVE station in Miami. He is frequently named in documents for AM/WORLD,[124] the CIA's codename for overthrowing Castro. (Cuban documents begin with the letters AM.)

In the summer of 1963, he worked closely with Morales to provide paramilitary training for Manuel Artime and Rafael 'Chi Chi' Quintero. He also become Quintero's handler.

Jenkins later worked with Shackley's organization in Laos; he was appointed Plans/Programs/Budget Management Officer in 1969 and was Chief of Base (1970-1973). He officially retired from the CIA in 1973 (at age 47).

But even later (in the mid-1980s), he played a major role in the covert efforts to resupply the Nicaraguan Contras, an effort led by Oliver North and Richard Secord – which violated Congressional proscriptions. [End of Wikispooks.]

---

121 See comments about Jenkins in (1) *The Death Merchant: The Rise and Fall of Edwin P. Wilson* (1985) by Joseph Goulden and Alexander W. Raffio *and* (2) *Manhunt: The Incredible Pursuit of a CIA Agent Turned Terrorist* (1986) by Peter Maas.

122 Carl Elmer Jenkins - Wikispooks.

123 Recall that Lansdale had picked Bill Harvey to head Task Force W, whose goal was to topple Castro. Harvey also ran the Executive Action attempt to kill Castro. Jenkins and his helicopter company were customers of Commercial Helicopters of Baton Rouge. This company got most of its funding from mobster Herman K. Beebe; one of its principles was CIA asset Barry Seal, who is discussed elsewhere in this book.

124 *Shadow Warfare: The History of America's Undeclared Wars* (2014) by Larry Hancock and Stuart Wexler.

The following is from a website "Carl Elmer Jenkins."[125] He finished first among 372 officers in a Marine Corps training program at Quantico, Virginia. In 1949, he was commissioned as Second Lieutenant in the marines. He served as chief of the CIA base in Guatemala, where he trained the leaders of Brigade 2506, the force that was slaughtered at the Bay of Pigs in April 1961.

He was recruited to the AMLASH team and worked very closely with David Morales – they had the same boss (Shackley).[126] Morales focused on development and deployment of security and intelligence forces, while Jenkins, as the military advisor, selected and prepared paramilitary cadre for small, individual missions. Meanwhile, David Phillips organized the safe houses.

The AM/WORLD memo (104-10315-10004) was declassified on January 27 (or maybe the 28th), 1999, and was discovered by Stuart Wexler in 2004; he showed it to Larry Hancock. With help from Malcolm Blunt, Hancock discovered even more CIA officers in AM/WORLD. Hancock points out that AM/WORLD had its own separate operations staff based in Miami and Mexico City. The head of AM/WORLD, and Artime's case officer, was Henry Hecksher. Hecksher had been head of the counter-intelligence section in Berlin (at BOB), where his colleagues were Shackley, Morales, and Bill Harvey.

While in Guatemala, Hecksher worked undercover as a coffee purchaser. He became part of PB/SUCCESS, a CIA operation (1954) that overthrew Jacobo Arbenz. Other CIA officers involved in this operation included David Atlee Phillips, Tracy Barnes, William "Rip" Robertson and E. Howard Hunt.

According to Phillips (read *Night Watch*[127]), Ike was so pleased with the overthrow of the democratically elected Jacobo Arbenz that he invited Hecksher, Tracy Barnes, Morales, and Allen Dulles to give a personal debriefing at the White House.

Richard Helms testified under oath to Congress[128] when he said that AMLASH "*...was not an assassination operation.*" However, Jenkins (at age 95 in June 2022), who surely knew better than Helms, snorted, "*Of course,*" when Jefferson Morley asked if it was an assassination program. Apparently, someone had forgotten to tell Dick Helms. In fact, Carl had provided Manuel Artime with a Belgian-made FAL rifle to kill Castro. It was to be fired by Rolando Cubela, a former medical student, who had been trained to preserve life.

---

125 https://spartacus-educational.com/JFKjenkinsC.htm

126 Shackley was also Tim Clines's boss.

127 Philips, David A., *The Nightwatch*, Ballantine Books (NY 1982).

128 *A Look Over My Shoulder: A Life in the CIA* (2003) by Richard Helms.

After divorcing his first wife (and their five children), Jenkins married again (in December 1965) – to the 29-year-old Elizabeth Starr Wilton (born April 1, 1936), who had more natural beauty and even more brains (as a Fulbright scholar) than did his first wife.[129] Elizabeth had previously been a translator for the CIA in Managua, Nicaragua.

Gene Wheaton (a close friend and colleague) described Jenkins as the head recruiter and trainer for the anti-Castro Cubans before the Bay of Pigs. Gene also recalled that Félix Rodríguez (a Cuban – and a good friend of George H. W. Bush) and Nestor Pino[130] were all in Vietnam with him (Jenkins) and even in the Congo during attempts to overthrow Lumumba. Incidentally, Gene added that Jenkins was the CIA liaison officer between CIA headquarters and Carlos Marcello. Quite calmly, Gene recalled that Carl had recruited Lee Harvey Oswald into the CIA while he was a marine [i.e., *before* he went to the USSR], but *"Lee was just a stooge they set up* [for later use – arbitrarily ***whenever***] *as part of an Operation Security Plan (for deniability) whenever they put a real dirty operation into place."*[131] *Quintero, when interviewed, stated, "If I was to tell what I know about Dallas and the Bay of Pigs, it would be the greatest scandal that has ever rocked the nation."*[132]

Jenkins, during an interview with Jeff Morley,[133] said, *"I was one of the handful of people in the agency that [sic] was trained and experienced in paramilitary operations. I could indeed bring down a government. Or I could protect the government by getting rid of the insurgents. And the word goes around* – 'Hey, if you need a dirty job done, call Jenkins.'"

In summary, Gene Wheaton (who had even contacted the ARRB[134] – more than once) asserted that Jenkins – and the anti-Castro Cubans, too – claimed that they had killed JFK. Apparently, Carl Jenkins has not

129 Elisabeth Starr Wilton (born April 1, 1936), American management consultant | World Biographical Encyclopedia. Paul Hoven (on the Education Forum, September 12, 2007) reports that she was raised in Wisconsin (as I was) but I don't recall ever hearing about her then. She received a PhD from the University of Maryland in 1978, seven years after my wife received her BS degree from the same university. She was a management consultant and a certified clinical hypnotherapist (National Board Certified Clinical Hypnotherapists, 2005). Unfortunately, despite Elizabeth's beauty and brains, she and Carl divorced in July 1990.

130 "A Witness List for House Hearings on Vol II of the CIA's Inspector General's Report on CIA Drug Trafficking" (https://www.copvcia.com/free/ciadrugs/witness_list.html).

131 Gene Wheaton, interviewed by William Matson Law and Mark Sobel, posted on YouTube on June 15, 2017. Also see https://www.maryferrell.org/pages/Essay_-_The_Wheaton_Lead.html.

132 Reinaldo Taladrid and Lazaro Barredo Medina, *Granma* (January 15, 2006).

133 JFKcountercoup: Jeff Morley with Carl Jenkins - w/ Commentary and Links (https://jfkcountercoup.blogspot.com/2022/06/jeff-morley-with-carl-jenkins.html).

134 Wheaton told the ARRB that he lived near Palm Springs, but I have never knowingly encountered him during the many years (since 1983) that I have lived here.

yet been buried in Arlington National Cemetery. In April 2025, a search engine could not locate his obituary, so Arlington must wait.

General Charles Willoughby (1892-1972)

Willoughby (see photograph below) may reside either inside or extremely near that the inner circle. During WW II he served as chief of intelligence for Douglas MacArthur. During the war, MacArthur said, *"There have been three great intelligence officers in history. Mine is not one of them."* Author John Ferris calls this an understatement. Although Willoughby was a bull of a man (at 6 feet 3 inches), MacArthur liked to call him "my little Nazi." Ironically, MacArthur was only 6 feet 0 inches tall. Willoughby was awarded the Distinguished Service Cross for his role in the Papuan campaign and he established Nagell's Field Operation Unit in the Far East. (Nagell is the primary subject of Dick Russell's 1992 book.) Near Manila on August 16, 1945, he met the Japanese surrender delegation. After the war, some of his old team joined the Skorzeny network in Europe. By 1952, Otto Skorzeny (see photograph below) had made his home in Madrid. Also recall that Jean Rene Souétre reportedly had met with E. Howard Hunt in Madrid during March-April 1963.[135] After his army retirement, Willoughby worked with H. L. Hunt on the International Committee for the Defense of Christian Culture. He frequently corresponded with Allen Dulles and H. L. Hunt. During the Jim Garrison investigation, he urged H. L. Hunt to make a compelling case for Soviet complicity in the JFK murder. His files also show correspondence with Hoover. A 1970 letter to Willoughby from Mario Garcia Kohly (the anti-Castro Cuban exile) refers to Hoover as *"a good friend of yours."* Willoughby is also buried in Arlington National Cemetery. But notice this: Dick Russell (in 1992) cites Willoughby on *48 pages!*[136]

From left to right: Willoughby (twice), Jean Rene Souétre, Robert Maheu, Larry Hancock

135 On 11/22/1963, E. Howard Hunt was meeting with Richard Helms and other CIA officials in a house in northwest DC (ZR Rifle: *The Plot to Kill Kennedy and Castro: Cuba Opens Secret Files* (1994), p. 163). Howard was obviously close to the top CIA leadership.

136 Russell 1992.

Johnny Roselli (1905-1976)

In 1928, Al Capone invited Roselli to work for the Chicago Outfit. By 1956, Roselli was the chief representative in Las Vegas for the Los Angeles and Chicago mafia. Roselli introduced Robert Maheu to Sam Giancana and to Santo Trafficante (Santo may have arranged the hit on Sam). Roselli was recruited by Harvey to assassinate Fidel Castro (thereby provoking RFK to rage[137]). Despite receiving six poison pills from the CIA, Giancana and Trafficante failed in this task. In 1963, Frank Sinatra sponsored Roselli for membership in the Friars Club. Soon after this, Roselli discovered a card-cheating operation run by one of his Las Vegas friends (Maurice Friedman). So, Roselli asked for his cut. This cheating was discovered in July 1967 by FBI agents, who had tailed Roselli. Scores of wealthy men, including millionaire Harry Karl (aka Mr. Debbie Reynolds) and Zeppo Marx were bilked of millions. Roselli was convicted and fined $55,000.

Some Likely "Mechanics"

Other nominees: Roscoe White, Harry Weatherford, James Files, Sergio Arcacha Smith, Jack Lawrence, Tony Izquierdo, Mac Wallace, Frank Sturgis, Lucien Sarti, Michele Nicoli. The global pool of available assassins likely numbered in the thousands.

H.D. Garcia Souétre Nicoletti Jack Canon

Charles Nicoletti

On March 29, 1977, Nicoletti was shot three times in the back of his head while in his Oldsmobile in a parking lot. His car was never turned off, so it overheated and caught on fire. He was soon to testify before the HSCA. George de Mohrenschildt died on same day.

Sam Giancana's demise had been similar: on June 19, 1975, just before his Church Committee testimony, someone crept into his basement and shot him in the head and neck seven times with a .22 caliber pistol. John Black (LBJ's next door neighbor) had warned him in advance – to no avail.

137 A new record release (March 2025) confirms Bill Kelly's previous conclusion: RFK did not order Castro's assassination: https://www.archives.gov/files/research/jfk/releases/2025/0318/124-10280-10030.pdf.

On June 24 and September 22, 1975, Roselli testified before the Church Committee (see photograph of Frank Church right) – about the CIA plan to kill Castro. Just before Roselli testified, Giancana was shot to death (June 19, 1975) in the basement of his Illinois home. Then (the next year), just ten days after Roselli disappeared, his body was found (on July 28, 1976) by a fisherman in a 55-gallon steel fuel drum floating in Dumfounding Bay near Miami. He had been garroted. His arms and legs had been cut off and he had a bullet hole in his head.[138] Bill Bonanno, the son of Cosa Nostra mafia boss Joseph Bonanno, claimed in his memoir (*Bound by Honor: A Mafioso's Story*, 1999) that Roselli and he had discussed the JFK assassination. According to Bonanno, Roselli fired at JFK from a storm drain on Elm Street.

In 2006, the Discovery Channel aired *Conspiracy Files*: *JFK*. Based on *Ultimate Sacrifice* (2008) by Lamar Waldron, Roselli had supposedly framed Abraham Bolden. In 2010, *Playboy* published an article by Hillel Levin; Roselli (see photographs below) was implicated there in the JFK assassination by William Robert "Tosh" Plumlee and by James Files, then an Illinois inmate.

138 In 1977 – during the HSCA – Nicoletti was murdered on the same day that de Mohrenschildt suspiciously died. A decade earlier, another death had been suspect; less than a week after the Garrison probe was announced, David Ferrie was found dead in his apartment (on February 22, 1967). For more strange deaths, see "30 Watergate Deaths" - JFK Assassination Debate - The Education Forum (https://educationforum.ipbhost.com/topic/4526-30-watergate-deaths/).

MULTIPLE TEAMS – PER ROB REINER

Anti-Castro Cubans (Herminio Diaz Garcia) – recruited by Morales
Corsican (Jean-Rene Souétre) – recruited by Harvey
Mafia (Charles Nicoletti) – recruited by Giancana
Military (Jack Canon) – recruited by Willoughby

Reiner selected these four characters for his podcast: Who Killed JFK? Podcast – Apple Podcasts

NOTE: I (not Rob) imagined the "recruited" pathway.

MULTIPLE SNIPER TEAMS WERE ISOLATED FROM ONE ANOTHER

John West: The most important aspect was using contract killers, i.e., sniper teams with deniable connections. They included the Corsican mob, the American mafia, Cuban exiles, and domestic trigger men. These teams were compartmentalized, probably not in sync with each other – which compromised the operation.

John West has been a sniper.

Bill Simpich proposes that the JFK hit was "piggybacked"[139] on top of a previously existing operation. Most likely this was the molehunt that used Oswald's (deliberately misstated) name. The perpetrators in this second operation were likely invisible to those in the first operation. The failure of the CIA Mexico Station promptly to report the Oswald visit to headquarters is consistent with this. It also explains why CIA headquarters (including Angleton) seemed so flummoxed by these fake telephone calls. Hancock even confirms this disconnect of the Mexico CIA station from CIA headquarters: *"…in many instances the Mexico City CIA station appears to have pursued its own interests regarding Lee Harvey Oswald."* So, here we may well have proof that David Phillips had an ongoing *independent* "Oswald" project (Hancock 2025, Kindle, 36). Even many years later, Anne Goodpasture would assert that headquarters *"had no need to know all those other details"* (Morley, *Our Man in Mexico*, p. 237). To make matters (of communication) even worse, the HSCA concluded that Phillips did not know what he was talking about: *"I knew him in Havana. His reports were unreliable."*[140]

139 A piggyback mortgage, or an 80/20 mortgage, occurs where the first mortgage accounts for 80% of the debt while the second covers the remaining 20%. John Newman notes that Bruce Solie (Newman's designated mole) did not favor killing JFK. In Newman's view, Solie *"was aghast to discover the plot to assassinate JFK may have been **hidden inside** [emphasis added] of his false molehunt"* (Newman, p. 58).

140 https://www.maryferrell.org/showDoc.html?docId=41321#relPageId=4.

Now think about this: JFK's autopsy was under tight military control.[141] Logically then, a conduit must have existed from the core assassins to the military. After all, how else could the autopsy have been so tightly controlled? In fact, on Sunday, November 24, 1963, Rear Admiral Calvin Galloway (the commanding officer of the National Naval Medical Center) – who although not a pathologist – had mandated that James Humes seriously revise the autopsy report. In fact, a "decoy ambulance," had been driven around the medical center (in a deliberately misleading manner) the night of the autopsy. Galloway personally rode around the medical center grounds in that decoy ambulance as a passenger.[142] So, if the military supervised the autopsy, are we to believe that they had no link to the Dealey Plaza murder? And if the military was innocent, why was Army Intelligence officer James Powell taking photographs in Dealey Plaza? Also recall that army reserve intelligence officer Jack Crichton arranged for Marina's translator.[143] It is even possible that the Dallas police first heard Oswald's name via Military Intelligence.

Peter Dale Scott has reported that at least two representatives of US military intelligence were on the scene. One was the 112th Military Intelligence Group from Fort Sam Houston in San Antonio. Lt. Col. Robert E. Jones had informed the HSCA of this. The second group was the 488th Military Intelligence Detachment; these were supervised by the two men in the pilot car of the motorcade that day – Jack Crichton and Colonel George Whitmeyer. Of the latter group (the 488th), about 40% were active duty policeman in Dallas.[144]

Then there is Eugene Dinkin, a US army code breaker, stationed in France; he was effectively part of the NSA. During October 1963, he discovered cable traffic from the OAS[145] (the French underground), of

---

141 Willoughby might have been a conduit to the military. Curtis LeMay, in particular, would have welcomed news of a JFK plot. LeMay had been in Canada that day, but made an urgent flight to observe the autopsy. Paul O'Connor recalls seeing him at the autopsy with his cigar. LeMay blew smoke into his face after Paul asked him to put it out.

Also recall that Colonel William C. Bishop had served under Willoughby in the Pacific. And here is another possible conduit: Gerry Patrick Hemming told Greg Burnham that he (Gerry) introduced Angleton to Oswald.

142 Recently discovered newsreel footage proves that Galloway was merely a passenger (and not the driver) in a navy ambulance that night. This corrects an error of interpretation originally made by researcher David Lifton about the precise meaning of a vaguely worded article (of 11/23/1963) in the *Washington Post*.

143 Otto Skorzeny had a secure channel to Crichton in Madrid – via the General American Oil Company (*The Skorzeny Papers* (2018) by Major Ralph Ganis, p. 313).

144 *The Devil is in the Details* (2020) by Alan Dale with Malcolm Blunt, p. 27. For the presence of multiple colonels in Dealey Plaza that day see "JFKcountercoup: Colonels at Dealey Plaza" (https://jfkcountercoup.blogspot.com/2021/04/colonels-at-dealey-plaza-updated.html).

145 This OAS must not be confused with the Organization of American States.

whom Jean Rene Souétre was a member.[146] As a result he mailed a letter to RFK saying that a JFK assassination would be attempted on November 28, 1963, and that it would be blamed on a communist or a Negro. He suspected that the US military was involved. He was so concerned that he abruptly absconded from his unit. He then tried to contact European ambassadors, to no avail. He eventually told the owner-editor of the *Geneva Diplomat.* The CIA verified this in a document (May 19, 1964) prepared for the WC – by Richard Helms! This was released in 1976, but Dinkin's name was omitted. On November 13, 1963, he was locked up at the Landstuhl General Hospital as a supposed psychotic.

We conclude then that the 11/22/1963 operation primarily had two men at its inner core – Harvey and Morales (with likely on-site supervision by Edward Lansdale – see part II). But they likely had critical assistance from Roselli – and also from Willoughby, Robertson and Jenkins. Harvey's interminable friendship with Roselli (a Mafia man) was clearly an alliance with the devil. As further support for such a small *initial* conspiracy, think about this: after Giancana was killed (with a revolver from Miami), Santo Trafficante confirmed that only two other men still knew who had killed JFK. Most likely he meant Harvey and Morales (or possibly Roselli). On the other hand, after the fire was lit for the JFK assassination (most likely after the Cuban Missile Crisis), this small group must have metastasized – rather widely.

As an example of this rapid diffusion, Adele Edisen, PhD,[147] a scientist (then at Tulane in neurophysiology) delivered a talk at a New Jersey meeting on April 17, 1963. While there, she was asked by "Dr. Jose A. Rivera"[148] (a Hispanic with an obvious accent) if she knew Lee Oswald, or the Carousel Club, or John Abt.[149] So, by then, the cat was well out of the bag.[150] My associated PowerPoint presentation cites 20 persons with

146 Russell 1992, p. 552 ff.

147 *A Secret Order* (2013) by H. P. Albarelli, Jr., Chapter Three. At the time, Adele was 35 years old, married, with three children. On 11/22,1963, when Adele heard the news, she said, *"I felt like I had been kicked in the stomach, my knees buckled."* She later told her story to the ARRB.

148 Col. Jose Rivera USAR- Bethesda, MD, a medical officer with foreknowledge of Oswald and assassination; he worked on special research projects at Fort Detrick, MD. (See link: "JFKcountercoup: Colonels at Dealey Plaza".)

149 After 11/22/1963, Oswald requested a lawyer named John Abt. From jail, Oswald apparently tried to call John D. Hurt, who revealed, *"I was in the counterintelligence corps in the Army during World War II"* ("JFK, Oswald, & the Raleigh Connection" by Randolph Benson in *Garrison: The Journal of History and Deep Politics*, Issue #2, June/July/August 2019, pp. 14-19).

150 Note that this encounter occurred *four days before* Lisa Howard first met with

foreknowledge. There are likely even more. In addition, it should not escape our attention that, inside this inner circle, in all probability, each man (i.e., Harvey, Morales, Roselli, Willoughby) had easy access to his own pool of "mechanics," i.e., the assassins in the multiple teams (probably at least four teams) in Dealey Plaza.[151] In other words, this core group of four individuals knew everyone worth knowing. No additional recruits were needed.

Foreknowledge – 20 Who Knew

- Richard Case Nagel
- Silvia Odio
- John Martino
- Eladio del Valle
- Ralph Yates
- Homer Eschevarria
- Adele Edisen, PhD**
- Garrett Trapnell
- John Garret Underhill
- Wayne January
- Rose Cheramie
- Joseph Milteer
- Santo Trafficante
- Eugene Dinkin*
- Jimmy Hoffa
- Marty Underwood
- Will Somersett
- Gerry Patrick Hemming
- Mario Garcia Kohly, Sr.
- David Christensen

*Dinkin predicted November in Texas, with a communist as a patsy.

**Edisen's amazing story was re-told by H. P. Albarelli. She also informed the ARRB: Testimony of Adelle Edisen.[1]

*** The new JFK releases (March 2025) have focused on this "Gary": Gary Underhill Memo in JFK Files Causes Stir.[2]

Meditate on this...

If 20 or more (mostly non-government) people knew in advance, what are the odds that the top CIA officials knew less than these 20 did, e.g., Cord Meyer, Ted Shackley, Phillips, Helms, and Angleton?

And think about this: Giancana died in June 1975, Harvey in June 1976, Roselli in August 1976, and Morales in 1978. The HSCA was established on September 15, 1976, and ended in late 1978. In 1977 – during the HSCA – Nicoletti was murdered on the same day that de Mohrenschildt died. Furthermore, a decade earlier, on February 22, 1967, less than a week after the Garrison probe was announced, Ferrie was found dead in his apartment.

1 https://www.jfk-assassination.net/arrb/index65.htm

2 https://www.msn.com/en-us/news/world/gary-underhill-memo-in-jfk-files-causes-stir/ar-AA1BdOgJ?ocid=BingNewsSerp

Castro, to initiate JFK's peace overtures to Cuba. So, it appears that plans had been developed well before Howard walked into Castro's embrace. Unfortunately, like so many others in this dismal assassination tale, she committed suicide – on July 4, 1965.

151 For more insight into (likely) at least four Dealey Plaza teams, read *Fry the Brain: The Art of Urban Sniping and its Role in Modern Guerrilla* (2008) by John West. The author has been a professional sniper.

The more difficult question though is this: Did Harvey truly initiate the plot on his own, or did he receive encouragement from higher up? Curiously, Bobby Baker is reported to have predicted that JFK would die a violent death while in office.[152] See Part II of this book for more insight into the transnational character of this assassination.

LBJ's contact with the assassins remains the darkest Black Hole of this entire JFK case. Many (if not most) history scholars accept his foreknowledge. That may be true. However, based on LBJ's sinister character, some historians believe that he may have been the primary trigger man in this chain of events. But see Part II of this book, where others seem intricately involved.

Yet, after all of this, it is impossible to totally exonerate the (other) top CIA officials in this murder – even though they were victimized[153] by the poison pill (the Mexico City calls were not their fault). We might describe these persons (those duped by the poison pill) as *accessories before the fact,* inasmuch as they did nothing to stop the murder – despite their likely foreknowledge (even if incomplete). Despite their prescience, they had nothing to gain by interfering with the murder – and probably much to lose, so why bother? Furthermore, they might well have worried that the Mexico City affair had identified them as active architects of the murder. The perfect example of this cover-up mode is Jeff Morley's *bête noire,* George Joannides.

152 Robert Morrow Political Research Blog: "LBJ's right arm Bobby Baker told Don Reynolds on Inauguration Day, 1961 that JFK would die a Violent Death and would not live out his term" (https://robertmorrowpoliticalresearchblog.blogspot.com/2022/05/lbjs-right-arm-bobby-baker-told-don.html).

153 Additional victims in this unmitigated charade were the autopsy pathologists, who were later presented with fake photographs (of the back of the head) and faked X-rays (the bogus 6.5 mm object and the White Patch).

But so also was the CIA overt decision in March 1964; Helms told Angleton's subordinate Ray Rocca that Angleton *"would prefer to wait out the Warren Commission."* Then think about this: when Oswald was captured, John Whitten said that the *"effect was electric"* on the top CIA officials – because they understood all too well who Oswald was. See the graph just below.[154] No doubt they were worried – after all, they had much to worry

This is how the US government monitors persons (i.e., Oswald) of "little interest"—Jeff Morley in JFK Facts

Pre-Assassination Oswald File Documents Seen by CIA Division

• Counterintelligence • Foreign Intelligence • Leadership • Records Integration • Soviet Russia • Support • Western Hemisphere

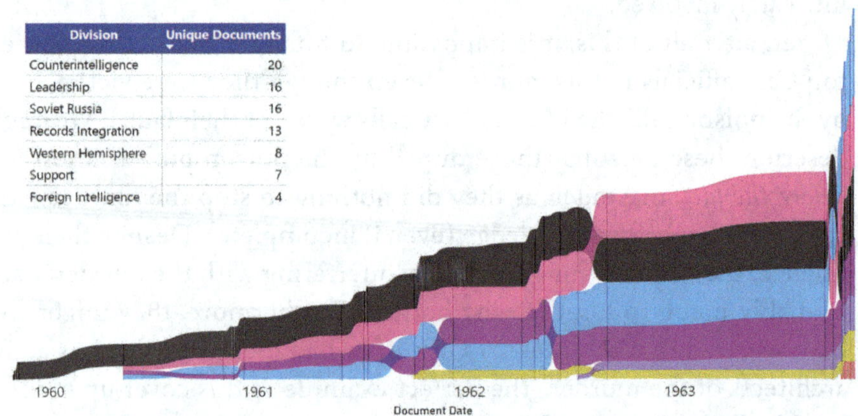

Division	Unique Documents
Counterintelligence	20
Leadership	16
Soviet Russia	16
Records Integration	13
Western Hemisphere	8
Support	7
Foreign Intelligence	4

154 (6) How the CIA Monitored Lee Harvey Oswald from 1959 to 1963 (https://jfk-facts.substack.com/p/how-the-cia-monitored-lee-harvey). Jefferson Morley, working with Michael Scott (the son of Winston Scott, the Mexico City CIA station chief in 1963), learned that Oswald was linked to four CIA operations: AMSPELL, LIERODE, LIENVOT, and LIEMPTY. The first two were supervised by Win Scott. But the last two were supervised by – guess who – David Atlee Phillips! (*LBJ: The Mastermind of the JFK Assassination* by Phillip Nelson (2011, 2013), pp. 348-349.) This is further proof of the "Bishop" ID as Phillips. David was indeed supervising Lee Harvey Oswald (but quite unconcerned about Lee's survival).

In 1963, Scott's colleague in Mexico City was Thomas Mann, the American ambassador to Mexico (May 1961 – December 1963). He been JFK's appointee, but only after some arm twisting by LBJ. Unlike the German writer (with the same name), this Tom was a Southern Baptist from Laredo; he believed (contrary to JFK) that nationalism and Communism were related. Mann was a longtime friend of LBJ and had served as Assistant Secretary of State for Inter-American Affairs during Ike's term, but he was discharged by JFK because of his strident anti-communist views (that would compromise JFK's Alliance for Progress).

Nonetheless, on December 14, 1963, LBJ re-appointed Mann to his former post as Assistant Secretary of State for Inter-American Affairs. A week later, Mann also became the head of USAID. This double-appointment was strongly opposed by the Kennedys and by their liberal supporters, which quickly demonstrated the chasm between JFK and LBJ on foreign affairs. As proof of this, Mann later supported the military overthrow of the democratically elected government in Brazil. Peter Dale Scott has confirmed that Mann *"...was a personal enemy of RFK."* Mann recalled that Hoover had told him to stop investigating the Oswald telephone calls from Mexico City. Ominously, Mann added that he about. Nonetheless, it is now over six decades later and the CIA has won this game; if we ever see the last of the sequestered (and *unredacted*) JFK documents, I will then believe it can snow in Death Valley.[155]

The photograph just above was taken at a nightclub in Mexico City on January 22, 1963. Daniel Hopsicker believes that all were members of Operation 40.[156] He suggests that the man closest to the camera on the left is Félix Rodríguez; next to him is Porter Goss[157] (CIA Director, 2004-2006), and then comes (drug smuggler) Barry Seal.[158] Hopsicker adds that the first person on the right is William Houston Seymour (sometimes

---

thought that Win Scott had been murdered (Tatro, November 2023, pp. 78-80). Mann Road in Laredo is named for the Mann family; while in Laredo (seeing patients as usual, but watching Mexico from my hotel room on weekends), I watched the Los Angeles Rams lose the 2019 Super Bowl.

155 "Snow in Death Valley, the hottest place on Earth? Not quite" - *Los Angeles Times.*

156 "Ted Shackley and the Secret Team" - JFK Assassination Debate - The Education Forum (https://educationforum.ipbhost.com/topic/5597-ted-shackley-and-the-secret-team/). *"Richard Nixon is generally given credit for planning Operation 40, during his 1959 campaign for president"* (Hopsicker, p. 143). The Mexico City photograph shown here has been adapted from the dust cover of Hopsicker's book. Hopsicker identifies the specific hotel where this photograph was taken (p. 246).

157 On the morning of 9/11/2001, Porter was having breakfast with a man who reportedly wired $100,000 to Mohamed Atta (Hopsicker, p. xi).

158 Lee Harvey Oswald and Barry Seal had been *fellow cadets* in the Louisiana Civil Air Patrol during a two week summer camp. This is where both of them met David Ferrie (Hopsicker, p. xxv). After Barry Seal was executed, the private telephone number of G. H. W. Bush was found in his (Seal's) wallet. Perhaps Porter Goss would not have been surprised about this after all. Besides knowing Oswald and the senior Bush, Barry Seal also knew Carlo Gambino (Hopsicker, p. 165). What an exciting guest list for a house party!

viewed as an Oswald lookalike – see William Seymour - Wikispooks), then next we see Frank Sturgis (on the right) attempting to hide his face with his coat. Other possibilities here are Albertao "Loco" Blanco (3rd right) and Jorgo Robreno (4th right). Type into a search engine: *"Operation 40 Spartacus."* But what would a drug smuggler (Seal)[159] discuss at dinner with a future CIA director (Goss)? Note that they were seated next to each other. [On October 5, 1986, Félix Rodríguez (who was obviously well-connected) made an emergency telephone call[160] to George H. W. Bush about a downed C-123k aircraft: George H. W. Bush.[161]]

On the next page is a photograph of (the same) Félix Rodríguez with George H. W. Bush (CIA Director, January 30, 1976–January 10, 1977). Félix was one of George's operatives.[162] The adjacent photograph shows

159 Barry Seal typically flew a Lear Jet for his drug drops. But it was later learned that he did not own it. Instead, the true owner was Paul Helliwell (via the CIA), who was the paymaster for the Bay of Pigs (Hopsicker, pp. 294, 354).

160 Félix Rodríguez telephoned the White House to report that the Eugene Hasenfus plane had been shot down (*Cocaine Wars* (1988) by Paul Eddy, pp. 338-339). Also see *Shadow Warrior: The CIA Hero of a Hundred Battles* (1989) by Félix Rodríguez and John Weisman. History afficionados will recall that the downing of the Hasenfus plane triggered the exposure of the Iran-Contra affair (Hopsicker, p. xiv).

On December 12, 1986, Daniel Sheehan submitted an affidavit to the court; it detailed the Irangate scandal. Danny also claimed that Thomas G. Clines and Ted Shackley had been running a private assassination program that had evolved from their own CIA projects. Others named by Sheehan were: Rafael Quintero, Richard Secord, Félix Rodríguez and Albert Hakim. But the two primary culprits were Gene Wheaton and Carl E. Jenkins (JFKCountercoup2: Larry Hancock on the Wheaton Names) (https://jfkcountercoup2.blogspot.com/2018/12/larry-hancock-on-wheaton-names.html). Also see Danny's scintillating book, with his further comments about Shackley and his training for assassinations by Otto Skorzeny: *The People's Advocate: The Life and Legal History of America's Most Fearless Public Interest Lawyer* (2013) by Daniel Sheehan.

In a stroke (this is almost a malicious pun – Casey did have seizures) of great fortune for him, just six days after Sheehan's affidavit was published, William Casey (CIA director, 1981-1987) had surgery for a "brain tumor." He *never spoke again*, thus making him the standard-bearer (for reticence) for all future DCIs (Director of Central Intelligence). On February 9, 1987, Robert McFarlane (another Iran-Contra character) conveniently overdosed on drugs. Bush later opened the pardon floodgates for these suspicious characters: Casper Weinberger, Robert McFarlane, Duane R. Clarridge, Clair E. George, Elliott Abrams and Alan D. Fiers, Jr. All had been charged with offences related to Iran-Contra, but Bush apparently knew better: George H. W. Bush (https://spartacus-educational.com/JFKbushG.htm). On the other hand, Bush could not save Catholic Casey: his funeral was led by Bishop John R. McGann, who used his pulpit to castigate Casey for his ethics and actions in Nicaragua!

161 https://spartacus-educational.com/JFKbushG.htm

162 *Compromised: Clinton, Bush, and the CIA – How the Presidency was Co-opted by the CIA* (1994) by Terry Reed and John Cummings. The Bush-Rodríguez alliance is documented on pp. 355, 357, and 370 – and on many more pages. Hopsicker notes the existence of documents, which imply that Félix was recruited into the CIA by Bush in 1961 (Hopsicker, p. 141). *"There is extensive documentation of Rodríguez's ties to US Vice-President George H. W. Bush during the Iran–Contra affair from 1983 to 1988"* (Félix Rodríguez (soldier) - Wikipedia). Félix actually admitted to the Kerry subcommittee that he knew George H. W. Bush through

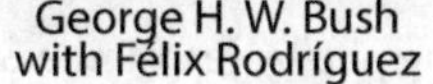

George H. W. Bush with Félix Rodríguez

Félix Rodríguez with Che Guevara

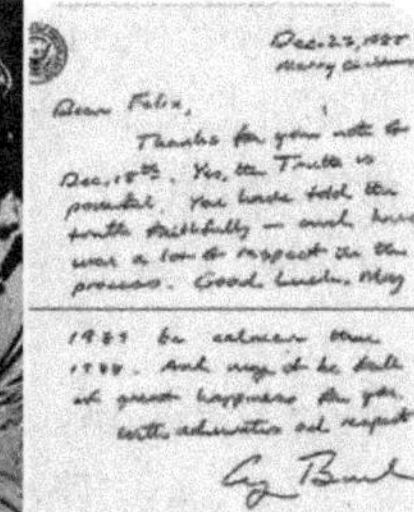

Dec. 22, 1988

Dear Felix,

Thanks for your note of Dec. 15th. Yes, the Truth is powerful. You have told the truth faithfully — and have won a ton of respect in the process. Good luck. May 1989 be calmer than 1988. And may it be full of great happiness for you. With admiration and respect

Geo Bush

A Christmas letter from George to Félix

Don Gregg, who was Bush's National Security Advisor during the 1980s (Scott 1991, p. 210).

Che's "hand operation" is cited by Terry Reed on p. 370. The photograph of this dubious pair was taken while Bush was vice-president (of the US!). Hopsicker emphasizes that both Bush and Rodríguez were members of an infamous clique who could not recall where they were on 11/22/1963 – this includes Richard Nixon and E. Howard Hunt. Trying to be helpful, the *Nation* magazine (November 29, 1963) described a memo by J. Edgar Hoover – about the briefing given to *"Mr. George Bush of the CIA."* Later research documented that only one George Bush qualified for this designation; he was indeed the son of Prescott Bush. George (wisely) refused to comment further.

Daniel Hopsicker cites Barry Seal as a pilot for a "getaway" plane from Redbird Airport in Dallas on 11/22/1963 (Hopsicker, p. 139). Seal died in a hail of bullets; in his wallet was George H. W. Bush's private telephone number (Hopsicker, p. 379). In this insane and chaotic underworld, Rodríguez (a notorious braggart) even supposedly declared that he had helped to kill Barry Seal (Reed and Cummings, p. 355). Recall that they both appear in the January photograph in Mexico City shown here, where a future CIA director sat precisely between them!

There seems to be some disagreement about who actually killed Che. Dick Goodwin reports that it was the Bolivians who captured and wounded Che, took him prisoner, and shot him (Goodwin, p. 207).

Wikipedia provides more details.

> About 30 minutes before Guevara was killed, Félix Rodríguez attempted to question him about the whereabouts of other guerrilla fighters who were currently at large, but Guevara continued to remain silent. Rodríguez, assisted by a few Bolivian soldiers, helped Guevara to his feet and took him outside the hut to parade him before other Bolivian soldiers where he posed with Guevara for a photo opportunity….
>
> A few minutes later, Sergeant Terán pointed his self-loading M2 carbine at Guevara and opened fire, hitting him in the arms and legs. Then, as Guevara writhed on the ground, apparently biting one of his wrists to avoid crying out, Terán fired another burst, fatally wounding him in the chest. In all, Guevara was shot nine times by Terán. This included five times in his legs, once in the right shoulder and arm, and once in the chest and throat (Che Guevara - Wikipedia).

Here is more on Che. What are the odds that Treasury Secretary Douglas Dillon (a multimillionaire) and Che Guevara (an Argentine revolutionary) would appear in the same photograph? Here it is: 1961 Orig Photo Cuban Leader CHE GUEVARA & DOUGLAS DILLON Punta Del Este Metting | #1910776410 (https://www.worthpoint.com/worthopedia/1961-orig-photo-cuban-leader-che-1910776410).

In August 1961, 33 US delegates flew to Montevideo, Uruguay, for a conference sponsored by the Al-

Félix (on the left) with Che Guevara, just before Che's death (October 9, 1967).[163] Per Hopsicker, Félix murdered Che[164] and cut off his hands (for fingerprint IDs). It would have been mesmerizing to eavesdrop while Félix regaled George H. W. Bush about his "hands-on operation" on his patient (Che).

One final thought – about Charles de Gaulle

- He survived 30+ assassination attempts
- Likely including one by Jean-Rene Souétre (Otto Skorzeny's hit man). Souétre (or someone using his name) was reported in Dallas on 11/22/1963.
- JFK could not survive even one (supposed) attempt by Oswald.
- So, why didn't the OAS just hire Oswald?

Is there any lesson in this? I think so. The NSA (John Newman's former workplace) was created by the National Security Act of July 26, 1947. Regrettably, as Harry Truman explained exactly *one month after* 11/22/1963, he never anticipated that the CIA would conduct operations. It was created solely to gather intelligence. Alas for America, Allen Dulles vetoed this,[165] and so his inexorable foolhardiness, followed for nearly eight decades now, has plunged us into a national security state.

The decisive blow to our republican government was fatally delivered via "The CIA Act of 1949," also called Public Law 110 (but more aptly named a *"non-public law"*). This law was passed while Allen Dulles was still CIA deputy to Walter "Beetle" Smith (see Beetle's photograph in this book). This new law essentially *prohibited CIA accountability*! Public disclosure would no longer be required. Fiscal and administrative information would be con-

---

liance for Progress. Dick Goodwin listened as Dillon offered one billion dollars per year (not his money – he assumed that US taxpayers would volunteer their own money!) to begin US support of Latin America. Che was also present as an observer. Che sent Dick a large polished, mahogany box, inlaid with the Cuban seal – and a handwritten note. It was full of the finest Havana cigars – with a request to meet. Dillon initially agreed, but then he soon retracted. Nonetheless, they soon met informally – for 3 hours. Dick later presented the cigars to JFK, who was the first to smoke them. Ten days later, their encounter became front page news (Goodwin, pp. 190-202). Also see "Che Guevara, Richard Goodwin, and the Almost Peace of 1961" (https://midnightwriternews.com/che-guevara-richard-goodwin-and-the-almost-peace-of-1961/).

163 "The last photograph of a live Guevara shows Rodríguez beside him, but Dino Brugioni suggests that this is a photomontage" (Félix Rodríguez (soldier) - Wikipedia). Also see "Documentary alleges last photo of Che is fake" (https://www.dnaindia.com/world/report-documentary-alleges-last-photo-of-che-is-fake-1126943). Highly sensitive heat-sensing equipment was developed in Ann Arbor; this was only a short jog from my residence during medical school. This high-tech gear was successfully used to track Che Guevara (Hinckle and Turner, p. 369). But since Che was killed five years before I started medical school, I claim innocence.

164 Reed and Cummings, p. 370.

165 Talbot 2015, p. 570.

fidential. The use of federal funds would be concealed. Exceptions (to public disclosure) included the budget, any activities, and even personnel. As a result, the operations section of the CIA grew noticeably larger compared to the analysis section – even though the latter was the CIA's *original purpose* (virtually its sole purpose). Soon after this, the ghastly medical experiments began, culminating in the 1953 death of Frank Olson.[166]

And here is Max Boot's take (Boot, Kindle, 575) on the CIA's accountability: *"...since its founding in 1947, as a freewheeling organization with no accountability to any outsider other than the commander in chief."* Of course, Arthur Krock's October 3, 1963, editorial in the *New York Times* seriously challenged the CIA's obedience to the "commander-in-chief" (Documents – The JFK Assassination).[167] We can only wonder what Boot had been smoking – or perhaps he had merely developed indigestion due to reading too many lone gunman books.

This curt dismissal of accountability is a *direct violation of human nature.* The website of the National Library of Medicine surveys this most fundamental dictum of accountability. But first notice that – quite contrary to the composition of congress in 1949 as well as the composition of the CIA in 1949 – *none of these three* (immediately below) *2021 authors are white males.*[168] The congressional (male) framers of this anti-republican act were grossly ignorant of this most basic principle of human psychology. Here is the verdict of these three (female) experts.

Practitioners and academics alike treat accountability as a means of directing and correcting individual and organizational efforts and performance and encouraging ***socially responsible behaviors*** [emphasis added]. *Accountability may be thought of as the "adhesive that binds social systems together"*[169,170] *and as such is not only a* ***fundamental principle*** [emphasis added] *of the organizational sciences, but is also a necessity for the effective operation of enterprise."*[171]

James Douglass was precisely on point:[172]

---

166 *A Terrible Mistake: The Murder of Frank Olson and the CIA's Secret Cold War Experiments* (2009) by H. P. Albarelli, Jr.

167 https://thejfkassassination.com/documents/.

168 *J Bus Ethics.* 2021 Nov 18;183(3):691–712. doi: 10.1007/s10551-021-04969-z. "We Hold Ourselves Accountable: A Relational View of Team Accountability" by *Virginia* R. Stewart, *Deirdre* G. Snyder, *Chia-Yu* Kou. PMCID: PMC8600914 PMID: 34812211. [I have italicized their first names to emphasize their genders.]

169 Frink & Klimoski, 1998, p. 3.

170 https://www.researchgate.net/publication/248126011_Toward_a_Theory_of_Accountability_in_Organizations_and_Human_Resources_Management

171 https://projects.iq.harvard.edu/lernerlab/files/lerner_tetlock_1999.pdf

172 *JFK and the Unspeakable: Why He Died and Why it Matters* (2008) by James Douglass, Kindle, "Afterward." This is a foundational reference book; Jim unmasks the

> What George Kennan and Harry Truman realized much too late was that, in the name of national security, they had unwittingly allowed an alien force to invade a democracy. As a result, we and the world had to deal with a U.S. government agency authorized to carry out a broad range of covert, criminal activities on an international scale, theoretically accountable to the president but with no genuine accountability to anyone.

Today therefore, short of a bloody revolution, this state of affairs has become irreversible. Just read *Legacy of Ashes* (2007) by Tim Weiner. Or recall the infamous words of Senator Chuck Schumer (to host Rachel Maddow on MSNBC):

> *Let me tell you: You take on the intelligence community – they have six ways from Sunday at getting back at you.*

In closing, listen to Bob Dylan.[173]

'Twas a dark day in Dallas, November '63
A day that will live on in infamy
President Kennedy was a-ridin' high
Good day to be livin' and a good day to die
Being led to the slaughter like a sacrificial lamb
He said, "Wait a minute, boys, you know who I am?"
"Of course we do, we know who you are"
Then they blew off his head while he was still in the car
Shot down like a dog in broad daylight
Was a matter of timing and the timing was right
You got unpaid debts, we've come to collect
We're gonna kill you with hatred, without any respect
We'll mock you and shock you and we'll grin in your face
We've already got someone here to take your place
The day they blew out the brains of the king
Thousands were watching, no one saw a thing
It happened so quickly, so quick, by surprise
Right there in front of everyone's eyes
Greatest magic trick ever under the sun
Perfectly executed, skillfully done
Wolfman, oh Wolfman, oh Wolfman, howl
Rub-a-dub-dub, it's a murder most foul.[174]

---

zeitgeist of the Cold War era. He also cites my expose of the JFK autopsy skull X-rays.

173 Bob Dylan 'Murder Most Foul' Song Review (https://www.vulture.com/2020/03/bob-dylan-murder-most-foul-song-review.html) *and* Bob Dylan – Murder Most Foul Lyrics | Genius Lyrics.

174 Excerpted from Bob Dylan © Universal Music Publishing Company.

APPENDIX I-A

A POISON PILL IN MEXICO CITY (1963)

SEPTEMBER

Su	M	Tu	W	Th	F	Sa
22	23	24	25	26	27	28
29	30					

OCTOBER

Su	M	Tu	W	Th	F	Sa
		1	2	3	4	5
6	7	8	9	10	11	12

See the (Ed) Lopez Report: 2003 Release: Oswald, the CIA, and Mexico City ("Lopez Report").

NOTE: Both Larry Rivera[175] and David Josephs[176] have argued

175 "The Mexico City Tapes" – The New JFK Show Blog (https://merdist.com/wp/2024/07/09/the-mexico-city-tapes/). Also see "The Twin 'Lee Oswald' Cuban Consulate Visa Applications" by Larry Rivera in *Garrison: The Journal of History and Deep Politics*, Issue #3, October 2019, pp. 196-202. Larry adds that the audio tapes of Boris and Anne Tarasoff (recorded by Kenneth Brooten) prove that both Tarasoffs stated it was not Lee Oswald on the LIENVOY Soviet Embassy wiretaps. Larry also notes that three Mexican presidents (1958-1976) were CIA assets, who had been active in and essential to implementing the Agency's plans ("Fifteen Finds of the JFK Files," *Garrison: The Journal of History and Deep Politics*, Issue #2, June/July/August 2019, pp. 100-107).

176 "Mexico City, Part 2 – The Trip Down, Part 1" (https://www.kennedysandking.com/john-f-kennedy-articles/mexico-city-part-2-the-trip-down-part-1). Also see "The Evidence

compellingly that Oswald (i.e., the man who Ruby shot) never visited Mexico City that month. Gerry Hemming also swore that Oswald never went.[177] Meanwhile, Fabian Escalante is certain he went![178] As for me, I have no horse in this race. In any case, the real person may not matter. The poison pill had been planted – based solely on the *Oswald name;* the physical body was not required. Of some note, in a different situation, the CIA (via Phillips) had used impersonation just two months before this. Oswald's name in the Mexico City affair therefore might best be seen solely as a placeholder.[179]

August 9 and 16: Oswald litters the New Orleans sidewalks with his pamphlets.

Aug 19: Garrett Trapnell alerts the FBI that an anti-Castro Cuban group had tried to recruit him for a plot against JFK.

Aug 29: The FBI interviews Trapnell.

September (early in the month): Oswald visits Clinton, Louisiana, likely with Clay Shaw and Guy Banister.

Sept (uncertain date): Tracy Barnes tells Robert Morrow about a possible plot to kill JFK.[180]

is the Conspiracy," by David Josephs, *Garrison: The Journal of History and Deep Politics*, Issue #8, November 2021, pp. 161-178. Then see *The Last investigation* (2013) by Gaeton Fonzi and *The Oswald Puzzle* (2025) by Larry Hancock and David Boylan and *Our Man in Mexico: Winston Scott and the Hidden History of the CIA* (2008) by Jefferson Morley and *Oswald and the CIA* (2008) by John M. Newman and *Oswald, Mexico, and Deep Politics* (2013) by Peter Dale Scott and *The CIA Killed Camelot, Didn't They?* (1997) by William Bobo (aka Roy Schaeffer).

177 Twyman, p. 748.

178 *The Plot to Kill Kennedy and Castro* (1994) by Claudia Furiati, p. 149.

179 This approach (i.e., Oswald's name – not his body – as a placeholder) was confirmed in 1978 by Veciana's comments to Anthony Summers: *"I asked him whether it was true that Oswald had been at the Embassy a few weeks before the assassination…and Bishop replied that it* ***did not matter*** [emphasis added] *whether he had or not – what was important was that my cousin, a member of the Cuban diplomatic service, should confirm that he had been"* (Tatro, 2023, p. 80).

It is striking that Mark Lane had reached this same conclusion (i.e., no Oswald visit) before anyone else (*Last Word: My Indictment of the CIA in the Murder of JFK* (2011) by Mark Lane, Mark Boyett, et al., pp. 201-202).

Here is the bottom line: No extant photograph of Lee Harvey Oswald has ever shown him at either the Cuban embassy or at the Soviet embassy. Ed Lopez had spoken to one of the Mexico City photographers, who insisted that the cameras had been *"working 20-30 days in a row at that time, without a day off, so there had to have been weekend coverage."* When this cameraman was told that the camera was broken, he laughed and said, *"Well, of course, we would have more than one camera. We never just had one camera"* (Tatro November 2023, p. 100).

Incidentally, Richard Sprague had wanted an authentic investigation. As an example, he wanted to see the repair bills for Phillips's allegedly broken camera. He also wanted to compare the typeset of the Mexico City transcript to the actual typewriter that was used by official stenographers. (Sprague interview with John Williams.)

180 *First Hand Knowledge: How I Participated in the CIA-Mafia Murder of President*

Sept 17: In a letter, Nagell warns Hoover about Oswald.

Sept 20: Nagell fires two shots into an El Paso bank ceiling.[181]

Sept 26: The FBI writes to the CIA about the Fair Play for Cuba Committee.

Sept 26 or 27: (Silvia was uncertain of the exact date – maybe it was even Sept 25): Three anti–Castro sympathizers (two Hispanic men and one American), visit Silvia Odio in Dallas. The American is introduced to her as "León Oswald." When Odio soon sees Oswald on TV (as JFK's alleged assassin), she promptly recognizes him (she faints!),[182] as does her sister Annie, who had opened the door.

Sept 27: 10 AM: Oswald (supposedly) arrives in Mexico City – from New Orleans.

> 10:30 AM: Oswald calls the Soviet Military Attache from the Hotel Comercio.
>
> At about 11 AM, Sylvia Duran supposedly sees Oswald (his first visit) at the Cuban Consulate. He is advised to return later with four photographs, but first to get his Russian visa from the Soviet Consulate.
>
> At 1 PM, Oswald returns to the Cuban Consulate with the requested four photographs.[183]
>
> Around 4 PM, Oswald visits the Cuban Consulate for the third time – after visiting the Soviet Consulate. Now he supposedly submits a complete application, including photographs and signature. (David Josephs and Larry Rivera critically dispute the authenticity of this submission.)
>
> At 4:05 PM, Sylvia calls the Soviet Consulate.

Ed Lopez: Sylvia's description of Oswald seems inaccurate, i.e., not the real Oswald.

Sept 28: At 9:45 AM, Oswald personally appears (a second time) at the Soviet Consulate – the evidence is an audiotape taken by the

Kennedy (1992) by Robert D. Morrow.

181 Nagell supposedly died from a heart attack on November 1, 1995, in Los Angeles, California, despite no history of heart disease. The letter to him from the ARRB (a request for information) was dated October 31, 1995. One of his footlockers (full of documents) had simultaneously disappeared from a storage facility (Twyman, p. 615).

182 Hinckle and Turner, p. 252. Also see *On the Trail of JFK Assassins* (2008) by Dick Russell, p. 143.

183 Jim DiEugenio reports that a search of photography shops within a 6-mile radius of the Consulate could find no evidence that Oswald had his photographs taken in any of them (e-mail to me, November 17, 2024).

CIA. This is Saturday, so both the Soviet and Cuban Consulates are officially closed.

At 11:51 AM, "Sylvia" is heard on a telephone recording of the Soviet Consulate. "Sylvia" puts an American (later said to be Oswald) on the phone. Oswald's Russian accent is terrible – but the real Oswald was a Russian translator!

However, the real Sylvia later claimed that neither Oswald, nor any American, visited the Cuban Consulate that day (a Saturday). [Most likely the taped voices of both Sylvia Duran and Oswald were faked – probably by the AMOTs, who were led by Morales.]

This was the day of Oswald's supposed contact with Kostikov. That *same* day, the Mexico City legat *immediately* contacted FBI headquarters, i.e., Hoover's office. See Larry Hancock's *Someone Would Have Talked* (2006), pp. 216-210. Also see Exhibits 15-19 for Larry's book: larry-hancock.com.http://www.larry-hancock.com/documents/index.html. So, Hoover knew about this contact, or did he promptly (or merely conveniently) develop senile dementia?

Ed Lopez: Oswald has now failed to obtain either a Cuban or a Soviet visa.

Sept 30: Phillips leaves Mexico City for a nine-day tour to DC and Miami, returning on Oct 9.

Awaiting him in DC is a pouch; this was probably a transcript of the fake October 1 telephone call (see just below). Phillips soon lies, claiming that the actual tape recording had been erased. In fact, David Slawson and William Coleman (for the WC) listened to these tapes on April 9, 1964, in Win Scott's office. The tapes were played for them by Alan White. These WC staffers understood that Phillips had lied about the persistence of these tapes. *"Unfortunately, we don't know which of the seven purported Oswald calls this was…."* (Hancock 2025, Kindle, 283).

October 1: A man (claiming to be Oswald) calls the Soviet Consulate, saying that he had been at the Consulate on Sept 28. Unlike the real Oswald, though, the caller on Sept 28 spoke "terrible, hardly recognizable" Russian. On Oct 1, the translator (of this tape) confirmed that this same man had called "a day or so" ago. Of course, the real Oswald spoke quite intelligible Russian. In fact, there are two recorded calls to the Soviet Consulate on this day. On one of them the caller asked a question to which the recipient answered with the name of Kostikov. This Soviet official was purportedly associated with assassinations (by the USSR). If true, this would totally safeguard the poison pill – by connecting Oswald to a Soviet man who oversaw Soviet assassinations. This scenario would, of course, imply that the Russians lurked behind JFK's murder.

Oct 2: Oswald (supposedly) leaves Mexico on a bus and arrives in Dallas on the next day (Oct 3). Since Sept 29, Oswald had possibly been sightseeing in Mexico City. He was supposedly seen at a twist party (by Elena Garro – a Mexican playwright and cousin to Sylvia's husband) on Sept 30 or Oct 1.[184]

Oct 2: JFK signs NSAM 263 – 1000 troops are to leave Vietnam by the end of 1963.

Oct 8: Bobby Baker resigns. *Life* magazine is preparing a major article.

Oct 9: Gheesling lifts the watch on Oswald, while Phillips returns to Mexico City.

The Poison Pill: No Russians or Cubans Faked the Calls

CIA memo: *"Following a thorough review and study of all available material, the Agency was unable to prove that Oswald had been acting under the direction of the KGB."*

The same was true for Cuba. That left only domestic suspects (including the anti-Castro Cuban exiles).

Summary: The Oswald impersonation acted like a poison pill for the Feds – both for the CIA and for the FBI. This was an astonishingly creative stroke, deliberately designed to protect the gruesome guys who would soon execute the hit job.

Oct 10: The CIA alerts the FBI about Oswald's visit with the Soviets in Mexico City.

Oct 14-16: Willoughby's International Committee meets in Switzerland. Several Germans in attendance are linked to the Munich newspaper that *first* broke the story of Oswald's supposed attempt on General Edwin A. Walker.

Oct 16: To his eternal regret, Oswald begins work at the TSBD.

Oct 22: Eugene Dinkin writes to RFK about Oswald.

November 1: Diem is assassinated.[185] Lansdale resigns.

184 2003 Release: Oswald, the CIA, and Mexico City ("Lopez Report") (https://www.history-matters.com/archive/jfk/hsca/lopezrpt_2003/contents.htm#:~:text=The%20%22thirteenth%20appendix%22%20to%20the%20HSCA%20Report%20on,less%20than%20two%20months%20prior%20to%20the%20assassination.)

185 FRUS 1961-1963, Vol IV: Vietnam August-December 1963 - III. The Coup

Nov 7-8: Jack Ruby has long telephone calls with two Hoffa associates.

Nov 9: FBI informant Willie Somersett tapes Joseph Milteer's conversation about plans to kill JFK. Hoover receives a copy of this tape.

Nov 14: A Ku Klux Klan member informs the FBI about a right-wing plan to hit JFK.

Nov 21: Jack Ruby and Hale Brading (separately) visit the office of H. L. Hunt.[186]

Nov 22: "The Big Event." Lots of strange characters unexpectedly materialize in Dealey Plaza.[187]

Nov 23: Hoover calls LBJ about Mexico City. A transcript exists for this 14-minute call, but the original tape has been erased – as Rex Bradford discovered.[188] The transcript concludes that Oswald had been impersonated in Mexico City.

The Mexico City Escapade: My Summary

Next to the JFK medical evidence, the Mexico City spectacle is the most confusing and perplexing aspect of the entire case. It is most unfortunate that the translators were not interviewed for many years. Nor did the Russians contribute until decades later. Peter Dale Scott has noted that the WC was presented with *four different versions* of Sylvia Duran's statements! Peter speculates that new versions were required to match the WC's final conclusion that Lee had acted alone, i.e., *without Soviet support*. For example, one late version conveniently omitted his American communist party card.

Several groups, as well as individuals, had competing goals and some were positioned to alter evidence, which likely occurred. So, there was some lying, some manipulation, as well as a few honest facts. But to disen-

Against the Diem Government, October 23-November 2 (https://history.state.gov/historicaldocuments/frus1961-63v04).

186 "The Nazi Connection to the John F. Kennedy Assassination by Mae Brussell" (http://www.maebrussell.com/Mae%20Brussell%20Articles/Nazi%20Connection%20to%20JFK%20Assass.html).

187 "Familiar Faces in Dealey Plaza" (https://www.memresearch.org/econ/faces/familiar_faces.htm). Just for starters, Hemming declares that Roy Hargraves and Vidal (Santiago) were there: "Gerry Hemming's Swamp, the Dark Side of Madame Nhu, Gordan McLendon, and Other JFK Assassination Sponsors" by Edgar F. Tatro in *Garrison: The Journal of History and Deep Politics*, Issue #15, November 2023, pp. 22-124.

188 "The Fourteen Minute Gap" (https://www.maryferrell.org/pages/The_Fourteen_Minute_Gap.html).

tangle the truth from fiction here requires some bravado as well as some quixotic courage. So, here is my take, but it probably does not matter very much – Oswald 's name alone was likely sufficient to provide the required poison pill.

The man who Ruby shot probably visited the Cuban and Soviet consulates on Friday, September 27. After all, Sylvia Duran saw the man – and his passport photograph – at the same time. And she did not blink. Nor did she promptly declare any discrepancy between these two images. In fact, the WC concluded that Oswald's application had been completed with Duran's assistance, and then submitted to Havana – where it was approved![189] So, how could Sylvia Duran do this and yet not notice a discrepancy between the two faces, i.e., the real physical person versus his photograph?

Hancock claims that Oswald's passport photograph was found in his possessions at Beckley St. – and so was the sweater he wore in that photograph. Even Marina recognized it.[190] His clothes that day do not match his passport photograph, but of course they need not match if he had brought photographs with him. And indeed he had come prepared – with lots of documents.

At about 9 AM the next day (Saturday), this same Oswald likely appeared at the Soviet embassy. This early morning visit is not documented in a telephone call. The three Russians who later remembered him surely knew (by then) how he looked. And none of them overtly complained about his atrocious Russian. But all of the supposed "Oswald" telephone calls after that morning were likely fake. My impression is that Hancock and Newman agree with this scenario. The HSCA also agreed: "*…Oswald had personally visited both the Cuban and Russian diplomatic facilities….*" (Hancock 2025, Kindle, 281).

Further support for his actual presence in Mexico City derives from both Elena Garro and her daughter. After they saw him on TV, they both immediately recognized him. Sylvia Duran is all over the map about whether she saw Oswald socially that weekend, but she likely had good reasons to lie. In fact, she was severely beaten in the process. But then Winston Scott had heard the same story (about the party with Oswald) from June Cobb, who had no good reason to lie. According to Peter Dale

189 Hancock 2025, Kindle, 324.

190 Hancock 2025, Kindle, 251. Also see *Warren Commission Hearings*, Volume 16, Commission Exhibit 161, Clothing found at Beckley; also personal communications [with Hancock] via Steve Roe, August 2023: https://www.maryferrell.org/showDoc.html?docId=1133#relPageId=544.

Scott (a relative of Win? – or a possible fellow diplomat?), Winston Scott kept a vinyl recording of Oswald's voice in his locked safe. This was later retrieved by the ever-diligent James Angleton.

Jefferson Morley reports that two CIA employees, Stanley Watson (Win's deputy) and Joe Piccolo, had each seen two photographs of Oswald, so perhaps these were later destroyed. One photograph was a three-quarters full shot. A likely candidate for performing such destruction, of course, is David Phillips, who was in charge of the monitors and their films. Ed Lopez (HSCA) saw zillions of photographs from that time, so the cameras were working. But why would Phillips destroy evidence of Oswald's actual presence? Isn't that what David wanted – as proof? Well maybe not quite. After all, surely not all of the "Oswald" entries were by the man Ruby shot. So, if just some entries showed that man,[191] but the other entries showed someone else, Phillips (if asked) would have been nonplussed. So, he might well have decided that it was better not to save any Oswald photographs at all, and just report broken cameras everywhere.

In fact, everywhere we turn here, we encounter David Phillips (who was quite fluent in Spanish); he lied – blatantly and often. In fact, Dan Hardway viewed him as the culprit.

As they interviewed him, the HSCA staffers were amused – and amazed – that Phillips often kept three cigarettes going at the same time! Under severe duress, he simply forgot that he had just lit one. The absurd Gilberto Alvarado allegation[192] about the red-haired Negro paying off Oswald – and the Cubans in the cafeteria – this all fits with David's psy ops. Furthermore, these psy ops fit with the scheming of Joannides and Phillips in collusion with their DRE affiliates. It also fits with the DRE's prompt identification of Oswald as the lone (communist sympathizer) gunman – Phillips may have prepared the DRE precisely for this moment. David's connection to Morales and the AMOTs could explain the fake telephone calls as well – they had likely been initiated by Spanish speakers, whose Russian skills were awful. But that did not matter, because Oswald's name (especially after the Kostikov connection) had by then been locked into the record and the poison pill was lying latent.

---

191 The CIA (see the Lopez Report) concluded that Oswald had entered and exited the embassies (plural) a minimum of five times (https://history-matters.com/archive/jfk/hsca/lopezrpt_2003/html/LopezRpt_0094a.htm).

192 Gilberto Alvarado Allegation (https://www.maryferrell.org/pages/Gilberto_Alvarado_Allegation.html).

The last question is whether that other Silvia (Odio) had encountered the man who Ruby shot. If they had met on September 25, this might be feasible. Roy Schaeffer has proposed that Oswald's trip to Mexico City could have accommodated a side trip to Dallas – if he had been driven to Dallas from New Orleans, presumably by his two associates from that night. But good photographs would surely help.

Appendix I-B

The Zapruder Film(s) and Those Other Films

The word "stop" in the subtitle of this book, *"Dealey Plaza was Just the Final Stop,"* is an allusion to the limousine stop. Despite the (manipulated) images of the extant Zapruder film, the limousine really did stop (or nearly stop) on Elm St. that day. My November 2023 Pittsburgh lecture (with assistance from Douglas Horne) presents overwhelming evidence that the extant film in the National Archives cannot be the original film: "A Closer Look at the Zapruder Film: The Case for Alteration – The Future of Freedom Foundation."[193] Also see the dazzling websites of "John Costella: The JFK assassination,"[194] *and* "(58) Zapruder Film - John Costella - YouTube,"[195] *and* "John Costella's Home Page."[196]

Due to my nine visits to the National Archives, we now know that the autopsy X-rays and photographs have been critically altered. The subsequent "experts" based their entire case on two objects that were literally *invisible* to the autopsy pathologists! The two culprit images were the Red Spot (on a photograph) and the 6.5 mm apparent bullet cross section on the AP X-ray. Nothing like these follies had ever occurred before (or since) in the entire history of forensic pathology or in all of diagnostic radiology. So, it should really be no surprise that the Zapruder film also required alteration. After all, the gaping hole at the back of JFK's head declared – for all the world to see – that he had been shot from the front. What was a surprise (this week, just before Christmas 2024), is that Orville Nix's granddaughter won a verdict in court over the Department of (in)Justice – about the famous Nix movie film: "Court Rejects Government's Bid to Stiff Owner of JFK Assassination Film."[197]

Acting on behalf of H. L. Hunt, Paul Rothermel (a former FBI agent and CIA asset) reportedly purchased a first-day copy of the Zapruder film

193 https://www.fff.org/freedom-in-motion/video/a-closer-look-at-the-zapruder-film-the-case-for-alteration/.

194 https://johncostella.com/jfk/.

195 https://www.youtube.com/playlist?list=PLh8S8qYKHminprt2uawGKhDbL3z0BzlYl.

196 https://johncostella.com.

197 https://jfkfacts.substack.com/p/court-rejects-governments-bid-to.

(*The Man Who Knew Too Much* (1992) by Dick Russell, p. 607). These images surely must differ from the extant film in the National Archives.

If a copy of an original film had leaked out that day, it might indeed explain why 5-6 individuals (e.g., Rich DellaRosa, Greg Burnham, and Mildred Cranor) have seen a Zapruder-like film that contains more frames, including the limousine rounding the corner at Houston and Elm – as well as a limousine stop. What is remarkable about these witnesses is their agreement with one another – and their disagreement with the extant film.

In 2005, with delicious condescension, Richard Trask had declaimed:[198]

> *...it boggles my mind how complex the "alterationists" conspiracy had to be and the seeming superhuman luck and professionalism the conspirators possessed in being to locate, acquire, transport, and have the knowledge concerning what films and photographs needed to be changed. So many variables. So little time.*

Of course, it is now twenty years since Trask wrote this, but still – even in 2005 – we knew that Orville Nix was upset about his film; he knew it was not the original. And the Muchmore film showed an obvious splice – precisely where a headshot had occurred. What are the odds of both of these simultaneous events?

And even in 2005, evidence for a limousine stop was already quite overwhelming, but none of this mattered to Richard[199] (or to Josiah Thompson). Of course, we don't know how Richard would now respond to my 2023 Pittsburgh PowerPoint presentation (cited above). Perhaps he would be more open-minded today than before, but that attitude is nowhere evident in his books.

In retrospect, Richard appears to have modeled himself after (Saint) Robert Bellarmine, who educated Galileo on how the sun spun circles around the earth. Nevertheless, despite voting (in 1600) to burn Giordano Bruno at the stake, Robert has been duly canonized, an award which (fortunately – or perhaps not) Richard has evaded. But we know so much more today than we did even twenty years ago. Perhaps it is unfair to crucify "Poor Richard."

After all, Richard did not then know that at least six films from that day show *the identical pergola site as blacked out*. This can only have been deliberate. Even worse, the most obvious altered film is the Moorman Polaroid, which Roy Schaeffer had identified as altered at the *Dayton Daily News* early on the morning of November 23, 1963.[200] Every extant image of this famous

198 *National Nightmare on Six Feet of Film* (2005) by Richard Trask, p. 371.

199 Just to be clear, this is not the same Richard Trask (an FBI agent) who beat his wife after a sex party: FBI Agent Richard Trask Beat Wife After Sex Party: Sheriff (https://lawandcrime.com/high-profile/lead-fbi-agent-on-whitmer-kidnapping-case-allegedly-beat-wife-until-she-had-blood-all-over-after-sex-party/).

200 From: r_schaeffer@att.net
To: DAVID W MANTIK Thu, Feb 27 at 8:16 AM [2025]

photograph contains the alteration. Judge for yourself. That same Saturday morning, Roy also noticed the obvious fingerprint (which obscures the policeman on the viewer's left) – and that same fingerprint has persisted for six decades. If you prefer to challenge yourself (in spotting the masked area), first view the Moorman photograph online – and do not proceed here! On the other hand, if you cannot wait, just view the image below.

Five other films (*from that same day*) show obliteration of *this same site* in the pergola. These are the Mark Bell movie, the Nix movie, the Rickerby still photograph, the Bronson movie, and the Betzner still photograph. Here are the images, with each redaction circled in red.

First is the Nix film, where we see a very black (absurd) rectangle – in several successive frames. Only one frame is shown here. I have never seen anyone else display this – or even cite it.

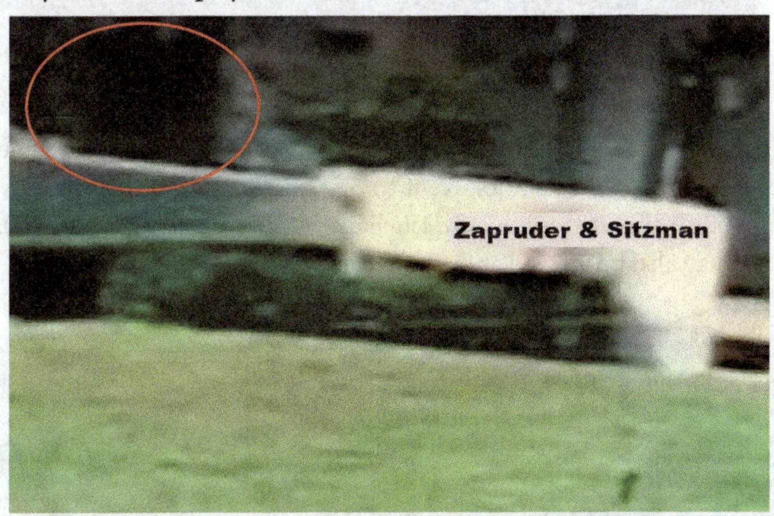

In the Moorman photo fax, I first noticed the black opaque mask when taking the Moorman fax to engraving on 11/23/1963 at 7:30 am.

For the Mark Bell film, two different sources are utilized here. The one on the left was lifted from the internet (note the sharp corner on the black rectangle), while the one on the right is from – you guessed it – the book by Richard Trask!

And here is the fourth film, taken by Arthur Rickerby:

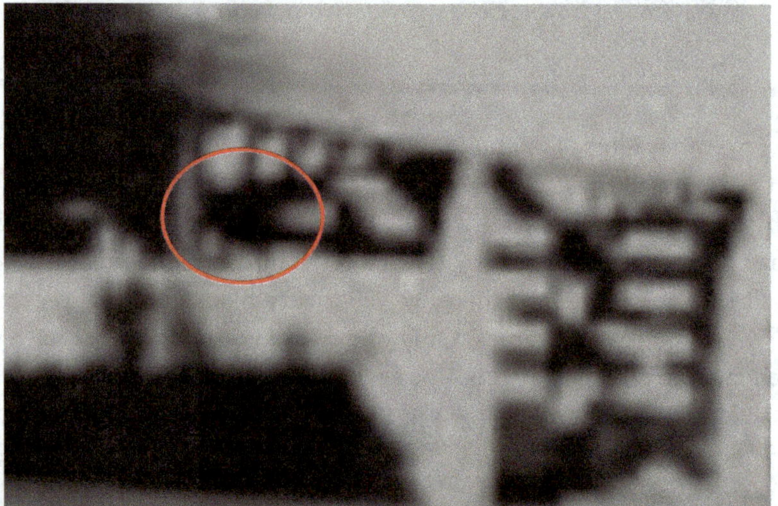

And here are the fifth and sixth films: Bronson is on the left, while Betzner is on the right. [As this book went to press, I discovered that Jim Towner's photograph shows the *same redaction* as Betzer (Trask 1994, p. 218). This image may also be viewed at the Sixth Floor Museum in Dallas.]

Just in case this seems dubious, let's view reality. Here are photographs taken by Wilma Bond (*on 11/22/1963*).[201]

In particular, notice how easy it is to see the window identified by the red arrow; that same window is obscured in the Moorman photograph.

From the collection of J. Gary Shaw.

For comparison, here are internet images (obviously taken at other times).[202] The arrows identify the transparent window that was wiped out (deliberately) in the Moorman photograph.

And here are two photographs with human figures so that you can judge for yourself: Moorman's Black Patch was large enough to obscure a human figure.

201 https://www.bing.com/search? - wilma bond Photgraphs

202 images of the pergola at dealey plaza - Search (https://www.bing.com/search?q=images+of+the+pergola+at+dealey+plaza&qs=RI&pq=dealey+plaza+pergola&sk=UT1&sc=9-20&cvid=0E13FC862FA14269BE2BBB0F43FF96BF&FORM=QBRE&sp=2&lq=0&ntref=1).

Meanwhile, Roy Schaeffer has enlightened me about alteration of Polaroid photographs. An appropriate 1963 device for this is shown here (with a contemporaneous Polaroid camera); these were owned by Roy Schaeffer.[203] A current device is shown next (polaroid copy machine - Search Images). Furthermore, even today websites still offer precise instructions for altering Polaroids.[204]

To my amazement, Roy next located a copy of a 30-year-old photograph from Dealey Plaza; he took this while standing *directly behind me*[205] while I replicated Moorman's location of 30 years before that. Roy's photograph is shown on the left here (ignore Roy's distracting X and his encircling ellipse) while Mary's (colored) photograph is on the right. Roy's photograph (taken 30 years after Mary) closely duplicates Mary's view that day – but Roy's has no circled black mask.

203 According to Roy, this device projects a magnified image (usually 10" x 12") that is then captured by the wire services machine. As the image is projected, it can be altered and then recopied.

204 "can a polaroid photograph be altered?" - Search (https://www.bing.com/search?pglt=427&q=can+a+polaroid+photograph+be+altered?&cvid=7ee639209cd547689c01c5eefb8438ad&gs_lcrp=EgRlZGdlKgkIABBFGDsY-QcyCQgAEEUYOxj5BzIGCAEQABhAMgYIAhBFGDkyBggDEAAYQDIGCAQQABhAMgYIBRAAGEAyBggGEEUYPDIGCAcQRRg8MgYICBBFGDzSAQgzNzIyajBqMagCALACAA&FORM=ANNTA1&PC=U531).

205 That precise photograph of me (mimicking Mary) appears in *Murder in Dealey Plaza* (2000), p. 347.

The Russians were infamous for faking and altering images. From my personal library, the cover of *The Commissar Vanishes* (1997) by David King is shown here. This cover displays a four-set sequence of deliberate alterations, in which one character after another disappears, until only Stalin is left.

Amazingly, Dino Brugioni (the CIA's master photo-interpreter) wrote the book on *Photo Fakery* (1999), as displayed here. Dino, of course, had helped to identify the Russian missiles during the Cuban Missile Crisis. He also recognized that the Zapruder film had been altered – as he demonstrated in his video interview, which appears in my 2023 Pittsburgh lecture (previously cited).[206] So, while Trask blithely belittles "alterationists" (like Brugioni), the reader is faced with a distinct choice: Do you believe Brugioni – or do you believe Trask (and Thompson)? You cannot believe both. So, who is more likely to know?

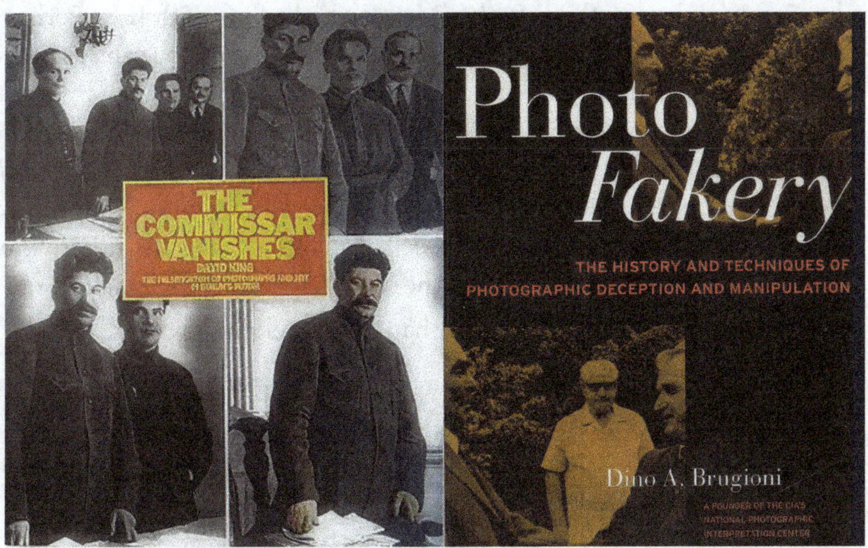

Roy Schaeffer, who promptly (on 11/23/1963) identified the Moorman photograph as manipulated, sent me the *Dayton Daily News* history book shown here. But we simply cannot escape altered images – even the cover of this history book has one (identified by the arrow)! But you must scrutinize this very closely or you will miss it.

206 "dino brugioni zapruder film" - Search (https://www.bing.com/search?pglt=427&q=dino+brugioni+zapruder+film&cvid=6cd5ca5bf06b441397c522b720dc95ba&gs_lcrp=EgRlZGdlKgYIARAAGEAyBggAEEUYOTIGCAEQABhAMgYIAhAAGEAyBggDEAAYQDIGCAQQABhA0gEINzQ1OGowajGoAgCwAgA&FORM=ANNTA1&PC=U531).

Dayton Ink

THE FIRST CENTURY OF THE DAYTON DAILY NEWS

Dear David Mantik,
There are two types of
in the ITU.
Job printing + newspapers.
I graduated in 1965
from New York Tech
Computer programmer
and finished my
apprenticeship
in 1969
at the Dayton Daily News
63 74 —
74-86
Job printer
Ray

Published by the

Dayton Daily News

Text by Teresa Zumwald
Photo research by Marvin Christian
Edited by Ron Rollins
Designed and produced by Sol Smith

Everyone knows that Marilyn Monroe had a fling with JFK. Perhaps this couple even danced in the Lincoln bedroom. But as you can see in the images below,[207] Marilyn also had a crush on another president. (Brugioni displays this dancing image in his book.) What would have been more appropriate than for Marilyn to dance with Abe in *his own (Lincoln) bedroom*? That bedroom is a historic site; it is where Bill Clinton entertained his wealthy donors (and *others* – like Sharon Stone), and also where Lincoln signed (on this very table) the Emancipation Proclamation, and around which Nixon and Kissinger had once knelt to pray.

Digital forgery can create photographic evidence for events that never happened.

207 I was able promptly to pull this February 1994 *Scientific American* issue from my 31-year-old files. It has superior resolution compared to the image that Brugioni displayed on p. 79.

But I have strayed from the main thoroughfare here – thanks to Brugioni. The real question is obvious: In Moorman, what did this Black Patch cover?[208] Surely not a gunman – that location would have been far too visible. So, perhaps a famous person who was part of the plot? Well, it was not Milteer who was probably elsewhere in Dealey Plaza that day.[209] In any case, it is almost impossible (at that distance) to identify a human face in Mary's photograph given its low resolution. But what else could it be? How about another photographer? But why would anyone knock a public photographer out of a film?

Think about this. If this book has established anything, the CIA knew that a hit was coming – *that day*. Good heavens, by April 1963 even Dr. Adele Edisen suspected something. Now if the CIA knew, surely they would have ordered a high quality movie film of their biggest hit. In fact, to omit this would have been gross negligence – and yet, and yet, no one has ever spotted this photographer. Why is that?

We also know that 5-6 individuals have seen a Zapruder-like film. It showed the turn at Houston and Elm and – quite astonishingly – these viewers (independently) all reported a limousine stop. Rich DellaRosa added one additional clue – he said that the viewpoint seemed slightly different from Zapruder's.[210] So, look again at the Black Patch (in Moorman) and notice its location relative to Zapruder – it matches DellaRosa's recollection. And in this map of Dealey Plaza, note the location of this CIA photographer and compare it to Zapruder's site.

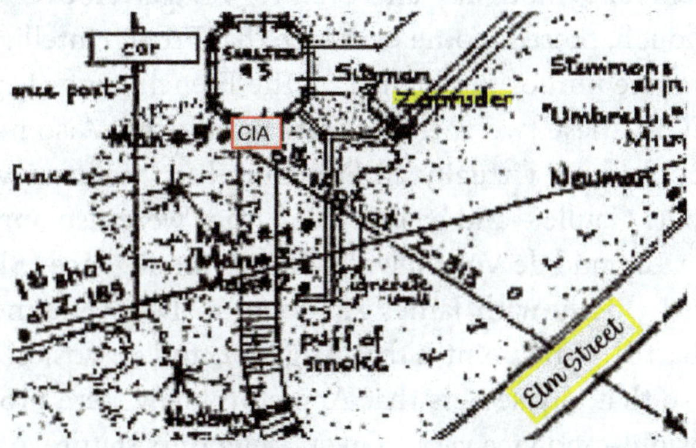

208 We know what the Black Patch in Zapruder frame 317 covered – it was the gaping hole at the back of JFK's head. See my essay, "Masquerade at the Museum" in *The JFK Assassination: Criminal Forgery in the Autopsy Photographs and X-rays* (2023).

209 J. Gary Shaw reports that Milteer was in Dallas on 11/22/1963. Milteer called the police at 10:30 AM that day. Although I am not sure why it was so urgent for them to know about Miami, Milteer advised these police that JFK would never again appear in Miami! See *Cover-up* (1992), p. 89.

210 "Rich DellaRosa Describes What He Saw In The Other Zapruder Film" (https://www.youtube.com/watch?v=XrRbkY9gEnQ).

Roy Schaeffer was the first to suggest a CIA photographer at that specific site, as described in this annotation in his book, which he gave me 5-10 years ago. William Bobo is actually Roy Schaeffer.[211]

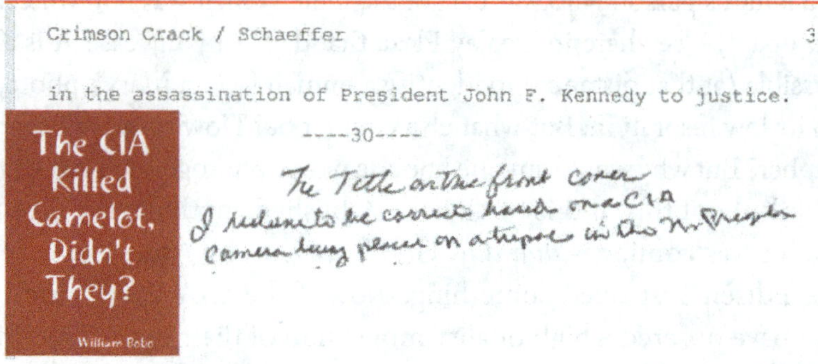

This annotation [boldface added by me] is here transcribed word for word: ***"The title on the front cover I believe to be correct based on a CIA camera being placed on a tripod in the N. Pergola…"***

So, perhaps copies of this Zapruder-like film descended from the original CIA film (rather than Zapruder's film) and were viewed by Burnham, DellaRosa, Cranor, et al. Paul Rothermel claims to have purchased a copy (of a movie film) that day – for H. L. Hunt, so which one was it? Now this gets interesting – because this Hunt was close to Allen Dulles; he was also close to General Willoughby and even to J. Edgar Hoover. To really stir this pot, though, there is some evidence that French intelligence eventually got a movie film of the big hit.[212] The French equivalent of the CIA is the SDECE. These two agencies were tightly knit. Also recall (see Part II in this book) how virtually all French military officers were violently opposed to de Gaulle – and by extension, they were also opposed to JFK.

Philippe Thyraud de Vosjoli was a French intelligence (SDECE) agent who worked closely with James Angleton in DC. (See more about de Vosjoli in Part II.) The point is that Angleton and de Vosjoli were personally close, so that any secrets that Angleton knew were probably shared with de Vosjoli – and vice versa. Given Angleton's stature in the CIA, and his persistent and fervent interest in Nosenko (and by extension, also an unrelenting interest in Oswald), as well as his never-ending conviction of

211 Roy's clever mind is also shown by this: he was the first to recognize that JFK's throat wound had been caused by a glass shard from the windshield. Years later, I (independently) made the same observation. No other explanation comes remotely close to solving this mystery. Welcoming William Bobo to BSSM! | College of Medicine.

212 The "Other" Zapruder Film (https://www.youtube.com/watch?v=hSdyqDBTpeo).

a (Soviet) JFK conspiracy, does it seem likely that Jim knew about this CIA film? Of course, he did. And if he did, would he have told de Vosjoli – and shown it to him? After all, for years these two had been blood brothers in the Cold War. So, this may be how French intelligence came into possession of the film.

We have also recently learned that Chana Gail Willis recalled her father's experience in Dealey Plaza that day[213]--he was *coerced* into filming the motorcade. But how was he overlooked by the film collectors, who had scavenged every conceivable film?[214] Recall that the federal agencies vigorously collected *all* Dealey Plaza films. They even *relentlessly pursued* that other Morman (a pun – he was on a mission), a young man named Robert Croft. They eventually located him en route to his new mission, as Trask himself tells us (pp. 43, 44, 63).[215]

However, if the images of a film gave away too much detail, then that film had to be lost (e.g., Beverly Oliver), or confiscated (e.g., Croft – **including a head shot**),[216] or else altered (e.g., Zapruder, Muchmore and Nix). To that altered list we can now add more: Bell, Rickerby, Betzner, and Bronson. In the Nix film, given the Black Patch (actually a sharply defined black rectangle), we now know that Orville was correct after all – his film had undeniably been altered. But the core question is this: Given that photographs were deliberately altered **during that same day** (i.e., the plotters were prepared) why would the federal agencies bother to *publicize* a CIA photographer?

Most likely, on that very day, they learned who this photographer represented. After all, the purpose of the feds was not to enlighten, but rather to obscure. And how is it possible that each of these altered photographs shows precisely the **same site of alteration** in the pergola? This

213 JFK Magazine: "Chana Gail Willis: Her Father's Life Story" (July 16, 2017) (https://www.jfkmagazine.org/2023/07/chana-gail-willis-her-fathers-life.html#/page/2). *"Her father worked for the CIA and was a U.S. Navy MASTER CHIEF photographer for U.S. intelligence. His daughter, Chana Gail Willis alleges he was forced to film President Kennedy's assassination from behind the picket fence for the CIA."* In this talk (and to me subsequently), Chana added that her father was also embedded at that time in Texas Instruments, which is still located in Dallas, Texas.

214 List of 500+ Photos Taken in Dealey Plaza (https://www.jfk-info.com/photos1.htm).

215 Serendipitously, my wife and I will see a live production of the musical, *The Book of Mormon*, tomorrow – for the first time.

216 *"Robert Croft stood on the grass opposite the TSBD and took the last picture of JFK before he was shot dead. The other three pictures Croft took were confiscated by the FBI because one was the fatal shot. The FBI claimed that photo was a blank"* (20+) Facebook) (https://www.facebook.com/maff.matthewman/photos/robert-croft-the-key-to-the-whole-thingrobert-croft-was-stood-on-the-grass-oppos/854005095602264 3/).

cannot be random. These alterationists knew who had stood there. Their manipulation was deliberate – and precisely directed – as if by GPS guidance. Someone on site guided them, but who played this role – perhaps the CIA photographer? The real alterationists (despite Trask, there were some – and they weren't folks like me) knew exactly where to look in each photograph. Their mission was well defined – and paid for with our tax donations – although they forgot to send you and me a thank you note.

In summary then, after identifying the fake 6.5 mm bullet cross section (on the AP skull X-ray), the artificial White Patch (on both lateral JFK X-rays), the forged Red Spot (in the autopsy head photograph), the geometric Black Patch (e.g., in Zapruder frame 317), and now the Black Patches in Moorman, Nix, Bell, Rickerby, Betzner, and Bronson, perhaps we should retitle the JFK execution and cover-up as "The JFK Assassination Follies." If so, the motto of these worker bees should have been "Have Brush, Will Travel."

Appendix I-C

The Hoover Memo (1960): Two Oswalds?

UNITED STATES DEPARTMENT OF JUSTICE
FEDERAL BUREAU OF INVESTIGATION

In Reply, Please Refer to
File No. 105-82555

WASHINGTON 25, D. C.

Date: June 3, 1960

To: Office of Security
Department of State

From: John Edgar Hoover, Director

Subject: LEE HARVEY OSWALD
INTERNAL SECURITY - R

Reference is made to Foreign Service Despatch Number 234 dated November 2, 1959, concerning subject's renunciation of his American citizenship at the United States Embassy, Moscow, Russia, on October 31, 1959.

It is noted that among other items, subject surrendered his United States Passport Number 1733242 to an American Embassy official. His last known residence as indicated in your despatch was The Metropole Hotel, Moscow, where he was residing in a nontourist status.

Your attention is directed to the report of Special Agent John W. Fain, Dallas, Texas, dated May 12, 1960, entitled "Funds Transmitted to Residents of Russia; Internal Security - R," a copy of which was furnished to the Department of State on May 24, 1960.

In that report you will note that subject's mother, Mrs. Marguerite C. Oswald, Fort Worth, Texas, advised that she recently received a letter addressed to her son from the Albert Schweitzer College in Switzerland indicating that Lee Oswald was expected at the college on April 20, 1960. She stated subject had taken his birth certificate with him when he left home. She was apprehensive about his safety because three letters she had written him since January 22, 1960, have been returned to her undelivered.

Since there is a possibility that an imposter is using Oswald's birth certificate, any current information the Department of State may have concerning subject will be appreciated.

1 - Director of Naval Intelligence

39-61981

Appendix I-D

Otto Skorzeny (1908-1975)

Skorzeny was Hitler's top commando. In 1952, he moved to Madrid, where he set up a school for training assassins. Read *The Skorzeny Papers: Evidence for the Plot to Kill JFK* (2018) by Major Ralph Ganis. Also watch *Europe's Most Dangerous Man: Otto Skorzeny in Spain* (on Netflix). Meredith M. Mantik also has an extensive video interview with Ganis, which still awaits release. It may appear in 2025 in her JFK documentary, *Conspiracyland.*

The Warren Commission: Left to Right: Gerald Ford (R-Michigan), U.S. Representative (later 38th President of the United States), House Minority Leader (1913–2006); Hale Boggs (D-Louisiana), U.S. Representative, House Majority Whip (1914–1972); Richard Russell, Jr. (D-Georgia), U.S. Senator (1897–1971); Earl Warren, Chief Justice of the United States (chairman) (1891–1974); John Sherman Cooper (R-Kentucky), U.S. Senator (1901–1991); John J. McCloy, former president of the World Bank (1895–1989); Allen Dulles, former Director of the CIA (1893–1969); General Counsel J. Lee Rankin (1907–1996).

Colonel Edward Lansdale with CIA Director Allen Dulles and United States Air Force Chief of Staff General Nathan F. Twining and CIA Deputy Director Lieutenant General Charles P. Cabell at The Pentagon in 1955.

Appendix I-E

Allen Dulles (1893-1969)

Allen Dulles is a curious case. Unless he was totally senile, he surely knew in advance about the plot. However, his mental faculties in 1963 (at age 70) were already in serious decline. Here are some excerpts from *The Brothers: John Foster Dulles, Allen Dulles, and Their Secret World War* (2013) by Stephen Kinzer. Cited pages are from my Kindle: 188, 214, 289, 302, and 306. After reading these, it is hard to picture Allen as the consummate mastermind of "The Big Event." After all, even two years earlier, he had already abandoned his personal involvement in the Bay of Pigs. Recall that he was calmly giving an irrelevant talk in Puerto Rico that very day!

Although David Talbot (in *The Devil's Chessboard,* 2015) focuses on Allen Dulles, he cites Stephen Kinzer on only *one page* (p. 230), where Kinzer is a "*noted Dulles biographer.*" But the title of Kinzer's book is not even cited in Talbot's 686-page book. Even more stunning, Talbot seems quite unaware of the following comments. (Kinzer's book was published two years before Talbot's.)

> This Indented Section Is From Kinzer (as cited above)
>
> During the late 1950s, Allen ceded his power to Bissell. Allen even turned the Castro planning over to Richard Bissell and "*withdrew into a private cocoon ... he was entirely detached. He never focused on the plot.... This was a remarkable fade. A deepening of character traits – distraction, inability to focus, lack of attention to detail, aversion to rigorous debate – that people around him had long observed.*"
>
> "*Stories of Allen's behavior circulated quietly. One day in 1958, an analyst brought him a new batch oof U-2 photos but found him unwilling to switch off his radio, which was broadcasting a Washington Senators game. He paid little attention to the photos.*"
>
> Allen was a poor administrator. Many around him also noted his lack of intellectual engagement.... His mind was undisciplined. By one account he was almost scatter-brained. A senior British agent who worked with him for years recalled "*...being seldom able to penetrate beyond his laugh, or to conduct any serious professional conversation with him for more than a few minutes.*"

> Bill Bundy: *"I had the feeling that by then he was slowing down a little.... I came to the conclusion that he hadn't been quite the man I had known. All through, he hadn't been as much on top of the* [Bay of Pigs] *operation as I had expected."*
>
> Admiral Burke was withering in his judgment of Allen. *"The fact is that he just wasn't involved in that operation. He showed up at meetings and sat there smoking his pipe.... I blame him for not being there."*
>
> In 1965, Schlesinger and Sorensen published articles blaming Allen for the Bay of Pigs fiasco. So, Allen began work on a rebuttal, but it was never published. His sister Eleanor believed that he *"... had already begun to lose his command over his memory and ideas."* She persuaded him not to publish.
>
> In the late 1960s, Allen began losing his way on the Georgetown streets. *"Perhaps it was what we call Alzheimer's disease today,"* a relative reported.

Allen died on January 29, 1969 – nine days after Nixon's inauguration. (Nixon was just one more All-American faux pas.) Before we leave Allen though, we shall review here his (tragic) role in Indonesia, a tale often overlooked in JFK assassination accounts. As usual, Allen's foreign policy position radically disagreed with JFK's position. For this analysis, we are mostly indebted to Greg Poulgrain for *The Incubus of Intervention: Conflicting Indonesian Strategies of John F. Kennedy and Allen Dulles* (2015).[217] I purchased the book on Kindle (2020), where Oliver Stone wrote the Introduction and James DiEugenio wrote the Afterword. Both are highly insightful and their words make for valuable reading. The following is a summary of Poulgrain's book; references are from my Kindle.

As yet another failure by Allen Dulles, he failed to inform JFK of the Sino-Soviet split. And JFK did not even realize that his support for the charismatic Muslim president of Indonesia (Sukarno) would endanger Allen's plans for regime change – Allen wanted access to Indonesia's vast natural resources. JFK's attitude would also jeopardize the Rockefeller plans for splitting Moscow from Beijing.

Another Allen (surnamed Pope – a CIA pilot), had been shot down (on May 18, 1958) during "The Indonesian Crisis," while Sukarno was president (1945 to 1965).[218] So, JFK asked Allen for a review of this case. In typical fashion, Allen gave the president of the US a **redacted copy**!

---

217 On Amazon, a used paperback was recently listed for $101.77.

218 CIA expenses in Indonesia (in 1958) were second only to Vietnam. Recall that the US was mostly financing French efforts in Vietnam until 1954, after which the US assumed responsibility for Vietnam.

Neither JFK nor Sukarno were then aware that Indonesia was awash in billions of dollars of natural resources (especially oil and gold).[219] But the Dutch did know, so they vigorously opposed Sukarno's move for independence. But JFK was sympathetic with Sukarno, so naturally Sukarno loved JFK.

During the Truman administration, Beetle Smith was CIA director, while Allen was his deputy. Peter Grose[220] describes Allen's tenure with Beetle as *"marred by tension."* In particular, Beetle did not approve of Allen's love for covert action. Beetle had even warned Ike about Allen's dangerous proclivities. As a result, Ike delayed Allen's appointment for *"long and agonizing weeks"* before finally consenting to it. Poulgrain concludes that Beetle was correct about Allen – and that Ike had made a grievous mistake. JFK would later agree with Beetle – he fired Allen after the Bay of Pigs. Even Joe Kennedy seemed to know about Allen's careless and risky fixations – well before JFK did.

Of the 418 WC witnesses, one of the most thorough interviews was with George de Mohrenschildt.[221] George's interactions with Allen during this WC encounter would have been priceless to observe – because these two men *had known one another for 40 years*![222]

Poulgrain reminds us that Allen had been in Dallas just five weeks before 11/22/1963; he had given a talk for the Dallas Council on World Affairs. Astonishingly, de Mohrenschildt was also a member of this group.

In his Afterword to this book, DiEugenio examines Sukarno's overthrow in 1965. He astutely notes that the slaughter of *hundreds of thousands* of innocent civilians *"filled the White House* [i.e., LBJ] *with incontinent delight."* Jim cites the pleasure taken by Cyrus Leo Sulzberger (publisher of the *NY Times*) in the news from Indonesia. Jim also emphasizes that infamous (June 19, 1966) column by James Reston in the *Times*: "A Gleam of Light in Asia." Furthermore, in 1969, after a visit to Jakarta, even Richard Nixon praised Indonesia's new leader (Suharto).[223]

219 Indonesia's gold proved to be twice that of South Africa's richest gold mine; Indonesia's natural resources even surpassed those of the Congo.

220 *Gentleman Spy: The Life of Allen Dulles* (1995) by Peter Grose, p. 310.

221 De Mohrenschildt did not believe that Lee was the lone gunman. Nor did Allen Dulles. Nor did Ernst Titovets. But David Kaiser does.

222 Allen lobbied for Standard Oil in their negotiations with the director of the Nobel interests in Russia; this director was Baron Sergius Alexander von Mohrenschildt – George's father! In a subsequent legal verdict, a $50,000 fine was levied because Allen had arranged for Vichy (Nazi) France to import oil from Standard Oil; in effect Allen was aiding an enemy of the US – while Germany was at war with American allies! We can only wonder which side Allen was on.

223 Poulgrain concludes that Suharto would never have become dictator if JFK had lived. Apparently, no one had informed Nixon about this.

The Times continued by quoting Suharto (no surname), who became an authoritarian dictator after Sukarno was deposed: *"Indonesia is a state based on law, not on mere power."* This was the same man who tried fiercely to live up to his own "democratic" billing – by killing one hundred thousand (mostly very poor peasants) during the annexation of East Timor. His vicious program had received approval from my future neighbor, Gerry Ford, and also from Henry Kissinger.[224]

For more in-depth analysis of Indonesia and Freeport McMoRan,[225] read the insightful 1996 article by my esteemed colleague, Lisa Pease: "JFK, Indonesia, CIA & Freeport Sulphur."[226] These corporate leaders profited handsomely while Suharto sold off portions of Indonesia. As a result, except for ordinary Indonesians, everyone was thrilled. Suharto reversed almost all of Sukarno's previous nationalizations of businesses. DiEugenio concludes: *"there was a large, almost canyon size, difference between how Allen Dulles viewed the Third World and how President Kennedy looked at it."* Even the Rockefellers would have agreed with this statement; so would Henry Kissinger, who played henchman for the Rockefellers.

---

224 "Henry Kissinger and the Murder of Timor-Leste" – The Diplomat (https://thediplomat.com/2023/12/henry-kissinger-and-the-murder-of-timor-leste/). See a photograph at that website of Suharto, Gerald Ford, Henry Kissinger, and Indonesia's foreign minister (Jakarta, December 6, 1975). Indonesia invaded East Timor the very next day – on the 34th anniversary of Pearl Harbor! I also suggest reading *The Trial of Henry Kissinger* (2012) by Christopher Hitchens and Ariel Dorfman (Kindle, 2012). You will enjoy Chris's biting sarcasm.

225 When I was still young and innocent, I happily took profits on my investments in Freeport McMoRan. Perhaps readers can advise me how to make restitution for my political naivety: who do I reimburse? But even the Tosefta Baba Metzia 8:26 (date: 3d CE, Hebrew) recognizes that it can be difficult to identify victims: Tosefta Baba Metzia 8:26 | Judaism and Rome.

226 https://www.kennedysandking.com/john-f-kennedy-articles/jfk-indonesia-cia-freeport-sulphur.

Acknowledgments – Part I

As prominently noted in my conjoined PowerPoint presentation, Bill Simpich was the primary provocateur for many of these thoughts. He deserves a 21-gun salute. After Ed Lopez and Dan Hardway (for the HSCA), it was Anthony Summers (*Conspiracy*, 1980) and Gaeton Fonzi (for the HSCA) who began to focus on Bill Harvey as a key conspirator. Many other contributors (listed in my PowerPoint) have confirmed these suspicions, but special kudos must go to David Talbot, Noel Twyman, Larry Hancock, and Dick Russell. Heather Fear provided photographs of Jane Roman and Bruce Solie, which I could find nowhere. Inquisitive readers might also review my "uncommon" bibliography in *The Assassination of John F. Kennedy: THE FINAL ANALYSIS* (by Jerome Corsi and me). Thoughtful insights can materialize from unanticipated sources. Open minds are also useful.

Intermission: A view from my bedroom.

Part II: The Sponsors

All the Way – with LBJ![227]

"Absolutely not," Connally said. *"I do not, for one second, believe the conclusions of the Warren Commission."* Thompson asked why he had not spoken out about this. Connally replied: *"Because I love this country and we needed closure at the time. I will never speak out publicly about what I believe."*

–In 1982, Doug Thompson asked John Connally if Lee Harvey Oswald had fired the gun that killed JFK.[228]

"Maybe it was the Russians. Could have been the Cubans. Might have been the Mafia.... Oliver Stone's JFK films [sic] are fantasies."

–Tim Weiner[229]

"Lee Harvey Oswald did kill President Kennedy all by himself.... Nothing suggests that the CIA was involved...."

–David Kaiser[230]

"Johnson knew about the assassination in advance but was not involved in its original inception."

–Noel Twyman[231]

"We know the CIA was involved, and the Mafia. We all know that."
–Richard Goodwin, former Deputy Assistant Secretary of State for Inter-American Affairs[232]

---

227 *All the Way* (2016) is an American biographical LBJ drama, made for TV.

228 John Connally (https://spartacus-educational.com/JFKconnally.htm).

229 "The Origin Story of Oliver Stone's Loony JFK Conspiracies" (https://www.rollingstone.com/politics/politics-features/jfk-oliver-stone-conspiracy-theory-russian-disinformation-1260223/).

230 *The Road to Dallas: The Assassination of John F. Kennedy* (2008) by David Kaiser, p. 416.

231 *Bloody Treason* (1997) by Noel Twyman, p. 823. Noel was one of my best friends; especially for his era, he had amazing insight into the major players in the JFK assassination. Noel gave me a copy of his book; when I read his lavish inscription I was stunned.

232 But David Kaiser does not know that it was a conspiracy! Talbot's quotation is from *Brothers* (2007), p. 303. Richard Goodwin joined JFK's speech writing staff in 1959. In August 1961, he met secretly with Che Guevara in Uruguay. His wife (Doris Kearns Goodwin) helped LBJ draft his memoirs. But Dick apparently did not tell Doris about the JFK plotters! Her book (*Lyndon Johnson and the American Dream* (2015)) fails to mention Billie Sol Estes, Cliff Carter, H. L. Hunt, or J. Edgar Hoover. To her (minimal) credit though she does cite Bobby Baker once.

But Johnson was certainly not the mastermind. And, yet loyal to the end, even on his deathbed [E. Howard] Hunt could not bring himself to name Dulles…."

–David Talbot[233]

"Over the final months of JFK's presidency, a clear **consensus** *[emphasis added] took shape within America's deep state: Kennedy was a national security threat. For the good of the country, he must be removed. And Dulles was the only man with the stature, connections, and decisive will to make something of this enormity happen. He had already assembled a killing machine* **overseas** *[emphasis added]. Now he prepared to bring it home to Dallas. All that his establishment colleagues had to do was to look the other way – as they always did when Dulles took executive action."*

–David Talbot[234]

(L–R) Jay Roach, Bryan Cranston, Anthony Mackie and Robert Schenkkan at the *All the Way* premiere in Austin.

All the Way With LBJ | Busy Beaver Button Museum

LBJ's Black Halo—and His Vanishing Act (at Houston & Elm)

Although Bill Harvey and David Morales (likely with assistance from Ed Lansdale – more follows below) supervised the successful exe-

After she left Brooklyn, Doris jilted the Dodgers without any guilt; then like Gertrude (Hamlet's mother) she married the local Boston Red Sox. So, she became the first female journalist to enter the Red Sox locker room. After a barren interval of 86 years (during the curse of the Babe) the Red Sox finally won the Series again in 2004. Despite 1951 (due to the home run heard around the world – by the Giants) and the 2018 World Series, Doris should have remained a Dodger fan (as I am).

233 *The Devil's Chessboard* (2015) by David Talbot, p. 504. For readers who want to view both sides of an issue, read "A Review of David Talbot's *The Devil's Chessboard*" by Phillip F. Nelson. This appears as Appendix A in *JFK: Who, How, and Why* (2017) edited by James Fetzer and Mike Palecek. Nelson believes that Talbot was wrong to place Dulles at the center of the plot. But we can still wonder why Dulles visited the LBJ ranch shortly before 11/22/1963. After all, JFK had fired Dulles, so he was no longer in office – and so he had no official business to discuss. Dulles's pending trip to the ranch was reported in the *Fort Worth Press*, shortly before JFK's own Texas trip. But this visit was omitted from Dulles's travel records (Fetzer and Palecek, p. 464).

234 Ibid., p. 560.

cution in Dealey Plaza,[235] one question remains: Did these men act independently – or did they merely follow orders? Harvey insisted that he had always followed orders.[236] On the other hand, we know that he did step out of line (and thereby lost his job) as a result of his commando raids during the Cuban Missile Crisis. As for Morales, he claimed that LBJ (1908-1973) had approved the plot.[237] If true, the looming question then becomes: *Who ordered this murder?* So, Part II is chiefly about the *sponsors,* i.e., those with the political and financial power to issue such an order. On the other hand, Part I was about those who carried out the order.

The Summum Malum: Lyndon Baines Johnson (LBJ)

LBJ Allen Dulles

235 See Part I in this book – about David Morales and Bill Harvey, who planned the events in Dealey Plaza (probably with Lansdale), and who were paid from taxpayer funds. David Denton emphasizes Harvey's astuteness:

> *Harvey had an eye-opening interview with the HSCA in 1976, when he suggested that to ensure success in an assassination attempt, one should "simply appoint a single senior officer to do everything to run the operation, kill the person, bury the body, and tell no one* (*Essays on the Assassination of President John F. Kennedy* (2020) by Professor David Denton, p. 47).

For the record, we should note that Ed Lansdale did survive 11/22/1963, although he was probably on site that day. After all, someone had to supervise "The Big Event." If not Lansdale, who then? We know that Harvey was at a Gladio base in Sardinia. The whereabouts of David Morales that day are uncertain, but he did die rather mysteriously some years later – in 1978, just before he was to appear before the HSCA.

236 Talbot 2015, p. 508. Talbot states that Harvey was *"probably telling the truth."* Of course, Bill wasn't exactly following orders in Rome in 1963. While in the eternal city, he persisted in his sexual (mis)adventures, chronic alcoholism, and compulsive antipathy for the Romans. Although he later became a Lutheran, in 1963 Bill had not yet read Paul's *Epistle to the Romans.*

237 Ibid., p. 503. Harvey had been CIA since 1947 (its first year). William Weston suspects a CIA shooter in the Book Depository that day, so perhaps Bill was just following orders: ("A CIA Shooter in the TSBD? – On the CIA & the TSBD" by William Weston in *Garrison: The Journal of History and Deep Politics*, Issue #11, September 2022, pp. 84-96).

LBJ's link to the conspirators is the darkest Black Hole of the entire JFK case. Many (if not most) history students accept (at least) LBJ's foreknowledge.[238] I concur with this. For example, in order to share his intimate thoughts while at his ranch, LBJ sometimes waded with confidants into the middle of the Pedernales River.[239] But, with respect to the JFK assassination, whether (1) he was merely being queried or (2) was an instigator – that issue shall remain a mystery. In any case, one of oft-cited clues to LBJ's foreknowledge is this photograph from Dealey Plaza, just as LBJ's car was rounding the corner at Elm and Houston.[240]

Dallas Police Officer Billy Joe "B. J." Martin said that according to his fellow motorcycle cops "who were escorting [the Vice-Presidential car,] he [LBJ] **started ducking down in the car a good 30 or 40 seconds before the first shots were fired...."** He said, in reflection upon the moments before the shooting, "our new president is either one jumpy son of a bitch or he knows something he's not telling about the Kennedy thing."

Senator Yarborough:
"Let me tell you one thing that didn't happen: that cock and bull story he (Johnson) told about Agent Youngblood pushing him down and jumping over and sitting on him. It's just plain... a fabrication. It didn't happen at all. Youngblood turned around. He [LBJ] had a little box—I guess it was an information box from the radio—and he leaned over... [listening to it]."
~interview with Jim Marrs in *Crossfire*, 1989

238 Here is a pertinent excerpt from *Bloody Treason* (1997) by Noel Twyman, pp. 768-769. Vince Palamara reported that Marty Underwood (an honorary SS agent) was the advance man for the SS. Vince was told that JFK never kept SS agents off the limousine. Twyman reports:

> *...Underwood stated that the CIA, the FBI, and the mafia "knew* (JFK) *was going to be hit" on 11/22/1963 – this information came from his direct contacts with CIA officer Win Scott, the Mexico City station chief during Oswald's* [supposed] *visit to that region! In addition, Underwood stated that, eighteen hours before Kennedy's murder, "we were getting all sorts of rumors that the President was going to be assassinated in Dallas; there were no if's, and's, or but's about it."*

For more on Underwood, see Jim DiEugenio's comments: "Who Is Gus Russo?" (https://www.kennedysandking.com/john-f-kennedy-articles/who-is-gus-russo-2).

J. Garrett Underhill, a former military affairs editor at *Life* (and CIA informant) stated that *"A small clique in the CIA"* killed JFK. Garrett knew the people involved and they knew he knew. Before he could blow his whistle, he was found in bed (May 8, 1964) with a bullet hole behind his left ear (Mellen 2013, p. 181). He then stopped being a whistleblower. Also see "Clint Hill's guilty verdict on LBJ: Circa year 2000: Clint Hill strongly implied that LYNDON JOHNSON was behind the JFK assassination" - JFK Assassination Debate - The Education Forum.

239 *"In time, LBJ insisted upon meeting Tex Brown* [the bounty hunter] *in person on the banks of the Pedernales River near LBJ's ranch. Apparently, to assure himself of absolute privacy and 'no recorders,' the president of the United States and Tex Brown stripped naked and stood waist high in the famous river in Texas"* ("LBJ & the Bounty Hunter" by Edgar Tatro, *Garrison: The Journal of History and Deep Politics*, Issue #5, August 2020, pp. 18-23).

Tatro also describes the relationship of Big Ray "Tex" Brown to Ruby and to Oswald. Brown claimed that they practiced shooting together, but that, although Ruby improved, Oswald did not. Tatro also claims that Ruby offered Brown a million-dollar contract for a "hit." Tatro cites John Connally as a conspirator and notes that Connally helped to keep Tex Brown silent after 11/22/1963. Also see *Broken Silence* by Ray "Tex" Brown (1996).

240 Lady Bird sat between Ralph Yarborough and LBJ (directly behind the driver). LBJ was on the far right side. Yarborough recounts, in great detail, the bizarre – and very

LBJ's foreknowledge: According to his escorts, LBJ had been ducking for 30-40 seconds before the first shots. He should be visible inside the far left, yellow circle, but where is he? After all, Lady Bird is trivial to spot inside the center circle.[241]

Edward Baker: The red ellipse circles LBJ's back (colorized for clarity) – he is leaning way over, with his head toward the right side of the limousine, but we cannot see his head. The image directly above his back is most likely a person in the background, i.e., someone standing on the sidewalk. Faces are colorized for clarity.

LBJ should clearly appear in this photograph (as shown here) where he was actually bent way over. After all, he was seated just to the right of Lady Bird (in the white hat). Faces are colorized for clarity. Type into a search engine: **"Proof LBJ Ducked."**

---

telling – events that he observed in LBJ's car that day. See *Into the Nightmare: My Search for the Killers of President John F. Kennedy and Officer J. D. Tippit* (2013) by Joe McBride. Joe (a fellow Badger) gifted me with a copy of his book in 2013.

241 LBJ ducking DOWN before the shots (https://www.youtube.com/watch?v=IJedJOAlcR8).

NSAM 273 (approved November 26, 1963)

National Security Action Memorandum 273[242] was an update to NSAM 263;[243] the latter was dated October 11, 1963. According to Wikipedia, this new NSAM *"was approved with minor changes,"* but John Newman fiercely challenges this farcical conclusion. NSAM 273 is included in this book because it reveals the cunning and duplicity of LBJ, who had claimed this:

> *"Kennedy's principal foreign policy advisors" agreed that it was important to show Johnson was continuing Kennedy's Vietnam policy....*[244]

Newman brutally disagrees:

> *...the NSAM he [LBJ] approved on November 26 had been altered – significantly – to open the door wide to the Americanization of the war.... These revisions were escalatory, and were based, according to McGeorge Bundy, upon directions given to him by President Johnson on Sunday, November 24.... The substantive changes made to paragraph seven, on operations against North Vietnam, were colossal. They were a fundamental reversal of Kennedy's policy.... The final NSAM opened the door for the use of US armed forces in direct attacks against North Vietnam.*[245]

Newman concludes: *"Johnson's claim that he and Kennedy's foreign policy advisors were continuing Kennedy's Vietnam policy was absurd."*[246] You won't find this in Wikipedia. Newman adds this: *"The fate of NSAM-273's provision for cross border operations into Laos was embarrassing."*[247] Of course, LBJ never bothered to mention this fact to the American public. Nor did Robert McNamara.

What is also remarkable is the sequence of declassification dates. Based on an e-mail from Greg Burnham (January 12, 2025), the draft version was only declassified 15 years *after* the final version was declassified! So, it was trivial for LBJ to say whatever he liked about the entire NSAM 273 process – and its contents. Recall that LBJ died on January 22, 1973, *three years before* the final version was available to the public. So, he could rest in peace.

242 nsam 273 conein - Search.
243 National Security Action Memorandum 263 - Wikipedia.
244 Newman 2016, Kindle, 461.
245 Newman 2016, Kindle, 462.
246 *JFK and Vietnam*, second edition (2016) by John Newman, Kindle, 463.
247 Newman 2016, Kindle, 465.

The DRAFT version was declassified on January 21, 1991.

```
[DECLASSIFIED - was classified TOP SECRET
Auth: EO 12356, Sec. 3.4
Date: 1/21/91
By: SKF, NARA
==========================================
```

The FINAL version was declassified on June 6, 1976

```
[DECLASSIFIED - was classified TOP SECRET
Auth: EO 11652
Date: 6-8-76
By: Jeanne W. Davis
NATIONAL SECURITY COUNCIL ]
```

On November 12, 1963, at a press conference, JFK had clarified his goals in Vietnam. His objective now was to bring the troops home – *not to win the war,* as John Newman clarifies.[248] JFK also agreed to lift the security requirements on his proposal to bring home 1000 troops (of about 16,000 total).

The first draft of this new policy was devised at Fort Smith on Oahu on 11/21/1963. About one hundred individuals were present, but the chief advisors were McNamara, National Security Advisor McGeorge Bundy, Secretary of State Dean Rusk, General Maxwell Taylor, Admiral Harry Felt, and General Paul Harkins. These men sometimes held their own private sessions. Although William Colby (as CIA chief in Saigon) was present he was not invited to these. Bundy had never before attended such a conference; he had been sent explicitly by JFK to implement the new presidential directive. But McGeorge was in an awkward spot – he had to reconcile JFK's pacific intentions with the militaristic goals of the Joint Chiefs. In any case, this new NSAM was finally signed by Bundy, who usually signed such items. Newman notes, however, that this draft, which approved unilateral attacks against North Vietnam, was *"**definitely not in line** with what Kennedy would want to say"*[249] [emphasis in the original].

Even before this conference, Henry Cabot Lodge (Ambassador to South Vietnam) had been pessimistic, but he became shocked during the conference as he heard more. Even McNamara planned to return to DC with *"growing concern."*

248 Ibid., 434-435.
249 Ibid., 448.

On Sunday, November 26, LBJ revised this original draft, but Newman notes that the final document was far different from the original draft. Newman includes all of these documents, even the handwritten annotations that revised the original draft, so the reader can observe how this process evolved.

One of Newman's huge surprises, when he researched this conference, was that the 1000-man *"withdrawal had been gutted."*[250] He discovered this in a tabbed enclosure (TAB E). (For amusement, the reader might search for this item in the Wikipedia article.) The *Pentagon Papers* concluded that this 1000-man withdrawal was merely an accounting exercise; there would be no meaningful reduction of actual troop strength. JFK would have been furious about this, as he had even anticipated such machinations. Newman notes that McNamara was probably ignorant of this "evisceration;" Taylor (JFK's "intellectual") alone was responsible for this deception.

At the conference, Bundy later said that he had learned – for the first time – that the military reports were finally realistic (i.e., very pessimistic) about the Mekong Delta. Newman pertinently asks why the truth was finally allowed to emerge. The answer was ironic: JFK was now using that truth to support his plans for disengagement, which the military clearly opposed. In other words, the false story of progress now had to be killed, in order to continue military engagement.

Although LBJ was quite pleased (with the *impression*) that he would merely continue JFK's policies, the facts were otherwise, as Newman reports:[251]

> *I'm going to give those fellas out there the money they want.... I told them they got it – more if they need it. I told them I'm not going to let Vietnam go the way of China. I told them to go back and tell those generals in Saigon that Lyndon Johnson intends to stand by our word, but by God, I want them to get off their butts and get out in the jungles and whip the hell out of some communists. And I want 'em to leave me alone, because I've got some bigger things to do right here at home.*

After these conversations (which included Bill Moyers) *that day,* LBJ's new edits to NSAM 273 were incorporated; he approved it the next day (Tuesday, November 26).

E-mail of Greg Burnham (December 5, 2024)

Greg Burnham has also explored NSAM 273 in great detail. Here is his response to my e-mail:

250 Ibid., 441.
251 Ibid., 461.

Yes, it changed NSAM 263. On November 21, 1963 – the evening that McGeorge Bundy signed NSAM 273 (DRAFT) – it was the current policy of the USGOV (regarding involvement in Vietnam) to begin the withdrawal of ALL US personnel from that country by the end of 1965, beginning with the first 1,000 by the end of 1963, as per NSAM 263….

Yet, item number one of the DRAFT of NSAM 273 states:

It remains the central object of the United States in South Vietnam to assist the people and Government of that country **to win their contest** [emphasis added] *against the externally directed and supported Communist conspiracy. The test of all decisions and US actions in this area should be the effectiveness of their contribution to this purpose.*

Burnham continues:

This is grossly inconsistent with the existing NSAM 263! That was NOT the central object of the USGOV on November 21st. **Withdrawal was** [emphasis added]. *How could this new central object "remain" when it was never in place to begin with?*

In his meetings with LBJ, McGeorge Bundy looms large in the immediate aftermath of 11/22/1963. Given the promptness and frequency of these meetings, this Bundy (i.e., not his brother Bill) requires much closer assessment for his role in this complex spider web. Alen Salerian has promised me that he will do this. Here is a photograph of the pervasive McGeorge Bundy.[252]

---

252 McGeorge proved to be so loyal to LBJ that the JFK aides began to accuse him of being a *"sellout"* (*My Brother Lyndon* (1970) by S. H. Johnson, p. 198). So, we agree with Sam that LBJ had focused on McGeorge Bundy in the immediate aftermath of 11/22/1963 (Talbot 2015, p. 407). On the other hand, early in 1965, LBJ proudly called Bundy *"my intellectual."* As proof of this, LBJ took Mac's briefings while he (LBJ) sat on the toilet. Such is life in high-ranking places. Dick Goodwin recalls being tested by LBJ in similar fashion.

Although Mac forcefully argued (initially) for escalation of the Vietnam War, he resigned in early 1966 (*nine years* before the end!) to become president of the Ford Foundation. After he resigned, he advised against further escalation of the war. Although (in 1953) he had become the youngest dean ever (at age 34) of Harvard's Faculty of Arts and Sciences, by the 1960s he had obviously mutated into a slow learner – such is the reward of sitting next to political power (or perhaps too long near someone else's toilet seat).

> *"Mac, what about you and Vietnam?"*
> *"I still don't understand," Mac said.*
> *"But Mac, you fucked it up, didn't you?*
> *The glacial silence that followed was broken only when Mac smiled and said,*
> *"Yes, I did. But I'm not going to waste the rest of my life feeling guilty about it"*
>
> –Bird, Kindle, 518.

My response to this is simple: *"Ah yes Mac, but what did you learn?"* In June 1965, Mac had warned McNamara that his plan for Vietnam was *"rash to the point of folly."* But Mac

McGeorge Bundy

Calvin Galloway

Lyman Lemnitzer

Phillip E. Tourney

In the Cabinet Room, just days after 11/22/1963: McGeorge, his mother, and LBJ.

In the interest of time and space, this essay will assume that LBJ knew in advance. But he was not the "mastermind." LBJ was not fit for that role. But he was absolutely critical in the cover-up. Only he had the power to control each relevant agency. He might rather be called the "linchpin." But

---

did not tell LBJ about his radical view! (Bird, Kindle, 523.) So what Mac had learned, but would not admit, was this: *He was too cowardly to tell the truth to power!* And this may very well explain why JFK had misjudged Mac; while in the White House, Mac was simply afraid to tell JFK what he truly believed. Dick Goodwin observed a similar psychology at play: "[Mac] *Bundy and McNamara were more anxious to serve the wishes of their new master than the memory of their dead one*" (Goodwin, p. 373). As historians have learned over and over again, the human race suffers interminably from sycophants.

Contrary to the college's history, Mac had tried to remodel Harvard into a class-blind, merit-based institution with a reputation for stellar academics. But if he had seen the Harvard women's rugby team recently defeat the Princeton women's team 102-0, he might have questioned his success on that score as well (*Revenge of the Tipping Point* (2024) by Malcolm Gladwell, Chapter Five, "The Mysterious Case of the Harvard Women's Rugby Team"). *In Veritas*, if you truly want to speak the truth, Harvard is now (in 2023) the *worst* college in the country for free speech – Mac would not be pleased: 'Abysmal': Harvard Named Worst School for Free Speech, Scores Zero Out of 100 (https://freebeacon.com/latest-news/abysmal-harvard-named-worst-school-for-free-speech-scores-zero-out-of-100/).

he likely knew little of the operational details.[253] There was no need for that; in fact, it could have been counterproductive.

The obvious question is this: How exactly was LBJ linked into this dark web? As we shall demonstrate here, multiple avenues exist. Most probably, more than one was used. This remarkable multiplicity may well explain why that first step will remain hidden forever. As an analogy, consider a hockey or a basketball scrum, where referees must decide who the real villain is. Often this is not obvious, even after a video review. Or ask a spouse: Who actually proposed marriage? Often, they truly do not know – as I do not!

Landslide Lyndon (the 1948 primary election)[254]

In order to fairly assess LBJ, we must first understand his character (or more aptly, his *absence* of character). He was elected to the US House in 1937 – as an FDR progressive. Texas Governor W. Lee "Pappy" O'Daniel had resigned the governorship in order to run for the US Senate, which allowed Coke Stevenson to become governor on August 4, 1941. But O'Daniel then had to defeat LBJ in a special election for this senate seat, which he did, so LBJ was forced to stay in the House.

In 1948, LBJ again ran for the senate – in a Democratic primary against Coke Stevenson. LBJ could not afford to lose a second time, but on election day *he did lose* (literally by only several votes).[255] Then *six days after* the polls closed, LBJ was miraculously gifted with 202 additional votes from Precinct 13 of Jim Wells County (see the photograph of the gang in this book). Stevenson only got 2 more votes from that site. After the subsequent statewide recount, LBJ won by 87 votes – out of 988,295.[256] Suspicions quickly arose that the 202 late votes were fraudulent; these 202 names were in alphabetical order and written with the same pen and handwriting! Some of the list-

---

253 As just another example, Gerry Hemming (who reported to James Angleton) told Dick Russell that H. L. Hunt (and his cohorts) *"...did not want to know operational plans"* (*The Man Who Knew Too Much* (1992) by Richard Russell, p. 301). This is likely true for most names linked to "The Big Event." So, Gerry can now enter a chain...

Hemming → Angleton → Allen Dulles → LBJ

254 LBJ did win one election in a landslide – in 1964, he won the national popular vote (60% – the largest margin in US history) and all but six states. At the same time, RFK barely won his New York Senate seat.

255 *Flawed Giant: Lyndon Johnson and His Times, 1961–1973* (1998) by Robert Dallek, p. 340.

256 That is only a difference of 0.0088%. For comparison, in 1960 (a year that is a model of the close election), JFK won the national popular vote by 112,827, a margin of 0.17%. The ratio of these two difference margins is 1700 ÷ 88 = 19. So, by this standard, the 1960 election was hardly close.

ed individuals claimed that they had not voted. And the last listed man (just before those specious 202 names) stated that he had voted right before the polls closed, and that no one was behind him.

A private, non-official investigation found that LBJ had conspired with George Parr, a Democratic Party leader in Texas, to falsify the vote totals. The US Supreme Court ruled that jurisdiction lay with the party, but not with the federal government, so LBJ absconded with the primary win and justice was never served. Nor would the US ever be the same. Later, author Robert Caro agreed that LBJ had stolen the election in Jim Wells County.[257] Coke Stevenson also agreed with this verdict. LBJ's at-

Precinct 13: LBJ's (illicit) Victory Party in 1948
Left to right: Deputy Sheriff Stokes Micenheimer, Hubert Sain, Givens Parr, Ed Lloyd and Barney Goldthorn

257 *The Years of Lyndon Johnson: Means of Ascent* (1990) by Robert Caro, p. 394. Caro emphasizes this ballot box atrocity with a hilarious story (p. 399):

"As Lyndon told the story [while LBJ mimicked the accent of a small Mexican-American boy], Manuel was sitting on a curb in a little town near the Mexican border one day and crying. Then a friend came up and asked him what the trouble was.

'My father was in town last Saturday, and he did not come to see me,' Manuel replied.

'But Manuel, your father has been dead for ten years.'

Manual just sobbed louder. 'Si, he has been dead for ten years. But he came to town torney in this fiasco was John Cofer,[258] who was assisted by Leon Jaworski[259] (later famous in the Watergate prosecution). At the Supreme Court level, Abe Fortas (as usual) also did his bit for LBJ.

For decades in Washington, DC, insiders had wondered how LBJ, who had always been only a professional "public servant," had acquired an enormous fortune including a radio and television station, considerable real estate, and bank assets totaling $15,000,000. (Multiply by at least 10 for 2024 values.) LBJ caused the whispers himself. He made no attempt to hide his wealth; instead, he flaunted it. He owned a 414-acre ranch in Texas. This included a 6300 ft landing strip and two planes. Meanwhile, he owned an enormous estate (The Elms) in exclusive northwest Wash-

---

last Saturday to vote for Lyndon Johnson, and he did not come to see me.""

258 Billie Sol Estes claimed that Cliff Carter (LBJ's right hand man) had instructed him to hire Cofer as his personal attorney. In a transcendent moment of enlightenment, Billie later realized that Cofer had only protected LBJ's interests (*A Texas Legend: The Man Who Knows Who Shot JFK* (2005) by Billie Sol Estes, pp. 106-107). When Ed Tatro personally asked Billie Sol who had actually killed JFK, Billie said, *"Cliff Carter"* (personal correspondence from Ed to me). Cliff Carter had also (conveniently) declared the death of Henry Marshall to be a suicide, even though he had five bullet wounds! *Mirabile dictu* – this JFK case is jam-packed with overt magic. Also see Full text of "Billie Sol Estes: A Texas Legend" (https://archive.org/details/billiesolestes--atexaslegendbilliesolestes2005/mode/2up?view=theater) and *Billie Sol: King of Texas Wheeler-Dealers* (1984) by Pam Estes.

Billie Sol had manipulated the Department of Agriculture in order to steal federal funds. Orville Freeman, the Secretary of Agriculture, had confirmed Billie's appointment to the National Cotton Advisory Committee. Freeman had done this despite a (negative) secret report on Billie Sol's cotton manipulations. This 140-page document (October 27, 1961) clearly warned that Estes was a sleight-of-hand wheeler-dealer (Investigations: Place in History | *TIME*). Freeman later admitted his mistake (*Desert Sun* 28 June 1962 – California Digital Newspaper Collection).

When I was a senior in a Wisconsin high school, Freeman (then the governor of Minnesota) was tasked with shaking my hand in Duluth after I won a regional public speaking contest (along with a scholarship that accompanied it). Here is just one source about the relationship between the CIA and the USDA: "OFFICIAL SAYS CIA EMPLOYS GRAIN SPIES" | CIA FOIA (foia.cia.gov) (https://www.cia.gov/readingroom/document/cia-rdp90-00806r000100200009-9). Phil Nelson has emphasized that the USDA was utilized by the CIA for global operations. Under the guise of workers or scientists, they would masquerade in multiple situations (*LBJ: The Mastermind of JFK's Assassination* (2010), p. 227). Nelson also claimed that LBJ persuaded Freeman to relax regulations in order to assist Billie Sol's frauds (pp. 660 ff). Despite Freeman's questionable decisions, he was devastated by JFK's death (Manchester, p. 357), so I don't want him to live in ignominy. Incidentally, the CIA also used the United States Agency for International Development (USAID) as a CIA cover *in that era*. Even David Morales worked for this agency! (Hancock 2006, p. 135.)

259 "Leon helped the CIA to launder funds:" Jaworski Reportedly Had Role In Setting Up C. I. A. Aid Conduit - The *New York Times*. After Jaworski died, George H. W. Bush (former CIA director) was a pallbearer at his funeral. A second pall bearer was Lewis Powell, whose official WC role was to protect Oswald's rights; we all recognize how well Lewis performed that role.

ington, DC,[260] next door to Fred Black and Bobby Baker.[261] See the photograph below.

The Elms in northwest DC: home to LBJ, Fred Black and Bobby Baker

LBJ Decapitates Leland Olds (1949)[262]

As definitive evidence of LBJ's mendacity, the tragic 1949 case of Leland Olds (1890-1960), during LBJ's first year as senator, is the *summum malum* (i.e., the greatest evil). The ensuing summary is from Robert Caro.[263] He discusses this quite brilliantly in his chapters 10, 11, and 12 – over a total of 72 *pages!* Caro obviously deems this to be a major insight into the character of LBJ. I concur.

---

260 "Current owners feel the history in LBJ's former home" - The *Washington Post*. Bobby Baker's business associate and partner (Fred Black) was a longtime, close personal friend of Johnny Roselli (*Someone Would Have Talked* (2006) by Larry Hancock, p. 310). Trying to be helpful, Fred Black had even telephoned Roselli several days before his (Roselli's) murder: Trafficante had a contract on him! Unfortunately, we have no record of what Black told his other next-door neighbor (LBJ) about this accurate prophesy. But Trafficante did have one regret about his role in the assassination. The dying don said, *"We should have killed Bobby"* (Hinckle and Turner, p. 419).

261 On 11/22/1963, Baker's friend, Don Reynolds, told B. Everett Jordan and his Senate Rules Committee that he saw a suitcase full of money that Baker described as a $100,000 payoff (to LBJ) for his assistance in securing the TFX contract. See: John Delane Williams Blog: "The Don Reynolds Testimony and LBJ" (https://johndelanewilliams.blogspot.com/2010/11/don-reynolds-testimony-and-lbj.html) and "Don B. Reynolds and LBJ" - JFK Assassination Debate - The Education Forum and "The TFX Decision: The Joint Canard" (https://apps.dtic.mil/sti/tr/pdf/ADA440831.pdf).

262 It was a very busy year. Giving the CIA a "Get out of jail free card," Congress passed the CIA Act of 1949. In September, the USSR had exploded an atomic bomb, while in October, communists had taken over China. The next year was noteworthy as well. On February 9, 1950 (in honor of Lincoln's birthday), Senator Joseph McCarthy "identified" 205 communists in the State Department and then in June 1950, North Korea invaded South Korea.

263 *Master of the Senate* (2002) by Robert Caro.

Olds had been a brilliant mathematics college student, graduating *magna cum laude.* After receiving his BA in 1912, he worked in a social settlement in Boston; he then did graduate study at Harvard and Columbia. He spent a few months during 1918 in the army. Later, he became the chair of mathematics at Amherst College, and in 1924 he became president of the college. After two years at Union Theological Seminary (Dietrich Bonhoeffer also studied there during 1930-1931), he was ordained a Congregational minister in Brooklyn.[264] His life was devoted to fighting poverty and injustice; FDR was his hero and so he became active in the American Labor Party, for whom he delivered the 1938 keynote address. In 1939 (two years after LBJ won election to the House), FDR named him to the Federal Power Commission (FPC), where he became chairman in January 1940. Olds began using the Natural Gas Act of 1938 to regulate gas prices on the pipeline from Texas to the Northeast. But this greatly displeased Herman and George Brown, who had purchased Texas Eastern Transmission[265] for $143 million (via intervention from LBJ) – a huge discount from its true value. The FPC allowed the Browns a 9.5% return, but that was much lower than they wished. *"Olds was the symbol of everything they* [the oilmen] *hated,"* recalls Posh Oltorf, the DC lobbyist for the Browns. *"So, for LBJ, this was the way to turn it around: **take care of this guy**."*[266] This was a critical crossroads for LBJ; he not only needed to take care of Olds, but he also needed to receive credit for this mean feat.

Harry Truman had renominated Olds; his confirmation was expected to be automatic. Before these hearings began (on September 28, 1949 – 3 months *after* his official term, during which interval Olds had no salary), Olds viewed LBJ as a personal friend. After all, they both (ostensibly) adored FDR and both were seen as vigorous advocates for rural electrification. Nonetheless, LBJ knew what to do with Olds – his strategy was based on surprising Olds at the confirmation hearings. During that summer, as his first step in decapitating Olds, LBJ had asked to chair the pertinent subcommittee. That part was easy – no one else was especially interested. Next, he switched committee members so that they could lynch Olds; LBJ wanted a unanimous decision. But Olds's 10-year record was impeccable; he was quite brilliant as well as honest, and he had many strong allies. Although Truman was a strong backer, Olds no longer had any remaining allies on this subcommittee – LBJ had moved all the chess

264 We can only wonder if Olds ever crossed paths in Brooklyn with Doris Kearns (who was born in 1943).

265 Ed Clark owned 40,000 shares (Caro, p. 250).

266 Ibid., p. 248.

pieces. Another strong backer, Senator Paul Douglas, was so confident that he did not even attend the hearings. Meanwhile, LBJ enlisted Alvin Wirtz (a member with LBJ of the Suite 8F Group – see more below), an Austin lobbyist for oil and gas, to exercise his cruelty and guile. Over the decades, Olds had written more than 1800 articles. Of these, LBJ and his cronies selected 54, mostly from the 1920s; their intent was to paint Olds as Red. LBJ also selected – and *coached* – his primary witness, John Lyle.

During the hearings (Sept 28 – Oct 3, 1949) Olds was accompanied by his wife and one FPC employee – but no attorney – so he was an innocent lamb going to the slaughter. Lyle opened with a 90-minute statement including, *"...his* [Old's] *objectives are basically hostile to our American way of life...."* Lyle would supposedly prove this with photostats – *"words of his* [Old's words] *own pen"* – that had been published in the communist newspaper, *Daily Worker.*[267] Although Olds had no idea what Lyle had planned, Olds had nonetheless prepared a powerful 12,000-word autobiographical statement. This summarized in great detail just how his thinking had evolved over the decades. He clearly stated that he had never believed in communism; in fact, he held that it was antithetical to American values. Alas, LBJ never allowed Olds to read his statement without interruption. One (senate) member after another persistently interrupted, but LBJ never tried to stop these interruptions (although, paradoxically, he had protected Lyle while he read his statement). So, finally, Olds resumed reading. But then, after just 6 minutes, LBJ himself interrupted – to accuse Olds of sharing a platform with Earl Browder.[268] This process went on and on and on,[269] so that Old's statement, for an exceptionally long while, remained unread on the table before him. Whenever the senators' attacks faltered, LBJ would renew them. This became so ferocious that on one occasion, two members were shouting, one with a very red face.

---

267 These articles had not been written for the *Daily Worker*; that paper merely subscribed to a press service for which Olds worked.

268 Browder was the General Secretary of the communist party (CPUSA) during the 1930s and first half of the 1940s. LBJ did not explain why this was still relevant in 1949. In any case, other Democrats had also incidentally (perhaps accidentally) shared a podium with Browder. So what?

269 This storybook device (of repetition more than twice) was powerfully employed in the movie, *Gandhi*, to emphasize the lengthy 1919 massacre of entire (innocent) families at Amritsar in the Punjab. The English officer in charge (the temporary brigadier general R. E. H. Dyer, born in the Punjab) was eventually removed from his appointment, passed over for promotion, and then prohibited from employment in India. He died in 1927, but he never did regret the firing: *"...if you want peace, then obey my orders and open all your shops; else I will shoot. For me, the battlefield of France or Amritsar is the same."*

Three members were almost simultaneously using the same brush to tar Olds. When no other senator was present (they had left on official business elsewhere), LBJ finally allowed Olds to finish reading his statement. As further humiliation (for Olds), LBJ gave photostats of these articles by Olds to each senator – but Olds got nothing. Later that day, a committee member (Senator Charles Reed) told the United Press: *"Here is a man who is a full-fledged, first-class communist."*[270]

Finally, the subcommittee voted unanimously against Olds: 7-0. Next, the full Commerce Committee was also nearly unanimous: 10-2. When this news arrived at a Fort Worth meeting (the International Petroleum Association of America), the 800 attendees broke into cheers – and a rebel yell was heard. Soon after this, following LBJ's speech to the full senate, they voted 53–15 against Olds. Truman could persuade only 15 of the 96 senators! Richard Russell (the future Warren Commissioner, not the JFK author) was beaming: *"I've never heard a more masterful speech against a nomination."* [On the contrary, Thomas K. McCraw stated, *"Lyndon Johnson's unbridled floor speech against Olds was one of the least creditable performances of his career."*[271]] Even the *Dallas Morning News*, which had opposed LBJ's run for the Senate less than a year earlier, was now on LBJ's side. Although he was only 41 years old, and still a junior senator, LBJ was now known as someone to fear.

The liberals were less enthusiastic. LBJ's liberal luster had been scraped off; liberals felt betrayed. After all, LBJ had spoken eloquently about rural electrification and cheap public power. Tommy Corcoran, LBJ's chief fund raiser said (about LBJ's hatchet job): *"I thought it was the rottenest thing he'd ever done … the committee did as dirty a job of trying to crucify this guy a la McCarthy* (who became famous in 1950, i.e., the very next year) *as I have ever heard."* Joe Rauh (who had saved the 1948 senate election for LBJ) said that Leland Olds *"was a great American. What Johnson did to him was really vicious … one of the dirtiest pieces of work ever done. I felt sort of dirty…."*

Years later, Senator Paul Douglas said, *"Olds was crushed by the experience, and I do not think that he and his family ever recovered from the blow."* His daughter recalls that her father had lost his *"buoyancy"* and his energy. A friend reported that Olds was financially poor for the rest of his life. (He never received any of those three months of back pay either.) His wife

270 Ibid., p. 266.
271 Narrative Biography Display (https://dillonreadandco.com/wp-content/pdf/leland_olds.pdfZ).

craved for revenge until she died at the age of 90. As a final illustration of LBJ's "empathy," during a break in the hearings he had stopped behind Olds; while putting his hand on Olds's shoulder, he said:

> *Lee, I hope you understand there's nothing personal in this. We're still friends, aren't we? It's only politics, you know.*[272]

Olds died on August 5, 1960. In a tribute, the Democratic nominee (JFK) said, *"In a sense, developments such as the St. Lawrence waterway and power projects are a personal memorial to him."* But in memory of a former "friend," the VP nominee (LBJ) said zilch.

LBJ Sacrifices the Sailors of the USS *Liberty* (1967)

As just one more illustration (of many possible[273]) of LBJ's (absent) code of ethics, we focus on the USS *Liberty* incident of 1967, during the Six-Day War.[274] This was an attack on a US Navy technical research ship (a spy ship), by Israeli Air Force jet fighter aircraft and Israeli navy motor torpedo boats – on June 8, 1967. The attack killed 34 crew members (naval officers, seamen, two marines, and one civilian NSA employee), wounded 171 crew members, and severely damaged the ship.[275]

Israel apologized for the attack, claiming that it was an error (they *supposedly* thought it was an Egyptian ship). Both the Israeli and US governments conducted inquiries and issued reports. Both concluded that it had been a mistake. Others, especially the survivors, still – to this day – vigorously reject these conclusions. They persistently maintain that the attack was deliberate. Even Thomas Hinman Moorer, 7th Chairman of the Joint Chiefs of Staff, pinned this tragedy – and coverup – *on LBJ*, i.e., the attack was deliberate and quite witting.

In May 1968, the Israeli government paid US $3.32 million (equivalent to US $29.1 million in 2023) to the US government for the families of the 34 dead men. In March 1969, Israel paid a further $3.57 million ($29.6 million value in 2023) to the wounded men. In December 1980, it paid $6 million ($22.2 million value in 2023) as the final settlement for

272 Ibid., p. 303. So, we now know how LBJ treated his "friends." On the other hand, Billie Sol Estes claims to know how LBJ treated his *enemies* – Billie attributed 17 murders to LBJ (one dead victim in Billie's story was LBJ's own sister): "Federal Official Killed During Inquiry 24 Years Ago : Estes Investigator's Death Ruled Murder" - *Los Angeles Times.*

273 For a comprehensive list, see "LBJ – Master of Outrageous Acts" by Edgar F. Tatro in *Garrison: The Journal of History and Deep Politics*, Issue #13, May 2023, pp. 34-114.

274 USS *Liberty* incident - Wikipedia. For the Israeli attack on the USS *Liberty,* also see *Body of Secrets* (2001) by James Bamford, pp. 187-239, 494.

275 Ibid.

the ship (plus 13 years of interest). For an excellent analysis, likely superior to any government report, read *Blood in the Water: How the US and Israel Conspired to Ambush the USS* Liberty (2019) by Joan Mellen. She agrees with Thomas Moorer – LBJ deliberately, and unnecessarily – sacrificed these American patriots. After all, LBJ (as usual) had more important priorities. From Mellen's Amazon website:

> *The facts said otherwise* [than an accident]. *So intense and sustained was the attack – it lasted for nearly an hour and a half – so specific was the aiming for the antennae and satellite dish on deck, that it was scarcely credible that Israel's aggression was not deliberate; such was the view of Marshall Carter, the director of the National Security Agency, his deputy director Louis Tordella, and Richard Helms, the Director of Central Intelligence.*

Watch Candace Owens (online in late 2024) read a letter from a USS *Liberty* survivor (Phillip E. Tourney); she also interviewed him.[276] LBJ played a critical role *during* this 90-minute cataclysm. Over a loudspeaker on the ship, Tourney actually heard LBJ say, *"I don't give a goddamn if all those sailors die, I'm not going to embarrass my ally, Israel."* Tourney reports that even the secretary of defense knew what the real situation was. (Robert McNamara resigned on Leap Year Day, 1968, so he was on duty during the Six Day War,[277] but he later claimed to know nothing about the USS

276 https://www.youtube.com/watch?v=PD5gtM1A990. Phillip Tourney's book is for sale on Amazon (December 11, 2024) for $1,732.45 (used): *What I Saw That Day: Israel's June 8, 1967, Holocaust of US Servicemen Aboard the USS* Liberty *and its Aftermath* (2011). For McNamara's strange role, see Robert Strange McNamara (1916-2009) – 2009 September-October - WRMEA (https://www.wrmea.org/2009-september-october/robert-strange-mcnamara-1916-2009.html).

Of course, we know that McNamara was quite capable of lying. For example, he had testified to congress about the Gulf of Tonkin Resolution. Contrary to Bob's assertions to congress, there was no clear evidence of an attack in the gulf. Johnson even claimed in private, *"Hell boys, for all I know they could have been shooting at whales out there."* Dick Goodwin (who knew Bob well) wrote, *"McNamara knew this when he testified, and lied about what he knew – or didn't know. Then, heaping fraud upon fraud, he misrepresented the conditions of combat in the Gulf of Tonkin"* (*Remembering America: A Voice from the Sixties* (1988) by Richard Goodwin, p. 359). So, why would Bob suddenly reform and tell the truth about the USS *Liberty*? Bob was also highly accomplished at forgetting. *"McNamara had a penchant for forgetting inconvenient conversations, as, for example, when he had suggested killing Castro or bombing Cuba"* (Boot, Kindle, 409).

277 Like McNamara, Yitzhak Rabin was also on duty. Under his command, the Israel Defense Forces (IDF) achieved victory over Egypt, Syria and Jordan in the 1967 Six-Day War. He later served twice as Prime Minister. Reports suggest that Rabin was in Texas sometime during November 1963. Because of his efforts for peace (the Oslo Accords), he won the 1994 Nobel Peace Prize. As a further, but unwanted, reward he was assassinated on November 4, 1995, by Yigal Amir, a right-wing extremist. So, JFK and Rabin

Liberty.[278]) Unbelievably, the survivors had to wait an unconscionable 17 hours for their rescue – which is highly suspicious in itself. Two-thirds of the crew were dead or injured. Highly reminiscent of the JFK autopsy, the survivors were ordered (*by the military*) never to speak of this tragedy again. So, once again, LBJ's dishonorable career was saved.

Secretary of State Dean Rusk angered the supporters of Israel – he also believed the attack had been deliberate:[279]

> *Accordingly, there is every reason to believe that the USS* Liberty *was or should have been identified, or at least her nationality determined, prior to the attack. In these circumstances, the later military attack by Israeli aircraft on the USS* Liberty *is quite literally incomprehensible. As a minimum, the attack must be condemned as an act of military irresponsibility reflecting reckless disregard for human life. The subsequent attack by Israeli torpedo boats, substantially after the vessel was or should have been identified by Israeli military forces, manifests the same reckless disregard for human life. At the time of the attack, the USS* Liberty *was flying the American flag and its identification was clearly indicated in large white letters and numerals on its hull. It was broad daylight and the weather conditions were excellent. Experience demonstrates that both the flag and the identification number of the vessel were readily visible from the air. At a minimum, the attack must be condemned as an act of military recklessness reflecting wanton disregard for human life. The silhouette and conduct of the USS* Liberty *readily distinguished it from any vessel that could have been considered as hostile. The USS* Liberty *was peacefully engaged, posed no threat whatsoever to the torpedo boats, and obviously carried no armament affording it a combat capability. It could and should have been scrutinized visually at close range before torpedoes were fired.*

In 1990 Rusk wrote:

> *I was never satisfied with the Israeli explanation. Their sustained attack to disable and sink* Liberty *precluded an assault by accident or by some trigger-happy local commander. Through diplomatic channels we refused to accept their explanations. I didn't believe them then, and I don't believe them to this day. The attack was outrageous.*

---

each had their own far right-wing enemies.

278 McNamara clearly played a major role in the Six Day War – his goal was to keep the USSR at bay: "Former US secretary of defense Robert McNamara dies at 93" - *The Jerusalem Post*.

279 Dean Rusk - Wikipedia.

Wikipedia continues:

> *After an Israeli claim appeared in* The Washington Post *that they had inquired about the presence of U.S. ships in the area before the attack, Rusk telegrammed the U.S. embassy in Tel Aviv and demanded "urgent confirmation." U.S. Ambassador to Israel (Walworth Barbour) confirmed that Israel's story was bogus:* "No request for info on US ships operating off Sinai was made until after the *Liberty* incident. Had Israelis made such an inquiry it would have been forwarded immediately to the chief of naval operations and other high naval commands and repeated to dept" [sic].

J. Evetts Haley described LBJ as entirely pragmatic and thus totally devoid of principle. Furthermore, he had no loyalty to his lieutenants. On the contrary, he often seemed to delight in particularly *"cruel and boorish behavior."* Once at a party at his ranch, where John Connally and his wife had arrived as guests, LBJ cursed John in front of the other guests as being a *"sorry s-o-b."* So, John and Nellie quickly grabbed their bags and left. On another occasion, Connally was brooding over a typical LBJ double-cross: *"I knew Lyndon Johnson would do it to others; I did not think he would do it to me."*[280]

The best description of LBJ is Barry Goldwater's incisive analysis:[281]

> *Johnson was a master of manipulation. He solved tough public issues through private plotting. His answer to almost everything was a deal – an air base here or a welfare project there…. Johnson was the epitome of the unprincipled politician…. He was a wheeler-dealer. Any campaign with him in it would involve a lot of innuendo and lies. Neither he nor anyone else could change him. That was what he was. And LBJ was treacherous to boot…. The last thing he wanted to do in his life was talk political principles or beliefs. He wouldn't do it. He never believed in it. His only political dogma was expediency. Things were never right or wrong. Most problems in this country could be fixed with cunning and craftiness.*

---

280 *A Texan Looks at Lyndon* (1964) by J. Evetts Haley, pp. 235-241. For his loyalty to LBJ, Connally was rewarded (on 11/22/1963) with a fractured rib and a pneumothorax. His death was due to pulmonary fibrosis from this singular event.

281 *Goldwater* (1988) by Barry Goldwater with Jack Casserly, pp. 190-192. Barbara Tuchman also had a candid opinion of LBJ – she called him both a "bully" and a "scoundrel" (Tuchman, pp. 252-253). And then she added (p. 319), *"No one is so sure of his premises as the man who knows too little."* But M. Scott Peck added the most devastating comment of all: *"…almost all of the evil in this world is committed by people who are absolutely certain that they know what they are doing"* (*The Road Less Traveled and Beyond* (1997), p. 165).

And here is a vibrant snapshot of LBJ's character:

> LBJ: *John* [McCormack], *that son of a bitch* [Bobby Baker] *is going to ruin me. If that cocksucker talks, I'm gonna land in jail.... Tell Nat to tell Bobby that I will give him a million dollars if he takes the rap. Bobby must not talk.*[282]

Context: LBJ Dodges the Bullet

On November 1, 1963, the Senate voted $50,000 to fund an expanded investigation of the Baker Scandal and a major Congressional hearing was scheduled for the morning of November 22, 1963. After triggers were pulled in Dealey Plaza, this never happened.

Baker's financial statement (Sept 1963): Net worth of $2+ million on a salary of $20,000. Between January 1962 and November 1963, he deposited $1.5+ million into his bank account.

Life: November 8, 1963

Bobby had resigned a month earlier.

Now at six decades removed from the assassination, no documents will ever identify the chief plotters. It is also most unlikely that any eyewitnesses will now step forward – after all, most (if not all) are dead. As with Hansel and Gretel, the bread crumbs are gone. However, the circumstantial evidence against the plotters is quite astounding. To initiate this trail, we first note the manner in which each relevant federal agency promptly fell into line; it is almost beyond belief.

The JFK Autopsy and the Military (1963)

As just one example, the military supervised the autopsy. Admiral Calvin Galloway,[283] although *not a pathologist*, demanded on Sunday (November 24, 1963) that the chief pathologist, James Humes, make critical revisions to the autopsy report.[284] Furthermore, during the autopsy,

282 LBJ to John McCormack (speaker of the House) as reported by Robert Barger in 1972 in the *Washington Payoff: An Insider's View of Corruption in Government* (Dell). Also see Hancock 2006, p. 308.

283 Rear Admiral Calvin B. Galloway, MC, USN, Elected President of Association | Military Medicine | Oxford Academic (https://academic.oup.com/milmed/article-abstract/127/12/985/4920112?redirectedFrom=PDF).

284 In his own report, Galloway noted that the throat "exit" wound was four inches higher than it was at Parkland Hospital. This was – quite literally – a moving experience. Despite this egregious blunder (or more likely a deliberate misdirection), he is in the military hall of honor: RADM Calvin Burrel Galloway. FBI agents Sibert (whom I have met) and O'Neill claim that Galloway even overruled Admiral Burkley, the president's physician,

Galloway personally rode around the medical center grounds in a decoy ambulance (as a passenger). James Jenkins served as a diener all night long at the autopsy. I have met him on multiple occasions, and have even recorded a long video interview with him and Mike Chesser.[285] We agree quite thoroughly on what happened at the autopsy. Just recently, Mike Chesser (who debriefed me within minutes of his telephone call with Jenkins) reported that when he (Jenkins) and Pierre Finck spotted an obvious entry site in JFK's right temple, Humes was called to the gallery, where he was warned, by a flag officer, to simply ignore that site. So, he did. Based on powerful, corroborative medical data (shown in my essays and lectures) we now know that this entry was authentic. It was due to an *oblique shot* from the right front, quite possibly from the Grassy Knoll, totally consistent with Malcolm Kilduff's *overt demonstration* at the news conference – just minutes after the murder. This shot caused the gaping hole at the back of JFK's head, which the conspirators found so difficult to cover-up. Their inept and hapless efforts help to explain the confounding – but long-lasting – mysteries of the autopsy.

Much of my prior work on this case has been devoted to sorting out the medical gobbledygook. Unfortunately, due to no fault of their own, the pathologists' predicament was only made worse because of alteration (by outsiders) of the autopsy X-rays and photographs, which totally bamboozled these physicians. I doubt that they ever truly understood what had occurred – either in these images, or even in JFK's body. After all, they tried *four times* to get their autopsy report right, yet their final version is still wrong. And then later, after they had (again) viewed the altered X-ray and photographic images, things went totally off the rails. So, that was not their fault, but they did lie. During their review of the autopsy X-rays (shortly before the Clark Panel), they claimed that no part of a bullet was visible on the X-rays. This was an absurd lie – even my 7-year-old son immediately spotted the 6.5 mm "cross section" on X-ray images in Lifton's book. They also fraudulently substituted someone else's brain for JFK's

during the autopsy ("Blaming the Victims: Kennedy Family Control Over the Bethesda Autopsy" by James Folliard, in *The Fourth Decade*, Volume 2, No. 4). But Burkley, after all, was not in the chain of command at Bethesda; later he implied that he accepted a JFK conspiracy. Galloway could never do that. Amazingly though, Burkley, the only physician at both Parkland and Bethesda, was never called by the WC: "The Missing Physician" (https://www.maryferrell.org/pages/The_Missing_Physician.html). Astoundingly, the WC found 553 witnesses more interesting than Burkley: "Warren Report - Appendix V. List of Witnesses" (https://aarclibrary.org/publib/jfk/wc/wr/pdf/WR_A5_ListWitnesses.pdf).

285 Michael Chesser, MD, "The JFK Autopsy Evidence – Part 1: The Skull X-Rays," *Garrison: The Journal of History and Deep Politics*, Issue #3, October 2019, pp. 184-193.

brain. ***This was hardly a mistake due to ignorance!*** Curiously, that evening a well-covered "lump" on a litter was seen near the morgue (Manchester, p. 399). Some observers have wondered if this was the pending replacement brain (in liquid inside a container), just waiting to be introduced to (perhaps "into") the body.

But even the subsequent government "experts" were consistently – and relentlessly – hoodwinked by that 6.5 mm fake and also by the forged Red Spot in the photograph of the back of the head. So then, it is not surprising that nine visits (nine *full* days) were required for me to fully unravel what had transpired, but we have now finally reached that point. My background in both physics and medicine was fully deployed (and required) to disentangle this mystery.

So, who was Galloway's superior? As Chief of Naval Operations in charge of the US quarantine of Cuba during the Cuban Missile Crisis in 1962, George Anderson (according to the media) distinguished himself. *Time* magazine featured him on the cover and called him *"an aggressive blue-water sailor of unfaltering competence and uncommon flair."* **Robert McNamara did not agree!** Here is the dialogue between McNamara and Anderson, as cited by Twyman.[286]

> *"I don't give a damn what John Paul Jones would have done,"* said McNamara. *"I want to know what you are going to do, now. What if they don't stop?*
>
> Anderson: *"We'll send a shot across the bow."*
>
> Mac: *"Then what, if that doesn't work?"*
>
> Anderson: *"Then we'll fire into the rudder…* ***This is none of your goddamn business, Mr. Secretary.*** *This is what we are going to do."*
>
> *"You're not going to fire a single shot at anything without my express permission, is that clear?"* said McNamara, walking out….
>
> *"That's the end of Anderson… He won't be reappointed,"* McNamara said to [Roswell] Gilpatric as they walked back to the Secretary's office….

McNamara viewed Anderson's actions as mutinous and *forced him to retire in 1963.*

286 Twyman, pp. 514-515. Noel was actually quoting *President Kennedy: Profile in Power* (1993) by Richard Reeves, p. 402.

Adm. George Anderson | Nov. 2, 1962
Anderson's boss was the Secretary of the Navy, Fred Korth, who reported to Robert McNamara.

Fred Korth	4 January 1962	1 November 1963

Anderson's superior was Fred Korth,[287] who on December 11, 1961, had been appointed Secretary of the Navy by JFK – apparently after some JFK arm twisting by LBJ. Korth was not a natural ally of JFK. (John Connally had resigned after one year in office to return to Texas, which he preferred to govern.)

Those Co-opted Federal Agencies

I am forever astonished at the alacrity exhibited by these federal agencies. Just to begin, the Secret Service (SS) at Parkland hastily washed out the limousine. Then they destroyed the film from a little boy's camera and, after the windshield hole was noticed, they immediately removed the limousine. It is difficult to imagine that each SS man independently made these decisions – which clearly violated the rules of evidence for a murder scene. A wide-ranging order must have existed – to include most of the SS. Furthermore, during the Assassination Records Review Board (ARRB), the SS deliberately destroyed records of JFK's trips during 1963 – even *after* they were specifically ordered to retain all of them. Jack Tunheim, chair of the ARRB, recalled that they *"were the most difficult of all government agencies involved."*[288] (Clarence) Douglas Dillon held final responsibility for the SS. One can only wonder: what was so essential for Dillon to hide?[289]

287 In an apparent coincidence (of many in this JFK case), Korth left office on the same day that Lansdale resigned: Fred Korth - Wikipedia. Here is another one: Korth served as attorney for Edwin Ekdahl (Oswald's stepfather) in his divorce from Marguerite Oswald!

288 *J. Edgar Hoover: The Father of the Cold War* (2000) by R. Andrew Kiel, p. 309. Twyman displays an extremely useful checklist; this list compares the predictions of Dinkin and Milteer (separately) with the actual outcome (Twyman, p. 525).

289 In 1975, C. Douglas Dillon testified before the HSCA about assassinations (during Eisenhower's term) of foreign leaders. He reported that Allen Dulles *"felt very*

The SS also controlled the autopsy materials. From my own work (during nine visits to the National Archives), we now know that both the autopsy photographs (the Red Spot) and the autopsy X-rays (the 6.5 mm bogus cross section) were modified after the fact – in order to implicate a lone gunman. These two faked images later persuaded the Clark Panel and the HSCA to raise the posterior entry site by *half the height of the head*. In other words, two objects that were *invisible* at the autopsy determined the final conclusion of these distinguished government "experts"! After I asked the autopsy radiologist, John Ebersole, about the 6.5 mm object, he forever stopped speaking about the autopsy. Ebersole alone had the expertise and experience to create this 6.5 mm forgery; ironically, he told me that he liked to write mystery novels. In any case, he himself had created a mystery that forever evaded all government "experts."

J. Edgar Hoover played his role, too. Although he had known about two Oswalds as early as 1960,[290] he advised his FBI men (*within just hours* – obviously via inconceivable ESP) to report only evidence that incriminated Oswald.[291] This is particularly astonishing because he surely knew about the predictions of Eugene Dinkin and Joseph Milteer.[292] Moreover, he actually *had possession* of Milteer's tape![293] We can only wonder if Edgar's memory was already fading – or was he solely malicious?

---

strongly that we should not involve the president directly in things of this nature." Dillon added that Ike would simply order, *"Do what is necessary,"* and Dulles would then carry out Ike's order (*The Crimes of Patriots* (1987) by Jonathan Kwitny, p. 24). See these two sites for oral history interviews with Dillon: JFKOH-CDD-04-TR.pdf (https://www.jfklibrary.org/sites/default/files/archives/JFKOH/Dillon,%2520C.%2520Douglas/JFKOH-CDD-04/JFKOH-CDD-04-TR.pdf) and Interview with C. Douglas Dillon (https://tile.loc.gov/storage-services/service/mss/mfdip/2004/2004dil04/2004dil04.pdf). Also note that Dillon and McGeorge Bundy and Allen Dulles and John Foster Dulles had worked together on Thomas Dewey's presidential campaign. In fact, Allen directly supervised McGeorge.

In the Brendan DuBois novel, *Resurrection Day* (1999), the Cuban Missile Crisis becomes a full-scale nuclear war. Washington, DC is destroyed and JFK and LBJ are both killed, so Douglas Dillon, the Secretary of the Treasury, becomes the 36th President of the United States.

290 View this document in Part I of this book.

291 See *The Oswald Puzzle: Reconsidering Lee Harvey Oswald* (2025) by Larry Hancock and David Boylan.

292 Tatro notes that Milteer was close to Guy Banister, who was a close ally of both General Walker and J. Edgar Hoover. Banister performed security services for both Clint Murchison and for H. L. Hunt ("Gerry Hemming's Swamp, the Dark Side of Madame Nhu, Gordon McLendon, and Other JFK Assassination Sponsors" by Edgar F. Tatro in *Garrison: The Journal of History and Deep Politics*, Issue #15, November 2023, pp. 48-50). Banister was also close to G. Wray Gill, a lawyer for Carlos Marcello (Tatro, November 2023, p. 83). McLendon was also friendly with Hoover (Tatro, November 2023, p. 84).

293 Kiel, p. 471.

Texas Connections (up to 1963)

From John Simkin[294]--posted January 11, 2005.

We now exit the navy and turn to the insightful research of John Simkin. He has outlined Texas connections in 1963. I have highlighted (in red) the names that seem most pertinent. The comments below are extracted (mostly verbatim) from Simkin's report.

[Simkin begins.] Over the last few weeks I have been researching the Suite 8F Group, a collection of right-wing political and business men. The name comes from the room in the Lamar Hotel in Houston where they held their meetings. Members of the group included George Brown and Herman Brown [effectively LBJ's godfathers], Jesse H. Jones, Gus Wortham, James Abercrombie, Hugh R. Cullen, William Hobby, William Vinson, James Elkins, Morgan J. Davis, Albert Thomas [disgraceful for the wink photograph on AF-1[295]], Lyndon B. Johnson. John Connally, Alvin Wirtz [infamous for the Leland Olds affair] and Edward Clark [featured in Phil Nelson's book] were also members of the Suite 8F Group

Suite 8F helped to coordinate *the political activities* of other right-wing politicians and businessmen based in the South. This included Robert B. Anderson [Secretary of the Treasury during 1957-1961], Robert Kerr,[296] Billie Sol Estes, Glenn McCarthy, Earl E. T. Smith, Fred Korth, Ross Sterling, Sid Richardson, Clint Murchison, Haroldson L. Hunt, Eugene B. Germany, Lawrence D. Bell [founder of Bell Aircraft Corporation], William Pawley [a close friend of Allen Dulles – and also of Meyer Lansky[297]],

---

294 Suite 8F Group - JFK Assassination Debate - The Education Forum (https://educationforum.ipbhost.com/topic/2868-suite-8f-group/)

295 *Best Evidence* (1980) by David Lifton; see the photograph opposite p. 589. Horne notes that this photograph is the only one of *"thirteen 35 mm negatives and eight 120 mm format negatives"* by Cecil Stoughton that "disappeared." The LBJ library claims to have "lost" only that photograph. When Lifton questioned Cecil about this photograph, Cecil reacted with alarm; he asked Lifton how he even knew about it!

Albert Thomas had helped to land NASA's Manned Spacecraft Center in Houston; this assured his further support for the Apollo program, which was a favorite of JFK (*Inside the ARRB* (2009) by Douglas Horne, Volume V, p. 1388). On the evening of November 21, 1963, at a Houston banquet in honor of Albert Thomas, JFK had lavished praise on Albert (*Kennedy* (1965) by Theodore C. Sorensen, p. 847). Despite this, on the following day, on AF-1, Thomas winked at LBJ, as seen in that infamous photograph.

296 The US Congress never disclosed the 1970s illegal smuggling of plutonium into Iran from the Kerr-McGee Corporation (in Oklahoma) – while Senator Robert Kerr (yes, it is the same cur) chaired the US Senate Armed Services Committee. The CIA directly supervised the transfer of this 98% bomb-grade plutonium to the Shah of Iran. This illegal operation was personally led by Ted Shackley, who had been – *on 11/22/1963* – the CIA station chief in Miami, where he assisted Lansdale and Harvey in Operation Mongoose. Kerr's photograph (with LBJ) appears in this book.

297 *Gold Warriors* (2005) by Sterling and Peggy Seagrave, Kindle.

Gordon McLendon,[298] George Smathers,[299] Richard Russell [Warren Commissioner], James Eastland, Benjamin Everett Jordan, Fred Black,[300] and Bobby Baker.[301]

---

298 Clint Murchison, Jr., with Gordon McLendon, owned the Dallas Cowboys. Gordon was a co-founder, with David Phillips, of the Association of Former Intelligence Officers (AFIO), where Burris's friend (Col. Delk Simpson) was a board member. Gordon was known for his elaborate practical jokes, even executed on Nixon and J. Edgar Hoover, both of whom he called friends. Jack Ruby was both an admirer and friend of McLendon, who allowed Ruby to advertise on his radio station, KLIF.

Before I forget, listeners heard McLendon call Bobby Thomson's home run on the Liberty Broadcasting System on October 3, 1951; this won the pennant for the Giants (over the Dodgers) to the dismay of Doris Kearns. I missed it because I was outside during a break, playing softball at my one-room country school in northern Wisconsin. I remember Bobby because I was listening to the radio when he fractured his ankle in 1954 during spring training; then a rookie (Henry Aaron) replaced him in the Braves' lineup and they could never get him out (a pun). Ironically in 1951, Andy Pafko had watched Bobby's home run sail over his head while he stood helplessly in left field; but in 1954, he and Bobby were Braves' teammates. Baseball is not irrelevant – even Abner Doubleday is buried at Arlington National Cemetery; he fired the first shot in defense of Fort Sumter. Joe Louis, my father-in-law (Edward Everett James), and Lee Marvin (but not John Wayne) are also quietly there, keeping JFK and RFK company.

Even Oswald was once captain of his Texas softball team: "The Serious Tip: Did Joe DiMaggio order John F. Kennedy killed?" (https://theserioustip.blogspot.com/2008/11/did-joe-dimaggio-order-john-f-kennedy.html). And Castro tried out as a pitcher for the Washington Senators (Allen Dulles's favorite team). Castro's photograph as a pitcher is here: Fidel Castro and Baseball – Society for American Baseball Research (https://sabr.org/bioproj/topic/fidel-castro-and-baseball/). If he had been a better pitcher, would we have had a Cuban Missile Crisis?

And here are two more arguments for baseball: (1) Even Allen Dulles preferred to listen to broadcasts of the Washington Senators than to review U-2 photographs (Kinzer 2013, Kindle, 289). And (2): Moe Berg was a professional baseball catcher, who was recruited to assassinate Werner Heisenberg. Watch *The Catcher Was a Spy*, a 2018 film about WW II. Moe was a close relative of my professional partner, Peter Greenberg, MD. (At my request, Peter recently radiated and totally cured my right hip arthritis.) While dining at Berg's Landing (a restaurant in Menominee, Michigan) I was sorely tempted to donate (to the restaurant) my copy of the paperback edition of *The Catcher Was a Spy*, which I serendipitously just happened to be reading at dinner while dining there.

299 LBJ brought Smathers into his inner circle as Secretary of the Senate Caucus, the third most powerful position in the party caucus. When LBJ suffered a heart attack in 1956 (at age 47), Smathers became acting Senate majority leader while LBJ was hospitalized. He eventually died of yet another heart attack (possibly #5). If you work 20 hours a day, rarely sleep, chain smoke, drink regularly to excess, are constantly overweight, do not exercise, persistently invent falsehoods, murder US sailors, and relentlessly screw your friends (and their wives) – then bad things just might happen.

300 Fred Black (LBJ's next-door neighbor in DC) had warned Roselli about Trafficante's morbid plan for him, so (given Black's mob connections), perhaps Fred also knew in advance about 11/22/1963. To inform LBJ, he merely had to walk next door!

Trafficante → Black → LBJ

301 In Washington, DC, Bobby Baker and Fred Black and LBJ lived in back-to-back-to back houses on the same block (in the order listed here). See Hancock 2006, p. 407. Baker had introduced JFK to Ellen Rometsch (Hancock 2006, p. 314).

The wink—Albert Thomas (no doubting Thomas)

The official photograph—no wink

January 3, 1949. Arthur Vandenberg swears in the new senators: Allen Frear, LBJ, Paul Douglas, and Robert Kerr.

In this essay we look for possible information conduits (about the JFK assassination) among the villains in this case. Of course, it is understood that such conduits are not always just one-way streets. And we must also

---

Baker's business partners were linked to Meyer Lansky and Moe Dalitz (Hancock 2006, p. 319).

Lansky (± Dalitz) → Baker → LBJ

Fred Black met with LBJ in the EOB in August 1963 – along with Bobby Baker. Hancock emphasizes that Black's knowledge of LBJ's affairs gave him "tremendous leverage" over LBJ (Hancock 2006, pp. 311-313).

Mafia → Black → Baker → LBJ

emphasize this: these conduits are merely suggestions. Any proofs would require documentation, which almost surely does not exist.

William Pawley

Lucien Conein

E. Howard Hunt

Mitchell WerBell

Based on this (Suite 8F) mélange, here are four possible chains…

Lansky → Pawley → Allen Dulles → LBJ

McLendon → Murchison → Clark → LBJ

Mafia → Roselli → Fred Black → LBJ

H. L. Hunt → Ed Clark → LBJ

Based on the relationships among Allen Dulles and Meyer Lansky and William Pawley,[302] we might also picture…

Allen → Dulles → Pawley → LBJ

Lansky → Pawley → Allen Dulles → LBJ

[Simkin resumes.] I am particularly interested in the possible links between this group and the General Dynamics Corporation and the $6.5 billion contract for the TFX jet fighter.[303] I have reason to believe that this contract played a factor in the Kennedy cover-up of the assassination. This involves an ex- FBI agent called I. B. Hale. He was head of security at General Dynamics. He was also caught bugging Judith Exner's apartment.

Posted January 11, 2005 (edited) by Stan Wilbourne, from Livingstone's new book, p. 84:

[Wilbourne begins.[304]] Fred Korth, also of Fort Worth (like Connally) took Connally's job as Secretary of the Navy under JFK,

302 Dulles, Allen – HISTORY HEIST (https://historyheist.com/glossary/dulles-allen/).
303 "The TFX Scandal's Link to the JFK Assassination Conspiracy" by Edgar F. Tatro in *Garrison: The Journal of History and Deep Politics*, Issue #12, January 2023, pp. 70-154.
304 Suite 8F Group - JFK Assassination Debate - The Education Forum

who then prepared to dump him [Korth] because, as Seth Kantor wrote, he was taking advantage of his job to *"further some of his Fort Worth banking investments."* Korth showed favoritism to the Continental National Bank of Fort Worth, of which he had been president until his appointment as Secretary of the Navy in 1961.

The Continental National Bank was one of twenty banks that loaned $200 million to Ft. Worth's General Dynamics to start building the TFX fighter plane. The TFX became one of the biggest boondoggles and scandals in American history and threatened the entire JFK administration, as did so much else that originated in Texas from Bobby Baker[305] and Howard Hughes[306] and LBJ.

When the scandal got out of control, *Korth was asked to resign* by Robert McNamara, Secretary of Defense. The request for his resignation came *just six weeks before* JFK was assassinated; probably by this time, the military (including Bethesda) already had its marching orders. Korth had helped to award the TFX contract to General Dynamics instead of Seattle's Boeing, whose bid was much lower. (Robert McNamara actually awarded the contract to General Dynamics despite the charge that he was wasting an unnecessary four hundred million dollars and would give navy fliers an inferior carrier plane.[307]) In 1961, Korth was on the board of directors of Bell Aerospace (formerly Bell Helicopters) where Michael Paine worked.[308] [Wilbourne ends.]

Besides George Anderson and Fred Korth (in the navy), we should also note the role of Navy Surgeon General Edward C. Kenney. He ordered two naval physicians, Commander James Humes and Commander J. Thornton Boswell, to conduct the autopsy. Humes was the lead pathologist. Boswell called the Bethesda choice *"stupid;"* he argued that it should instead have been done at the more specialized Armed Forces Institute of Pathology (AFIP) just five miles away. Although both had conducted autopsies, neither was well trained nor certified in forensic pathology.

---

305 During the investigations of Bobby Baker's finances (in September and October of 1963), the wife of the government accountant (Lorin Drennan) was found dead in the bathroom by her young children, with the unlocked front door open (Hancock 2006, p. 309).

306 The Hughes Tool Company was located in Houston, Texas. Howard racked up about $6 billion in contracts for paramilitary and clandestine warfare hardware (Hinckle and Turner, p. 16).

307 Tatro, January 2023, pp. 70-154.

308 Marina deleted Ruth Paine from her circle of friends because Ruth *"was sympathizing with the CIA"* (Mellen 2013, p. 275). Watch *The Assassination and Mrs. Paine* | Prime Video (https://www.amazon.com/Assassination-Mrs-Paine-Ruth/dp/B09Q34NCPP).

Dick Davis, MD (at AFIP), was later reported as prepared that night to assist with neuropathology. We later became colleagues at the Los Angeles County/USC Medical Center.

C. Douglas Dillon (1909-2003)[309]

Douglas Dillon, Secretary of the Treasury, was responsible for the SS; LBJ was his direct boss. James Rowley, head of the SS, reported to Dillon.[310] During *"The Big Event"* (of 11/22/1963), Dillon was safely in Hawaii with other cabinet members. When the Warren Commission (WC) interviewed Dillon, Allen Dulles addressed him familiarly as "Doug."[311] Republican Dillon (who had campaigned for Ike with John Foster Dulles) had been inside Ike's inner circle, apparently even during discussions about Lumumba's future.[312] Dillon was close to both Dulles

309 Like so many other Americans of his era, *Douglas Dillon had served in the OSS*. Curiously, his *Wikipedia* entry does not cite this fascinating connection. This OSS list includes Supreme Court Justice Arthur Goldberg, movie director John Ford, and Sterling Hayden (who later spoofed military bravado as Brigadier General Jack Ripper in Stanley Kubrick's *Dr. Strangelove*). Others were UN diplomat Ralph Bunche, Princeton historian Carl Schorske, Yale historian Sherman Kent, Harvard historians H. Stuart Hughes and William Langer, political theorist Herbert Marcuse, music critic Edward Downes, poet Stephen Vincent Benét, philanthropist Paul Mellon, mobster Charles "Lucky" Luciano, columnist Joseph Alsop, Julia Child, and even the major-league catcher Moe Berg (a relative of my professional partner, Peter Greenberg, MD). See the enlightening *New Yorker* article by Louis Menand (March 6, 2011): Wild Thing | *The New Yorker* (https://www.newyorker.com/magazine/2011/03/14/wild-thing-louis-menand). For more on C. Douglas Dillon, here is Wikipedia: "A close friend of John D. Rockefeller III, he [Dillon] was chairman of the Rockefeller Foundation from 1972 to 1975. He also served alongside John Rockefeller on the 1973 Commission on Private Philanthropy and Public Needs, and under Nelson Rockefeller in the Rockefeller Commission to investigate CIA activities." Online sources report that Dillon resigned in 1965 in order to return to private finance. D. Frank Cormier begs to differ. He states that *"...after a bathroom conference* [with LBJ], *he resigned rather than endure more of them"* (LBJ: *The Way He Was* (1977), p. 135).

310 RFK affirmed, *"Dillon will do what he thinks is right. He's my friend"* (Goodwin, p. 462). Goodwin adds that RFK was also mistaken about his relationship with Robert McNamara; this supposed friendship obscured (for RFK) McNamara's "duplicity." But RFK was not solely blameless. JFK had chimed in, *"James Rowley is most efficient. He has never lost a President"* (*Kennedy* (1965), by Theodore Sorensen, p. 843).

311 Dulles apparently liked to use first names. After Ike named him CIA director, *New York Times* general manager (Julius Ochs Adler) congratulated his friend "Allie" while Allen reciprocated with "Julie" (Talbot 2015, p. 48).

312 Talbot 2015, p. 379. In August 1960, Ike gave Dulles approval to "eliminate" Lumumba. Robert Johnson had been taking notes at this NSC meeting, so everyone was stunned. This was not supposed to be so public. Well, actually it wasn't. Lumumba's murder occurred just 3 days before JFK was inaugurated – he was totally stunned, almost as much as Lumumba was.

Just before Lumumba was killed, Louis Armstrong had given a concert there, and then he had dinner with Devlin, who (at that very moment) was planning to kill Lumumba! (Kinzer 2013, Kindle, 247.) Obeying Ike, Allen had sent a cable to Devlin, ordering a strike against Lumumba (Kinzer 2013, Kindle, 248) – and then Sidney Gottlieb promptly showed brothers; Foster spent his dying days in 1959 (from colon cancer – for which he got radiation therapy from my own specialty) at Dillon's Florida retreat. (John Foster Dulles is buried at Arlington National Cemetery.) Meanwhile, Allen Dulles had previously stayed at the legendary vineyard owned by Dillon in the Bordeaux country (near the home of my centuries-ago, ancient ancestors). He recalled this visit as among the most "delightful" of his life.[313]

---

up with poison for the job (Kinzer 2013, Kindle, 249). Allen had dispatched Devlin to the Congo, but he [Devlin] was ignorant of the country. *"They were puppeteers of power."* And regarding Lumumba, *"None of us* [CIA officers] *had any real concept of what he stood for,"* one of them later said (Kinzer 2013, Kindle, 266). Quite unlike Ike, JFK had planned to free Lumumba and then integrate him into a new congress (Kinzer 2013, Kindle, 280).

After Lumumba, the Soviets' next African aid project sent snowplows to Guinea (Kinzer, Kindle, 281) – so we cannot claim that the Soviets lacked a sense of humor. And then they (with quite straight faces) sent wheat to the Congo, even though the Congo had no wheat mills! Their next farce was to distribute pamphlets in English – even though most Congolese were illiterate. The Soviets might as well have used Russian. In 1960 – after 52 years of Belgian rule – the Congo had 17 college grads in a population of 13 million. They had no doctors, lawyers, or engineers (Kinzer 2013, Kindle, 257). [The French in Vietnam were equally irresponsible; one doctor served 38,000 people. For comparison, the Philippines had one doctor per 3000 persons.] More seriously, two years after Lumumba's murder Allen admitted that he might have exaggerated the danger from Lumumba (Kinzer 2013, Kindle, 283). Ike wisely remained silent about this, but many historians agree with Allen, who paradoxically kept his job. In the decades that followed Lumumba, *"the Congo became a hell of repression, poverty, corruption, and violence"* –all engineered by the incorrigible Allen Dulles (Kinzer 2013, Kindle, 281). Does anyone recall Mobutu Sese Seko, president of Zaire (now the Democratic Republic of the Congo), who seized power in a 1965 coup and ruled with an iron fist for 32 years? That is Allen's legacy.

Ike was focused on the then-Belgian Congo because of its uranium reserves. The core of the first atomic bomb had come from Lumumba's Congo ("The forgotten mine that built the atomic bomb" – https://honorsofdistinctionmag.com/the-forgotten-mine-that-built-the-atomic-bomb/#:~:text=The%2520Shinkolobwe%2520mine%2520%25E2%2580%2593%2520named%2520after%2520a%2520kind,the%2520atomic%2520bombs%2520dropped%2520on%2520Japan%2520in%25201945). So, Ike was naturally worried that the Russians would displace the US in that country. On the other hand, Hillary Clinton later disagreed with Ike. Via her machinations with Uranium One and with Rosatom (with their major holdings in Kazakhstan), her foundation was rewarded with a generous piece of cake (echoes of Marie Antoinette), while she also gave the Russians their share of "yellow cake." As a result the Russians now control 20% of US uranium reserves ("Does Russia Really Own 20% Of The US' Uranium Reserves?" | OilPrice.com). Despite this national faux pas, Hillary won the Presidential Medal of Freedom ("Cash Flowed to Clinton Foundation Amid Russian Uranium Deal" - *The New York Times*). Ike would have been stupefied.

313 Talbot 2015, p. 554. Talbot emphasizes that Dulles, even though CIA director, answered to men with far more wealth, and in some ways, even more power than his own. Douglas Dillon fills that bill.

Dillon had been active in Republican politics since 1934. He had worked for John Foster Dulles in Thomas E. Dewey's 1948 presidential campaign. He also assisted Eisenhower in his 1952 campaign, and so became one of Ike's close advisors. But "Foster" (as he was called) had one obsession – he wanted (only) to be Secretary of State. For this, he

By the time that Dillon appeared before the WC, their staff had tried for months to get SS records. But Dillon stonewalled them. When the staff would not quit, Dillon huddled with his *old friend* John McCloy[314] – and then appealed directly to LBJ! WC staff member Willens marveled at Dillon: *"I still can't believe he involved President Johnson in this."*[315] Later, LBJ put Dillon *in charge* of implementing the Warren Report's recommendations! Presumably, this did not include impeaching a criminal president.[316]

But we are not done with "Doug." In 1975, President Gerald Ford[317] (who knew better) appointed Dillon (who also knew better) to the

was willing to sacrifice his dignity and anything else. When he felt that he might lose his job (due to the antics of Joe McCarthy), he folded like a limp flower – and did everything to placate Joe. So, Foster's groveling encouraged my Wisconsin senator to ransack the State Department (Talbot 2015, p. 216).

314 In September 1945, after Truman discontinued the OSS, it was McCloy who insisted on creating the CIA: *"The continuing operation of the OSS must be performed in order to preserve them"* ["them" presumably meant the *operations*]. (*Legacy of Ashes* (2007) by Timothy Weiner, p. 10.) And so Truman eventually – and to his everlasting regret – bit the bullet offered by John McCloy.

McCloy had worked with Bill Donovan, the Dulles brothers, and Meyer Lansky to set up the global network of secret funds and black banks (Sterling and Peggy Seagrave 2008, Kindle, p. 465); this implies two Warren Commissioners in the same chain (just below)!

Lansky → McCloy → Allen Dulles → LBJ

315 Talbot 2015, p. 584.

316 If Dillon had really done the job that LBJ had given him, he would also have indicted his good friends (the Dulles brothers) for their WW II activities that favored the Nazis (Talbot 2015, p. 29). For example, Sullivan and Cromwell had long done legal work for I. G. Farben; during WW II, Farben manufactured Zyklon B gas. Before WW II, John Foster Dulles had signed "Heil Hitler" on his correspondence to Farben. At the same time that John Foster was genuflecting, the Nazi authorities (in 1936) had forbidden Lutheran pastor Dietrich Bonhoeffer (one of my all-time heroes) to teach. His book, *Cost of Discipleship* (1937) clarified his rejection of the Nazis. In fact, just *two days* after Hitler became chancellor, Bonhoeffer had delivered a radio address in which he attacked Hitler and warned Germany against slipping into an idolatrous cult. But no one was listening – except for Winston Churchill.

Bonhoeffer was hanged on April 9, 1945; Germany surrendered on May 7, 1945. He was sentenced without any legal defense. There were no witnesses. There was no evidence against him and no records were kept of the proceedings. I would have paid (a lot) to listen to Bonhoeffer interrogate the (Presbyterian minister) father of these Dulles brothers about his sons' Nazi hospitality. (Foster was on the Union Theological Seminary board.)

317 In 1976, Gerald R. Ford (my fellow Michigan alumnus and former near neighbor in Rancho Mirage) told the former French president (Valéry Giscard D'Estaing): *"It wasn't a lone assassin. It was a plot. We knew for sure that it was a plot. But we didn't find who was behind it"*: http://jfkfacts.org/president-ford-spoke-jfk-plot-says-former-

Valéry D'Estaing, Gerald Ford & Mickey Mantle

Gerry told Valéry that JFK had been killed by conspiracy. But Mickey was only concerned with his personal domestic affairs and with alcohol. On the other hand, after Marilyn was murdered, Mickey's former teammate (DiMaggio) prayed daily for vengeance against his fellow Catholics, JFK and RFK

Rockefeller Commission (Nelson also knew better – see more below) to investigate possible CIA involvement in JFK's murder. This was a natural fit for Dillon since his wealth lay in nearly the same stratosphere as Nelson Rockefeller's (over $1 billion at death) – and, of course, these two *had also been lifelong friends.*[318] Another appointee was almost unbelievable – but

french-president-/. When I asked Gerry to sign his Oswald book (*Portrait of the Assassin*, 1965) for me, he promptly did so (with his left hand). And then he turned to me – to remind me that he was the last surviving member of the WC. But I escaped safely; he did not recognize me.

In 1942, Ford had applied to be an FBI agent, but he was rejected and his application was withdrawn. Ironically though, as a member of the WC, he was able to play pathologist: he deliberately moved the back wound entry into the neck – to facilitate the Single Bullet Theory ("Gerald Ford's Role in the JFK Assassination Cover-up," *Crime Magazine*) (https://crimemagazine.com/gerald-fords-role-jfk-assassination-cover).

I subsequently bequeathed Ford's signed book to my daughter, who is doing a JFK documentary. Gerry included classified documents in his book, for which Harold Weisberg did not receive official clearance until ten years later! Laws had been passed to target Daniel Ellsberg's *Pentagon Papers*, but Ford violated these same laws. By denying that he had published classified material, he also committed perjury before the Senate Judiciary Committee on May 3, 1974 (Edgar F. Tatro, "An outsider's look at the insufferable Leon Jaworski" in *Garrison: The Journal of History and Deep Politics*, Issue #010, June 2022, pp. 76-156).

> *Ford committed the final act of the Watergate cover-up when he sent those records and papers and tapes to Nixon in California. In addition, "Mr. Becker went so far as to order the Secret Service to stop an army truck that was being loaded with records from leaving the White House ground, an order [that was subsequently] affirmed by President Ford:"* Benton Becker, Ford Aide, Dies at 77; Negotiated Nixon Pardon - *The New York Times*

318 Nelson Rockefeller was also an intimate friend of Ed Lansdale! Even more stunning, the Seagraves claim that Nelson was involved in overt operations (Sterling and Peggy Seagrave, Kindle, p. 462).

N. Rockefeller → Lansdale → Colby → Allen Dulles → LBJ
N. Rockefeller → Lansdale →C. Cabell → LBJ

On August 21, 1993, Trenton Parker (once part of the CIA counter-intelligence unit Pegasus) told author Rodney Stich that he had listened to his unit's taped conversations about the JFK assassination. (The tapes had previously been turned over to congressman Larry McDonald.) Parker recalled a discussion between [Nelson] Rockefeller and [J. Edgar] Hoover. Rockefeller asks, *"Are we going to have any problems?* And he [Hoover] replies, *"No, we aren't going to have any problems. I checked with Dulles. If they do their job we'll do our job."* Parker emphasizes that Hoover did not realize that his phone had been tapped by the CIA (*Defrauding America: Encyclopedia of Secret Operations by the CIA, DEA, and Other Covert Agencies* (1998), p. 638). I own an author-signed copy of Stich's book, which Oswald LeWinter gave me. Oswald also inscribed it: *"To David Mantik, from an admirer who contributed. Oswald LeWinter."*

LeWinter was featured in two documentaries. *Gladio*, the first (1992), was a three part BBC documentary about Operation Gladio. In this, LeWinter is identified as *"Colonel Oswald Le Winter, CIA-ITAC liaison officer, Europe."* LeWinter is also cited in the 1998 ARRB report: Oswald LeWinter - Wikipedia. On one occasion, LeWinter revealed to Robert Parry how he had undermined the work of Barbara Honegger on the "October Surprise: Teacher, sailor, soldier, spy: the remarkable Oswald LeWinter" | www.italianinsider.it (https://www.italianinsider.it/?q=node/2964).

During the late 1990s, I chauffeured my daughter Meredith to LeWinter's house for playdates with his daughter, Yael. (I noticed that Oswald had many books on the JFK assassination.) In the book of *Judges* (chapters 4 and 5), we encounter yet one more temple it was Lyman Lemnitzer! (Lyman also knew better – more to follow.) But Peter Clapper, director of public affairs for the Rockefeller Commission, had no illusion that their work was aimed at reforms. He stated, *"Like it or not, we are engaged largely in a public relations job."*[319]

SS chief James Rowley (who reported to Dillon) was the first person to greet LBJ when his plane touched down at Andrews Air Force Base that night. Rowley (like Admiral George Burkley, MD) stayed on for the rest of LBJ's term. Intriguingly, Rowley had previously served the FBI under J. Edgar Hoover; Rowley had even remained a close friend of Hoover. But the FBI also had another ready conduit with the CIA – James Angleton had a back channel with Hoover. During the WC, Jim often met with FBI contacts William Sullivan and Sam Papich.[320] Bill Harvey also served as a direct contact with Sullivan and Hoover while he was on the CIA payroll.[321] So, we can now imagine…

Hoover → Rowley → Dillon → LBJ

Sullivan → Angleton → Allen Dulles → LBJ

But Dillon was caught between a rock and a hard place. While his boss (LBJ) publicly proclaimed his belief in conspiracy on multiple occasions, Dillon's own subordinate, James Rowley – that same evening (11/22/1963) – told RFK that his brother had been cut down in a crossfire by three, or perhaps four, gunman.[322] Furthermore, at least 21 officers confirmed hearing shots from the front. Are we truly to believe that "Doug," surrounded by such

---

wound (besides JFK's). In her tent, Jael (aka Yael – a historic Jewish heroine) tricks her runaway enemy (General Sisera) with deceptive kindness, and then she covers him gently with a rug. But after he falls asleep, she drives a tent peg through his temple with a mallet. Yael was so forceful that the peg pinned Sisera's head to the ground. View the painting just here: *Jael and Sisera* by Jacopo Amigoni (1682–1752) – or watch *Nailed It* on Netflix. As if foreordained, the locations of the temple wounds for Sisera and JFK are almost identical.

319 Rockefeller Commission, Peter Clapper to David Belin, "Public Affairs Considerations in Report," May 2, 1975. | National Security Archive (https://nsarchive.gwu.edu/document/21504-document-11). The final report of the Rockefeller Commission was heavily influenced by two former WC activists – Gerald Ford and David Belin. Both (at least publicly) were fervent lone gunman supporters. Furthermore, Ford asked Dick Cheney (!) to edit the final report.

320 Talbot 2015, p. 578.

321 Hopsicker, p. 144.

322 *Brothers* (2007) by David Talbot, p. 14. Rowley told RFK of his belief in conspiracy, i.e., three gunmen. And Jerry Behn told Forrest Sorrels, *"It's a plot."* And Sorrels replied, *"Of course"* (Hinckle and Turner, pp. 273-274).

well-informed insiders, remained forever naïve in the face of this crime?[323] And if he truly was so innocent, why did he obfuscate for the WC – when he should promptly have complied? Even later, according to Jack Tunheim (chair of the ARRB), the SS was the most obstinate federal agency in releasing records. Furthermore, they were the only known agency to *deliberately* destroy records. How likely then is it that "Doug" literally knew nothing?

But Rowley and LBJ (and Dillon, too) are not the only ones who knew that the WC was an unmitigated sham. Even Roy Kellerman knew; his widow said that *"he always accepted that there was a conspiracy."*[324] In fact, virtually anyone who knows anything about this case readily admits to conspiracy. I posted a long list of such enlightened characters in "The Silence of the Historians" from *Murder in Dealey Plaza* (2000) edited by James Fetzer, pp. 404-405. This is reproduced below as Appendix II-G.

Shown on the next page is a 1963 treasury note, with Douglas Dillon's signature highlighted. JFK had initiated this printing by the Treasury Department, in an apparent attempt to decrease the Federal Reserve's powers.[325] Some historians have argued that this encroachment on the Reserve system angered these *private bankers,* who relied on printing federal reserve notes for their own profits – and that this attack on their system then fueled their flames for assassination.[326] That discussion, however, lies

323 RFK, of course, considered McNamara to be his friend. In retrospect, this is bizarre, especially since RFK would eventually come out strongly against "McNamara's War."

324 Ibid. For Kellerman's true belief, see *The Assassination of John F. Kennedy: THE FINAL ANALYSIS* (2024) by David Mantik and Jerome Corsi, p. 11. For more insight into Kellerman, read my previous book, *The JFK Assassination Decoded: Criminal Forgery in the Autopsy Photographs and X-rays* (2023), pp. 267, 360. For the SS destruction of the motorcade windshield (Dillon must have known), read my chapter ("The JFK Limousine Redux") in my immediately above cited book.

325 In 1816, Thomas Jefferson had warned, *"Private banking establishments are more dangerous than standing armies; and the principle of spending money to be paid by posterity, under the name of funding, is but swindling posterity."* Today's monetarists would laugh Tom right off of his lectern. Of course, the Federal Reserve is a *"...private banking cartel, whose books are not open to the public"* (Sterling and Peggy Seagrave, Kindle, p. 435).

In 1982, the 9th District Court of Appeals said: *"Federal Reserve Banks are not federal instrumentalities... but are independent, privately owned, and locally controlled corporations...."* (Sterling and Peggy Seagrave, Kindle, p. 455). But Henry Ford said it best (*My Life and Work* (1922), p. 179):

> *The people are naturally conservative. They are more conservative than the financiers. Those who believe that the people are so easily led that they would permit the printing presses to run off money like milk tickets do not understand them. It is the innate conservation of the people that has kept our money good in spite of the fantastic tricks which financiers play-and which they cover up with high technical terms. The people are on the side of sound money. They are so unalterably on the side of sound money that it is a serious question how they would regard the system under which they live, if they once knew what the initiate can do with it.*

326 *Executive Order 11110: Did the Fed Kill JFK?* (2013) by James L. Paris and Robert

well beyond the scope of this essay. Even aside from that though, Dillon's role in the JFK plot may well be overdue for examination by historians.[327]

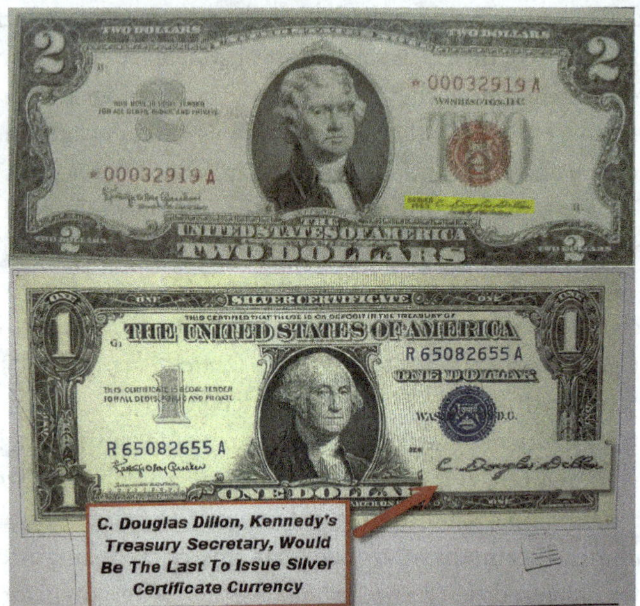

August 18, 1961

C. Douglas Dillon: Annual Assay Commission
United States Mint Philadelphia

G. Yetman, Jr. On June 4, 1963, JFK signed this executive order, which gave the US Treasury authority to print money totally independently of the Federal Reserve. This was an end run around the Fed – so there would be no related profits for Reserve-affiliated member banks. The order authorized $4.3 billion dollars of silver-backed currency, but Dillon killed this order in less than four months after JFK's death.

327 On March 25, 1964, Dillon announced that silver certificates would no longer be redeemable for silver dollars. Silver certificates could only be exchanged for an equivalent dollar amount of silver bullion until June 24, 1968. After that, silver certificates would only be considered legal tender for their face value. *"On June 24, 1968, thousands of people swarmed assay offices in the United States, anxious to unload their holdings of silver certificates. The US Treasury had deemed this to be the final date on which the certificates could be exchanged for silver bullion. People camped out overnight to ensure that they would beat the deadline, and the resulting lines stretched for hours.* Life *magazine covered the story, and offered a history of silver certificates in the United States."* Historical Echoes: The Demise of Silver Certificates - Liberty Street Economics (https://libertystreeteconomics.newyorkfed.org/2015/01/historical-echoes-the-demise-of-silver-certificates/). Treasury notes have red US Treasury Seals and serial numbers in place

So, the foreknowledge of the SS, the FBI, and the military is inescapable. How likely then is it that LBJ was totally oblivious?[328] Would each of these agencies have acted – in a coverup *in concert with one other* – without protection from their respective superiors? In addition, the buck must stop somewhere – even if signed by Douglas Dillon.

Those Weird LBJ Telephone Calls

Then there are those eccentric telephone calls that LBJ made that night; if he knew nothing, no reason existed for any of these calls.[329] While Hoover quietly went home and enjoyed a night off, LBJ (usually via his aide Cliff Carter) called John W. Fritz (captain of Homicide and Robbery Bureau of the Dallas Police Department) and District Attorney Henry Wade.[330] Cliff Carter called Wade 3-4 times that night![331] Police Chief Jesse Curry must have gotten the word, too, as Hoover refused to work with him on law enforcement after 11/22/1963. LBJ felt that any word of

of the green ones on Federal Reserve notes. At least Dillon did not suffer the indignity of the 39th Treasurer of the United States (1989-1993) under George H.W. Bush. Catalina Vasquez Villalpando went to jail for tax evasion: Stephen Koschal, Autograph Authenticator, Quality Historical Autographs and Signed Books Bought and Sold (https://www.stephenkoschal.com/villalpando.html).

328 In my conjoined PowerPoint for Part I of this book, I listed twenty who had foreknowledge, including some private citizens. One of the more remarkable characters was Adele Edisen, a neurophysiologist from Tulane. If a private citizen like Adele knew, how likely then is it that LBJ (or Dillon) was kept so naïvely in the dark?

329 For more on these telephone calls, see "LBJ & the Bounty Hunter" by Edgar Tatro, *Garrison: The Journal of History and Deep Politics*, Issue #5, August 2020, pp. 18-23.

330 Before Henry Wade got his marching orders from LBJ, he claimed that preliminary reports indicated more than one person was involved in the assassination. His initial (unbiased) quotations appeared in the *Dallas Morning News* on 11/23/1963: "*They* [sic] *should all go to the electric chair.*" Unfortunately, by that morning Wade had learned much (about political power – but not much about actual new evidence).

Years later, Wade recalled: *"Cliff Carter, President Johnson's aide, called me three times from the White House that Friday night."* We should recall that Wade had been an FBI agent during 1939-1943; in his office he had hung portraits of LBJ and J. Edgar Hoover. Wade had made multiple trips to DC, where he had met privately with LBJ and appeared at political parties at LBJ's house. Mark North (*Betrayal in Dallas: LBJ, the Pearl Street Mafia, and the Murder of President Kennedy* (2011)) has even published a series of letters between the two men: ("David Letterman, Arsenio Hall, & the JFK Assassination" by Edgar F. Tatro in *Garrison: The Journal of History and Deep Politics*, Issue #16, March 2024, pp. 50-81). See a photograph here of LBJ giving Wade a bear hug.

LBJ and Henry Wade

Brandstetter

Gordon McLendon

331 Hancock 2006, p. 305.

conspiracy would shake the nation to its core; according to LBJ, charges of an international communist conspiracy had to be stopped. But LBJ never publicly speculated on the possible national consequences of his own confession of guilt – after all, he needed to totally "CYA."

The Johnson diary (at the Johnson Presidential Library) shows no contact betwween LBJ and Hoover on 11/22/1963, but in *Death of a President* (by William Manchester),[332] LBJ calls Hoover at his home at 7:25 PM. And then, before midnight (11/22/1963), Hoover orders some Oswald evidence items to be sent promptly to the FBI from Dallas. Later, to further confuse matters, items received back in Dallas from the FBI were not a good match to those originally sent from Dallas.

And then, during Oswald's short sojourn in the operating room, LBJ spoke to Charles Crenshaw, MD (whom I have met).[333] If LBJ truly knew nothing, what possible reason could trigger such a call to the operating room?

Ed Clark (1906-1992)

Phil Nelson[334] has proposed that Ed Clark, the perpetual "Boss of Texas" was LBJ's link to the plotters. Since LBJ had worked hand-in-glove with Clark for many years, that seems plausible. For example, Clark was even on the board of a Murchison oil company! And Murchison knew H. L. Hunt, whose son employed Willoughby – and also Jack Y. Canon.[335] Years later, attorney Barr McClellan[336] observed the clever payment (via a highly devious accounting maneuver) of $2 million

Ed Clark LBJ

332 Hancock 2006, pp. 305, 403.

333 *JFK: Conspiracy of Silence* (1992) by Charles A. Crenshaw, with Jens Hansen and J. Gary Shaw, pp. 186-188.

334 *Blood, Money & Power: How L. B. J. Killed J. F. K.* (2003) by Barr McClellan.

335 Rob Reiner has proposed Jack Y. Canon as one of the Dealey Plaza gunmen. He might be right – listen to his podcast: Who Killed JFK? Podcast - Apple Podcasts (https://podcasts.apple.com/us/podcast/who-killed-jfk/id1714611578). For more on Jack, see "Inside story of US black ops in post-war Japan" - *Asia Times* (https://asiatimes.com/2020/08/inside-story-of-us-black-ops-in-post-war-japan/). Canon shot himself (apparently accidentally) on May 8, 1981, at his home in McLean, TX: Jack Y Canon (1914-1981) - Find a Grave Memorial.

336 His son, Scott McClellan, was White House Press Secretary for G. W. Bush. Scott's brother (Mark) was the head of Medicare; he had formerly been FDA commissioner.

to Ed Clark for services rendered (for 11/22/1963). Finally, the law firm of Allen Dulles (Sullivan and Cromwell) provided legal services to Murchison's oil company! (See more below.) We also know that Willoughby regularly corresponded with Allen Dulles,[337] so we can imagine…

Canon → H. L. Hunt → Clark → LBJ

Willoughby → Helliwell → LBJ

Willoughby → Lansdale → C. Cabell → Allen Dulles →LBJ

Willoughby → H. L. Hunt → Murchison → Clark → LBJ

Murchison → Allen Dulles → LBJ

Gordon McLendon (1921-1986)[338]

From Wikipedia, we learn the following. McLendon fought in World War II and was commissioned as a Japanese-language intelligence officer in the Office of Naval Intelligence (ONI). He was a co-founder (with David Phillips[339]) of the Association of Former Intelligence Officers (AFIO). He was a member of the board of stewards of Highland Park Methodist Church in Dallas and the board of directors of the Dallas Symphony Orchestra. Liberty was the second largest radio network in the US at the time with over 458 affiliated stations. In 1960, McLendon and his close friend Clint Murchison owned Radio Nord which broadcast from an offshore facility; it was called a pirate radio station by the Swedish government because it was located on a ship that was outside their legal jurisdiction. McLendon especially attracted attention for his stern denunciations of French president Charles de Gaulle, whom he described as *"an ungrateful four-flusher"* who could *"go straight to hell."* [If so, Gordon and de Gaulle can now share a drink.] McLendon, a conservative Democrat, garnered 43% of the vote in a primary race against liberal incumbent US Senator Ralph Yarborough in 1964.

Ruby was both an admirer and friend of McLendon; he told the FBI that McLendon was one of his six *"closest friends,"* and McLendon allowed Ruby to advertise on his radio station, KLIF. So, Ruby's apparent affiliation with KLIF allowed him easy access to the Dallas Police Department. After Ruby's arrest, he asked George Senator to contact McLendon – to

337 Russell 1992, p. 707.

338 *Gordon McLendon: The Maverick of Radio* (1992) by Ronald Garay, p. 179.

339 McLendon and Phillips had been friends in Fort Worth ever since junior high school (Tatro, November 2023, p. 68).

let him know where he was. Ruby testified that on 11/23/1963, he attempted to call McLendon but could not reach him; the last letter Ruby wrote before he died was to McLendon. While Earl Warren interviewed him, Ruby even asked Earl if he knew either Robert Storey or McLendon.

After Bobby Baker was released from prison in 1972, he stayed at the Cielo Ranch, owned by McLendon. J. Edgar Hoover was also a guest at McLendon's house on many occasions.

Bill Pulte was a former professor of teaching and learning. Bill summarized what happened on 11/22/1963:[340]

> *Gordon was supposed to attend the lunch in JFK's honor. Notoriously late for events, a couple of his staff reminded him to get ready. Later, they reminded him again and said that he was going to be late if he didn't leave right away. He replied,* "Yeah, let's go now and see the SOB get his brains blown out." *The staff members told* [Charles W. (Bill)] *Weaver* [who managed KLIF in Dallas] *about this shortly after the assassination.*

Jones Harris confirmed this story to Ed Tatro; his source was a McLendon secretary.[341] Gaeton Fonzi[342] claims that Phillips was responsible for the infamous Mexico City (fake) telephone calls that were designed to link Oswald to the Cubans and Soviets. This is a colossal conclusion; if this is true, then Phillips was party to the piggy-backed operation discussed in Part I. That means that Phillips was fully cognizant – more so than Angleton was. Most likely Fonzi was on target; almost certainly, Phillips had actually created these fake calls. If that is true, then the Mexico City scenario can be unraveled.

Consider this. From 1961 through the fall of 1963, David Phillips was *in Mexico City* – as Chief of Covert Action.[343] We also know that David Morales was often in Mexico City that summer.[344] The notion of a pig-

340 Ibid., p. 66.

341 Ibid., pp. 67-68. Jones Harris told Ed Tatro that he personally knew Phillips; he also claimed that Phillips had recruited McLendon into CIA enterprises. I once visited Jones Harris at his Manhattan apartment next to Central Park. He liked to keep up on my work. His son is still on the physics faculty at Yale, which was yet one more connection for us: Harris Lab | Yale (https://harrislab.yale.edu). Jones also told me that he had once dated Pamela Turnure, Jackie's press secretary. Jones routinely insisted that we investigate the Honest Joe Pawn Shop, because their vehicle had been parked prominently and conveniently in Dealey Plaza that day. Jones also alerted me to Bagley's book, *Spy Wars*.

342 *The Last Investigation* (2013) by Gaeton Fonzi, pp. 196-197, 266, 278-297.

343 Fonzi, p. 266.

344 Ibid., p. 376. Brad Ayers had learned this directly from Bob Wall, who was Morales's Assistant Chief of Operations at JM/WAVE.

gy-back operation (e.g., one superimposed on a pre-existing molehunt) was beyond the grasp of Morales (he was not even a good student in high school); Morales was an action figure, not a theorist. On the other hand, Phillips was the master of psy-ops. Another individual with the mental flair to invent such a devious scheme is Bill Harvey. But Bill, since his contretemps with JFK during the Missile Crisis, had been banned to Rome, where his primary exercise was getting drunk and pursuing international affairs with Roman (or perhaps roamin') women. So, sometime during that summer or early fall in Mexico City, Phillips passed this clever scheme on to Morales, who assigned it to one of his Spanish-speaking AMOTs (perhaps Jose Sanjenis – see Part I).

If we accept this role for Phillips, it explains why he so relentlessly lied about it – even against all reason. His trip to CIA headquarters was designed to assess his own success at this rogue operation – he wanted to leave no time for headquarters to fabricate its own explanation (and he kept it hidden from them – as Angleton's ignorance confirms). Recall that Phillips had left Mexico City for DC on September 30, only to return on October 9 – the same day that Gheesling lifted the watch on Oswald. Since Phillips was so focused on Oswald, he surely knew what Gheesling had done to his (David's) own minion (Oswald). If this scenario is accepted, then David Phillips should have been indicted for murdering Lee Harvey Oswald.

There is another corollary. Recall that Antonio Veciana had supervised a sketch of "Bishop." When this sketch was shown to family members of David Phillips (and to a secretary), they immediately recognized this image as their relative, David Phillips. Joseph Burkholder Smith (Phillips's supervisor during the Bay of Pigs) also confirmed the ID.[345] What are the odds of this – unless the ID was real? Another well-placed CIA officer ("Ron Cross"), who handled one of the most active anti-Castro groups, was certain that Phillips had used the pseudonym of Bishop. And Escalante, based on two independent Cuban sources, confirmed that Phillips had used the name "Maurice Bishop."[346] So, the evidence for Phillips as "Bishop" is quite overwhelming.

John Newman's opposition to this ID is based on documents that showed Veciana's connection to a different agency than the CIA. Quite likely, however, Veciana was double-dipping as a "bilateral agent," i.e., collecting support (and possibly funds) from more than one US agency (likely

345 Tatro, November 2023, p. 70.
346 Twyman, pp. 356-357.

the CIA and Army Intelligence). I attended the Bethesda conference (September 25-28, 2014), where Veciana confirmed his ID as David Phillips.

It was at this conference that neurologist Michael Chesser, MD, first introduced himself to me. Soon afterwards, Mike confirmed my critical optical density data from the extant JFK autopsy X-rays at the National Archives – these had been focally altered so as to incriminate Oswald.[347]

Of course, this collaboration between Phillips and Morales went way back. They had both participated in the Guatemala coup.[348] Others in this coup included Allen Dulles, Richard Bissell, Tracy Barnes, and E. Howard Hunt (Talbot 2015, p. 261). Helen Phillips, David's first wife, also reports that E. Howard often visited them in Mexico City (Fonzi, p. 280).

During 1958-1960, Morales worked out of the American Embassy in Havana, while Phillips worked there (under cover) in his public relations business. Then, during the Bay of Pigs, they again worked together. Immediately after this, they coordinated operations via JM/WAVE, the CIA station in Miami. Next, Morales showed up in Vietnam and Laos with Ted Shackley, but after that he appeared in Latin America, a CIA division headed by – you guessed it – David Phillips.[349]

This entire scenario is consistent with the recollections of E. Howard Hunt.[350] But he described himself as merely a "benchwarmer." He believed that the JFK plot centered on the CIA's Cord Meyer, David Atlee Phillips, David Morales, and William Harvey.[351]

The primary evidence that implicates Cord Meyer derives from Peter Janney.[352] His father (Wistar) had called Ben Bradlee early in the afternoon

347 "The JFK Assassination: Cause for Doubt" in *Assassination Science* (1998) edited by James Fetzer, pp. 93-139.

348 Amazingly, Nelson Rockefeller was included in this chain of command. His economic interests were being put at serious risk by Juan Jacobo Árbenz Guzmán. Furthermore, Allen Dulles was seated on the board of the United Fruit Company (Hopsicker, p. 72). In Guatemala, 3% of the landowners owned 70% of the land. Nelson was likely included in this 3%. Allen's favorite bank – J. Henry Schroder Banking Corporation (a Sullivan and Cromwell client) – served as agent before 1954 for *all three major firms in Guatemala*. So, Allen had much at stake in Guatemala.

349 Fonzi, p. 383. But this is all in the public record.

350 *Bond of Secrecy: My Life with CIA Spy and Watergate Conspirator E. Howard Hunt* (2012) by Saint John Hunt, Eric Hamburg, et al.

351 "So Who Killed JFK?" – The JFK Historical Group (https://www.jfkhistorical.com/blog-1/2018/8/2/so-who-killed-jfk)

352 Peter accompanied me on a visit to the Sixth Floor Museum in Dallas; together we viewed the MPI images – *after* they had been altered. See "Masquerade at the Museum" in *The JFK Assassination Decoded: Criminal Forgery in the Autopsy Photographs and X-rays* (2023) by David W. Mantik, pp. 31-44. Peter's recollections of his father's suspiciously early knowledge of the death of Mary Meyer (and his early communication with Cord Meyer about her death) are detailed in *Mary's Mosaic* (2012) by Peter Janney, pp. 340 ff.

of Mary's murder (October 12, 1964). Wistar then called Cord Meyer (Mary's former husband) to inform him. Peter still wonders how his father could have known so early – well before the police had even identified the victim! [Perhaps Wistar had borrowed some ESP from J. Edgar Hoover, who immediately knew that Oswald was the lone gunman.]

What Gordon McLendon knew about Mexico City, we will never know. It depends on how well Phillips trusted his old friend, but that is no longer very relevant.

One final comment about Gordon; in fall 1963, he went on a secret trip with his family to Mexico City.[353]

Lt. Col. O'Wighton Delk Simpson (1911-1999)

The following is excerpted (and slightly paraphrased) from the *Los Angeles Times* (see the footnote after this section).

Minutes before midnight on Jan. 12, 1953, John Arnold and 13 of his men in a B-29 bomber – its belly painted black to match the night sky – were shot down over China's border with North Korea. They made headlines around the world when Washington eventually negotiated their release. But the story behind their ordeal – the hidden CIA connection – is only now emerging from behind a veil of official secrecy.

By daylight, at least eleven of the men had been captured by Chinese troops and taken to the river city of Andung, China, the base for the main Soviet military force during the Korean War. After brief questioning at Andung, they were taken north by train to Mukden, where they spent 16 days in prison. The next stop was Beijing, where they remained behind bars until released at a Hong Kong rail stop on Aug. 4, 1955. An Air Force intelligence officer, *Delk Simpson,* who was stationed in Hong Kong, was the first to greet the released men. Close behind, Simpson said in an interview, were CIA officials. A few days later, in Japan, the men would be interviewed by an Air Force team that included CIA psychologist John Gittinger; Arnold later was debriefed at CIA headquarters.[354] [End of *LA Times* article.]

Delk Simpson served with Howard Burris on LBJ's inaugural committee. On August 20, 1977, Delk's son (Delk, Jr.) was interviewed by Robert D. Morrow. The son stated, *"Dave Phillips and my father communicate all the time."* The son claimed that his father and Howard Burris had foreknowl-

353 Scott 1993, p. 124. Also see "Overview: The CIA, the Drug Traffic, and Oswald in Mexico" by Peter Dale Scott in "Deep Politics III" (December 2000, https://www.history-matters.com/pds/dp3.htm). Peter credits Mary Ferrell, who (apparently) was friendly with McLendon's children.

354 "Soldiers' Cold War Ordeal Tied to CIA Link, Mysterious Leak" - *Los Angeles Times.*

edge of 11/22/1963. Then to this plot he added Charles Cabell. [Charles (and probably Earle, too) was a tenth-generation descendant of Pocahontas,[355] so how much more American can this plot get?] Simpson and Burris were affiliated with Clint Murchison and other oil men on worldwide oil leases. Nonetheless, HSCA investigators concluded that these characters could contribute nothing to the case. But Simpson admitted his involvement in the plot to his son's girlfriend (Didi Hess), who worked for the Pentagon. He said to Didi, *"I did it because it was necessary... and I got myself involved.... The whole thing's true, Didi.... I did it for the total good."* Robert Morrow confirmed this during an interview on September 25, 1977. Delk later admitted to Gus Russo and Jim Marrs that he and General Sam Anderson had toasted JFK's death while in Paris (France).[356] Delk had obviously not appreciated the opening quote from C. S. Lewis in Part I.

This son, O'Wighton Delk Simpson, Jr., died in 1982, in Florida at age 39 (DOB: 6/27/43). Junior had claimed that senior (his father) was the "bagman" for the JFK assassination. But junior was only 10 years old on 11/22/1963, so he must have learned this later (and likely shared it then with his girlfriend, Didi). He believes that the payoff occurred in Haiti, where the Baron was then located; this was also where Jacqueline Lancelot witnessed too much (see more later on Lancelot). Recall that de Mohrenschildt was in Haiti during 1963-1964, probably dining at Jacqueline's restaurant (see below). Later in Paris (France), Delk, Sr. and his close friend Howard Burris worked together in the import-export business.[357]

Like so many others in this sorry tale, Delk (senior) is buried at Arlington National Cemetery, not so far from JFK (and Jackie, too).

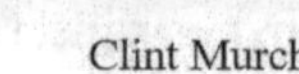

Delk Simpson, Sr. Clint Murchison, Jr. Col. Wm. C. Bishop General Charles Cabell

355 https://en.wikipedia.org/wiki/Charles_P._Cabell

356 Tatro, November 2023, pp. 113-114. See: Transcript of Kennedy Assassination Workshop conducted by John Newman and Gus Russo entitled, "Major General Edward G. Lansdale, Colonel Howard Burris and Air Force Intelligence Connections to the Kennedy Assassination" at the Hyatt Regency Hotel at Reunion Square, Dallas, Texas, October 24, 1992.

357 Type into a search engine: "Mary Farrell Col Delk Simpson"

Colonel Howard Burris, Sr. (1918-2009)[358]

Beginning in 1961, Colonel Howard Burris became LBJ's military aide; he also had a fairly direct line to Allen Dulles. LBJ clearly relied on input from Burris,[359] as Newman makes quite clear.[360] Burris's superior was General David Burchinal; he was Curtis LeMay's protégé. Recall that LeMay, always at loggerheads with JFK,[361] had attended the autopsy only via a last-minute flight from Canada. At the autopsy, he blew smoke into the face of Paul O'Connor after Paul asked him to extinguish his lit cigar. It stayed lit.

From Jim DiEugenio: Posted November 14, 2019[362]

Dulles and LeMay were pals, on a first name basis and exchanged gifts I have never thought that the JFK murder worked, through any kind of formal channels.

LeMay → Allen Dulles → Burris → LBJ

Burchinal → LeMay → Allen Dulles → LBJ

Burris had participated in the 1953 coup in Iran against Mohammad Mosaddegh.[363] Since this coup was directed by Allen Dulles (CIA director, 1953-1961) and by Kermit "Kim" Roosevelt, Jr. (Teddy's grandson), there can be no doubt that – already *a decade before* 11/22/1963 – Allen Dulles and Burris were longtime close colleagues in covert action.

Dulles was in Texas shortly before the assassination. During October 25-29, 1963, he met with old friends in Houston and Dallas and he spoke before the Dallas Council on World Affairs. His stopover in Texas was an anomaly for a book tour (for his *Craft of Intelligence* – an "autobiography" ghostwritten for Dulles by E. Howard Hunt and perhaps by others like Howard Ronan)[364] that otherwise focused on the two coasts. Dulles's date book during his Texas trip omitted much, with big gaps in his schedule.

358 Also see Appendix II-H

359 Col. Burris was in the oil business with Mickey Wiener. He also served as military attaché at the US Embassy in Geneva, Switzerland. In Paris, he was in the import-export business with Col. Delk Simpson; but then Burris was called to Switzerland after Nosenko defected. Burris supposedly was Nosenko's original case officer (A Record from Mary's Database) (https://www.maryferrell.org/php/marysdb.php?id=1730&search=delk).

360 Newman 1992, pp. 161, 225.

361 LeMay was Chief of Staff of the US Air Force (1961–1965); there was never any love lost between JFK and LeMay.

362 https://www.cia.gov/library/readingroom/docs/CIA-RDP80B01676R001200020047-8.pdf. Unfortunately, that link (on Dec 4, 2024) did not provide any useful information on the relationship between LeMay and Dulles, but that is no surprise; links mutate much faster than Darwin could have imagined.

363 *Our Man in Haiti* (2012) by Joan Mellen; see the center photograph section.

364 As just more evidence of E. Howard Hunt's close relationship to top CIA offi-

But Dulles was wired into the Texas oil industry – for which his own law firm, Sullivan and Cromwell, *had provided legal counsel* for many years.[365] He was also wired into the local political hierarchy, including Dallas mayor Earle Cabell (officially a CIA asset), who was the younger brother of Allen's former CIA deputy (Charles).[366] The latter had been a fellow victim of JFK's post–Bay of Pigs housecleaning.[367] [JFK had fired both Allen Dulles and Charles Cabell. Despite this humiliation, their family names got forever trapped onto public structures – see the photographs below.] So, now we have a connection between *Texas oil* and the prior law firm of *Allen Dulles!*

Murchison → Allen Dulles → LBJ

J. Edgar Hoover Building   Dulles International Airport

Earle Cabell Building   General LeMay Building: US Strategic HQ

cials, on 11/22/1963 he and Richard Helms were meeting in a CIA safe house in northwest DC, presumably not far from the Elms, where LBJ lived (Hinckle and Turner, p. 251). Of course, Howard was also close to Willoughby (Lernoux, p. 79). Prior to the 1964 election, Howard was downgraded and shipped to the CIA base in Madrid (the home of Otto Skorzeny since 1952).

E. H. Hunt → Helliwell → Lansdale → C. Cabell → LBJ

365 Talbot 2015, p. 488.

366 Charles Cabell was intimately familiar with the CIA's use of Otto Skorzeny (*The Skorzeny Papers* (2018) by Major Ralph Ganis, p. 181).

Skorzeny → C. Cabell → Allen Dulles → LBJ

367 The LBJ/ Dulles photo - JFK Assassination Debate - The Education Forum (https://educationforum.ipbhost.com/topic/27642-the-lbj-dulles-photo/).

The following is from https://erenow.net/modern/the-devils-chess-board-allen-dulles-the-cia/19.php:

> *"Dulles was among those who maintained warm relations with the vice president* [LBJ], *even as both men's stars declined during the JFK era. In retirement, Allen continued to invite Johnson to Washington, DC, functions. So, during the summer of 1963, Johnson hosted Dulles at his ranch in the Texas Hill Country, sixty miles west of Austin. Dulles's visit to the LBJ Ranch did not appear in his calendar, but it was briefly noted in a syndicated news photo, i.e., in the* Chicago Tribune *of August 15, 1963.*[368] *It shows LBJ astride a horse, while a beaming Lady Bird and Dulles look on. Considering how JFK was estranged from both men – and how notoriously conniving both were – the picture could only have produced a sense of puzzlement in the White House"*[369] – especially because *Allen Dulles* was then *out of office.* (See this startling photograph near the beginning of Part II.)

Lee Shepherd: Col. Howard Burris's visit to Texas just before 11/22/1963

Douglas Caddy Posted July 3, 2021 (edited). Lee Shepherd posted this on Facebook on 7/2/2021:[370]

In July 1961, a National Security Council meeting was attended by Gen. Lemnitzer, Dulles, and Burris. At this meeting, Gen. Thomas F. Hickey (Staff Director for the National Security Council's Net Evaluation Subcommittee Staff) *"presented a plan for nuclear surprise attack on the Soviet Union."*

Acting as LBJ's military advisor, Col. Burris had accompanied Johnson to Vietnam during the same year (1961), where these two men convinced Prime Minister Ngo Dinh Diệm to petition JFK to train 16,000 US troops; JFK denied this request. As John Newman points out, in all likelihood, it was Burris who was a CIA back-channel to LBJ; therefore, Burris was likely LBJ's liaison to Allen Dulles. Burris's commander was none other than Gen. David A. Burchinal, a protégé of Gen. Curtis LeMay.

LeMay → Allen Dulles → Burris → LBJ

---

368 Talbot 2015, p. 493.

369 https://erenow.net/modern/the-devils-chessboard-allen-dulles-the-cia/19.php

370 Lee Shepherd on Col. Howard Burris' visit to Texas just before JFK was assassinated - JFK Assassination Debate - The Education Forum (https://educationforum.ipbhost.com/topic/27226-lee-shepherd-on-col-howard-burris-visit-to-texas-just-before-jfk-was-assassinated/). Type into a search engine: *"jfk assassination symposium lee shepherd"*

A letter written to George de Mohrenschildt from LBJ's office reveals that it was Walter Jenkins who first introduced the Baron to Burris.[371] Roger Stone notes: *"Following his mysterious death, the unlisted phone number of Colonel Burris was found in Mohrenschildt's address book alongside that of Judge Sarah Hughes."*[372] Sarah had sworn LBJ into office on AF-1.[373]

Just before the assassination, LBJ's military attaché, fellow Texan and *friend of over thirty years,* Col. Howard Lay Burris, flew to Texas on an unconfirmed mission that he later chose to lie about. Thanks to John Newman, we now suspect its purpose: Burris was to brief and oversee the [illegal] transition of LBJ into the White House.[374]

In 1993, Richard Bartholomew wrote an article that mostly focused on Burris.[375] This next segment is a summary of that piece.[376]

[Bartholomew begins.] The last of the Baron's letters to LBJ (June 13, 1969) emphasized their mutual friends, including Barbara and Howard Burris, as well as George Brown and the late Herman Brown. (LBJ's term ended on January 20, 1969.) Lansdale's private letters imply that LeMay needed help from Allen Dulles to promote Lansdale from colonel to general; this implies that Lansdale was CIA. Judging from common social events, Lansdale and Charles Cabell (CIA) were very close. After reading a pre-galley copy of *JFK and Vietnam,* Daniel Ellsberg (who had worked closely with Lansdale) called the author (John Newman) and said, *"This is the first time I've ever thought that Lansdale might have been involved in the assassination."*

George Brown → Burris → LBJ

Lansdale → C. Cabell → Allen Dulles → LBJ

---

371 Joan Mellen adds that Burris had met this wife, Barbara Jester, at the University of Texas. She was the daughter of the former governor of Texas, Beauford Jester (Mellen 2012, p. 195). Ironically like JFK, Beauford also died young while in office.

372 Stone, Roger with Mike Colapietro. *The Man Who Killed Kennedy: The Case Against LBJ,* 2013.

373 LBJ later appointed Sarah to the US National Commission of UNESCO. LBJ was a fanatical devotee of *quid pro quo.*

374 https://jfkjmn.com/new-page-42/#. The military has marvelous memories of Howard; notwithstanding his 1963 visit to the LBJ ranch, *"his actions on all these occasions reflect the highest credit upon himself and the Armed Forces of the United States.":* Howard Burris - Hall of Valor: Medal of Honor, Silver Star, U.S. Military Awards (https://valor.militarytimes.com/recipient/recipient-99004/).

375 Quixotic Joust: Excerpt from Manuscript by Richard Bartholomew (https://quixoticjoust.blogspot.com/2011/10/excerpt-from-manuscript-by-richard.html).

376 Also see *The Deep State in the Heart of Texas* (2018) by Richard Bartholomew and Edgar Tatro.

[Bartholomew continues.] Lansdale's travel records include a Cuban-exile camp.

Cuban exiles → Lansdale → C. Cabell → Burris → LBJ

During April-May 1963, Lansdale visited a sniper school in Panama. His record included a cover note: the visit was not to be discussed. In the months just before 11/22/1963, Newman noticed *"a lot of Spanish names. I found names that were reminiscent of CIA type folks."* But why would Lansdale suddenly develop an interest in persons with Spanish names? Beginning in September 1963, in up to ten letters to friends and associates, Lansdale reports his intention to visit Texas in November.[377]

Spanish names → Lansdale → C. Cabell → Allen Dulles → LBJ

In *JFK and Vietnam,* Newman cites Burris for gross deceptions about progress in the Vietnam War. LBJ learns the truth via a back channel, while JFK learns the opposite via official channels.

Robert Morrow (*The Senator Must Die,* 1988) described two unnamed colonels. In 1977, Morrow had picked up a hitchhiker (a young man) who said that his father had been involved in the JFK assassination. His father was a former Air Force intelligence officer,[378] who was very close to LBJ. In 1963, the hitchhiker had seen his father receiving money in Haiti; he also heard relevant conversations about this.

Gus Russo discovered the identities of the two colonels [who are not reported in this piece by Bartholomew, but the first colonel must be Delk Simpson]. One of them [Simpson] wanted to talk about his good friend, Howard Burris, who he said served on LBJ's inaugural committee with him; they were also both friends of Charles Cabell. When this colonel [Simpson] worked for Martin Marietta, he was liaison to NATO during the late 1950s and early 1960s. Russo discovered that Burris was from Texas and that he had oil money. They all knew each other and they were all tied into the NATO network that was defying JFK. Gus also learned that Burris, Sr. was a close friend of Richard Helms. In fact, in September 1976, Howard L. (sometimes A.) Burris, Jr. had married Princess Shahrazad Pahlbod, the niece of the Shah of Iran![379] They divorced in 1982,

---

377 https://quixoticjoust.blogspot.com/2011/10/excerpt-from-manuscript-by-richard.html

378 Colonel O'Wighton Delk Simpson fits this description rather well. He and Burris had served together on LBJ's inauguration committee and they later went into business together.

379 Howard L. Burris, Jr. weds Shahrazad Pahlbod_1976 - Newspapers.com™ (https://www.newspapers.com/article/honolulu-star-bulletin-howard-l-burris/20101494/?cj_pub_cid=5250933&cj_pub_name=Microsoft+Shopping+(Bing+Rebates,+Coupons,+etc.)&cj_

while Howard Jr. (born 1950) was just beginning medical school. In an astonishing concurrence, Richard Helms (the former ambassador to Iran) had been a lifelong friend of the Shah.[380]

NATO → GLADIO → BARTOLOMEW'S COLONEL → C. CABELL →A. DULLES →LBJ

HELMS → BURRIS →LBJ

Dr. Howard A. Burris, MD | Nashville, TN | Oncology

Howard Burris, Jr. and the Princess

WASHINGTON — Princess Shahrazad Pahlbod, a niece of the shah of Iran, and Howard L. Burris Jr. of Washington were married in Rome on Friday, the Iranian embassy said.

The princess is the daughter of the shah's eldest sister, Princess Shams Pahlavi, and her husband, Minister of Culture Mehrdad Pahlbod. A former student at the Chapin School in New York, she was graduated in 1974 from Washington's Mount Vernon Junior College. Burris, a 1972 Princeton graduate, is the son of a retired Air Force Colonel and a grandson of the late governor of Texas, Beauford H. Jester. They will live in Washington, where Burris will work with his father, a business consultant, and in Teheran.

***Honolulu Star-Bulletin*, Honolulu, Hawaii • Tue, Sep 21, 1976, p. 16.**

pub_site_id=100357191&cj_link_id=11455311&cj_pub_sid=oc5A05L8E_cFrofF6SHThE-ZLrUhzO2XyqSv6Pv83KxS8E-oA14Y-AKzXvorasEJA&cjevent=b89b7488d17211ef83a-339c10a1cb82a) and IICHS - Institute for Iranian Contemporary Historical Studies (http://www.iichs.org/index_en.asp?id=1817&img_cat=110&img_type=0).

380 The Style Section of the *Washington Post*, March 17, 1982: Princess Ashraf Pahlavi, "Faces in a Mirror." This is cited in *The Senator Must Die* (1988), p. 11n. "Helms and the Shah had been schoolmates at Le Rosey in Switzerland: The Rise and Fall of Richard Helms": https://www.rollingstone.com/culture/culture-news/the-rise-and-fall-of-richard-helms-191224/. Incidentally, David Rockefeller was the Shah's banker; he made more loans to Iran than any other US banker. But David had caused the hostage crisis – he persuaded Jimmy Carter to admit the Shah into the US for medical care. Carter complied and so he got his own reward – a loss in his next election (to Reagan during the October Surprise).

Somewhat curiously, Bartholomew reports that David H. Byrd supported the concert pianist Van Cliburn. So did Barbara Jester Burris, the wife of Howard Burris, Sr. I have no idea of how, or if, this is related to the JFK assassination. But then, the age of 23, Cliburn did win the inaugural International Tchaikovsky Competition in Moscow in 1958 during the height of the Cold War.

Bartholomew adds the following morsels. Burris appears in the Baron's address book four times, once as *" Howard Burris/Haiti."* The infamous troopship for the Bay of Pigs was called the *"Barbara J."* Given the relationship between Barbara (née Jester) Burris and Jorge Mas Canosa (a Brigade 2506 veteran), this just might trigger some uplifted eyebrows. Barbara was a fund raiser and supporter of the Cuban American National Foundation run by Jose S. Sorzano. The chairman of the foundation was Jorge Mas Canosa.

During 1954-1957, Burris was attaché to the US embassy in Switzerland.[381]

George de Mohrenschildt (the Baron) received at least two letters from Col. Howard Burris. In addition, in spring 1963, the Baron claimed to know LBJ.[382] The Baron's address book also includes George H. W. "Poppy" Bush (with the nickname)[383] and William Paley (the head of CBS).

According to Robert D. Morrow,[384] in February 1991, Bud Fensterwald[385] arranged *"to interview an Air Force colonel* [likely Delk Simpson]... *who I had identified as the possible bagman (responsible for paying the conspirators) for the JFK assassination."* Morrow told Gus Russo that *"Bud is going to get himself killed"* if he went ahead with this interview. On April 2, 1991, Bernard Fensterwald, 69, died at his home in Alexandria, Virginia. Robert D. Morrow is convinced that Bud was murdered, but his wife insists he died of natural causes, i.e., a heart attack.

Meanwhile, in August 1962, General Burchinal (Howard Burris's superior) became deputy chief of staff for plans and programs for the Joint Chiefs. He held this position until February 1964, so he was in office on 11/22/1963. He soon became director of the Joint Chiefs of Staff.

---

381 That Swiss location must have given Burris access to the Gladio network. Likewise, as a NATO liaison, Delk Simpson surely would have known about Gladio.

382 *The Road to Dallas* (2008) by David Kaiser, pp. 173, 189. George de Mohrenschildt was also the mediator for the CIA in their plan to oust Haitian dictator "Papa Doc" Duvalier: https://spartacus-educational.com/JFKdemohrenschildt.htm.

383 As DCI, George H. W. Bush obfuscated civilian requests for CIA files on Oswald and Ruby; in particular, he downplayed CIA involvement. Bush memoranda show that he was especially interested in what the CIA knew about 11/22/1963 and didn't report to the WC; he was also curious about whether the CIA was complicit in the murder. Clearly, as DCI, Bush must have known that the CIA persistently hid information that refuted the WC verdict (IN THE COMPANY OF FRIENDS) (https://www.cia.gov/readingroom/print/1938068).

384 This Robert Morrow is the author of *First Hand Knowledge: How I Participated in the Cia-Mafia Murder of President Kennedy* (1992). A somewhat different Robert Morrow is currently active on JFK online forums.

385 Bernard Fensterwald - Wikipedia. His clients had been James Earl Ray, James W. McCord Jr., Mitch WerBell, Richard Case Nagell, and John Paisley's widow.

Delk Simpson, Jr. no longer lives, but Dr. Howard Burris, Jr. does. Their fathers were very close, so we would expect that these two sons knew one another rather well. Burris, Jr. was born in 1950, so he was about 13 on 11/22/1963. Delk, Jr. would have been about 10 that day. Especially in view of Delk, Jr.'s knowledge, did these two sons ever discuss events from their fathers' lives? And has anyone lately asked the good doctor – or maybe even Didi (Delk's girlfriend – if she still lives) what Dr. Burris knows?

Here is a remarkably puzzling record from Mary Ferrell's files:

> *Colonel Burris was supposedly the original case officer for Nosenko. When Nosenko defected, Burris was called back to Switzerland. He was the intelligence officer who ran Nosenko in Switzerland in Jan. 1964.*[386]

I have no idea what to make of this. I have found no other source to confirm this. I have only ever encountered Tennant Bagley as Nosenko's case officer. *Help!*

Like his lifelong colleague (Delk Simpson), Howard Burris, Sr. is buried at Arlington National Cemetery.

Lucien Conein (1919-1998)

Lucien Conein ("Black Luigi") was born in Paris, France, but was raised in Kansas. During WW II he served in the French army for a year before switching to the US army. As a native French speaker, he was asked to volunteer for the Office of Strategic Services (OSS) – the predecessor of the CIA. In 1944 he assisted the French Resistance during the Allied landings in Normandy. He worked with a group directed by the OSS; he also assisted the British effort. In effect, at that time he was working and living with the *Corsican Mafia.*[387]

In 1951, Conein and Ted Shackley[388] worked together in Nuremberg. Conein also worked with Bill Harvey in Germany during 1949-1953. In

386 https://quixoticjoust.blogspot.com/2011/10/excerpt-from-manuscript-by-richard.html

387 Lucien Conein - Wikipedia. *"The CIA assistance was channeled to a new Bureau of Narcotics and Dangerous Drugs (BNDD) intelligence office established under Lucien Conein, a veteran CIA covert operations specialist, who boasted of the trust he enjoyed in the Corsican underworld:" (Cocaine Politics: Drugs, Armies, and the CIA in Central America* (1991) by Peter Dale Scott and Jonathan Marshall, p. 28). E. Howard Hunt reported that Corsicans had been recruited as Dealey Plaza gunmen (Talbot 2015, p. 501). Also see *Surprise, Kill, Vanish: The Secret History of CIA Paramilitary Armies, Operators, and Assassins* (2019) by Annie Jacobsen.

388 Shackley was eventually forced out of the CIA in 1979 when a scandal (about the sale of arms) finally exploded and tarnished his reputation (IN THE COMPANY OF FRIENDS, https://www.cia.gov/readingroom/print/1938068). For all of his "heroic" work, he received the Distinguished Intelligence Medal from the CIA. On the other hand, when David Corn interviewed him, Ted answered fewer than 1/5th of Corn's written questions (*Blond Ghost: Ted Shackley and the CIA's Crusades* (1994) by David Corn, pp. 77, 407). Even-

1954, Conein and Lansdale served together in Vietnam. In the late 1950s, he also worked with William Colby (CIA director, 1973-1976) in Vietnam. In 1963, he worked as a liaison officer for Henry Cabot Lodge, Jr. He gave $42,000 to the leader of a military coup, General Dương Văn Minh. In November 1963, Nhu Ngo Dinh Diệm and his younger brother Ngô Đình[389] were assassinated. JFK was stunned, as he had ordered these two fellow Catholics to be airlifted to another country. JFK's orders had been ignored.

Later in 1963, Conein worked with Ted Shackley and William Harvey at JM/WAVE (the CIA station in Miami).[390] Allen Ginsberg described him as *"the crucial person"* in the CIA's link to the Southeast Asian opium trade.[391] He was also closely connected with E. Howard Hunt[392] and Mitchell WerBell,[393] two suspects in the JFK plot. Furthermore, Twyman reports that Conein and WerBell had a working relationship with Carlos Marcello.[394] Gerald Patrick Hemming (more below) claimed that if you wanted to understand the JFK assassination, you should just take a close look at Mitchell Livingston WerBell. Mitchell's specialty was assassination weapons, including silencers. His machine

---

tually, in a fit of justice delayed, Mother Nature caught up with Ted – by repaying him with cancer. Soon after this, he died at his home in *Bethesda, MD*.

389 Alfred McCoy has shown that these two brothers got rich by trading dope. But this was quite typical – other US-backed Vietnamese leaders did the same. Opium was regularly flown out by the CIA's Air America (formerly Civil Air Transport) and so the Montagnard villages flourished – without US taxpayer dollars. As Wilfred P. Deac explained, *"Their mission was to get people to fight against communism, not to stop the drug traffic"* (Kwitny, p. 50-51).

Before being flown home, the bodies of GIs were cut open, gutted, and then filled with up to 50# of heroin. This priceless item was then tagged with an ID number, so that these hard-working officers could claim their just reward, e.g., at Norton Air Force Base, just down the street from where I would soon work at the Loma Linda University Medical Center (Kwitny, p. 52).

390 In 1974, Victor Marchetti reported that the CIA's covert operations utilized 2/3 of CIA's total budget of about one billion dollars per year. An additional $5 billion (for covert operations) was hidden inside other federal agencies. Victor noted that these operations employed 11,300 of the 16,500 total CIA employees. But this did not include employees of contract companies or of proprietary companies – which may have been double the aforementioned size (*The Cult of Intelligence* (1974) by Victor Marchetti).

391 Lucien Conein - Wikipedia

392 *Bond of Secrecy: My Life with CIA Spy and Watergate Conspirator, E. Howard Hunt* (2012) by Saint John Hunt.

393 Mitchell WerBell - "The Man Who Was Involved in Everything" | The Vintage News (https://www.thevintagenews.com/2018/10/17/mitchell-werbell/). WerBell was a notorious arms dealer. He had worked with Helliwell during WW II, specifically with the OSS China section (Lernoux, p. 158).

WerBell → Helliwell → Colby → Allen Dulles → LBJ

394 Twyman, p. 701.

guns were said to be quieter than an IBM Selectric typewriter. A pulp magazine once described Mitch as *"The Wizard of Whispering Death"* (Hinckle and Turner, p. 393). In November 1963, Conein gave the green light for Diệm's assassination; as a result, Lansdale became furious. (Diệm and Lansdale were friends.) Hemming had his own connections as well.[395] He once pitched Clint Murchison, Jr. and Nelson Bunker Hunt and Gordon McLendon for donations to his (Gerry's) organization Interpen. So, we can now imagine these three chains...

CORSICAN MAFIA →CONEIN → LANSDALE → C. CABELL → E. CABELL →LBJ

MARCELLO → CONEIN (± WERBELL) → HARVEY → HELMS → LBJ

HEMMING → MURCHISON → CLARK → LBJ

Like many of his colleagues in this case, Conein is buried at Arlington National Cemetery.

PAUL HELLIWELL (1915-1976)[396]

Richard Goodwin

Paul Helliwell

David Burchinal

Billie Sol Estes

In China during WW II (and then afterwards), Paul Helliwell's immediate boss was William Donovan. He also worked with Ray S. Cline, Richard Helms (CIA director, 1966-1973), E. Howard Hunt, Jake Esterline, Mitchell WerBell, John K. Singlaub, Jack Anderson, Robert Emmett Johnson and Lucien Conein. Astute readers will recognize many CIA names here – so Paul clearly knew the CIA folks who mattered. In 1943, Colonel Paul Helliwell became head of the Secret Intelligence Branch of the OSS in

395 An EX-CIA Man's Stunning Revelations On "The Company," JFK's Murder, And The Plot To (https://www.latinamericanstudies.org/belligerence/argosy-hemming.htm). Twyman marveled at the incredibly numerous connections that Hemming possessed – more than any other character in this case, e.g., Angleton, Harvey, Giancana, Nicoletti, Trafficante, Martino, Pawley (Twyman, p. 681).

396 paul helliwell wiki - Search

Europe. In 1945, Helliwell was replaced in this post by William Casey (CIA director, 1981-1987). In 1947, Paul joined the CIA in its debut year, as did Bill Harvey and Winston Scott and J. Walton Moore. So, we can picture…

CONEIN → HELLIWELL → HELMS →LBJ

E. HOWARD HUNT → HELLIWELL → HELMS → LBJ

WERBELL → CONEIN → CLINE → HELMS →LBJ

CONEIN → CASEY → WIN SCOTT → LBJ

In 1960, Paul Helliwell was transferred in order to provide business cover for the CIA's Cuban operations. According to Peter Dale Scott,[397] Helliwell worked with E. Howard Hunt, Mitch WerBell and Lucien Conein to develop relationships with drug-dealing, anti-Castro Cuban veterans of the Bay of Pigs invasion. Helliwell met Ted Shackley (head of the Miami CIA station) and Thomas G. Clines during this time. Paul later became CIA paymaster for JM/WAVE, where David Morales was second in command. So, consider this option…

MORALES → HELLIWELL → HELMS → LBJ

According to Daniel Hopsicker,[398] Helliwell ran Red Sunset Enterprises in Miami. Hopsicker claims it was a CIA front company for recruiting frogmen and explosives experts for Operation Mongoose, which was led by Ed Lansdale and Bill Harvey; both were in Washington, DC, at the same time.[399]

HARVEY (± LANSDALE) → HELLIWELL → HELMS → LBJ

LANSDALE → C. CABELL → HELMS → LBJ

397 *The Iran-Contra Connection: Secret Teams and Covert Operations in Reagan Era* (1987) by Jonathan Marshall, Peter Dale Scott, et al. I do not know if Peter Dale Scott and Winston Scott are related, but Peter is a former diplomat and Winston might have fancied himself as one. Someone should ask Peter.

398 *Barry and the 'boys'* (2001, 2006, 2016) by Daniel Hopsicker, p. 358. Hopsicker reports that the Fontainebleau Hotel in Miami often hosted meetings that included Robert Maheu, Trafficante, Giancana, Roselli, Bill Harvey, and Lansky (p. 357). Robert Aime Maheu (1917–2008) had worked both for the FBI and the CIA, but also for Howard Hughes, so he was ideally situated to facilitate connections.

Trafficante → Maheu → Harvey (± Lansdale) → C. Cabell → Burris → LBJ

Lansky → Roselli → Harvey → Lansdale → C. Cabell → Burris → LBJ

399 On Nov 21, 1961, JFK, RFK, John McCone, Richard Goodwin, and Lansdale met to discuss plans for Operation Mongoose. RFK stressed the importance of immediate dynamic action to discredit the Castro regime. JFK officially authorized this on November 30, 1961. Burris would also have been in DC at the time – as LBJ's military aide.

A Mongoose loose in Cuba

Helliwell helped to set up Civil Air Transport and Castle Bank & Trust; both were CIA proprietary companies.[400] He was also president of the Castle & Trust Bank, which was convenient for transferring illicit funds.[401] So, here are four more options…

Helliwell → Shackley → Helms → LBJ

Helliwell → E. H. Hunt → Helms → LBJ

Helliwell → Conein (± Cline) → LBJ

Morales → Shackley → Helms → LBJ

400 *Cocaine Politics: Drugs, Armies, and the CIA in Central America* (1991) by Peter Dale Scott and Jonathan Marshall, p. 92. One of the chief sites of money laundering was in Chiang Mai in northern Thailand. Here was a colorful market for the drug crop grown in the local mountains. Like Newcastle is known for coal, or Chicago for cattle, Chiang Mai is known for dope. The local Nugan Hand bank office was located in the same suite as the DEA. The DEA receptionist even answered the telephone for the bank when necessary (Kwitny, p. 207). When the Castle Bank went under, the Nugan Hand bank assumed its role. William Colby provided their legal services (Kwitny, pp. 13, 71-74, 290-291). When Francis John Nugan was found dead (in Australia) in his Mercedes, Colby's card was found in his pocket (Kwitny, pp. 20-21). Ironically, William Colby himself was later murdered – and never finished his dinner. Regarding William Colby, see "The Man Nobody Knew: In Search of My Father, CIA Spymaster William Colby" | HuffPost Latest News (https://www.huffpost.com/entry/william-colby_b_970620).

401 The Castle Bank & Trust was located in Nassau. According to a government official close to the case, *"The CIA convinced Justice that exposure of Castle…and other Helliwell dealings, would compromise very sensitive and very significant intelligence operations"* (Hinckle and Turner, p. 387). Also see Lernoux, pp. 77-79, 83-94. The Pritzker family of Illinois was the primary investor, but others included Hugh Hefner, Tony Curtis, Robert Guccione, and Chiang Kai-shek's daughter. It would be interesting to ask the current Illinois governor, Jay Robert Pritzker, what he knows about this.

According to Paul Williams, Helliwell was legal counsel to Santo Trafficante,[402] but – incredibly – he also served as adviser to LBJ![403] He and Tommy "the Cork" Corcoran were two of the closest advisors to Senator LBJ. In case this seems dubious, here is the actual page:[404]

> In those years Helliwell was also the Thai consul in Miami. The consulate operated out of his offices; its registered foreign lobbyist was Washington lawyer James Rowe. And Rowe's partner was the more powerful lobbyist Tommy "The Cork" Corcoran, who at United Fruit's behest had helped trigger the CIA's overthrow of the Arbenz government in Guatemala. Corcoran also represented Chiang Kai-shek's relatives and the Civil Air Transport, a CIA front that, like Sea Supply, was involved in the Asian opium trade. At the time Helliwell employed Rowe, he and Corcoran were two of the closest advisers to Lyndon Baines Johnson, the rapidly rising Senate majority leader.[3]

Trafficante → Helliwell → LBJ

Helliwell later worked as a Miami lawyer and served as legal counsel to a Panamanian holding company that controlled a Bahamian gambling casino linked to Meyer Lansky. He also promoted land rackets associated with Lansky.[405] Furthermore, he knew Lucky Luciano[406] and Meyer Lansky.[407]

Lansky → Helliwell → LBJ

Luciano (± Lansky) → Helliwell →LBJ

Curiously, Tim Weiner omitted Helliwell from his *Legacy of Ashes* (2008). [That title was based on Ike's quote, which was cited above.] This omission (of Helliwell) may be one reason that so little seems known

402 In 1952, Santo Trafficante, Sr., turned his Havana concessions over to Santo Trafficante, Jr. After 1954, when the father died, the son became the Mafia boss of Florida. So junior inherited Lucky Luciano's heroin network.

403 *Operation Gladio: The Unholy Alliance between the Vatican, the CIA, and the Mafia* (2018) by Paul Williams, p. 146.

404 *The Great Heroin Coup* (1981) by Henrik Kruger, p. 131; also see *The War Conspiracy* (1972) by Peter Dale Scott, pp. 210-212.

405 Lernoux, p. 82.

406 In 1936, Lucky was not so lucky; Thomas Dewey locked him up. But Lucky was promised his release after WW II for his assistance with the Allied landings on Sicily. According to the *Chicago Tribune*, this is the same Dewey who (along with his VP- candidate *Earl Warren*) defeated Truman in the POTUS election of 1948: chicago tribune dewey defeats truman - Search

407 Lansky also knew Frank Sinatra. Once he gave Frank two kilos of heroin so that Sinatra would have a little "walking around" money" (Hopsicker, p. 168). But Frank never sang about this.

about Helliwell in this JFK case. Of course, readers of Lernoux's book (1984) knew otherwise, as Paul is featured there.[408] Penny emphasizes Paul's intellectual brilliance and also the fact that he was never charged with a crime. Although most of us would never boast about such a feat (i.e., no crimes), Helliwell had good reasons to boast.

Helliwell knew Bill Donovan (head of the OSS during WW II),[409] Angleton, Allen Dulles, and Sir William Stephenson;[410] they were all involved in opium sales. *"Donovan, Angleton, and Dulles viewed Helliwell's proposal* [to sell opium] *as answered prayer."* As a result of this new adventure, black musicians (especially in New York City) became addicted to heroin – but they did not regard this as answered prayer. (This was well before 1996, when Gary Webb published his "Dark Alliance" series in the *San Jose Mercury News.*) So, consider this…

ANGLETON (± ALLEN DULLES) → HELLIWELL → LBJ

Helliwell was a busy guy. He secretly purchased 27,000 acres for the Disney world resort. His law firm also advised Resorts International, which was linked to Eddie Cellini (a top Lansky associate), Robert Vesco, Howard Hughes, Bebe Rebozo, and Richard Nixon (yes, our POTUS).[411]

Also recall that, during WW II, "Wild Bill" Donovan and Luciano cooperated in Operation Husky.[412] Alfred McCoy[413] documents Donovan's

408 *In Banks We Trust – Bankers and Their Close Associates: the CIA, the Mafia, Drug-traders, Dictators, Politicians, and the Vatican* (1984) by Penny Lernoux.

409 A decorated veteran of World War I, Donovan is apparently the only person to deserve all four of the major decorations: the Medal of Honor, the Distinguished Service Cross, the Distinguished Service Medal, and the National Security Medal. He also got a Silver Star and Purple Heart, so he could never be called heartless. His character had been played in the 1940 Warner Brothers film, *The Fighting 69th*. Eventually, there were so many aristocrats in the OSS that it became known as "Oh, So Social." As just one example, Donovan was a classmate of FDR at Columbia Law. "Wild Bill" had also shared a box with Hitler at the 1936 Olympics (so did Inga Arvad, JFK's later mistress) and – unbelievably – Bill had been in contact with Rudoph Hess before his mysterious flight to England in 1941!

410 William Stephenson - Wikipedia.

411 Lernoux, p. 83.

412 Paul Williams, pp. 31, 37, 38. 42. New York crime boss, Vito Genovese, was right-hand man to Luciano. Also note the CIA-Mafia connection on p. 41 of the book by Williams. In particular, James Angleton would mediate any legal issues between the mob and the CIA via New York lawyer, Mario Brod.

Mafia → Angleton → Helms → LBJ

413 *The Politics of Heroin in Southeast Asia* (1972) by Alfred W. McCoy, p. 7. McCoy is the Fred Harvey Harrington Professor of History at my undergraduate alma mater, the UW-Madison. He wrote, *"The State Department provides unconditional support for corrupt governments openly engaged in the drug traffic."*

McCoy showed how opium production by CIA-backed warlords increased tenfold in a short period after the CIA moved in – and how heroin distribution to the West was facilitat-

reasoning: *"...any ally was welcome and any means was justified"* to fight communism. To appreciate the depth of this illicit commitment note that, during 1947-1967, no drug busts occurred, even though the number of addicts soared from 20,000 to 150,000! Later, Lucien Conein obtained an arrangement whereby the DEA would claim that any CIA asset busted for narcotics smuggling would be described as involved a deep-cover "investigation." In 1972, Nixon had appointed Conein to the DEA's Special Operations Group; this was designed as an international network to smash the drug trade (presumably Conein's WWII experience with the Corsicans had made him an expert); so, he collected a group of anti-Castro Cubans for this purpose...

Anti-Castro Cubans →Conein → Lansdale → C. Cabell → Burris → LBJ

---

ed by the Sicilian and Corsican Mafias' intelligence connections in Palermo and Marseilles (McCoy, p. 4). See the drawing below of Barthelemy Guérini, the Marseilles criminal leader, who captured control of that city's waterfront (from the Communist party) with the support of the CIA during 1950-1951. He was later sentenced to 20 years for a murder.

During WW II, the OSS supported Antoine Guérini (and his 3 brothers – Barthelemy, Francois and Pascal) and their allies who were fighting the Nazis in the south of France. After the war, the CIA funneled millions of dollars to the Guerini organization to fight the communist labor unions (especially on the Marseille docks). Guerini was also connected to the American Mafia, especially through Mexico City and Montreal; his illegal drugs were shipped to those sites from France. Two of Guerini's American allies were Carlo Gambino and Santo Trafficante (Kross, Kindle, 5579). For even more details about these criminals and their connection to American intelligence, read Twyman, Chapter 20.

Trial of Barthélémy, Pascal and François Guérini. Marseille, January 1969 (drawing by Calvi).

McCoy reported that South Vietnam's President Nguyễn Văn Thiệu, Vice President Nguyễn Cao Kỳ, and Prime Minister Trần Thiện Khiêm led a narcotics ring with ties to the Corsican mafia, the Trafficante crime family in Florida, and other high level military officials in South Vietnam, Cambodia, Laos, and Thailand. Those implicated by McCoy included Laotian Generals Ouane Rattikone and Vang Pao (see his photograph in this book) and South Vietnamese Generals Đặng Văn Quang and Ngô Dzu. He told a congressional subcommittee that these military officials facilitated the distribution of heroin to American troops in Vietnam and to addicts in the US. McCoy stated that the CIA chartered Air America aircraft and helicopters in northern Laos to transport opium harvested by their "tribal mercenaries." He also accused US Ambassador to Laos (G. McMurtrie Godley) of blocking the assignment of Bureau of Narcotics officials to Laos in order to maintain the Laotian government's cooperation in military and political matters (Alfred W. McCoy - Wikipedia).

Angleton[414] swore allegiance to the Holy Mother Church and became knighted by the Sovereign Military Order of Malta (SMOM).[415] Also knighted were William Casey, William Colby, John McCone (JFK's appointee as CIA director, 1961-1965), Vernon Walters (CIA Deputy Director, 1985-1989), William Buckley, Alexander Haig, and Bill Donovan.[416] Believe it or not, so was former Nazi, Richard Gehlen![417] As a result, we can now add another possible conduit…

GEHLEN → ANGLETON → ALLEN DULLES → LBJ

COLONEL FRANK "BRANDY" BRANDSTETTER (1912-2011)[418]

[The following comments are paraphrased from the biography by Carlisle – see the prior footnote.] Frank was born in Bratislava

414 Via his unrelenting molehunts, Angleton had poisoned the CIA from top to bottom so that William Colby had to force him to retire in 1974 (Weiner, pp. 276-277). Also see The mystery of disgraced CIA spymaster James Angleton's "retirement" • MuckRock (https://www.muckrock.com/news/archives/2017/oct/19/angleton-return/). Because of Jim's persistently reckless behavior, Congress was forced to pass the Mole Relief Act. Jim had destroyed the careers of at least 14 innocent CIA employees: "C.I.A. Dug for Moles but Buried the Loyal" - *The New York Times.*

415 These "knights" were linked to the Vatican secret services and to the Italian Mafia.

416 After he retired from the OSS (in late 1945), Donovan formed the World Commerce Corporation (WCC) with Nelson Rockefeller, Joseph C. Grew (nephew of J. P. Morgan), Alfred DuPont, and Charles Hambro (of the Hambros Bank). WCC was registered in Panama; it employed a mob figure (Satiris "Sonny" Galahad Fassoulis), who was also an international arms dealer (Fassoulis, Satiris "Sonny" | Air Forces Escape & Evasion Society) (https://airforceescape.org/afees-in-memoriam-obituaries/in-memoriam/fassoulis-satiris-sonny/#:~:text=%25E2%2580%259CSonny%25E2%2580%259D%2520Fassoulis%2520was). WCC provided services to Chiang Kai-shek's army; they did this by buying and selling surplus US weapons and munitions to underworld groups, including the Italian Mafia. In exchange, the national Chinese army provided the opium that helped to create the CIA (Paul Williams, pp. 56-57), thus saving American taxpayers millions of dollars. (I wonder if some of these funds went to the CIA account at Schroder's bank, which was controlled by Allen Dulles.) See the profound analysis by Peter Dale Scott: "Operation Paper: The US and Drugs in Thailand and Burma," *The Asia Pacific Journal*, 2008. Also see Sterling and Peggy Seagrave, p. 324.

N. Rockefeller → Donovan → Allen Dulles → LBJ

When Nelson Rockefeller ran for POTUS, he hand-picked the following men to assist him: Walt Rostow, Dean Rusk, Roswell Gilpatric, Edward Lansdale, Paul Nitze, Harland Cleveland, Roger Hilsman, Lincoln Gordon, Adolf Berle, McGeorge Bundy, and Henry Kissinger. All came directly from the Rockefeller Brothers' Special Studies Project. "What Did Otto Otepka Know About Oswald and the CIA?" (https://www.kennedysandking.com/john-f-kennedy-articles/what-did-otto-otepka-know-about-oswald-and-the-cia). Kissinger, in particular, spent many years subsisting on handouts from Rockefeller.

417 Reinhard Gehlen - Wikipedia. When ex-Nazi Richard Gehlen finally retired in 1968, Allen Dulles gave him an expensive Swiss chalet! (Twyman, p. 569.)

418 *Brandy, Our Man in Acapulco: The Life and Times of Colonel Frank M. Brandstetter* (1999) by Rodney P. Carlisle and Dominic J. Monetta.

into the Austrian-Hungarian nobility, but then he deserted that fine life to relocate to the United States, ironically as a penniless, teenaged *nobleman*. He volunteered for the US army in 1940. His knowledge of customs, traditions and fluency with Hungarian, Romanian, Austrian, Czech and German made him ideal for a career in intelligence.

After graduating from the US Army Intelligence School, he was trained by British military intelligence before he parachuted with the 506th Airborne Infantry Regiment on D-Day and led his IPW (Interrogation of Prisoners of War) team into WW II. He served General Matthew B. Ridgway as his trusted aide while with the XVIII Airborne Corps until the end of the war; later he served with General Ridgway in the Mediterranean Theater of Operations. His awards include the Silver Star and the Bronze Star.

Whether foiling a mass breakout plot by German POWs in England during WW II or leading a small party on a dangerous mission behind German lines (to deliver a surrender demand from Ridgway to Field Marshall Walter Model) or parachuting into battle on D-Day or confronting an angry Cuban mob that planned to destroy the Havana Hilton – Brandstetter evoked the highest commendations from all parties. Ridgway praised him as a *"man of unimpeachable integrity, and personal physical and moral courage to the highest degree."*

Brandy spent 40 years as a US Army Reservist, frequently assisting the Office of the Army Chief of Staff for Intelligence (ACSI), the Defense Intelligence Agency (DIA), the FBI, and the CIA. Unofficially, he provided reconnaissance (often at his own expense) for services in China, Greece, Cyprus, Morocco, South Africa, Spain, Argentina, Yugoslavia, and many other hot spots, especially whenever security threats emerged. [End of Carlisle biography.] Some researchers believe that one of the security threats that Brandy perceived was JFK's plan to stop the Cold War. More discussion follows below.

Crichton's collaborator in the 1950s study,[419] fellow 488th member Lt. Col. Frank Brandstetter, was in turn a friend to these men: David Phillips, Gordon McLendon, George de Mohrenschildt, and Philippe Thyraud de Vosjoli. Phillips had known Brandstetter since the 1950s, when both worked together in Havana. Gordon McLendon (the wealthy Dallas businessman) was cited by Jack Ruby as one of his six closest friends, a relationship that Gordon seemed reluctant to acknowledge.[420]

---

419 JFKcountercoup: Col. Frank M. Brandstetter (https://jfkcountercoup.blogspot.com/2010/11/col-frank-m-brandstetter.html).

420 20 WH 39 [WC Hearings, Volume 20, p. 39].

Brandy was also close to Sam Kail, the Army Intelligence person who coordinated George de Mohrenschildt's April 1963 visit with the CIA (and with Army Intelligence) in DC (after which the Baron landed in Haiti and became an active foe of Papa Doc).

Later in life, Brandy founded and operated the Las Brisas Resort in Acapulco, by turning a few undeveloped casitas into the top resort in the world by 1972.[421]

Philippe Thyraud de Vosjoli was a French intelligence (SDECE) agent who worked closely with Angleton in DC.[422] On 11/22/1963, de Vosjoli was reportedly panicked by JFK's murder, so he packed a few clothes and a few Gauloises, and then made a beeline for Brandstetter in Acapulco.[423] (We can only wonder how many other folks did precisely that.) In any case, de Vosjoli explained that he feared for his life (although he was probably more frightened of his own colleagues in the SDECE than he was about the JFK murder). The point is that Brandy was clearly in the loop – i.e., someone close to Angleton knew where to hide.

While enjoying Acapulco, de Vosjoli ran into Leon Uris, the novelist. Together they published a novel (*Topaz*, 1967), which became an international best seller. Thus the SDECE learned that de Vosjoli was still alive. Later Alfred Hitchcock turned this novel into a movie, which portrayed de Vosjoli, Angleton, and Golitsyn.[424]

According to Peter Dale Scott, Brandy had urged David Phillips to expand his group so that it included not just the CIA but also officers from other intelligence services. Gordon McLendon's best friend conveniently was Frank Brandstetter. When Brandy married his second wife, Marianne Porzelt, on December 26, 1978, the best men were Gordon McLendon and the ex-President of Mexico, Miguel Aleman.

---

421 FRANK BRANDSTETTER Obituary (2011) - New York, NY - *New York Times.*

422 The SDECE is the French counterpart to the CIA. Alfred McCoy notes that during the First Indochina War (1947-1954), the French were desperate to fund their intelligence services. So, they contacted the local opium producers in the Golden Triangle and created an international smuggling ring, which came to be known as the French Connection. This specifically included the Corsican Mafia ("The Politics of Heroin in Southeast Asia" - Wikipedia). So, the US intelligence services got into this game rather late, but de Vosjoli could have told Angleton all about it.

423 JFKCountercoup2: ACSI - Assistant Chief of Staff for Intelligence, USAR (https://jfkcountercoup2.blogspot.com/2014/03/acsi-assistant-chief-of-staff-for.html). Also see *Cold Warrior* by Tom Mangold (1992), pp. 131-133.

424 Mangold, p. 112-113. De Vosjoli makes one final comment: *"Listen, I'll tell you something. In the world of intelligence you have a lot of sick people. They cannot tell the truth."* Angleton would have agreed with his friend. See Appendix II-D below on Angleton.

Brandy routinely supplied the government with information on Frank Sinatra, Jimmy Hoffa, Sam Giancana, Morris Dalitz, Roy Cohn and others.[425]

While David Morales operated from the US Embassy in Havana, Brandy was an employee of the Hilton Hotel in Havana. Morales often met with Brandy, and sometimes with June Cobb, who was a public relations aide to Castro. Brandy was also quite close to Sam Kail (CIA), who was in the embassy with Morales. In addition, while in Havana, George Lumpkin became a good friend of both men. Lumpkin, of course, was later Deputy Chief of Police in Dallas. In 1963, he rode in the pilot car during the Dallas motorcade.[426] (Lumpkin also commanded the 488th US Army Reserve Intelligence unit.) Brandy was also very close to David Phillips (who was undercover in Havana at that time) and to Warren Broglie; Warren and Brandy later worked together in the hotel business in Mexico.[427]

Lumpkin →Brandstetter → Morales → Harvey → Helms → LBJ

Lumpkin was also close to Jack Crichton, who was Lumpkin's superior in the same military reserve division. Dallas police officers constituted about half of the entire unit.[428] Also note that "Dry Hole" Byrd was the Director of Crichton's Dorchester Gas Producing Company.[429] The LBJ Library contains several letters to Crichton from LBJ (1954-1960); these compliment him and promise to assist his efforts for the reserves.

Crichton → LBJ

Peter Dale Scott calls Brandy *"the connector."* Besides his friendships with Phillips, McLendon, Crichton, and Lumpkin – Brandy also knew FBI agent Vincent Drain rather well. Drain had been assigned permanently to the Dallas Field Office, conveniently before 11/22/1963. He accompanied all of the Oswald evidence while it was airborne to DC.[430]

---

425 *A Secret Order* (2013) by H. P. Albarelli, pp. 244-245. Also see "Frank Brandstetter Obituary," *The New York Times*, August 21, 2011.

426 Lumpkin had insisted on the dogleg turn at Houston and Elm. He also had received supervisor Roy Truly's list of employees at the TSBD, with Oswald's name on top – and with Ruth Paine's address. Douglas Horne told Oliver Stone that Roy Truly was not listed as an official employee, which raises a question about his intelligence connections. Incidentally (or maybe not), Roy was cousin to Fred Korth (Tatro, November 2023, p. 103).

427 Ibid.

428 Listen to the online speech by Peter Dale Scott for COPA in 2010. Type into a search engine: *"Peter Dale Scott, COPA speech, 2010."*

429 Ibid.

430 The Dallas police had taken five rolls of film to picture the 455 Oswald evidence items. These were also numbered and inventoried. When these items were returned to Dallas, none of the photographs – or any of the original five rolls of film – were included.

On 11/21/1963, Brandy had conducted a seminar in Dallas. While there, he got a telephone call from Drain; they were to discuss the bubbletop on JFK's limousine. A note appears in Albarelli's book that refers to a Dallas meeting on 11/20/1963:*"Frank B. here."*[431] According to Bertram Gross, *"Gerry Patrick Hemming says that Frank M. Brandstetter met with H. L. Hunt, Clint Murchison and Gordon McLendon on 11/21/1963."*[432]

On May 2, 1984, J. Gary Shaw met with Henry Hurt, who had interviewed Vincent Drain for three hours. Shaw's notes describe Drain as a close friend of J. Edgar Hoover and Cartha DeLoach (recall that Drain was FBI), as well as Sam Rayburn. Drain told Hurt that he had carved his initials deep into the stock of the supposed murder weapon. But when the weapon was returned to Dallas from the FBI, his initials had magically vanished! Drain concluded that it was not the same weapon.

Brandy was also close friends with Cartha DeLoach, who had seen the initial Zapruder film and described JFK as going *forward* (so did Dan Rather), contrary to the head snap seen in the extant film. But Brandy also knew the man who seemed to know everyone – it was the Baron! For example, the Baron knew LBJ, G. H. W. Bush, Oswald, Burris, and Murchison. There was once a plan to replace Papa Doc with Clemard Joseph Charles, who was the Baron's business partner. Incidentally (and probably not a surprise), G. H. W. Bush was also a good friend of Brandy.[433]

Before we leave Brandy, think about this: Brandy had at least one "one-on-one" meeting with LBJ in the White House. Tatro also reports that LBJ and his family often spent extended time at Brandy's Acapulco resort.[434] Conveniently, this required that Brandy become familiar with the security measures of the SS. (Has Vince Palamara reported on this? On

John Armstrong believes that the third mystery (spent) shell was surreptitiously inserted into evidence after the fact by Vincent Drain. Tatro muses that such an action was a "real drain" on the entire case. Drain may also have placed Oswald's palm print on the weapon (by visiting the funeral home and lifting it from Oswald's corpse). In fact, FBI agent Richard Harrison described Drain as personally driving to the funeral home (Tatro, November 2023, p. 106).

431 *Coup in Dallas: The Decisive Investigation into Who Killed JFK* (2021) by H.P. Albarelli, Jr., with Leslie Sharp and Alan Kent, pp. ix, 162, 360-361.

432 This information is from Ed Tatro, November 2023, p. 104. In turn he cites J. Gary Shaw as quoting Bertram Gross in his book, *Friendly Fascism*: [PDF] Friendly Fascism by Bertram Gross | 9781497689404 (https://www.perlego.com/book/2427522/friendly-fascism-the-new-face-of-power-in-america-pdf?campaignid=436439430&adgroup). As a disclaimer, this is one of the very few JFK books I have not read. (My wife thinks I have already read enough.)

433 Tatro, November 2023, p. 111.

434 Tatro (Ibid., p. 112) provides the source: Peter Dale Scott, in an online text: Dallas '63: The First Deep State Revolt Against the White House.

the other hand, Vince has reported on Douglas Dillon's WW II service for the OSS.) Brandy also reportedly told LBJ about his interactions with de Vosjoli and with Sam Kail. Finally, Lady Bird and Lynda Bird spent considerable time at the Brandstetter's home in Acapulco while they visited the Space Museum at Casa de la Tranquilidad.[435]

Like so many other enemies of JFK, Brandy is buried at Arlington National Cemetery.

Operation Gladio

Operation Gladio was the codename for clandestine "stay-behind" operations of armed resistance organized in 1948 by the Western Union, and subsequently subsumed by NATO (formed in 1949) and by the CIA (established in 1947).[436]

In 1963, when JFK fired Lyman Lemnitzer from his position as Chief of Staff for the Joint Chiefs, he unwisely made him head of NATO (in Europe). This meant that Lemnitzer had immediate access to Gladio's clandestine and terrorist activities – as well as its connection to the *Corsicans.*[437]

NATO → Gladio → Lemnitzer → Burris → LBJ

Corsicans → Gladio → Lemnitzer → Willoughby → H. L. Hunt → Clark → LBJ

Gladio → Angleton → Helms → LBJ

In Italy, Angleton rescued and recruited fascists who later served in Operation Gladio. One was Prince Junio Valerio Borghese (aka "The Black Prince"), commander of a campaign that murdered hundreds of Italian communists who had fought against Mussolini.

---

435 *Brandy--Our Man in Acapulco: The Life and Times of Colonel Frank M. Brandstetter* (1999) by Rodney P. Carlisle and Dominic J. Monetta, p. 235.

436 This was the same year as the Whittaker Chambers-Alger Hiss hullabaloo; HUAC had also cited the Hollywood Ten that year. Some readers may also recall 1947 because of Jackie Robinson, the Roswell incident, the Mt. Rainier UFO sightings, the Marshall Plan, the partition of India, the crash landing of the Kon-Tiki, the transistor's first demonstration, or the passage of the National Security Act. Paul Helliwell, J. Walton Moore, William Robertson, and William King Harvey also joined the CIA that year. Furthermore, Winston Scott became the CIA's first London station chief in 1947. And then my sister Sharon was born! (See Medical-Surgical Nursing - E-Book - Elsevier eLibrary.) (https://www.elsevier-elibrary.com/product/medicalsurgical-nursing-ebook). Oh, I almost forgot: Jack Ruby was an alumnus of the Chicago mob, class of 1947. So, Jack and Sam Giancana had been confrères in Chicago (Hinckle and Turner, p. 246).

437 For further discussion of Corsicans, see Stephen Rivele (https://spartacus-educational.com/JFKrivele.htm).

Later, Prince Borghese, *"in close collaboration with the CIA in Rome on the night of December 7, 1970, started the ... right-wing Gladio coup d'état in Italy, code-named Tora Tora"* (now known as the Borghese coup).[438]

Angleton became the key American figure controlling all right wing and neofascist political and paramilitary groups in Italy in the postwar period.[439]

Borghese → Angleton → Allen Dulles → LBJ

In 1964, Harvey recommended Colonel Renzo Rocca, Chief of the Italian Military Intelligence Division R, as liaison for building up the Italian Gladio network.[440] Harvey cooperated closely with CIA secret warfare expert Vernon Walters,[441] and with Renzo Rocca (Director of the Gladio units within the military secret service (SID)), and with Giovanni De Lorenzo – to escalate the secret war.[442]

Renzo Rocco → Harvey → Walters →Allen Dulles → Burris →LBJ

Once de Gaulle was informed (by 1966) about the secret Gladio network, he decided to remove France from the military side of NATO. In 1967, he evicted NATO from Paris in order to regain *"full sovereignty* [over] *French territory."*[443]

Allen Dulles reported to JFK:

---

438 *NATO's Secret Armies: Operation Gladio and Terrorism in Western Europe* (2005) by Daniele Ganser, p. 76.

439 Chapter 12 – "The Assassination of JFK, Gladio and Israel – The Terrorism Business" | by Brendan Devenney | Medium (https://medium.com/@dubhelloco/chapter-12-the-assassination-of-jfk-gladio-and-israel-the-terrorism-business-d26129f9bca2)

440 "Democratic State vs. Deep State: Approaching the Dual State of the West" by Ola Tunander. Peace Research Institute Oslo (2008).

441 During the fallout from Watergate, General Vernon Walters (CIA) ricocheted between Richard Helms and John Dean; but the CIA eventually won this battle and the agency ousted their old foe (Nixon) from the White House. [See *Silent Coup: The Removal of a President* (1991) by Len Colodny and Robert Gettlin; also read Hopsicker, pp. 178-179]. Nixon was a bit like my character (a special projects coordinator for the FBI), where the protagonist claims, *"Guys like Mantik can ruin careers"* (*The Last Corpse* (2023), a novel by Walt Brown (my JFK colleague), p. 149). More seriously, see Walt's "Master Chronology of the JFK Assassination," available on CD. Most likely, the CIA's major disagreement with Nixon (with the possible serious exception of détente with China) was over the control of drugs. Nixon tried to bring drug control into the White House (using Conein), but that would have shattered the CIA's prodigious profits from drug running. So, the CIA took serious notice of this attempt by Nixon to monopolize the drug market (Hopsicker, pp. 164, 195). G. H. W. Bush also paid attention; see *The Mafia, CIA & George Bush* (1992) by Peter Brewton.

442 Ganser 2005, Kindle. Renzo Rocca used this Gladio army to bomb newspapers and then blame the left, so as to discredit the communists and socialists.

443 Chapter 12 – The Assassination of JFK, Gladio and Israel – The Terrorism Business | by Brendan Devenney | Medium

> *At least 80 percent of the [French] officers are violently against him [de Gaulle]. They haven't forgotten that in 1958, he had given his word of honor that he would never abandon Algeria. He is now reneging on his promise, and they hate him for that. De Gaulle surely won't last if he tries to let go of Algeria. Everything will probably be over for him by the end of the year – he will be either deposed or assassinated.*[444]

The last known attempt to kill de Gaulle (July 1, 1966) occurred when he moved to expel NATO; at that moment, he was en route to Orly Airport to visit the Soviet Union.[445]

During a 1990 interview with Admiral Pierre Lacoste, the French chief of the secret services (DGSE), claimed the de Gaulle assassination attempts were orchestrated by members of the Gladio network.[446] F. Mark Wyatt,[447] an *acting* chief of station in Rome in the 1960s, who attended a secret CIA training camp for Gladio soldiers in Sardinia, says he believes the program was valid and important in its early days. But, he adds, *"in the sixties, the danger of Soviet invasion had lessened to the*

---

444 Ibid. JFK had spoken out incredibly early in favor of Algerian independence, thus promptly earning the scorn of right-wing French militarists, the OAS in particular. Ike also strongly disapproved of JFK's speeches on Algerian independence (*Odeal in Africa* (1983) by Richard Mahoney). Of course, Ike was wrong about this, just as he was wrong about deposing Mosaddegh and about killing Patrice Lumumba, who was Congo's *first democratically elected* prime minister.

After Mosaddegh fell from grace, Kim Roosevelt made an enemy of Richard Helms. Kim began to feel sorry for the deposed leader after his three-years in prison. Roosevelt arranged for Mosaddegh's release with a comfortable pension. However, he died soon afterward, a death possibly engineered by Richard Helms (https://quixoticjoust.blogspot.com/2011/10/excerpt-from-manuscript-by-richard.html). From Wikipedia … Mosaddegh was kept under house arrest at his Ahmadabad residence, until his death on March 5, 1967. He was denied a funeral and was buried in his living room, despite his request to be buried in the public graveyard, beside the victims of the political violence on July 21, 1952.

Lumumba's successor was Joseph Mobutu; by the 1980s, the Mobutu regime had become infamous for mismanagement and corruption. See "How the Congo Descended into Darkness" by Jim DiEugenio in *Garrison: The Journal of History and Deep Politics*, Issue #8, November 2021, pp. 277-289.

Ike was surely not perfect; he had once incongruously and ingenuously asked Holocaust survivor Siegfried Halbreich: *"Did it hurt you very much when they tattooed this number on your arm?"* (Gladwell 2024, p. 228). On the other hand, Ike was romantically on target with Kay Summersby; he just needed Mamie's obliviousness and some Viagra to counter his many years of smoking.

445 *The People's Almanac*, David Wallechinsky & Irving Wallace, 1975-1981.

446 Written by Jonathan Kwitny in 1992 for *The Nation*. "The C.I.A.'s secret armies in Europe" - Free Online Library (https://www.thefreelibrary.com/The+C.I.A.'s+secret+armies+in+Europe.-a012148091).

447 While Bill Harvey was Rome's chief of station in 1963, F. Mark Wyatt had served under him. Wyatt had (unexpectedly) encountered Harvey on a plane to Dallas in early November 1963 (Talbot 2015, p. 477). Harvey was cagey about his target in Dallas.

point that the Americans should have withdrawn. I think this thing should have been stopped long ago."[448]

Gladio's existence became public when Italian Prime Minister Giulio Andreotti revealed it to the Chamber of Deputies on October 24, 1990.

Paul Williams documents[449] that in 1967, Ted Shackley and Thomas G. Clines established heroin refineries with the assistance of the Corsican Mafia. In 1968, Ted (in a collegial mood) even arranged for Trafficante to meet the local Hmong drug lord, General Vang Pao (who commanded the CIA's secret army[450]) in Saigon, so we might see…

Corsican Mafia →Shackley →Lansdale → C. Cabell → Burris → LBJ

Dean Rusk

B. Guerini in Marseilles

Alfred McCoy

General Vang Pao

In 1990, Giulio Andreotti confirmed that a secret army existed in Italy and Western Europe. They were part of NATO and had been set up by the US Secret Service, the CIA, and Britain's MI6 after WW II in order to fight communism in Western Europe.[451]

As early as 1947, French Minister of the Interior (Edouard Depreux) had publicly exposed the existence of this secret army inside France. It included extreme right-wing elements, e.g., French Vichy collaborators (Nazi supporters). They were poised to impose a right-wing dictatorship in the event of a communist surge in elections.[452]

During this period, James Angleton, and his right-hand man Ray Rocca, ran Special Counter-Intelligence throughout Italy.[453] They worked closely with Italian counterintelligence to keep an eye on communists.

448 Chapter 12 – The Assassination of JFK, Gladio and Israel – The Terrorism Business | by Brendan Devenney | Medium

449 Paul Williams, p. 88.

450 *The Politics of Heroin: CIA Complicity in the Global Drug Trade* (1972 and 1991) by Alfred McCoy), the photographic section.

451 Ganser, p. 1.

452 Ibid., p. 88.

453 Angleton paid Sicilian and Calabrian Mafia figures to smuggle OSS agents into

Ray Rocco → Angleton → Helms → LBJ

Raymond Rocca remained in Italy and was Angleton's liaison with the Italian intelligence service until he returned to Washington in the summer of 1953. (Provocatively, Rocca had claimed that Jim Garrison would get a *"guilty"* verdict on Clay Shaw.[454])

In 1947, Angleton participated in an Office of Support Operation (OSO) where propaganda and other means were used to keep the Italians from voting any communists into office.[455]

The rigging of the 1948 Italian election was the first operation conducted by the (recently formed) CIA. Some supervision came from the law office of the Dulles brothers, Sullivan and Cromwell in New York City. James Angleton would play a vital role in helping to steal that 1948 Italian election.[456]

In September 1960, Richard Bissell and Allen Dulles initiated talks with two leading Mafia figures – Johnny Roselli and Sam Giancana. Later, other crime bosses such as Carlos Marcello, Santo Trafficante and Meyer Lansky became involved in this plot against Castro.

Giancana → Roselli → Bissell (± Allen Dulles) → LBJ

Marcello → Roselli → Harvey → Bissell → Allen Dulles → LBJ

Sicily and into the toe of Italy. As a reward, Donovan and Angleton put Sicilian gangsters into powerful political positions in Palermo and in Rome. Angleton also kept them well supplied with guns and gold (Sterling and Peggy Seagrave, Kindle, p. 467).

454 *Cold Warrior: True Story of the West's Spyhunt Nightmare* (1991) by Tom Mangold.

On May 9, 1961, at the Grand Ballroom of the Sheraton-Charles Hotel in New Orleans, Charles Cabell was guest speaker for the Foreign Policy Association. The person who introduced him was Clay Shaw!

Clay Shaw → C. Cabell → E. Cabell → LBJ

455 *The Man Who Kept the Secrets: Richard Helms and the CIA* (1979) by Thomas Powers, p. 35.

456 *James Jesus Angleton, the CIA, and the Craft of Counterintelligence* (2008) by Michael Holzman. The US was obviously no foe of stolen elections. According to the (congressional) Pike Report, after WWII the CIA (with Angleton's assistance) spent $65 million in Italy to be sure the right (the political right) people were elected. They usually succeeded. It would have been enlightening to hear Angleton explain exactly how he had persuaded American taxpayers to foot this bill – or how he had obtained the necessary funds.

Otis Pike (chairman of the congressional committee) was duly rewarded for his heroic efforts on behalf of ordinary Americans. He told the House that the CIA special counsel (whose salary was paid by US tax dollars) had told his committee staff director, *"Pike will pay for this, you wait and see – we'll destroy him for this."* In fact, Pike lost his next election for congress (Scott 1991, p. 250).

In 1963, JFK asked Lansdale to focus on Vietnam. However, Lansdale was soon in conflict with General Maxwell Taylor, JFK's representative. Taylor, contrary to JFK, believed that the war could be won by the military.[457] In the summer of 1963, he argued that 40,000 US troops could solve the Vietminh threat, and that another 120,000 could cope with any North Vietnamese or Chinese threat. JFK did not agree. Nor did history.

Lansdale also disagreed with "Max" Taylor. Lansdale had spent years studying the way Mao Zedong had taken power in China. He often quoted Mao as telling his guerrillas: *"Buy and sell fairly. Return everything borrowed. Indemnify everything damaged. Do not bathe in view of women.* [We can only wonder where Lansdale had tried this experiment – and what had happened.] *Do not rob personal belongings of captives."* The purpose of such rules, according to Mao, was to create a good relationship between the army and its people.

It was these heretical views that abetted Lansdale's path to unemployment. Nonetheless, after 11/22/1963, Lansdale continued to argue against LBJ's decision to use military force in the Vietnam War.[458]

---

457 Max was not alone. One of McNamara's closest aides told Dick Goodwin, *"Bob's greatest concern at the beginning of 1965 was his fear that he might not be able to talk the president into the bombing. He spent all his time preparing arguments and lining up allies"* (Goodwin, p. 375). JFK would have been dumbfounded.

458 https://spartacus-educational.com/COLDlansdale.htm. Of course, Lansdale was right about the Vietnam War. But even McNamara once briefly glimpsed his own errors. In 1966, he told Dick Goodwin,

> *You know, Dick, it might be a good idea if we had someone in these meetings who understood Vietnamese culture and politics.*

Goodwin adds, *"It was a moment of revelation …* [it] *demonstrated the danger of policies conceived and carried out by a small group of men in virtual secrecy. They began by lying to Congress and the public…."* Oddly, Dick says nothing about the *available* expertise of Senator Mike Mansfield of Montana. His service in the Marines had triggered a lifelong interest in Asia. He had visited China on a special mission for FDR in 1944. He had even been a professor of far eastern history. After a visit to Vietnam in December 1962, Mansfield advised JFK that US money given to Vietnam was being squandered and that the US should avoid further involvement there. So, he became the first American official to comment even mildly negatively on Vietnam involvement. However, as early as 1955, when General Joseph Lawton Collins left to take up his post in Vietnam, Foster Dulles told him, *" the chances of our saving the situation there are not more than one in ten."* Apparently Foster forgot to tell LBJ (Tuchman, p. 277).

However, even before that, in 1954, General Matthew Ridgway (see his photograph in this book) had told Senator George Aiken of Vermont that *"even if two million men were sent to Vietnam they would be swallowed up."* Matthew had fought in Korea, so he knew first-hand about the hazards of Asian warfare (Goodwin, p. 380). Furthermore, the French had just surrendered on May 7, 1954, at the Battle of Dien Bien Phu. Aiken did not retire until 1975, so he was in the Senate during the 1960s. Ridgway had retired from the army in 1955, but in November 1967, he joined LBJ's "Wise Men." Along with General James Gavin, these two generals advised Clark Clifford that victory in Vietnam was

General Lyman Lemnitzer (1899-1988)

Much of the following is from Chapter 12 – The Assassination of JFK, Gladio and Israel – The Terrorism Business | by Brendan Devenney | Medium.[459]

Lemnitzer served as Chairman of the Joint Chiefs of Staff (1960-1962), but (like Bill Harvey) he was relieved of his position by JFK shortly after Lemnitzer approved of the mad scenarios in Operation Northwoods. (Ed Lansdale had also supported these wild-eyed proposals.[460]) Casey Quinlan has proposed that Eisenhower actually planted the seed for some of Lemnitzer's hair-brained schemes. Casey also traces Otto Skorzeny's ties to US intelligence.[461]

Operation Northwoods was unearthed by my heroic colleague, Douglas Horne, during his service in the 1990s on the ARRB. It was a 1962 plan to stage false flag terrorist attacks inside the US and abroad to provoke *"military intervention in Cuba."*[462] The plan called for the CIA or other operatives to commit genuine acts of terrorism in US cities and elsewhere.

---

unattainable. In response, NSA advisor W. W. Rostow wrote a 5-page memorandum for LBJ, claiming that Ridgway and Gavin were ill-informed. Instead, he expressed supreme confidence that the bombing offensive would soon win the war (Matthew Ridgway - Wikipedia).

Incredibly, McNamara, by late January 1966 (22 months *before* Ridgway joined the "Wise Men" in November 1967), had already privately agreed with Ridgway that the war was *rubbish*. During a one-on-one interview with Dick Goodwin, McNamara swept his arm across an 8-foot map (in his office) of Southeast Asia and asked, *" Do you think it would make any difference to American security, Dick, if this entire place went communist?"* Dick was stunned, hardly knowing what to say, when McNamara concluded, *"It wouldn't make the slightest bit of difference,"* and then he sat down (Goodwin, p. 453). So, several days later, on January 31, 1966, the bombing resumed. McNamara eventually resigned on Leap Year Day 1968 – two years after this bombing resumed, but only a few months after the Wise Men appeared on the scene.

459 https://medium.com/@dubhelloco/chapter-12-the-assassination-of-jfk-gladio-and-israel-the-terrorism-business-d26129f9bca2

460 "JFK: His Life and Public Assassination" by Edward Curtin, *Garrison: The Journal of History and Deep Politics*, Issue #8, November 2021, pp. 15-31.

461 "Frontier Justice – JFK: A Targeted Kill" by Casey Quinlan in *Garrison: The Journal of History and Deep Politics,* Issue #3, October 2019, pp. 68-81.

462 The Dealey Plaza event may originally have been designed as a false flag attack (as in the Northwoods scenarios – with all shots deliberately designed to miss), and with someone like Oswald playing the patsy. It is even possible, if not likely, that many participants in the subsequent, authentic murder attempt were told that it was only a fake assassination – or some kind of "incident." In fact, it is often impossible to know just what a given participant believed. The gunmen must have known, of course, but beyond that, it is often a mystery. For example, Chauncy Holt (who claims to have provided illicit SS badges in Dealey Plaza) was told that *"an incident was going to be created which could be laid at the door of pro-Castro Cubans. The word attempted assassination was never used"* (Chauncey Holt – https://spartacus-educational.com/JFKholt.htm).

These acts were to be blamed on Cuba in order to create public support for a war with Cuba. One part of Operation Northwoods was to *"develop a Communist Cuban terror campaign in the Miami area, in other Florida cities and even in Washington."* Lyman Lemnitzer signed the document and presented it to Secretary of Defense Robert McNamara on March 13, 1962.[463] JFK was not pleased; in fact, he was horrified.

The "Years of Lead" [due to bullets][464] coincided with JFK's transfer of General Lyman Lemnitzer to Supreme Allied Commander Europe of NATO (SACEUR). In his position as SACEUR (1963-1969), Lemnitzer would have the final word on activities of Operation Gladio.

> *In 2000, an Italian parliamentary investigation concluded that the US had supported the "strategy of tension" in order to "stop the PCI [Italian Communist Party] and to a certain degree also the PSI* [Italian Socialist Party] *from reaching executive power in the country."*

A US Senate report concluded:

> *Those massacres, those bombs, those military actions had been organized or promoted or supported by men inside Italian state institutions and, as has been discovered more recently,* ***by men linked to the structures of United States intelligence*** [emphasis added].[465]

So, in summary, Lemnitzer, as head of NATO, had ready access to Gladio files, including the Corsican connection. Surely, JFK had not anticipated this outcome, just as he surely did not foresee Harvey's geographical proximity to the Corsicans after Bill's late June 1963 transfer to Rome. Bill Harvey's connections to Gladio are no secret. In fact, on 11/22/1963, Harvey and his deputy, F. Mark Wyatt, were in Sardinia – *at a Gladio base!*[466]

Harvey → Lemnitzer → Allen Dulles → Burris → LBJ

Corsicans → Shackley → Allen Dulles → LBJ

463 http://www.gwu.edu/~nsarchiv/news/20010430/index.html. Also see *Body of Secrets* (2001) by James Bamford, pp. 82-91, 300, 301.

464 The "Years of Lead" (from bullets during the late 1960s to the late 1980s) in Italy were filled with political violence and social upheaval, marked by both far-left and far-right political terrorism. Although I visited Italy in 1970, I remained blissfully unaware of my own risk. Sometimes it is better simply to remain ignorant, but I passed that frontier long ago.

465 Ganser, p. 82.

466 Talbot 2015, p. 476. When Wyatt died in 2006 (at age 86), he still believed that Harvey had foreknowledge of 11/22/1963 – or was actually involved. Even during the HSCA, Dan Hardway had written a memo that targeted Harvey as a likely suspect for the Dealey Plaza event. Hardway had also incriminated David Phillips for the madness in Mexico City (*The Other Oswald* (2019/2020) by Gary Hill, p. 142).

Otto Skorzeny (1908-1975)

In early 1945, Bill Donovan (head of the OSS) first interviewed (Nazi SS) Lt. Col. Otto Skorzeny, chief of Hitler's commandos. Donovan retired that December, so it is likely that Allen Dulles promptly became aware of Skorzeny.[467] On August 19, 1948, Frank Wisner[468] became head of the Office of Policy Coordination (OPC),[469] the (subsequent) CIA division for covert action.[470] Wisner had served briefly in covert action under Dulles right after the war and Skorzeny had served in virtually every one of Wisner's operations.[471] It is almost certain that Angleton and

---

467 "Allen Dulles OSS and nazi war criminals dynamics selective prosecution"| History after 1945 (general) | Cambridge University Press (https://www.cambridge.org/us/universitypress/subjects/history/history-after-1945-general/allen-dulles-oss-and-nazi-war-criminals-dynamics-selective-prosecution).

468 Wisner worked with C. D. Jackson in Operation Mockingbird. According to Wikipedia, *"Operation Mockingbird was an alleged [sic] large-scale program of the United States Central Intelligence Agency (CIA) that began in the early years of the Cold War and attempted to manipulate domestic American news media organizations for propaganda purposes."*

Jackson would later arrange for *Life*'s purchase of the Zapruder film, which the public viewed for the first time – with explosive repercussions – in 1975. Jackson had successfully kept this secluded for 12 years. Contrary to Wikipedia, the activities of Mongoose were not merely "alleged." In fact, Allen Dulles himself had initiated Mockingbird in 1953 (Paul Williams, p. 59). Wikipedia needs to study some history.

At age 56, Frank Wisner committed suicide on October 29, 1965. Lisa Howard barely preceded him (also from suicide) on July 4, 1965. Wandering into this JFK case has not always been healthy, especially if you lived in the 1960s and the 1970s (specifically during the HSCA).

469 The OPC, a Cold War outfit for dirty tricks, had been created by Harry Truman independently of the CIA. In 1947, OPC was absorbed into the CIA.

470 In 1948, E. Howard Hunt was in Paris, to assist with classified programs for the Marshall Plan. So, he likely knew of the OPC contact with Otto Skorzeny (Ganis, p. 118). In the early 1950s, Ben Bradlee took over control of the Internation Organizations Division (IOD) within the CIA; it handled covert operations for global corporate entities. Bradlee was later replaced by his deputy, Cord Meyer (Mary's husband). These men worked on Wisner's covert activities at the same time that Donovan used Skorzeny as an asset (Ganis, p. 128). Ben Bradlee would later (1968) become the executive editor of the *Washington Post*.

On November 1, 1950, Ben had exited a streetcar in front of the White House just as two Puerto Rican nationalists shot at President Harry Truman. In 1957, Ben married Antoinette 'Tony' Pinchot Pittman (the sister of Mary Pinchot Meyer). So, Ben was brother-in-law to Cord Meyer, one of the CIA's top officials; Cord is also a suspect in the JFK assassination. Ben won the Walter Cronkite Award for Excellence in Journalism in 1998 – but he forever refused to look into the JFK assassination, even though he had been one of JFK's closest friends. Ben found his indifference embarrassing to explain.

471 Eisenhower was no stranger to Skorzeny; during the Battle of the Bulge, Skorzeny was rumored to have led an assassination team that targeted Ike. As a result, Ike was tightly confined to his headquarters and heavily guarded. Skorzeny later denied that the rumor was true, but Ike kept a photograph of Otto on his White House desk (*The*

Harvey knew who Skorzeny was soon after Donovan's initial interview, if not during WW II itself.[472] After all, Ike (during the Battle of the Bulge) surely knew who Skorzeny was. Almost certainly, by August 4, 1953, Harvey (and/or Angleton) had met Skorzeny – likely face to face in Madrid. In fact, Skorzeny cites a visit from "BOB."[473] Otto had written a letter to his wife, Ilse, in which he described showing a letter to BOB (that he had received from Gamel Nasser). He specifically cited current news from the Middle East. That is highly significant since Skorzeny was working, at that moment, on *a CIA-related mission* directly involving Egypt. Furthermore, when Harvey was working on QJ/WIN,[474] it is quite likely that he had thoroughly reviewed Skorzeny's file, because, according to Ralph Ganis, the letters QJ refer to Spain.[475] In any case, this review supposedly included a (March 1958) report from the CIA station in Madrid.

Skorzeny not only knew Bill Harvey, but he had also been approached by a certain major general of the American army who knew MacArthur; this must have been General Charles Willoughby, who officially retired from the Army on September 1, 1951. Furthermore, the Portland *Oregonian* reported on his visit with the headline, *"Mac's Aide in Spain."* Major Ralph Ganis concludes that the Skorzeny-CIA alliance began in 1952, and that Otto was a clear asset of Angleton's Counterintelligence Staff.[476]

SKORZENY → HARVEY → LANSDALE → C. CABELL → ALLEN DULLES → LBJ

SKORZENY → WILLOUGHBY → H. L. HUNT → CLARK → LBJ

Skorzeny Papers (2018) by Major Ralph Ganis, Chapter 8). My daughter, Meredith Mantik, has a long video interview with Ganis, which is still awaiting release.

472 On October 3, 1949, the NATO military assistance program for Europe (*Paix et Liberte*) met in Washington, DC, with CIA director Walter Bedell Smith, who was Allen Dulles's boss (Kinzer 2013, Kindle, 28). (See Beetle's photograph in this book.) Skorzeny soon became deeply involved in this program. CIA logs show that Bill Harvey was present for this 1949 meeting, so he clearly knew who Otto was (Ganis, p. 133). During this early post-war period, Conein worked closely with Bill Harvey and Frank Wisner, so he (Conein) would have known of Skorzeny as well. E. Howard Hunt had brought Lucien into the White House in 1970, so these two obviously knew one another…

Skorzeny → Harvey → Lansdale → C. Cabell → Burris → LBJ

Corsicans → Conein → E. H. Hunt → Helms → LBJ

473 Harvey was chief of "BOB," the Berlin Operations Base. Berlin Operations Base - Wikipedia.

474 Per Gerry Hemming, who told Greg Burnham in November 2018, QJ/WIN was Louis van Hooke; not everyone agrees. Twyman (p. 396) created an excellent table on QJ/WIN. Also see *The Other Oswald* (2019/2020) by Gary Hill, p. 174.

475 On the other hand, the MFF site has identified QJ as Luxembourg; QU is provisionally tagged as Spain: https://www.maryferrell.org/php/marysdb.php?id=7793.

476 Ganis, pp. 184-187.

Astonishingly, another person who knew Skorzeny was Ava Gardner, who lived in a luxury apartment directly above him in downtown Madrid. In the apartment directly below Otto and Ilse lived Werner Voight, Sr. He was Otto's business partner, who is cited in the Skorzeny papers. Werner's son recalled that Otto was working for the US Air Force; Skorzeny's papers confirm that he had a contract for construction of a US base. Beguilingly, only a few years earlier, funding for BOB had also come from a USAF contract.[477] During 1954-1958, Otto apparently handled 20% of all subcontractor contracts for US bases in Spain, so it is likely that the US Air Force (as well as Curtis LeMay) knew who Otto was.[478]

Even more to the point, Skorzeny had many business connections in Dallas, where Earle Cabell (a CIA asset) was the mayor. Earle's brother (Charles) had been one of the first top intelligence officials to become aware of Otto. But Otto also had business connections in New York City, Miami, Chicago and the Bahamas. Enchantingly, some of these cities then harbored strong Mafia groups (and may still do so).

Mafia → Skorzeny → Earle Cabell → LBJ

Beginning in 1952, Otto invested in Spanish oil development projects with Brown, Raymond, Walsh (BRW), which later became Brown and Root (LBJ's effective godfathers).[479]

Skorzeny → Brown & Root → Clark → LBJ

Otto also had a secure channel to Jack Crichton in Madrid via the General American Oil Company.[480] Jack Crichton, reserve army intelligence, was one of the first to interview Marina Oswald. Jack also met with H. L. Hunt soon after 11/22/1963.[481]

477 Ibid., p. 301.

478 Ibid., p. 312.

479 In 1962, Brown and Root were taken over by Halliburton; Dick Cheney later became their CEO. Unlike Bill Donovan, Cheney really was heartless for a while – he used a mechanical pump instead of a biological heart. Nonetheless, the Brown Foundation continued to contribute to CIA-associated organizations. In 1963 (according to Robert Montenegro), Brigadier General Paul Francis Gaynor (CIA Chief of Security) identified several key members of Brown and Root as CIA assets, including its President, George Rufus Brown (Curious - JFK Assassination Debate - The Education Forum) (https://educationforum.ipbhost.com/topic/26536-curious/).

George Rufus Brown → Burris → LBJ

480 Ganis, p. 313.

481 Crichton was also a good friend of George H. W. Bush. In 1959, Crichton and Bush raised funds for Operation 40. Before too long, however, this group focused on assassinations; it is not known if Bush was told about this change in focus, but Crichton almost certainly was told (*The Secret War: CIA Covert Operations Against Cuba 1959-62* (1995) by Fabian Escalante, Mirta Muniz, et al.).

Skorzeny →Crichton → H. L. Hunt → Clark → LBJ

In 1960 (or before), the Mossad recruited Skorzeny. But it was not a *"one-off"* as apologists claim. One of his Mossad handlers attended his funeral 13 years later (in Spain in 1975); this implies that Otto was in their service for a long time – and that he was a valued asset.[482]

Skorzeny was a founding member of the "Die Spinne" network that aided the escape of Nazi SS members; this network formed "The Paladin Group" in 1970:

> *The Paladin Group ... was on the outside a legitimate security consultancy. However, the group's real purpose was to recruit and operate mercenaries for right-wing regimes and dictatorships ... worldwide, as well as serve the role of political subversion in Europe.*

The "Paladin Group" was an anti-communist organization which (according to SAS-founder, David Stirling), was Skorzeny's long-held idea of setting up an *"international directorship of strategic assault personnel"* whose objectives would enable it to *"straddle the watershed between paramilitary operations carried out by the troops in uniform and the political warfare which is conducted by civilian agents."*[483]

With recruits from a group that included former members of the Nazi SS, France's Service Action Civic (SAC), and the disbanded Organisation de l'Armee Secret (OAS), Paladin became a guns-for-hire body that catered to mercenaries for right-wing dictatorships. It provided training to security agencies of these dictatorships, but also to guerrilla organizations.

Skorzeny was a personal friend of Italian neo-fascists Prince Junio Borghese (a puppet of James Angleton) and also of Stefano Delle Chiaie.[484]

---

482 "The Strange Case of a Nazi Who Became an Israeli Hitman" by Chris Woolf (2016). "How a famous former Nazi officer became a hitman for Israel" - The World from PRX (https://theworld.org/stories/2016/03/30/how-famous-former-nazi-officer-became-hitman-israel).

483 Chapter 12 – The Assassination of JFK, Gladio and Israel – The Terrorism Business | by Brendan Devenney | Medium.

484 Klaus Barbie and Otto Skorzeny trained death squads in Bolivia. Klaus (under CIA protection) had recruited 600+ paramilitary, swastika-wearing, Nazi-worshipping mercenaries, who went on a shooting spree in the COB building in La Paz (*The Big White Lie: The CIA and the Cocaine Crack Epidemic* (1993) by Michael Levine, p. 57). In Spain they were assisted by Stefano Delle Chiaie (*The Essential Mae Brussell: Investigations of Fascism in America* (2014) edited by Alex Constantine, Kindle). See the photograph of Otto and Klaus here: Incredible photo of Otto Skorzeny and Klaus Barbie vida loca party - Axis History Forum (https://forum.axishistory.com/viewtopic.php?t=247808). I displayed this same photograph in *The JFK Assassination Decoded: Criminal Forgery in the Autopsy*

As exiles, both men spent time in Spain (where Skorzeny had his headquarters).[485]

Note that much of this information has been taken from Chapter 12 – The Assassination of JFK, Gladio and Israel – The Terrorism Business | by Brendan Devenney | Medium.[486]

So, we have another possible conduit…

Skorzeny → Borghese → Angleton (±Dulles) LBJ

Robert Gerald Storey, Sr., was one of three members of the Texas Court of Inquiry,[487] which ran concurrently with the WC; this Texas Court provided information to the WC. Storey had served under Charles Cabell in WW II, and he had also been a Nuremberg prosecutor and president of the American Bar Association. In 1947, Storey became Dean of Southern Methodist University's Dedman School of Law. He was also a documented member of the networks of Otto Skorzeny and Jean Pierre Lafitte.[488] His Texas associates were George H. W. Bush, Prescott Bush,[489] and Leon

Photographs and X-rays (2023) – on the last page of that book.

Chiaie was also known as the "Black Pimpernel." He assisted with the Bologna railroad station bombing and was also a colleague of Michael Townley, who masterminded the assassination of Orlando Letelier, the former Chilean ambassador to the US. Delle was associated with Salvador Allende's overthrow in 1973 (Lernoux, p. 177). Whatever the CIA told President Nixon about this coup is still TOP SECRET: "49 Years Later, Nixon's Knowledge of Pinochet Coup Remains Secret" – History News Network (https://www.historynewsnetwork.org/article/49-years-later-nixons-knowledge-of-pinochet-coup-r). *"Richard Helms holds the unsavory distinction of being the only director of the CIA ever convicted of lying to Congress. He did so regarding an attempt to prevent Salvador Allende from becoming president of Chile during the country's first successful open elections in 1970:* 'New Book Explains Why Ex-CIA Director Richard Helms Lied to Congress'" (https://www.usnews.com/news/blogs/washington-whispers/2013/01/11/new-book-explains-why-ex-cia-director-richard-helms-lied-to-congress).

485 "Otto Skorzeny and The Paladin Group" – By Mark David; "Skorzeny: The Mythical Nazi Commando (Part 2)," War History Online; June 24, 2017: "ODESSA: The Most Dangerous Man In Europe, Otto Skorzeny & The Paladin Group" – By Mark David (Archive) | RIELPOLITIK (https://rielpolitik.com/2020/04/09/odessa-the-most-dangerous-man-in-europe-otto-skorzeny-the-paladin-group-by-mark-david/).

486 https://medium.com/@dubhelloco/chapter-12-the-assassination-of-jfk-gladio-and-israel-the-terrorism-business-d26129f9bca2

487 Besides Robert Storey, the other two primary members were Leon Jaworski and Waggoner Carr (https://www.texastribune.org/2012/01/30/texplainer-what-court-inquiry/).

488 *Coup in Dallas: The Decisive Investigation into Who Killed JFK* (2021) by Leslie Sharp and Alan Kent, Kindle. Also see *The Skorzeny Papers* (2018) by Major Ralph Ganis.

489 *"Prescott, Sr., probably also had a part in the CIA's interest in young George. A managing partner of Brown Brothers Harriman and major benefactor of Yale, Prescott had been an Army Intelligence operative in World War I. He also ardently supported Eisenhower's covert Cold War policies and was a close friend of William Casey, an OSS veteran who went on to head the CIA from 1981 until his death in 1985"* (IN THE COMPANY OF FRIENDS) (https://www.cia.gov/readingroom/print/1938068).

Jaworski. When Dulles chose Charles Cabell as his deputy, Storey wrote a letter to Dulles to congratulate him on his wisdom.

Skorzeny → Storey → C. Cabell →LBJ

Skorzeny is one of the rare characters in this book who is not buried either at Arlington or in a military plot. His ashes lie at the family site in Vienna, Austria, the site of his birth. Like LBJ (and Mickey Mantle), he died at a young age (67).

Edward Lansdale (1909-1987)[490]

According to Sterling Seagrave, General Charles Willoughby sent Lansdale to the Philippines after WW II, so we might consider this…

Lansdale → Willoughby → H. L. Hunt → Ed Clark → LBJ

Lansdale → C. Cabell → Allen Dulles → LBJ

In the early 1950s, Allen Dulles gave Lansdale $5 million (or maybe $10 million) to finance CIA operations against the Hukbalahap movement.[491] These were Filipino peasant farmers fighting for land reform. Still during the 1950s, Dulles later asked Lansdale to provide similar services in Vietnam.

Lansdale (see his photograph in this book) was opposed to the Bay of Pigs operation because he knew that it would not trigger a popular uprising against Castro. JFK respected the advice of Lansdale and selected him to become overall project leader of Operation Mongoose. Bill Harvey directed the CIA side, but Lansdale may have been the primary leader.[492] Lansdale did reprimand Harvey for his commando raids during the Cuban Missile Crisis.

Lansdale resigned on October 31, 1963, or maybe McNamara fired him, as Lansdale claimed – see *Wikipedia.* The pressure to remove Lansdale came from Generals Curtis LeMay and Victor Krulak and other senior members of the military; apparently this pressure did not come

---

490 "In the Philippines, the CIA Has Found a Second Home" - *Los Angeles Times.* Greg Lavin (who knew Ed well) also sees him in Dealey Plaza on 11/22/1963; in particular he cites Ed's stooped (depressed) right shoulder, which does seem almost unique. Greg also cites Ed's deployment of the Golden Lily treasure in CIA escapades around the globe. See the very recent book, *Chasing Ed: Was Major General Edward G. Lansdale the Mastermind of the JFK Assassination?* (2025) by Gregory C. Lavin.

491 AD1112093.pdf. This seventh publication in the Historical Analysis Series addresses the American role in the Philippine Hukbalahap Insurrection. Lansdale enters the scene on p. 79. See p. 117 ff for the "Psychological Warfare Operations," including Lansdale's advice.

492 Bill Kelly argues that the Kennedys were not trying to kill Castro: "The Lansdale Memo of March 16, 1962, Re-Evaluated" by William Kelly in *Garrison: The Journal of History and Deep Politics*, Issue #8, November 2021, pp. 272-276.

from the CIA. In fact, *Lansdale and Charles Cabell were close friends.* Literally, just minutes separated Lansdale's resignation (or firing) from Diệm's assassination, which Lansdale had fiercely opposed.[493]

Daniel Ellsberg (famous for the *Pentagon Papers*) served under Lansdale at this time; he liked Lansdale because of his commitment to democracy. Ellsberg also agreed with Lansdale that the Vietnamese should run the pacification program. He argued that unless it was a Vietnam project it would never work. Lansdale knew that there was a deep xenophobia among Vietnamese. JFK agreed.

Daniel Sheehan is convinced that Lansdale appears in the photograph with the three tramps. Danny has spoken with Lansdale's former second wife (a Filipino).[494] This is Patrocinio Yapcinco Lansdale (also known as Pat Kelly), who has identified Lansdale in the "tramps" photo taken near the TSBD on 11/22/1963. She swears that it is Lansdale.[495]

Perhaps this should surprise no one – because Lansdale was Harvey's colleague (possibly his superior) in Mongoose, and Harvey said that he always followed orders. Furthermore, Harvey's fingerprints are all over the operation in Dealey Plaza. So, it would be no surprise (and not even a new relationship) if Lansdale had supervised Dealey Plaza during 11/22/1963. But Harvey was the one with contacts everywhere – Skorzeny, the Corsicans, the Mafia, Willoughby, and even the anti-Castro Cubans (the latter, especially during his time in Mongoose).[496]

493 The pope had ordered (the Catholic) Diệm to follow the orders of the US government (aka the CIA in this case). (Paul Williams, p. 58.) After the demise of the Diệm brothers, we can only hope that the pope had learned his lesson.

494 (49) Danny Sheehan on Ed Lansdale identification - YouTube (https://www.youtube.com/watch?v=JiRqNiG19dg).

495 Is the "Lansdale Hypothesis" of the JFK Assassination the Real Deal? - Page 11 - JFK Assassination Debate - The Education Forum (https://educationforum.ipbhost.com/topic/27123-is-the-lansdale-hypothesis-of-the-jfk-assassination-the-real-deal/page/11/).

496 Allen Dulles had his own contacts with anti-Castro Cubans. In April 1963, Allen met with Paulino Sierra Martinez, a former henchman for Fulgencio Batista. Sierra was funded in the US by the Mafia and US corporations. The SS suspected (but could not prove) that Sierra was associated with the Chicago plot to kill JFK. Although the Warren Report does not cite him, the HSCA was quite concerned about his "unsavory" connections – but that was where the trail ended. In any case here is the question: Why did Allen Dulles meet – *in April 1963* – with Sierra (who seemed to have no love for JFK) – and why didn't Allen tell his fellow WC members what it was all about? (Talbot 2015, pp. 7-8, 458-462.)

Regarding Paulino Sierra Martinez – Homer Echevarria had learned from him that JFK was to be killed on 11/22/1963. Homer was connected to the DRE, as was David Phillips. E. Howard Hunt confirmed David's connection: "*The DRE. Dave Phillips ran that for us. But that is classified, I think. He was the head of it….*" (Hopsicker, pp. 141, 146). So, if Paulino knew about "The Big Event," what exactly did he tell Allen Dulles in April 1963? Furthermore, the HSCA discovered that Paulino's organization was backed by organized crime (Hopsicker, p. 147). So, what exactly did Allen Dulles know?

Danny Sheehan on Ed Lansdale identification (May 23, 2016)[497]

From Greg Burnham (e-mail of December 3, 2024)

[Burnham comments.] Fletch [Prouty] told me the "flechette dart" weapon systems (there were several) were brought to his office by Lansdale and an attending operator. The meeting was intended to convince Fletch, who was the Military's CIA Liaison Officer at the time, to support the proposal by CIA that the Department of Defense (DoD) should fund the weapon's further development. After a brief demonstration of one of its functions, Lansdale wanted to show a more impressive example. So, they decided to helicopter to a government R&D facility for the demo. For reasons unknown, while en route the helicopter had a major mechanical malfunction. It pitched and rolled, so to speak, and the occupants were genuinely concerned. Ultimately, the pilot, who Fletch said did an excellent job, regained control and they arrived unscathed. But, en route, during the worst part, Lansdale urinated and defecated on himself! Fletch found poetic justice there. He said, *"Lansdale had been known to hang Vietnamese POWs by their heels outside of the open door of Huey* [Bell]

April 1963 was a remarkably busy month: Besides this mysterious Dulles encounter, Adele Edisen bumped into "Dr. Rivera;" Lisa Howard crossed paths with Castro; Vidal went to Texas; Oswald supposedly took a pot shot at General Walker; Lansdale visited a sniper school in Panama during April-May; and Jean Rene Souétre may have met E. Howard Hunt in Madrid during March-April 1963. Was all of this merely random? It was, after all, just seven months before 11/22/1963. Also recall this: Dulles was not in office in April 1963. JFK had fired him on November 29, 1961. So why was Allen meeting with Sierra at all? For Adele Edisen, see https://spartacus-educational.com/JFKedisen.htm.

Paulino Sierra Martinez → Allen Dulles → LBJ

497 https://www.youtube.com/watch?v=JiRqNiG19dg.

helicopters in order to force information out of them. Lansdale got great joy out of this sort of thing...."

FROM GREG BURNHAM (E-MAIL OF DEC 5, 2024)

[Burnham comments.] Fletcher Prouty: Was it Lansdale? - JFK Assassination Debate - The Education Forum.[498]

> KRULAK: *That is indeed a picture of Ed Lansdale. The haircut, the stoop, the twisted left hand, the large class ring. It's Lansdale. What in the world was he doing there? Has anyone ever asked him, and who was the photographer?*[499]

Fletch told me that it's literally impossible for someone with Lansdale's background and function within government Black Ops to be so close to the assassination of *any* country's leader and have nothing to do with some aspect of it.[500] [End of Burnham comments.]

Krulak's letter is dated March 15, 1985. Lansdale died almost two years later, on February 23, 1987. During this two-year interval, why didn't Lansdale correct Krulak's supposed (mis)recognition of him? Also recall that, years later, his second wife (Pat Kelly) recognized him [Lansdale] in that photograph – and she never reported that Ed had denied his presence there. The (previously cited) video by Danny Sheehan was from May 2016; Pat had died 10 years before that (in 2006). But Pat, during all of those years, had never disclosed whether she had even asked Lansdale about 11/22/1963. Perhaps these questions only occurred to her after his death in 1987. One last question about that "tramps" photograph: Why is that Charles Harrelson doppelgänger smiling?

Lansdale's whereabouts on 11/22/1963 are (otherwise) unknown. In his autobiography, *In the Midst of Wars* (1972), with an introduction by Cecil B. Currey, Ed does *not* cite his location on that day.[501] Lansdale does not even seem to know about the JFK assassination – that event is not in his index![502] Given the momentous impact of this All-American event on

498 https://educationforum.ipbhost.com/topic/21791-was-it-lansdale/.

499 Appendix D: Krulak Letter Re: Dealey Plaza Photos And Lansdale Identity, "Understanding Special Operations" (https://ratical.org/ratville/JFK/USO/appD.html).

500 "Ed Lansdale in Dealey Plaza Nov 22 1963" (https://www.youtube.com/watch?v=5ATbhCUZxjQ).

501 Prouty emphasizes that Lansdale's book, and also *Ed Lansdale* (1988) by Cecil B. Curry *"... are burdened with a heavy coating of 'cover story'"* (Prouty, pp. 65-66) and that they should not be taken as reality. In my opinion, the same is true of *The Night Watch* (1977) by David Phillips. He does not even cite his relationship to Brandstetter or McLendon. But he does cite Allen Dulles's tale about ignoring Lenin in order to play tennis (p. 87).

502 Lansdale's book has other nonappearances that are equally astonishing. His

everyone else, no one (except for Richard Nixon[503] and G. H. W. Bush[504] and E. Howard Hunt and Félix Rodríguez[505]) could possibly have overlooked this date – *but Lansdale did.* Even David Morales and Bill Harvey and Allen Dulles (and I) were able to recall where we were. (Although he had been fired, someone admitted Allen to the CIA's "Farm" in Virginia.)

Although Krulak (letter of March 15, 1985) and Prouty identified Lansdale in that "tramps" photograph, Ed never tried to deny it before his death in February 1987. In fact, there is no evidence that he was ever asked where he was. This was a major oversight by Fletcher Prouty – and by Victor Krulak, too. Prouty does not even discuss this identification in his 1992 book – even though Krulak had written this letter in 1985! Why was Lansdale never asked where he was on November 22, 1963?[506]

Although Boot (in his 2018 book about Lansdale) cites the tramps photograph, he then promptly claims – while totally ignoring the identification by Pat Kelly (Lansdale's second wife) – that no reason exists to identify Lansdale in that image. If that is true, Boot should at least attempt to offer an alibi for Lansdale, especially after multiple individuals had identified him, but Boot does not even try. This is not serious scholarship; at best, this is deliberate misdirection. In fact, until Ed's death in 1987 (24 years after 11/22/1963), no one had ever asked Lansdale for an alibi – even though his (multiple) letters had stated that he would be in Texas at about that time.

---

index does *not* include these names: McNamara, Bundy, LBJ, Lodge, MacArthur, the Golden Lily, Rockefeller, Rusk, Taylor, Harkins, Felt, or McCloy. Vietcong appears on as many pages as Adolf Hitler (or Paul of Tarsus) – just one page, while CIA occurs on only three pages. "Nicolai" Lenin is cited for one page, but on that page his first name is not even stated. (Like Putin, Lenin's first name, especially after his death, became Vladimir; he called himself N. Lenin, but the N did not represent any name at all.) Pat Kelly (Ed's second wife) is said to appear on p. vii, but she does not. Furthermore, Lansdale implies some animosity between the CIA Saigon station chief (COS) and himself. This is presumably in 1955, but Ed is ridiculously frugal with dates. Did the COS truly not know that Ed was CIA? If so, this is woeful CIA communication. Oddly, Ed refuses to name that COS, but Wikipedia cites Evan Parker. William Colby wrote the (glowing) Foreword for Ed's book, but note this: after WW II, Colby helped to establish the stay-behind networks of Operation Gladio, a covert paramilitary organization organized by the CIA to make Soviet occupation difficult. But neither Lansdale nor Colby mentions Gladio. Nor does Ed spend any time discussing his sabotage efforts, e.g., his destruction of trucks and railroads. Beginning in 1959 (until 1963), William Colby served as the CIA's deputy chief of station (and later COS) in Saigon, but Colby's name does not even appear in the index. So, Ed was either deliberately secretive – or merely forgetful and disorganized.

503 For a hilarious litany of Nixon's discordant memories, see Prouty, pp. 119-120.

504 Regarding the whereabouts of George H. W. Bush on 11/22/1963, read the comical anecdote by Russ Baker in his chapter 4 ("Where was Poppy?") in *Family Secrets* (2009).

505 Hopsicker, p. 140.

506 https://bit.ly/4k3mNXR

But someone had to coordinate the shooting sites for the mechanics that day – surely they could not all occupy the Grassy Knoll. If not Lansdale, then who? Paul Linebarger had written the *official textbook on propaganda*; after Lansdale, Linebarger's (sole) other favorite pupil for psy-ops was E. Howard Hunt, but Howard was meeting with Richard Helms in a CIA safe house in northwest DC that day. And Bill Harvey was at a Gladio base in Sardinia. Some folks see David Morales in a photograph from Dealey Plaza that day; his location otherwise is not known, but his confession implies that he was there. In any case, David was not known for his psy ops skills. Furthermore, Lansdale had just written to several friends of his plans to be in Texas in late November. Also recall that Lansdale had visited a sniper camp earlier that year – and his circle of acquaintances had recently expanded to include many Spanish names. Moreover, he had directed Operation Mongoose, where he had surely met many anti-Castro Cubans. Furthermore, his circle of close colleagues was highly suspicious: Willoughby, Nelson Rockefeller, and Charles Cabell. Why have none of them vouched for his presence somewhere else that day? Finally, isn't it likely that Earle Cabell, the mayor of Dallas would have known if he was somewhere else? Why didn't Earle speak up? Also consider this: in testimony before the Church Committee, Lansdale had admitted that he was the one to first suggest assassinating Castro. Clearly, Ed Lansdale walked under a very dark cloud. Even Allen Dulles (or John McCloy or Richard Nixon) have never offered an alibi for Ed for 11/22/1963. So, why can't we see Lansdale's November 1963 travel records? As he was an employee of Food for Peace (via USAID), this surely cannot be a national security issue. Finally, think about this: In his autobiography, he says absolutely nothing about the Golden Lily treasure vaults. So, we can conclude this: just like Bill Harvey, Ed Lansdale could keep secrets. Also see Edward Lansdale.[507]

Joseph Burkholder Smith, in *Portrait of a Cold Warrior* (1981), cites the primary CIA trainer in covert intelligence operations. It was Paul Linebarger, a former Army officer who wrote the *official textbook on propaganda* and psychological warfare. Linebarger was a college professor who gave private classes in covert intelligence procedures and techniques at his DC home. Among his students, Linebarger was especially proud of E. Howard Hunt and Edward Lansdale, who *"had black minds."*[508] Lansdale's advertising

507 https://spartacus-educational.com/COLDlansdale.htm

508 *"Portrait of a Cold Warrior"* (1976) by Joseph B. Smith, Chapter 6, "At the Foot of the Master:" JFKCountercoup2: Joe Smith on Paul Linebarger and David Maurer (https://jfkcountercoup2.blogspot.com/2017/07/joe-smith-on-paul-linebarger-and-david.html). This article also notes the CIA's detailed study of Valkyrie and its relevance to 11/22/1963.

background (like that of David Phillips) exploited his expertise: psychological warfare (or psy-ops). There are now manuals on psy-ops and Lansdale is considered the father of that type of warfare.[509] What other background would have been more ideal for 11/22/1963? Then consider this:

The (Frank) Church Senate Committee wanted to know who had authorized assassination (in general). In particular, in Mongoose there were plans and resources to assassinate Castro. So, Senator Howard Baker put the question to Lansdale:[510]

Senator Baker. In connection with Mr. Smothers' question, did you originate this idea of laying on the CIA a requirement to report on the feasibility of the assassination of Castro or did someone else suggest that?

General Lansdale. I did, as far as I recall.

UNCLASSIFIED

David Denton wonders if the initial point for a plot (within the military) could be the ACSI (Assistant Chief of Staff for Intelligence). This was a small, special-purpose military unit created in 1960 to coordinate the intelligence activities of the army technical services. Bill Kelly has described it as *"one of the most ubiquitous, but least known military intelligence agencies with offices in the Pentagon."* Colonel Fletcher Prouty described it as the *"black intelligence arm"* of the US military. Denton also notes a memo from Colonel Walt Higgins; its source was the ACSI. Higgins's memo suggested that the assassination plot could mimic Operation Valkyrie, the 1944 failed plot that used German Army members – while simultaneously keeping many of them ignorant.

On April 26,1963, in Washington, DC, ACSI member Colonel Sam Kail met with George de Mohrenschildt and Haitian businessman Clemard Charles. The Baron was promoting Charles as a replacement for then-President of Haiti, "Papa Doc" François Duvalier. Furthermore, Kail was *"on a covert detail to the Agency* [the CIA] *during 1962-1966."* Since the Baron had just moved to Haiti from Dallas, Denton wonders if the ACSI was tracking Oswald ("What the JFK Files Tell Us" by Professor David Denton in *Garrison: The Journal of History and Deep Politics,* Issue #8, November 2021, pp. 208-238).

509 https://quixoticjoust.blogspot.com/2011/10/excerpt-from-manuscript-by-richard.html.

510 Ibid.

John Newman found a paper that placed Lansdale in DC; it was dated November 14, 1963. It concerns running errands for his wife. After that there is no record of his whereabouts except for another piece of paper; on it was "Texas Hotel" and "Denton," a name, and phone number. The Texas Hotel is where Kennedy stayed on 11/21/1963; Denton, Texas is just north of Dallas,[511] while Professor David Denton is at Olney Central College in Olney, Illinois. Shortly before 11/22/1963, Lansdale had written several letters to friends in which he implied an imminent visit to Texas. Why the Food for Peace program required such a visit to Texas at that moment was never clarified.

Allen Dulles obviously admired Ed Lansdale and helped to propel his career. Even back in 1954 (shortly before Điện Biên Phủ), Dulles had asked that Ed be added to a group of American liaison officers, a unit that had been accepted by the French (*JFK: The CIA, Vietnam, and the Plot to Assassinate JFK* (1992) by L. Fletcher Prouty, p. 39).[512] And Dulles was responsible for Lansdale's final promotion – against the wishes of air force generals Victor Krulak and Curtis LeMay.

Two months after Điện Biên Phủ, Lansdale was the "unconventional warfare officer" attached to the Saigon Military Mission. He was the leader (with Lucien Conein) of a 12-man team. He then purchased (surely not via personal funds – but perhaps with the Golden Lily treasure) the defeated Vietnamese army (ARVN) and with them he fought a 6-day battle to take Saigon back; 500 people were left dead (Hopsicker, p. 159), but Lansdale survived.

But McNamara disliked Lansdale; in his own 1975 testimony before the Church Committee, Bob said, *"I am damn annoyed at the damage he* [Lansdale] *has done to dead people"* (*The Road Not Taken* (2018) by Max Boot, Kindle, 581).[513] For amusement, read about Lansdale's

511 Ibid. Also see Dale, p. 261. I am unaware of any link between David Denton and Denton, Texas. Stan Weber in "The Denton Connection" (*Garrison: The Journal of History and Deep Politics*, Issue #15, November 2023, pp. 212 ff) even credits David Denton for assistance but – incredibly – he offers no recognition for this bizarre name coincidence! Someone should ask David about this. (Prof. Denton was gracious enough to ask me to speak at his conference last November (2024)).

512 During the early 1950s, the US covered about 80% of all French military costs in their Indochina War.

513 Aside from the peculiar question of how dead people can ever be damaged, we can only wonder if McNamara was referencing Lansdale's active role in "The Big Event." Ironically, Bob seemed unconcerned about the 3 million humans who died from "McNamara's War" (how many vietnamese died in the vietnam war - Search). But of course, while at Berkeley, Bob had been seduced by mathematics, so it would be wrong to attribute any emotions to him (until he wrote *In Retrospect*, but by then it was far too late).

futile attempt to educate McNamara about Vietnam (Boot, Kindle, 364-368). Lansdale's retirement party (1963) was held in a large conference room between the offices of McNamara and Roswell Gilpatric. While the accolades were still gushing, McNamara marched directly through the festivities without a glance at Lansdale – and he said nothing (Boot, Kindle, 413).

But be aware of Max Boot's bias; he remains a fervent devotee of the lone gunman: *"...an assassin's* [just one] *bullets."* Also beware of Boot's announcement in his Acknowledgments: *"This is a Council on Foreign Relations book."* Boot also claims that the Kennedys had called for the assassination of Castro (Boot, Kindle, 582). Bill Kelly strongly disagrees with this, as do many other serious scholars.[514] So read Boot with great care. By 2018, he had had at least two years to think about Pat Kelly's [no kin to Bill] identification of Lansdale in Dealey Plaza – as well as eighteen years to meditate on our findings in *Murder in Dealey Plaza* (2000). Unfortunately, Boot seems totally oblivious to both of these items, just as he knows nothing about the voluminous anti-WC literature of the preceding

---

Over 24 months, McNamara had visited Vietnam five times. Nonetheless, Barbara Tuchman was precisely on point in her assessment of McNamara:

> Appreciation of the human factor was not McNamara's strong point, and the possibility that humankind is not rational was too eccentric and disruptive to be programmed into his analysis (Tuchman, pp. 288, 294).

Unfortunately for McNamara, near the end of his term in office, even his own beloved numbers finally told the truth: *"His own Systems Analysis at the Department of Defense concluded that military benefits were not worth the economic cost"* (Tuchman, p. 338). Of course, McNamara kept this a secret from the public. By 1967, McNamara had concluded that bombing had not worked – so the entire purpose of US strategy was finally admitted to be a failure by the Secretary of Defense (Tuchman, p. 345) – and yet the war did not officially end until eight years later (on April 30, 1975). In fact, during 1975, my future near neighbor (Gerald Ford) told Congress that their failure to vote for aid to South Vietnam would damage our credibility – and that this aid was *"essential to our national security."* Of course, Gerry was wrong while Matthew Ridgway was right: *"it should not have taken great vision to perceive... that no truly vital US interest was present"* (Tuchman, p. 375). But Gerry did not have great vision – not even while serving on the WC.

514 RFK (and JFK – and Catholic John McCone), quite unlike Ike, seemed quite opposed to violating the Fifth Commandment ("Do not kill"), perhaps based on the Catholic scruples of all three. If that is accepted, as I do, then RFK could never have ordered Marilyn's murder (let alone Castro's murder). Most likely the Mafia (e.g., Giancana) killed her (chiefly via a rectal suppository) – with the clear purpose of framing RFK. Almost surely they had wiretapped her residence, so they knew about RFK's visits that night; they merely seized this unexpected opportunity: "Why Frank Sinatra Believed Marilyn Monroe Was Murdered: A New Book Reveals" (https://people.com/movies/why-frank-sinatra-believed-marilyn-monroe-was-murdered-book/). Also see *Coroner: America's Most Controversial Medical Examiner* (1983) by Thomas Noguchi with Joseph Dimona Noguchi. Furthermore, even Joe DiMaggio was duped by this frame-up, and so he never forgave RFK (or JFK).

55 years. Since he is nearly 30 years younger than me, he still has time to catch up on his reading. I have already done mine.

After WW II, Lansdale and McCloy crossed paths on several momentous occasions. The following (rather lengthy) comments derive chiefly from Sterling Seagrave; a citation follows below. Lansdale and McCloy met in the mid-1940s in the matter of the Golden Lily treasure vaults. Lansdale and Severino Garcia Diaz Santa Romana (Santy) had been either observers or participants of the torture of Major Kojima Kashii before this time (Seagraves, p. 27). Later Kojima led Lansdale and Santy to more than a dozen Golden Lily treasure vaults in the mountains north of Manila. Captain Lansdale flew to Tokyo to brief Generals MacArthur and Willoughby about this stunning discovery, and then he went on to DC to brief President Truman.

After discussions with his cabinet, Truman decided to proceed with the gold recovery, but he kept it a state secret. Much of this war prize had originally been looted by the Nazis. To avoid a trace of initial ownership, the Nazis had melted the gold down, and then recast it as ingots marked with the swastika and black eagle of the Reichsbank. Original owners had died and pre-war governments had vanished, so this was hard to trace. Eastern Europe was sinking behind the Iron Curtain, so returning gold there was not feasible. Henry L. Stimson's special assistants on this project were his deputies John J. McCloy and Robert A. Lovett (and consultant Robert B. Anderson). Their solution was the Black Eagle Trust. The idea was first discussed secretly with the allies (in July 1944), when 44 nations met at Bretton Woods, New Hampshire. This is confirmed in documents from high-level sources, including a CIA officer based in Manila [perhaps Lansdale], and former CIA Deputy Director Ray Cline, who learned of Santy's recoveries in 1945. Even in the 1990s, Cline tried to control this Japanese war gold, which was then still in Citibank vaults.

After briefing President Truman and others in DC (including McCloy, Robert Lovett, and Stimson), Captain Lansdale returned to Tokyo in November 1945 with Robert B. Anderson. MacArthur then accompanied Anderson and Lansdale on a covert flight to Manila, where they toured the vaults; Santy had opened them for inspection. While inside, Anderson and MacArthur strolled down *"…row after row of gold bars stacked two meters tall."* Far from being bankrupted by the war, Japan had been greatly enriched, and (thanks to Washington's intervention) Japan used this treasure for its post-war recovery. To the delight of the Japanese citizens, this gold was *not* transferred to Fort Knox where it could have benefited

Americans. Furthermore, there has been no audit of Ft. Knox since 1950. But see "Donald Trump, Elon Musk want to visit Fort Knox gold depository"[515] *and* "Fort Knox vs. No Gold: The Truth About America's Gold Reserves."[516]

According to Ray Cline and others, during 1945-1947 this (Santy and Lansdale) gold was discreetly moved by ship to 176 accounts at banks in 42 countries. For example, some gold was trucked to warehouses at the US navy base in Subic Bay (west of Manila) and to the US air force base at Clark Field (north of Manila). Preference went to the navy because of the massive weight of this bullion. Secrecy was vital. If the recovery of a huge mass of stolen gold had become known, the market price of gold would have plummeted, and thousands of people would have tried to claim it. So then DC would have been bogged down while resolving ownership.

The secrecy surrounding these recoveries was total. Robert Anderson and Paul Helliwell traveled globally, setting up these black gold accounts, while providing cash for political funds throughout the noncommunist world. In 1953, to reward him, President Eisenhower nominated Robert Anderson to a cabinet post as Secretary of the Navy. The following year Anderson rose to Deputy Secretary of Defense. Later he became Secretary of the Treasury (1957-1961, just before Douglas Dillon assumed that position). After that, Anderson resumed private life, but remained closely involved with the CIA's global network of "black banks," as created by Paul Helliwell. Eventually, Anderson got embroiled in the scandal of the Bank of Credit and Commerce International (BCCI),[517] a bank with CIA ties – and Ike wondered why he had ever trusted him. BCCI had a major office in the Cayman Islands. Besides their superb scuba diving, the Caymans have been the third largest banking community in the world. Its GDP (per capita) of US $109,684 is one of the highest in the world. Immigrants from over 140 countries and territories reside in the Cayman Islands. This self-governing territory has 87,866 residents, but it is only 20 miles long![518]

But no one made better (political) use of these gold recoveries than Ed Lansdale. For his role in enabling the Black Eagle Trust, Lansdale became the darling of the Dulles brothers and their Georgetown crowd. Writing to the US Ambassador in Manila (Admiral Raymond Spruance), Allen

---

515 https://www.usatoday.com/story/news/politics/2025/02/28/donald-trump-elon-musk-want-to-visit-fort-knox-gold-depository/80067497007/?gnt-cfr=1&gca-cat=p.

516 https://www.usgoldbureau.com/news/post/fort-knox-vs-no-gold.

517 Regarding BCCI, see *False Profits: The Inside Story of BCCI, the World's Most Corrupt Financial Empire* (1992) by Peter Truell and Larry Gurwin.

518 Cayman Islands - Wikipedia. Also see Hopsicker, p. 355.

Dulles called Lansdale *"our mutual friend."* In the early 1950s, Allen Dulles gave Lansdale $5 million to finance CIA operations against the Hukbalahaps (rural farmers) in the Philippines. When he sent Lansdale to Vietnam in 1954, Dulles told Ike that he was sending one of his *"best men."* In the late 1950s, Lansdale was in and out of Tokyo on secret missions with a hand-picked team of Filipino assassins. Lansdale was also close to Richard Nixon. ***Without exception, Lansdale's Asian adventures were costly failures.***

In 1958, Joseph Mankiewicz directed the movie, *"The Quiet American."* (View the marquee here.) Amazingly, Lansdale persuaded Mankiewicz to change the script. The protagonist (Alden Pyle) was played by Audie Murphy, who became the hero. On the other hand, Thomas Fowler (played by Michael Redgrave) reverted to the bad guy. According to critic Robbie Graham (about Fowler), *"…this is instead now the man whose moral compass has gone awry."* Graham Greene disowned the film as a *"propaganda film for America."* My reaction is simple: This is Lansdale at his best – he turned the script upside down! After all, he was the psy op specialist.[519]

The above comments are chiefly adapted from Sterling Seagrave's comments on the Education Forum (as cited just above); Sterling and his wife Peggy had written *Gold Warriors: America's Secret Recovery of Yamashita's Gold* (2005).

In 2002, another movie version was produced, this time starring Michael Caine and Brendan Fraser: The Quiet American (2002) - IMDb. On this second occasion, Graham Greene (with others) – but not Ed Lansdale – was credited as a writer. Ed was not happy – well actually he was dead.

Before we leave Lansdale, also note the strong McCloy-Rockefeller connection. With offices in New York City, London, Tokyo, Hong Kong, Singapore, Moscow, and DC – Milbank, Tweed, Hadley & McCloy is still one of the world's oldest and most distinguished international law firms. It is famous for its historic representation of the Rockefeller family, and

519 "Edward Lansdale - JFK Assassination Debate" - The Education Forum: https://educationforum.ipbhost.com/topic/13678-edward-lansdale/.

especially for its relationship to the Chase Manhattan Bank. Their law firm also claims other prestigious clients, e.g., the New York Stock Exchange.

Before 1946, McCloy was Assistant Secretary of the War Department, where he met Nelson Rockefeller (Lansdale's good friend); Nelson eventually (in 1946) persuaded McCloy to join their law firm. Later McCloy became president of the World Bank (subsequently headed by McNamara), then high commissioner of Germany, and finally chairman of both the Ford Foundation (later headed by Mac Bundy) and the Chase Manhattan Bank, as well as JFK's special assistant on disarmament.[520] That concludes our summary of Lansdale, the Rockefellers, and McCloy.[521]

When Sam Helpern (who had known Lansdale for a decade) was the new deputy chief of the Cuba desk and an OSS veteran (in about 1962), he recalled Lansdale: *"Ed had this aura around him. Some people believed he was a kind of a magician. But he was basically a con man. You take a look at his proposed plan for getting rid of Castro. It's utter nonsense"* (slighted adapted from Weiner, p. 185).

Late in life Ed confessed that he had been CIA all along (Boot, Kindle, 101). Of course, he had never been a pilot. Here is a short excerpt from a twilight interview with him; the link is cited immediately below the excerpt (the yellow line is in the original transcript).

C: So you were never paid by CIA; you were paid by Air Force...

L: Yeah.

C: But for all intents and purposes, you were on detached service to CIA?

L: Yeah.

Edward Lansdale Interviews | Cecil B. & Laura G. Currey Archive | Fort Hays State University[522] *and* November 12, 1985 Interview with Edward Lansdale.[523]

---

520 Milbank, Tweed, Hadley & McCloy -- Company History.(https://www.company-histories.com/Milbank-Tweed-Hadley-McCloy-Company-History.html).

521 For more fascinating background on McCloy, see Milbank, Tweed, Hadley & McCloy -- Company NEW History (https://www.company-histories.com/Milbank-Tweed-Hadley-McCloy-Company-History.html) and https://kayej.substack.com/p/cia-connected-dc-hospital-chief-advised?

522 https://scholars.fhsu.edu/lansdale_interviews/.

523 https://scholars.fhsu.edu/cgi/viewcontent.cgi?article=1057&context=lansdale_interviews.

Cecil B. Curry used these interviews for his book *Ed Lansdale* (1988); I confess that I have not read it. But today (March 3, 2025) it can be purchased on Amazon for $55-95.

As we close this section on Lansdale, I would re-emphasize several points. Paul Linebarger was the former Army officer who *wrote the official textbook on propaganda* and psychological warfare; he recalled that Lansdale had been one of his top students. Lansdale supported the mad scenarios in Lemnitzer's Northwoods proposals. In the Philippines, Ed had worked with the arch-conservative Willoughby. He was also close friends with Nelson Rockefeller and Charles Cabell and even with Richard Nixon, while Allen Dulles always had his back. Prouty (who died in 2001 – five years before Pat Kelly) strongly suspected that Lansdale had sent him to the South Pole to isolate him from "The Big Event."

Furthermore, one of Lansdale's first decisions for Operation Mongoose was to appoint Bill Harvey as head of Task Force W. The operational headquarters for Mongoose was at the CIA JM/WAVE station in Miami (the largest CIA station in the world at that time). This station was directed by Ted Shackley, where David Morales was second in command.[524] So we promptly see multiple ominous connections, i.e., Lansdale, Harvey, Shackley, Morales – and even McCloy.[525]

In 1962, JFK chose McCloy as his personal representative to negotiate the removal of Soviet missiles and IL–28 bombers from Cuba. Since RFK had chosen Lansdale to direct Operation Mongoose (November 1961–April 1964),[526] how likely is it that these two men (Lansdale and McCloy) at least communicated about Cuba, if not about other matters (like the Golden Lily treasure vaults)?

Boot notes that Ed was a Christian Scientist; this cult was created in 1866 by Mary Baker Eddy. Ed (perhaps named after Eddy?) was also an adulterer (which that church permits – despite the Seventh Commandment); in 1946, he met his future second wife (Pat Kelly) a young, attractive Filipino widow with children. But he remained legally married to his first wife, Helen Batcheller, until she died in 1972. After his Asian

524 Operation Mongoose: https://spartacus-educational.com/JFKmongoose.htm.

525 For even more fascinating connections, consider this enlightening overview as presented by John Newman and Gus Russo: "Major General Edward G. Lansdale, Colonel Howard Burris and Air Force Intelligence Connections to the Kennedy Assassination" at the Hyatt Regency Hotel at Reunion Square, Dallas, Texas, October 24, 1992 (Tatro, November 2023, pp. 113-114).

526 Historical Documents - Office of the Historian. (https://history.state.gov/historicaldocuments/frus1977-80v23/d77)

debacles, his greatest failure was his abandonment of his first wife and their children back in the US.[527]

Ed smoked and drank, which is permitted by the Christian Science church (and is not prohibited by the Ten Commandments). But a belief in matter (as in *the physical world*) is *not* permitted by this church. So, if members of this church commit adultery, they have only to think spiritual thoughts and all will be well. Although they seem to enjoy physical pleasures, they do not believe in an afterlife.

Despite the Christian Scientists' disbelief in solid matter (only the spiritual world exists), Lansdale (like so many others in this JFK case) is buried under genuine earth at Arlington National Cemetery.

WILLIAM KING HARVEY (1915-1976)

As an operative, Harvey fits better into Part I. Part II is chiefly about the sponsors, but this section is useful inasmuch as it shows Harvey's connections to some powerful sponsors.

> *In close cooperation with CIA secret warfare expert Vernon Walters – William Harvey, chief of the CIA station in Rome, and Renzo Rocca, Director of the Gladio units within the military secret service, Servizio Informazioni Difesa (SID), and De Lorenzo escalated the secret war. Rocca first used his secret Gladio army to bomb the office of the DCI (Director of Central Intelligence) and the offices of a few daily newspapers and thereafter blamed the terror on the left….*[528]

RENZO ROCCA → HARVEY → WALTERS → HELMS → LBJ

Italian intelligence (SIFAR) recruited 4000 (sic) provocateurs to work with Rocca and his army. In 1968 Rocca was found dead (of a head shot) in his Rome office. It was ruled a suicide but his hands showed no trace of firing a gun, and bloodstains showed he had been lying flat on the floor. General Carlo Ciglieri began investigating the SIFAR, but then he was found dead on a dirt road outside Padua (where even today Galileo is still fondly remembered)![529]

RENZO ROCCA → HARVEY → LEMNITZER → LBJ

527 "The Mysterious American" (https://www.chron.com/local/the-observation-post/article/The-Mysterious-American-12822396.php).

528 Ganser, Kindle. Also see Paul Williams, p. 75.

529 Chapter 12 – The Assassination of JFK, Gladio and Israel – The Terrorism Business | by Brendan Devenney | Medium. (https://medium.com/@dubhelloco/chapter-12-the-assassination-of-jfk-gladio-and-israel-the-terrorism-business-d26129f9bca2)

When Bill Harvey arrived in Rome to assume his position as CIA station chief, he didn't waste any time.

> He ... *urged Col. Renzo Rocca,*[530] *a top SIFAR counterespionage chief, to sabotage the center-left partnership that had gained momentum with Kennedy's visit. Harvey pushed Rocca to use his 'action squads' to carry out bombings of Christian Party democrat offices and newspapers – terrorist acts that were to be blamed on the left.*[531]

Dulles was wired into the Texas oil industry. His law firm (Sullivan and Cromwell) had provided legal counsel for many years. Furthermore, the brother (Earle Cabell) of Allen's deputy (Charles Cabell) has been officially linked to the CIA via a recent document release, so we can now imagine four more possible chains...

Murchison → Allen Dulles → LBJ

E. Cabell → C. Cabell → Allen Dulles → LBJ

Lansdale → Colby → Allen Dulles → LBJ

Lansdale → C. Cabell → Allen Dulles → LBJ

530 Oddly then, Harvey worked with Renzo Rocca in Italy – at the same time that Angleton (with deep roots in Italy) worked with Ray Rocca in Washington, DC. Are these two Roccas related? I have no idea – but after WW II, Ray Rocca remained in *Italy* and was Angleton's liaison with the Italian intelligence service until his own (Ray's) return to Washington in the summer of 1953.

531 Talbot 2015, p. 475.

Col. Fletcher Prouty and Gen. Victor Krulak
both worked with Gen. Edward Lansdale in the Pentagon.
Both men identify him being in Dealey Plaza, Nov 22, 1963.

Gen. Lansdale specialized in political-psychological warfare operations and manipulation of governments

He worked for Allen Dulles, the Director of Central Intelligence. Although his cover story title was Air Force Colonel and later General, he was always working for the CIA.

The photo of him reveals deep involvement with certain members of the CIA in the planning, removal, cover story and cover-up of the assassination of President Kennedy in Dallas on Nov 22, 1963.

Planning and cover story for such manipulation of government personnel was Landale's forte.

Documents shown here are available at www.prouty.org

Mayor Earle Cabell

Ed Lansdale's book

Robert McNamara

In 1969, Henry Kissinger and US General Alexander Haig (who ran NATO as Supreme Allied Commander in Europe during 1974–1979) authorized Licio Gelli (fascist and former liaison officer between the Italian government and Nazi Germany) to *"recruit four-hundred high ranking Italian and NATO officers into his lodge."*

This lodge was a secret Masonic group called Propaganda Due (P2).[532]

---

532 Ganser, p. 74. Also note that Centro Mondiale Commercial (CMC) and P2 shared the *same office* space (Fred Litwin, "On the Trail of Delusion" - Part Three) (https://www.kennedysandking.com/john-f-kennedy-reviews/fred-litwin-on-the-trail-of-delusion-part-three). Also see *The Ghost: The Secret Life of CIA Spymaster, James Jesus Angleton* (2017) by Jefferson Morley. Readers interested in real detective tales will delight in "The Dangling Man," in *Coroner at Large* (1985) by Thomas Noguchi. (See https://archive.org/details/coroneratlarge00nogu/page/n5/mode/2up.) The protagonist is Roberto Calvi, who was known as "the Vatican banker." On June 18, 1982, he was found dangling (dead) from the Blackfriars Bridge in London. In his pockets were $20,000 in foreign currencies (probably enough to pay off St. Peter soon thereafter) and 12 pounds of bricks and stones. In order to achieve his final position (despite his known vertigo) he had to negotiate down a 20 foot ladder in order to reach the bridge scaffolding. Noguchi has

> *De Gaulle was convinced that the coup was supported by the Allen Dulles-led CIA – and the French press was filled with leaks alleging this secret US involvement.... But Kennedy took pains to assure de Gaulle that he did not back the coup, and in fact he offered to defend the embattled French government with US military firepower.*[533]

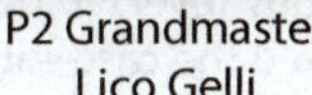
P2 Grandmaster Lico Gelli

The Dangling Man: Roberto Calvi

Mafia Conduit: Michele Sindona

Abe Fortas & LBJ "The Treatment"

solved this case (as a murder), which had remained open. In the 1990s, Tom had called me to hear my view of the JFK autopsy materials.

Thomas Noguchi had done the autopsy on RFK. He believed that all the evidence pointed to a second gunman, but he was not permitted to submit this during Sirhan's trial. In his 1983 memoir, Tom stated: *"Thus I have never said that Sirhan Sirhan killed RFK."* As RFK, Jr., has recently pointed out, the evidence implicated Thane Eugene Cesar. Noguchi noted that the pertinent gun was extremely *near the skin* when the bullet entered the right mastoid process. This could not have been Sirhan's gun (*Coroner* (1983) by Thomas T. Noguchi, MD, p. 108). Of course, Sirhan's lawyer, Grant Cooper, began the trial by asserting that Sirhan was just another lone assassin.

But Cooper had been blackmailed – he was facing an indictment for possessing stolen transcripts of a grand jury proceeding; it was a case of card cheating by Johnny Roselli at the Friars Club (*Who Killed Bobby? The Unsolved Murder of RFK* (2008) by Shane O'Sullivan). But even after RFK's death, LBJ could not leave well enough alone. He cancelled a flight for a brain surgeon for RFK (*RFK: A Candid Biography of RFK* (1998) by C. David Heyman) and he tried to prevent RFK's burial at Arlington! (*Mutual Contempt: LBJ, RFK, and the Feud That Defined a Decade* (1998) by Jeff Shesol).

P2 (Propaganda Due) had evolved from Catholic Gladio units that met in Masonic lodges. (The movie, *The Godfather III*, cites P2.) Their grandmaster was Lucio Gelli, who had met with George H. W. Bush in Langley (1980) to plan the October Surprise. (See *October Surprise* (1989) by Barbara Honegger.) The 953 members of P2 included Silvio Berlusconi (future prime minister), Michele Sindona, Robert Calvi, and top members of Italian intelligence, military, media, as well as select politicians (Ganser, pp. 109, 193 and Lernoux, p. 179).

Gelli had also arranged arms shipments to Muammar el-Qaddafi – to Libya via Argentina. Hillary Clinton (who assisted Libya's return to a slave market) was not pleased about these shipments – and the slaves did not cheer when Hillary was awarded the Presidential Medal of Freedom from Joe Biden. (Well, the English language is always ripe for ambiguity – I mean that she was awarded the medal by Joe, not that she was necessarily free of him!) Today, thanks to Hillary, hundreds of migrants are still bought and sold across the country every week: Slavery in Libya - Wikipedia.

533 "Fifty-five Years Ago: Attempt to Overthrow France's Charles De Gaulle. Was the CIA Involved?" - Global ResearchGlobal Research - Centre for Research on Globalization (https://www.globalresearch.ca/fifty-five-years-ago-attempt-to-overthrow-frances-charles-de-gaulle-did-cia-help/5521661).

See these footnotes on Gelli,[534] Calvi,[535] and Sindona.[536]

De Gaulle acknowledged that JFK himself was not behind the French officers' rebellion, but the incident clarified to both leaders that something was ominous: *"Kennedy was not in charge of his own government."*[537]

---

534 In 1973, Gelli flew to Argentina with Juan Perón. While in exile in Madrid, Juan had also been a good friend of Skorzeny; Gelli also often visited Juan in Madrid. In 1981, Gelli was the rare Italian invited to Ronald Reagan's inauguration – it was suspiciously on *the same day* that the American hostages in Iran were released! Three days after Calvi was hanged, Gelli was arrested in a Geneva bank while trying to withdraw $60 million; he was using an Argentine passport. After his incarceration, Gelli bribed his way out of prison, but he did not die until 2015 at the age of 96! So, some crimes pay more than others.

On July 19, 2005, Gelli was formally indicted by Roman Magistrates for the murder of Roberto Calvi (Licio Gelli - Wikipedia). This decision was subsequently reversed due to insufficient evidence. However, I believe that Tom Noguchi has solved the case – it was a murder, as most Italians promptly recognized. See a prior footnote.

535 Calvi knew what was coming. At the time of his death, he was on the run and using an alias. He had been a longtime member of P2, and was known as "the Vatican banker." Also watch the movie, *The Godfather III*. Hirohito also liked the Vatican bank; he once transferred $45 million to it (Sterling and Peggy Seagrave, Kindle, 428). For more on Gelli, Calvi and Sindona, read Lernoux's book, especially chapters 9 and 10.

In 2018, Paul Williams (pp. 45-46) wrote that the Vatican Bank (officially the IOR – for The Institute for Works of Religion) was the *"perfect place for the CIA and the Sicilian Mafia to launder their ill-gotten gains of the narcotics trade ... It remains one of the world's leading laundries for dirty cash under Pope Francis."* This conclusion was based on David Gibson, "Vatican Bank Needs More Transparency, Regulators Say," *Huffington Post*, July 18, 2012: Vatican Bank Needs More Transparency, Regulators Say | HuffPost Religion (accessed December 11, 2024) (https://www.huffpost.com/entry/vatican-bank-needs-more-transparency-regulators-say_n_1684198).

536 Michele Sindona was a banker with clear connections to P2 and to the Mafia. With Mafia and CIA funds, Sindona was able to purchase his first bank in Milan. This bank was then used to transfer funds from the Vatican bank to Gladio. Bill Harvey, the new CIA station chief in Rome, was delighted to invite Sir Jocelyn Hambros (of the Hambros Bank) and David Kennedy (of the Continental Illinois Bank) to become minority shareholders (Paul Williams, pp. 82-83). Kennedy had been Secretary of the Treasury under Nixon and also had been US ambassador to NATO. This Kennedy (surely no JFK kin) then became one of Gladio's key agents for the conduit of covert CIA funds; these funds assisted the 1967 coup d'etat in Greece, which was primarily a Gladio effort (Paul Williams, p. 83). As chief American intelligence officer during the Greek Civil War, Karamessines was instrumental in organizing the Greek Central Intelligence Agency (KYP) along American lines (Thomas Karamessines - Wikipedia).

In 1972, Sindona bought a controlling interest in the Franklin National Bank of Long Island, NY. Two years later (no surprise) the bank collapsed (see Lernoux, pp. 179 ff). Just before its collapse, its auditors had seen no problems! (Lernoux, p. 261.) That same year Sindona won the *"Man of the Year"* award from the American Club in Rome. For more about these three antic caballeros (Gelli, Calvi, and Sindona), see Lernoux, pp. 180, 188.

537 *The Devil's Chessboard: Allen Dulles, the CIA, and the Rise of America's Secret Government* (2015) by David Talbot. See a book review: https://www.kirkusreviews.com/book-reviews/david-talbot/the-devils-chessboard/.

> *The secret network, erected at the bosom of NATO and financed by the CIA ... had a branch in Portugal in the 1960s and the 1970s. It was called "Aginter Press" and was allegedly involved in assassination operations in Portugal as well as in the Portuguese colonies in Africa.*[538]

By early 1963, LBJ was a ghost; his once-commanding future grew dimmer by the day – and he knew it. In March, Susan Mary Alsop, Joe's (convenient) wife, told Arthur Schlesinger that LBJ had unburdened himself to her husband, while the columnist was dining "...*a trois* with Lyndon and Ladybird." According to Alsop's wife, *"Lyndon had been very dark and bitter about his frustrations and his prospects."* After recounting the confessional dinner in his journal, Schlesinger added his own observation about LBJ: *"He really has faded astonishingly into the background and wanders unhappily around, a spectral and premature elder statesman."* LBJ even began physically to fade as the months went by, losing so much weight that his suits hung loosely off his shoulders and his eyes seemed to sink inside their sockets.[539]

But if LBJ knew that JFK would be killed, why was he so depressed?[540] Although he must have known that a plot was brewing (at least after the Cuban Missile Crisis), perhaps he considered its odds of success to be dreadfully low. But sometime in the summer of 1963, especially after visits to the LBJ ranch from Colonel Howard Burris (LBJ's military aide since 1961) and Allen Dulles,[541] his faith seemed to increase.[542] But that is not to say that no plot was brewing – most likely, after the fuse had been brightly lit by the Cuban Missile Crisis, it must have begun to take specific

---

538 *On the Trail of Clay Shaw: The Italian Undercover CIA and Mossad Station and the Assassination of JFK* (2018) by Michele Metta, p. 130. Also see Michele Metta, "Clay Shaw, the CMC, and the Stay-Behind Network," *Garrison: The Journal of History and Deep Politics*, Issue #3, October 2019, pp. 205-206.

539 Talbot 2015, p. 490-491.

540 Ibid. This is Talbot's portrait of LBJ in 1963.

541 Although Dulles seemed to get on simply fine with LBJ, his relationship with Ike (as with JFK) had been tenuous, especially after the U-2 incident of May Day 1960. In particular, Dulles had assured Ike that the U-2 was safe. After this perceived betrayal, Ike told his aides that he never wanted to see Allen again. Ike added that Allen would leave the next president a *"legacy of ashes"* (Talbot 2015, pp. 366-367).

Of course, Allen Dulles had also lied to JFK about success at the Bay of Pigs. Unbelievably, the aborted Cuban invasion occurred while Allen was in Puerto Rico nonchalantly giving a talk as the main speaker for the Young Presidents Organization during April 15-16, 1961. Allen obviously never had any respect for JFK; in fact, he never even hung a portrait of JFK at CIA headquarters. But then JFK never hung Allen's portrait in the Oval Office either.

542 "The Big Event - The Devil's Chessboard: Allen Dulles, the CIA, and the Rise of America's Secret Government" (https://erenow.org/modern/the-devils-chessboard-allen-dulles-the-cia/19.php).

shape by the end of 1962.[543] But Twyman quotes Hemming as saying that Banister, in March or April 1962 (even before the Missile Crisis) had approached him to kill JFK. Hemming was stunned and declined. This occurred at the home of Luis Rabel in Metairie, a suburb of New Orleans.[544]

Doris Kearns Goodwin notes that, after he left office, LBJ suffered from depression for some years and was in "*extreme despair;*" he spoke excessively of conspiracy. He had even been seeing a psychiatrist.[545] Her impression was that LBJ, via his provocative lifestyle, was deliberately trying to kill himself. She also hints that he felt guilty – presumably for having illicitly seized the reins of power.[546] LBJ eventually got his wish – he died

543 Dick Russell implies that the plot began by late 1962. He hints that the Cuban exiles (during 1962-1963) lit the fuse. Furthermore, after the Missile Crisis, the Joint Chiefs were also quite upset (Russell 2008, p. 222). Daniel Ellsberg recalled the situation right after the Crisis: *"There was virtually a coup atmosphere in Pentagon circles.... The atmosphere was poisonous, poisonous."* Talbot emphasizes that the Air Force (under LeMay) was particularly virulent – and remained so for another 25 years! (Talbot 2015, p. 453.) On the other hand, Hinckle and Turner (p. 272) suspect that the decision to kill JFK was made in the spring of 1963. Oswald was then instructed by his "pro tem handler," Guy Banister, to advertise himself as a *"commie-nut."*

Russell also cites a quote from late 1962 made by a Miami Cuban, Jose Aleman: *"Mark my words. This man Kennedy is in trouble.... He is going to be hit"* (Russell 2008, p. 142). One of Eugenio Martinez's best friends was Aleman, who was the son of one of Cuba's wealthiest men: Eugenio Martinez. Aleman later claimed that the Mafia were after him, so he shot his family members and killed himself (*The Last Investigation* (1993) by Gaeton Fonzi, pp. 256-257). Also see *"The 'mentally unbalanced' son of a once-wealthy Cuban exile"* - UPI Archives (https://www.upi.com/Archives/1983/07/31/The-mentally-unbalanced-son-of-a-once-wealthy-Cuban-exile/4827428472000/). Finally, Aleman's father-in-law had been a lawyer for Lucky Luciano in Havana (Hinckle and Turner, p. 353).

On the other hand, Russell quotes Richard Case Nagell as saying that he had heard of a plot against JFK (using Oswald) – *before* the Missile Crisis. He claims to have reported this (via CIA channels) to Des FitzGerald on August 27, 1963 (Russell 2008, p. 228). Recall that Oswald had returned to the US in June 1962; Dick Russell implies that Oswald was inserted into the conspiracy just one month later, by July 1962 (Russell 2008, p. 212). [After Bill Harvey left for Indiana, FitzGerald took over Bill's leadership of Staff D.]

544 Twyman, p. 698.

545 See *Power Beyond Reason: The Mental Collapse of Lyndon Johnson* (2002) by D. Jablow Hershman, Ph.D. and Gerald Tolchin, et al., p. 6:

> Johnson may well have been the most psychologically unstable person ever to assume the presidency. He was a tragic figure pursued by demons, real and imagined ... It appears likely that Lyndon Johnson suffered from bipolar (manic-depressive) disorder throughout his life, a condition that grew worse as he grew older, peaking just as he reached the zenith of his influence and power.

546 *Lyndon Johnson and the American Dream* (2015), p. 366. On one occasion, LBJ told Doris Kearns Goodwin that (after he had become president) he had worried that his POTUS position had been wrongfully acquired, so that he would be cancelled once the truth became known. I wonder if he had been reading Shakespeare's *MacBeth* – or perhaps it was MacBird! (MacBird! - Wikipedia.) *Macbird!* opened at The Village Gate on February 22, 1967, and after 386 performances,

of a heart attack on January 22, 1973 (just two days after Nixon's second inauguration) at the young age of 64 – not even old enough for traditional Social Security payments.[547] Unfortunately, he died just a year before lithium was approved for bipolar disorder (manic depression). Had this drug been available earlier, world history would likely have been turned upside down.[548] Of course, lithium for Ivan the Terrible (1530-1584), or Napolean Bonaparte, or Hitler, or Stalin (all bipolar) would have transformed the world as well.[549] See my pending book for more about bipolar disorder and its havoc on world history.

Major General Charles A. Willoughby (1892-1972)

Willoughby said he was born on March 8, 1892, in Heidelberg, Germany, as Adolph Karl Weidenbach (or perhaps Tscheppe-Weidenbach). He emigrated from Germany to the U.S. in 1910, then in October 1910 he enlisted in the US Army, where he served in the infantry, initially as a private, later rising to sergeant. He was honorably discharged in October 1913. He was fluent in English, Spanish, German and French (and later Japanese).[550] Willoughby was connected to Allen Dulles, the Hunt Oil family of Dallas, and the anti-Castro Cuban exiles.[551] Rob Reiner has nominated Willoughby as the technician for the JFK assassination.[552] Dick Russell agrees.

Gen. Charles Willoughby, Gen. Matthew Ridgeway, Gen Walter Bedell "Beetle" Smith (CIA)

---

closed on January 21, 1968. While in medical school, I once (1973) thoroughly enjoyed the live play in Ann Arbor, Michigan.

547 Despite his undomesticated lifestyle, LBJ had a longer life than Mickey Mantle: LBJ lived 64 years, 4 months and 26 days, while Mickey lived only 63 years 9 months, and 24 days. But while Mickey only wrecked his knee (and his marriage and his children), LBJ managed to wreck the world. Of course, Mickey was not manic-depressive.

548 Hershman and Tolchin, p. 248.

549 *Brotherhood of Tyrants: Manic Depression and Absolute Power* (1994) by D. Jablow Hershman and Julian Lieb, MD.

550 In the early 1940s, he frequented the Spanish Club in Manila. Charles A. Willoughby - Wikipedia.

551 "Was General Charles Willoughby the Mastermind of the JFK Assassination?" (https://www.onthetrailofdelusion.com/post/was-general-charles-willoughby-the-mastermind-of-the-jfk-assassination).

552 "(6) Rob Reiner Names Four Shooters in the JFK Assassination" (https://randallbeach.substack.com/p/rob-reiner-names-four-shooters-in).

I concur – Willoughby had a well-nigh perfect resume for "The Big Event." Even Noel Twyman was (at least mostly) on board, as he states (about Willoughby): *"…was capable of planning an operation similar to the JFK assassination"* (p. 551). On the other hand, Twyman (p. 542) hints that the fuse (for "The Big Event") was first lit by Jimmy Hoffa and the Mafia. But I could then counter that the anti-Castro Cubans had first exposed their wrath to Phillips – or to Willoughby – or to Morales – or to Harvey (among others). It is not essential to know exactly who first lit the fuse – after all, someone was surely going to toss this match. Several serious options exist.

From Douglas Caddy: Lee Shepherd posted this on Facebook today (December 31, 2020). The reference to JFK appears near its end. Author Dick Russell wrote:[553]

> *While his mentor, General* [Douglas] *MacArthur, passed into quiet retirement and was occasionally sought by Kennedy for advice,* [Major General Charles A.] *Willoughby* [MacArthur's Chief of Intelligence] *approached his seventieth birthday with samurai swords placed strategically next to his desk. Willoughby's holy war against the "Red Menace" found him sitting on the boards of most of the major conservative groups, and reaching into Europe and Latin America to start his own International Committee for the Defense of Christian Culture….*

MacArthur (at 6' 0") often referred to his 6'3" aide as *"My little Fascist."* The World Anti-Communist League (WACL) was a far right-wing international, non-governmental organization of politicians; the group was the brainchild of Gen. Willoughby. Alongside Gen. Edwin Walker, he also sat on the board of the Young Americans for Freedom. He was also a good friend of H. L. Hunt. After WWII ended, Willoughby worked counterintelligence with Edward Lansdale to ruthlessly suppress the guerrilla resistance movement in the Philippines.

Walker → Willoughby → H. L. Hunt → Ed Clark → LBJ

Willoughby → Lansdale → C. Cabell → Burris → LBJ

In 1951, Gen. Willoughby retired from the army after 41 years, but he maintained a relationship with Military Intelligence (G-2). Willoughby was a staunch supporter of Sen. Joe "Tailgunner" McCarthy[554] and was

553 Major General Charles A. Willoughby - JFK Assassination Debate - The Education Forum (https://educationforum.ipbhost.com/topic/26882-major-general-charles-a-willoughby/).

554 While growing up in Wisconsin, I watched these Army-McCarthy hearings on

also associated with the American Security Council (ASC), founded in 1955 by ex-FBI agents. The ASC targeted nearly 20,000 leftists during the 1950s, the period of the McCarthyite witch-hunts, which was led by mob attorney Roy Cohn,[555] McCarthy's grand inquisitor and close friend of J. Edgar Hoover. Its policy-advising board, the National Strategy Committee, was managed by Gen. Curtis LeMay and supported by Gen. Lyman Lemnitzer. The ASC was the *"leading public group campaigning to use US military force to oust Castro from Cuba, and to escalate the war in Vietnam."*

Lemnitzer → LeMay → Allen Dulles → Burris → LBJ

Willoughby, the man the US Army Military Intelligence Hall of Fame calls *"The Most Prominent American Intelligence Officer of World War II,"* lobbied the US Congress to authorize $100 million for Gen. Francisco Franco's government in Spain,[556] which he described as *"a cradle of supermen,"* led by the "second greatest general in the world" (MacArthur was the greatest). E. Howard Hunt and William D. Pawley[557] helped to form the top-secret army unit called Field Operations Intelligence (FOI), which worked jointly with Willoughby and the CIA. Richard Case Nagell's connection to Willoughby has also been established. Dick Russell noted that Willoughby had ties to the anti-Castro Cuban exile community in the US[558] and served as a DC representative of the National Advisory Committee while *he was in Texas* between October 31 and *November 21, 1963.*

(black and white) TV.

555 JFK's father was a supporter of Joe McCarthy (i.e., both were Irish Catholics – and both were named Joe). RFK even worked for the much-despised Irish-American senator from my home state of Wisconsin.

556 By 1952, Otto Skorzeny was ensconced in Madrid, Spain. Ava Gardner arrived several years later – and lived in the same building as Otto.

557 William Pawley also knew that other Hunt (H. L.); Pawley helped to persuade H. L. Hunt to support the KMT regime (in China) with millions of dollars. Allen Dulles assisted them in this effort. Pawley also assisted in the CIA plot to overthrow the Guatemalan government of Jacobo Arbenz. After Pawley "retired," he went into business (again) with Meyer Lansky; in Cuba, he bought sugar plantations, an airline and a bus company (Sterling and Peggy Seagrave, Kindle, p. 470). For the KMT, see History of the Kuomintang - Wikipedia. Sun Yat-sen founded this party, but then Chiang Kai-shek assumed control in 1927. Today it is a major political party in Taiwan. The most powerful US voice during this era for Chiang was Henry Luce, the head of *Time/Life*. Henry (a staunch Christian moralist) and Clare were personal friends of Chiang and Madame Chiang (Kwitny, p. 48).

Pawley died in Florida (January 1977) of a self-inflicted gunshot wound. Since many thousands were killed in Guatemala after 1954 – mostly Indian peasants who were murdered by the army – it would have been spellbinding to hear Pawley explain why he still considered his Guatemalan adventure to be a success (Lernoux, p. 237).

Lansky → Pawley → H. L. Hunt → Clark → LBJ

558 Russell 1992, pp. 707-708.

E. H. Hunt → Pawley → Allen Dulles → LBJ

Anti-Castro Cubans → Willoughby → H. L. Hunt → Clark → LBJ

Cuban exile leader Vidal also traveled to Dallas during this time on several occasions, in order to "raise funds" for the anti-Castro exiles; he was under CIA control. Vidal was also a member of a paramilitary group, Intercontinental Penetration Force ("InterPen") that performed illicit deeds that the CIA would not. Authors J. Gary Shaw and Larry Harris note that Vidal's CIA contact, Col. William C. Bishop, often met with extremists Loran Hall, Lewis Bloomfield, Edwin Walker and Charles Willoughby. Three years after the events in Dallas, Willoughby began full time work for H. L. Hunt's son, Nelson Bunker Hunt. Sterling and Peggy Seagrave note in *Gold Warriors* (2005): *"For Willoughby, truth was always flexible."* [So, Willoughby and Angleton were "birds of a feather."] Military intelligence men like Willoughby were never called to testify before the WC, even though Willoughby had worked closely with George H. W. Bush's friend (Alfred Ulmer, former CIA station chief in Paris) and he was associated with Clint Murchison[559] and Bircher John Rousselot. Willoughby died at

559 For many years, Murchison, Jr. had squired Hoover and Clyde Tolson to their bungalow at the Del Charro Hotel in La Jolla, California. Even McNamara said, *"I can believe that"* (Twyman, p. 502). With overtones of Hillary's "expertise" in the cattle futures market (a $100,000 win for her), the rumor is that Hoover never lost a bet on that race track. Nor have I, but I have never bet there. On the other hand, I once found a $20 bill on the sidewalk just outside the track. During the month that Hoover annually vacationed at the Del Charro, his visitors included LBJ, Richard Nixon, John Connally, Meyer Lansky, Santo Trafficante, Johnny Roselli, Sam Giancana, and Carlos Marcello. Murchison, Jr. (who owned the Del Charro) was also involved (like Estes and LBJ) with Jimmy Hoffa and Frank Costello; Frank was a good friend of Sam Giancana and a former business associate of Joseph P. Kennedy (Nelson, Kindle, 144). So, we can now show one more connection:

Murchison → Hoover → LBJ

Murchison had other connections as well. After leaving the JFK administration, McCloy joined a law firm that represented Clint Murchison, Jr. and Sid Richardson. Furthermore, McCloy had done business with these oily men before – while he was at Chase Manhattan Bank. Even earlier, in 1954, Murchison and McCloy had cooperated in a shady deal to take control of the New York Central Railroad (*The Chairman: John J. McCloy and the Making of the American Establishment* (2017) by Kai Bird, pp. 286, 431).

McCloy also liked to relax by hunting whitewings with Murchison, Jr. at his ranch in Mexico. Nonetheless, McCloy had no scruple about serving on the WC. As Walt Disney would say, *"It's a small world, after all!"* [Ironically, this is precisely the title of Chapter 37 in Hopsicker's book.] Also note that, on the day after the WC first met, LBJ awarded McCloy the Freedom Medal in the State Dining Room. Unfortunately, this award still did not free McCloy from the clutches of LBJ. As further fare for reflection, Mae Brussell claims that *"McCloy had a lengthy career riddled with Nazi sympathies:* "The Nazi Connection to the John F. Kennedy Assassination by Mae Brussell" (http://www.maebrussell.com/Mae%20Brussell%20Articles/Nazi%20Connection%20to%20JFK%20Assass.html).

McCloy → Murchison → H. L. Hunt → Ed Clark → LBJ

his gated estate in Naples, Florida in 1972. A longstanding member of the Military Intelligence Hall of Fame, Gen. Willoughby was entombed with full honors in Arlington National Cemetery, ironically not far from the Kennedy brothers.

Vidal →W. Bishop → Willoughby → H. L. Hunt → Clark → LBJ

Murchison → Willoughby → H. L. Hunt → Clark → LBJ

The Women: Clare Boothe Luce, Madame Nhu, and Candy Barr

On November 1, 1963, Trần Lệ Xuân (aka *Madame Nhu* (1924-2011)) was resting from minor surgery at the Beverly Wilshire Hotel. She had just learned of the murder of her (decade-older) husband (Ngô Đình Nhu) and his even older brother (Prime Minister Ngô Đình Diệm). She commented: *"Whoever has the Americans as allies does not need enemies."*[560] She then (perhaps tongue-in-cheek) accused the fiery monks of using *"imported gasoline."* Then she added that she would clap for another monk barbeque show. She also (correctly) prophesied: *"Whatever happens in Vietnam will find its counterpart in the US."* JFK had called her *"that goddamn bitch."* In my opinion she had far too many IQ points (as well as *noblesse oblige* and a sharp tongue) for her limited role. On the other hand, during a visit to Vietnam in 1961, LBJ had called Diệm *"the Winston Churchill of Asia."* But LBJ was even more fond of Madame Nhu; his flirtatious behavior toward her can be appreciated in the image of this couple in this book.[561] During her (October 1963) US tour, Madame had rubbed shoulders with many right-wingers; Hemming even insists that she met with Clint Murchison, Jr.

So, after the Warren Report was issued (and seemingly speaking as a lawyer) McCloy asserted *"I never saw a case that was so completely proven"* (*The Essential Mae Brussell: Investigations of Fascism in America* (2014) edited by Alex Constantine, Kindle). Considering that McCloy had attended only 16 of the 51 formal sessions, and heard less than half of the witnesses, his ability to reach any conclusion at all was a historic feat. Would that modern juries could achieve such efficiency!

Incidentally, McCloy had supervised General Leslie Groves during the Pentagon construction – so that it was called "McCloy's Folly." Groves, of course, later supervised J. Robert Oppenheimer in the Manhattan Project. I still wonder if the US would have been better off without a McCloy.

560 Tatro, November 2023, pp. 38-45.

561 *Our Vietnam: the War 1954-1975* (2000) by A. J. Langguth, p. 131. "Letter to Madame Nhu from Lyndon B. Johnson," Texas Tech University Vietnam Archive, Douglas Pike Collection, Item # 236123070, September 20, 1963.

Tatro notes this:[562]

> *It is documented that the US Embassy* [in Vietnam] *was **electronically bugged*** [emphasis added] *by Nhu's counterintelligence operatives and it is known that Henry Cabot Lodge and Lucien Conein had discussed the impeding coup there, so Diệm and his brother could have theoretically been preparing a counter-attack against JFK long before their own murders.*

Tatro then cites Hemming: [563]

> *Some foreign* [ex- and current] potentates, *including the recently widowed Madame Nhu from Saigon* […who were present in Dallas on that fateful day] ***contributed funds*** [emphasis added] *and plotted separate operations against the president's life.*

During her 1963 US tour, *Time* magazine described Nhu as the guest of honor at Dudley T. Dougherty's Bee County Ranch, where he kept an oil well in his front yard. Then this Dougherty clan brought her to Dallas in October 1963, to be honored at General Walker's "US Day" rally, which Lee Harvey Oswald also attended![564] Also see Michael Griffth's essay on the Diệm family and their possible role on 11/22/1963.[565]

Although *Clare Boothe Luce* was the wife of Henry Luce (the owner of *Time/Life*) she was also widely understood to be a mistress of Allen Dulles. This alone qualifies her for an appearance in this book. But she was also responsible for her right-wing operatives, or *"my boys,"* as she called them. Like Hillary Clinton, she also won the Presidential Medal of Freedom – but she did not trigger the revival of slavery (as Hillary ironically did in Libya). Clare was Madame Nhu's most devoted promoter. In the *National Review* she castigated the US media for attacking the "Dragon Lady" for her remarks during her US tour. Clare described the Madame as a *"militant Catholic, mother of four, and a devoted and fiercely loyal wife."* (That was just before she was widowed.)

Henry Luce spent almost $¼ million during 1963-1964 on anti-Castro groups like Alpha 66. JFK was a prime target for Henry's *"paramilitary journalism."* Henry warned: *"If Jack turns soft on communism,* Time [the magazine – not Father Time] *will cut his throat."* And so Henry became

562 Tatro, November 2023, p. 46.
563 Ibid.
564 Tatro credits Peter Dale Scott's primary research for these scintillating jewels.
565 Michael T. Griffith, "Suspects in the JFK Assassination," Tripod Lycos, revised December 19, 2002.

a primary contributor to the JFK cover-up.[566] His publisher and personal emissary to the CIA (C. D. Jackson) had kept the Zapruder film so sequestered that Garrison had to win a Supreme Court case to use the film during his trial. Jackson kept in close contact with Allen Dulles and John McCloy during this critical period. Carl Bernstein discovered that Clare even knew about some of these machinations. Jackson was a close personal friend of Dulles; Jackson even knew about Allen's affair with Clare. We can only wonder what Jackson told Clover (Allen's wife).[567]

Clare was a former representative in the US House; she had also been an ambassador to Italy. Gaeton Fonzi described how she deliberately led them on a wild goose chase; this burned up US tax dollars as well as much needed investigative time.[568]

Vincent Salandria notes Clare's close relationship with William Pawley, the wealthy oilman with extensive Havana interests. (Recall that Pawley was especially close to Allen Dulles.) Pawley had financed a series of speedboat raids against Castro, and Clare had sponsored one of them. She became friends with one of the crews and even invited them to her New York townhouse. She called them *"my boys."*

Clare was a member of the Board of Directors for McLendon's and Phillip's AFIO. On one occasion she was a keynote speaker; she delivered a *"vigorous defense of the intelligence establishment and a historical review of its successes"* (Fonzi, pp. 58, 322-323). Unfortunately, she died in 1987, twenty years before *Legacy of Ashes* was published in 2007. Such is the bliss of dying early while still ignorant

William Pawley → Clare Luce *(while in the bedroom)* **→ Allen Dulles → LBJ**

And here is a final thought about Clare: in August 1963, Bill Harvey (from Rome) wanted to contact Clare.[569]

Candy Barr (aka Juanita Dale Slusher (1935-2005)) appears in this book because she knew both Jack Ruby and Mickey Cohen. (Candy and Mickey appear together in a photograph in this book.)[570] She had met

566 *Life's* first issue on the assassination required three successive attempts before Luce deemed it to be a satisfactory cover-up. This cost him millions of dollars, but (no worries) he still had residual funds.

567 Opinion | "When a C.I.A. Director Had Scores of Affairs" - *The New York Times.* According to his sister, Eleanor, Dulles had *"at least a hundred"* extramarital affairs, including some during his tenure with the CIA (Allen Dulles - Wikipedia). With so many domestic affairs, it is no wonder that he had so little time for international affairs.

568 *The Last Investigation* (2013) by Gaeton Fonzi.

569 *The Devil is in the Details* (2020) by Alan Dale with Malcom Blunt, pp. 75-76.

570 "Texas Stripper Candy Barr Dies; Had Dalliance With Vegas Mobster" (https://

Jack Ruby in 1952, but their friendship was casual and she rarely (if ever) worked for him.

At 14, she married a young Dallas safecracker named Billy Debbs. *"They became kind of like a teenage Bonnie and Clyde,"* Skip Hollandsworth wrote in a 2001 *Texas Monthly* article. He cracked the safes; she drove the getaway car.[571]

Cohen had contributed funds to "The Big Event." Tatro reports that Eugen Hale Brading called Mickey from the DalTex building that day to report on their success.[572] However, we do not know what Mickey had told Candy that day. But Candy, aside from Mickey's generosity to her, may have learned on other occasions about his charities for the "mechanics." Barr knew Mickey well enough that Cohen accompanied her to the Saints and Sinners testimonial for Milton Berle in April 1959.[573] Candy worked as a "technical adviser" on the 1960 movie, *Seven Thieves,* where she taught Joan Collins how to dance burlesque.[574] Barr was quoted, *"Anytime Miss Collins wants to leave the movies, she has it made in burlesque."*

In 1975, *Oui Magazine* paid this 41-year-old grandmother $5,000 to pose nude. (The average annual salary in the US in 1975 was $7700.) Soon afterward she was interviewed in *Playboy.* She had a casual sexual encounter with Hugh Hefner, who (in 1984) characterized their affair as *"a sort of Sex King and Queen kind of thing. She was wonderful."*

After release from prison, Barr was contacted several times by Jack Ruby. On May 8, 1963, he visited her ranch home in Edna, Texas (her birth city) and gave her a puppy. After Ruby killed Oswald, the FBI came to her home on Thanksgiving. She also testified to the WC. She later reported, *"They thought Ruby had told me names and places and people, which he didn't."* Notice (no surprise) that the FBI did not ask her about what Mickey Cohen had told her. (Recall that the Apalachin Meeting had occurred in late 1957.) She was pardoned by Governor John B. Connally in 1967. (Sarcastically, Ed Tatro believes that JBC himself needed a pardon.)

In 1984, despite the fact that (in 1960) she had served three years and 91 days in prison, the *Texas Monthly* listed her (along with Lady Bird Johnson) not as one of history's perfect prisoners, but rather as one of

---

www.washingtonpost.com/wp-dyn/content/article/2006/01/03/AR2006010301612.html).

571 Twyman, p. 664.

572 Tatro, November 2023, p. 34.

573 Candy Barr - Wikipedia.

574 1959 Photos: Candy Barr Teaches Joan Collins To Dance Burlesque - Flashbak (https://flashbak.com/1959-photos-candy-barr-teaches-joan-collins-to-dance-burlesque-5399/).

the *"perfect Texans."* I can only wonder if LBJ was also a "perfect Texan," especially since (on 11/22/1963) he had squandered his opportunity to be the perfect prisoner.

Juanita Dale Slusher Madame Nhu LBJ

Mickey Cohen and Candy Barr Clare Boothe Luce The Dragon Lady

Money for the Minions

A presidential assassination cannot possibly succeed without money – stacks of illegal money. In this case, three sources exist: Hoffa's pension funds, Mafia accounts, and Texas oil money. According to Twyman, Jimmy Hoffa sent funds via Carlos Marcello to the anti-Castro Cubans. He cites $500,000.[575] In addition (according to Colonel William C. Bishop), Rolando Masferrer transferred an additional $500,000 of Hoffa's funds.[576]

Twyman (citing Hemming) also implicates Mafia funds. Some came from Mickey Cohen on the west coast and from Jack Dragna, who represented the Los Angeles mob. More money came from Las Vegas, which was then forwarded to Carlos Marcello.[577]

575 Twyman, pp. 623, 664, 692. Lawyer Frank Ragano (a habitual liaison to Hoffa and Marcello) delivered a message from Hoffa: *"Tell Marcello and Trafficante that they had to kill the president."* MobMuseum10242017.pdf (https://www.moldea.com/MobMuseum10242017.pdf).

576 Ibid., p. 835.

577 Ibid., p. 664.

But this operation surely required much more than that – especially to pay off the multiple gunmen. A first guess would be $10 million total, but this is obviously difficult to pin down. Just for comparison, Roselli was offered $150,000 (plus expenses) for a hit on Castro, but he said he would not do it just for the money.[578] For comparison, Meyer Lansky had placed a million-dollar bounty on Castro's head.[579] McClellan suggests that Ed Clark alone appropriated $2 million for himself. (For current values multiple by a factor of 10.)

The truly deep pockets in this case must require the oil men who, by keeping their depletion allowance (for years), surely profited by at least hundreds of millions of dollars[580] – over a long time interval. And there is credible evidence that they were involved – after all, without such deep pockets, JFK would likely have survived. As just one example, Twyman cites an offer by H. L. Hunt to kill JFK.[581] According to Gerald Patrick Hemming[582] (who Twyman quotes), the following individuals were in the room during this offer: George de Mohrenschildt,[583] Lester Logue, and Howard K. Davis. Nelson Bunker Hunt was at the opposite end of the room, so he may not have heard this offer. But Twyman cites no specific dollar amount here. Then Twyman cites Hemming again: Larry LaBorde

578 Hinckle and Turner, p. 25.

579 Hinckle and Turner, p. 79. These authors also cite Mario Garcia Kohly, who told Nixon that Castro had put a million-dollar price tag on his (Kohly's) head (p. 198). Kohly once lost to Fulgencio Batista for a Cuban congressional seat, but then he did manage to play golf with *Charles Cabell* and Richard Nixon. After the Bay of Pigs, Kohly rented a large townhouse in Georgetown *next door to Allen Dulles!* (Hinckle and Turner, p. 199.) Furthermore, Robert Morrow once showed Kohly a flawless batch of [Cuban] ten-peso notes, created via the engravers at the US Bureau of Engraving and Printing (*Washington Observer*, October 1, 1966).

580 David Talbot suspects that it might have been billions of dollars (Talbot 2015, p. 488). In 1963, *World Petroleum Magazine* predicted that JFK's reforms could cost US oil up to $280 million every year (Twyman, p. 554). So, the oil men could easily pay for "The Big Event" – and for even more events if necessary!

581 Twyman, p. 699. In 1963, H. L. Hunt's personal fortune was estimated at $16 billion; that was *four times* the visible wealth of the Rockefellers! (In 1963, H.L. Hunt's personal fortune was estimated at $16 billion - Search). This was mostly due to the oil depletion allowance, which had shielded 30% of his oil profits – for decades. In 1968, H. L. Hunt gave Curtis LeMay $1 million (as a personal inducement) in order to recruit him to run on the ticket with George Wallace (Twyman, pp. 517, 550). Hunt also provided cash to Jimmy Hoffa (Twyman, p. 560).

582 Angleton was Hemming's handler! (Twyman, p. 734.)

583 The Baron had interesting fellow residents at the Republic National Bank building in Dallas: Mary Ferrell, Eugene Locke (JFK motorcade), Neil Mallon (Bush protégé), Harold Berman (Ruby lawyer), and Earl Mayfield (LBJ attorney). The latter reported that the building was also filled with CIA agents (*Blood, Money and Power* (2003) by Barr McClellan, p. 177).

was with him (Hemming) when Guy Banister made an offer.[584] Again, the dollar amount is not cited. Twyman (again quoting Hemming) cites Dallas meetings where fund raising for the murder was discussed. But Hemming declined to name these individuals.[585] Hemming also recalled a meeting at the house of John Martino (an electronics expert).[586] Attending were Nicoletti, Giancana, and Charles Tourine, Sr. *"And it was for a hit on Fidel. I passed on $15,000 directly to Felipe Vidal that night and another $15,000 was given to Felipe directly by Martino."* While Roselli lived in Key Biscayne, he was close pals with Martino; they hosted barbeques and raced around in speedboats. After Martino died (rather suspiciously), his private papers confirmed a long relationship with Santo Trafficante, Jr. (Hinckle and Turner, p. 405).

Martino → Roselli → Harvey → Lansdale → Burris → LBJ

Dick Russell (the JFK author) also interviewed Hemming, who recalled *"a retired armed forces type, a guy from the Klan."* Hemming claims that, over a period of time, he saw multiple offers: *"Some of the cheapos talked about $100,000; one said they'd pay a million."*[587]

584 Twyman, p. 682.

585 Ibid., p. 745.

586 Martino also had foreknowledge. FBI files describe Martino as *"a very close friend"* of Felipe Vidal Santiago (*On the Trail of JFK Assassins* (2008) by Dick Russell, p. 220). Furthermore, Loren Hall saw Giancana give $30,000 to Martino for their unsuccessful raid on Cuba on June 8, 1963 (Russell 2008, p. 140). This raid involved William Pawley, Shackley, Morales, Hemming, Felipe Vidal Santiago, Frank Sturgis, Richard Billings (of *Life*), and Rip Robertson. Operation Tilt (Bayo/Pawley Mission) (https://spartacus-educational.com/JFKtilt.htm). Like Giancana, Martino died in 1975 (supposedly of a heart attack). But he died at a dodgy moment; he had just spoken to a Texas business associate, Fred Claasen. He told Fred that he had been a CIA contract agent and that he knew about the JFK plot. And shortly after this conversation, he was dead.

Harvey died (of heart disease) in June 1976. Roselli was savagely murdered in August 1976 and Morales died (in mysterious circumstances) in 1978. The HSCA was established on September 15, 1976, and terminated in late 1978. In 1977 – during the HSCA – Nicoletti was murdered on the same day that de Mohrenschildt died. The HSCA era was distinctly unhealthy. (Nicoletti is sometimes discredited as a sniper due to his 20/200 vision without glasses. But my naked vision (before LASIK) was much worse than that. However, with eyeglasses, I could easily achieve 20/20 vision.)

Furthermore, ten years earlier, on February 22, 1967, less than a week after the Garrison probe was announced, David Ferrie was found suspiciously dead in his apartment. That *same* night, Eladio del Valle (an associate of both Oswald and Ferrie) was brutally murdered in Miami. He was shot, then hacked, and then abandoned (thoroughly dead) in his Cadillac – just as Garrison was looking for him. According to Claudia Furiati (*The Plot to Kill Kennedy and Castro*, p. 139), Eladio was a partner with Trafficante in smuggling operations before the Cuban revolution. He escaped to the US on January l, 1959 (the final day of the Batista regime).

587 Russell 1992, p. 60.

Finally, Felipe Vidal Santiago (hereafter called Vidal)[588] told Cuban General Escalante that, in early November 1963, he met with wealthy Texas businessmen at the Petroleum Club. Twyman notes that this is confirmed by an HSCA document that showed Vidal in Texas during November 6-11, 1963.[589] Furthermore, Colonel William C. Bishop (a CIA hit man)[590] told J. Gary Shaw of a similar trip by Vidal to Texas in April 1963. Twyman also reports that Bishop, Vidal, and Hargraves visited Dallas in 1963. Independently, Hemming told Dick Russell of a trip to Dallas by Vidal, in the week just before 11/22/1963.[591]

Vidal → Col. Bishop → Willoughby → H. L. Hunt → Clark → LBJ

Foreign Presses for American Currency

One final – and quite astonishing – source of funds came to my attention rather late; this has been long overlooked in the JFK literature. Allen Dulles controlled a CIA contingency fund with Schroder's Limited, a British bank.[592] At that time, this fund contained $50,000,000;[593] sixty years later, adjusted for inflation, this would be over $500,000,000. (It would be highly embarrassing to ask Allen how these funds had been collected.) It is shocking – even unconscionable – that in a so-called democracy a single American, unelected and unaccountable, had access to such funds – as well as control over them. What other government official has had sole discretion over such a vast sum of (supposedly) public funds? Furthermore, these funds were typically unaudited – and mostly hidden from Congress![594] Without congressional approval, not even JFK could unilaterally tap into such gargantuan figures.

---

588 Twyman also cites Vidal as being with Oswald during the (apparently staged) shooting of General Walker (Twyman, p. 836). Also see Vidal in this commentary: Doug Campbell Explains Who Was Most Likely to Go Rogue: AARC - JFK Assassination Debate - The Education Forum (https://educationforum.ipbhost.com/topic/31031-doug-campbell-explains-who-was-most-likely-to-go-rogue-aarc/#ipsLayout_mainArea).

589 I have not searched for this.

590 Authors J. Gary Shaw and Larry Harris note that Vidal's CIA contact, Col. William C. Bishop (who had served in the Pacific theater with Willoughby), often met with extremists Loran Hall, Lewis Bloomfield, Edwin Walker and Charles Willoughby.

Vidal → Col. W. Bishop → Willoughby → H. L. Hunt → Clark → LBJ

591 Twyman, p. 691.

592 This appears to be the same bank: About us | Schroders (https://www.schroders.com/en-us/us/individual/about-us/). As of June 2024, they managed nearly a trillion (sic) dollars. Their website describes two centuries of investing, and they still have a branch office in New York City.

593 Hinckle and Turner, p. 83.

594 The US constitution delegates spending authority to Congress; the CIA is not cited – nor is Allen Dulles. The Founding Fathers would have been horrified to see so

The CIA's connection to Schroder's went way back to 1937, when Allen Dulles (as a member of Sullivan and Cromwell) was named a Schroder bank director. When Dulles joined the CIA, other partners of his law firm took over his seat on the bank board. Hinckle and Turner (*Deadly Secrets*, 1981 and 1992) note that Schroder's had a New York branch (they still do), which clearly made business simpler for Sullivan and Cromwell, who were also located in New York City.[595] However, I have seen no clues that Allen Dulles used any of these funds for 11/22/1963. Of course, if he had, that would prove David Talbot correct, i.e., Dulles might then be considered the overall mastermind of 11/22/1963. Furthermore, insofar as I know, the ARRB did not ask Schroder's for assassination-related records. And I suspect that none of the still-sequestered (nearly 4000) JFK-related records (as of December 21, 2024) at the National Archives will be helpful either (visa vis Schroder's bank).[596]

To finalize this issue, I would emphasize one last point: even if each of these witnesses is discounted, someone had to pay these renegades. If those cited here were not involved, then someone else must have paid – or we would have skipped over "The Big Event" of 11/22/1963. Quite literally, millions of dollars (more likely at least tens of millions) were required. So, who donated at the office that day?

Well actually, for this purpose, the CIA may not have needed a domestic office. The US officially donated printing plates for US currency to other countries. About a decade ago, in an official publication, Iran claimed

---

much power and money allocated to the sole discretion of the (unelected) Dulles brothers. Perhaps even their father (a Presbyterian minister) would have objected.

Article I, Section 8, Clause 1: *The Congress shall have Power To lay and collect Taxes, Duties, Imposts and Excises, to pay the Debts and provide for the common Defence and general Welfare of the United States; but all Duties, Imposts and Excises shall be uniform throughout the United States….*

595 Home | Sullivan & Cromwell LLP (https://www.sullcrom.com). They are located in New York City. "Sullivan & Cromwell LLP is an American multinational law firm headquartered in New York City. Founded in 1879 by Algernon Sydney Sullivan and William Nelson Cromwell, the firm advised on the creation of Edison General Electric and the formation of U.S. Steel:" Sullivan & Cromwell - Wikipedia.

Ironically, Dietrich Bonhoeffer studied in New York City (at Union Theological Seminary) during 1930-1931, so behold a trifecta – Bonhoeffer, Schroder's Bank, and Sullivan & Cromwell were all in New York City at the same time! Furthermore, Bonhoeffer was also in the US during June 1939, by invitation from the Union Theological Seminary. After titanic inner turmoil, he soon regretted his decision and returned to Germany after only two weeks in New York (thus sealing his death).

596 "Why Did Trump Buckle With CIA Appointment?" - LewRockwell (https://www.lewrockwell.com/2024/12/jacob-hornberger/why-did-trump-buckle-with-cia-appointment/).

that *counterfeit money was being produced by the United States '**intelligence community**'* [emphasis added].[597] Here is one example.

> One operation ... regards the so called "Superbills," or "Supernotes" sting. Years earlier, in the late sixties or early seventies, *the CIA had secretly provided to the Shah of Iran a perfect set of printing plates that could reproduce US$100 bills **without blemish*** [emphasis added]. Also provided was an intaglio printing press. This special printing press ensures that the etched plate meets paper with tremendous force, creating the distinctive embossed feel of a genuine banknote. *In addition, the Shah was also given the ink and banknote quality paper enabling him to produce perfect counterfeit US Dollar banknotes. The Shah later fled Iran and left the plates and press behind in his confusion.* The whole caboodle sat in the mint at Tehran, according to some experts.

According to British Foreign Office files, as reported by Professor Richard Aldrich of Nottingham University, there is a precedent for this; during WW II, the CIA had judiciously re-located their printing plates for Chinese currency.[598]

Then in 1948, four US Air Force planes crashed into the mountains of Mindanao. Two B-29s were carrying thousands of Federal Reserve notes (American paper money); this money was inside boxes from Chase Manhattan and Wells Fargo. The boxes were sealed with wax and official stamps. The personnel wore the attire of Claire Chennault's Civil Air

597 united states - Did USA send Federal Reserve System officers to Iran to print cash for Iranian oil - Skeptics Stack Exchange (https://skeptics.stackexchange.com/questions/17960/did-usa-send-federal-reserve-system-officers-to-iran-to-print-cash-for-iranian-o) and Iraqi Banks Used U.S.-Created System to Funnel Funds to Iran - WSJ(https://www.wsj.com/politics/national-security/iraq-banks-u-s-fed-iran-financing-0c3e740c?msockid=1ee4a76cedd8652b0363b223ec5b64dc). This latter (*Wall Street Journal*) article is dated Sept. 8, 2024. Also see *The Crimes of Patriots: A True Tale of Dope, Dirty Money, and the CIA* (1987) by Jonathan Kwitny. For a cogent summary see *In Banks We Trust: Bankers and Their Close Associates: The CIA, the Mafia, Drug Traders, Dictators, Politicians, and the Vatican* (1984) by Penny Lernoux, pp. 65-76. Lernoux provides an excellent summary of the Ambrosiano-Calvi-Vatican Bank affair, including the links between Italian right-wing organizations and their South American counterparts. And here is another captivating article (from 2007) that asks about CIA culpability in printing: "US currency: Is the CIA counterfeiting US currency?" – Newslog: (https://newslog.cyber-journal.org/is-the-cia-counterfeiting-us-currency/).

598 Sterling and Peggy Seagrave, Kindle, p. 443. Aldrich was co-editor of the journal *Intelligence and National Security*; he described the strategic situation in 1948 in testimony before a British court (in 2003). Britain's Special Operations Executive (SOE) had printed and circulated massive amounts of *counterfeit* currency and bonds during the war. Aldrich explained that the CIA was only imitating British practice.

Transport (CAT), which was partly owned by the CIA. This currency was printed by the US Government at the *Bureau of Engraving and Printing in Washington, DC*. According to a source that the Seagraves interviewed, the CIA even *has* (note the present tense) a full-time office there.[599]

So, mistrust begins to creep in: if the CIA had access to perfect printing plates (which may well be true), what would stop them from printing their own perfect US currency – in order to fund their own adventures? In fact, this precise scenario was raised by Hinckle and Turner for the CIA's (currency-printing) projects in southeast Asia. If the CIA can obtain free (as well as tax-free) money, would they truly be able to resist this temptation? In view of the CIA's chronic secrecy, the full truth may never be known.

Dealey Plaza Redux: Who Supervised This Execution?

One additional point must be recognized: to succeed, the assassination had to be thoroughly professional. After all, recall that 30+ attempts on de Gaulle – during this same time period – *were all unsuccessful*, despite professional teams. In Dealey Plaza, one rule was critical – these multiple teams must not occupy the identical site. Therefore, someone must have directed each team to a specific site. John West, who has been a professional sniper, focuses on this.[600] He suggests likely shooting sites in Dealey Plaza; he also speculates (credibly) on the backgrounds of the various (four) teams.[601] He also emphasizes the critical role of signalers in Dealey Plaza. He cites the two men sitting on the curb; one had a radio while the other had an umbrella – in clear sunshine![602] As the limousine

599 Sterling and Peggy Seagrave, Kindle, pp. 443-446.

600 *Fry The Brain: The Art of Urban Sniping and its Role in Modern Guerrilla Warfare* (2015) by John West, Kindle. Gerry Hemming and John West agree on the lack of coordination between the teams. Hemming adds: *"The teams don't know who the other teams are. They don't even know they exist"* (Tatro, November 2023, p. 34). I would add this, however: some supervision must have occurred – or else two teams might have competed for the same site. Hemming stated that the targeted cities were Chicago, San Antonio, Tampa, Miami, and Dallas (Tatro, November 2023, p. 37).

601 Gerry Hemming also cites four teams, although their backgrounds differ from those of John West. Hemming claims that the teams were unaware of one another, but this does not seem quite right – someone had to keep them from occupying the same site. He also notes that silencers (from Mitch WerBell) were extensively used (Twyman, pp. 664-665). Hemming added General John McGruder and Charles Siragusa to the mix (as sponsors) Charles ran the Federal Bureau of Narcotics, which had assassination capability. He had been in the OSS, and his immediate superior was James Angleton. Hemming himself had connections; his uncle had been a business partner with John McCone (Tatro, November 2023, pp. 27-28).

602 The Cuban-appearing man may be Vidal, while his partner may be Hargraves

passed, one of them extended his arm. But he also notes an unidentified woman, who walked onto the infield grass of the central plaza as the motorcade approached Dealey Plaza from Main St. She waved a white handkerchief over her head. What common bystander would do this? Most likely, she acted as a signaler for the teams – to advise them of the motorcade's arrival at Dealey Plaza. These actions were useful, if not essential, in order to update the gunmen on JFK's status (i.e., dead or alive). They needed to decide on further shots.

This is where Lansdale comes into focus. Recall that he had retired (or had been fired) on October 31, 1963. So, he was free to take on another job during November.[603] Since it now seems likely that he was in Dealey Plaza – and a veteran event manager was required – he fits the bill rather well. His resume includes precisely this set of skills. Moreover, he had personal motives: (1) he had been denied an appointment as ambassador to Vietnam, which he strongly believed he had earned and (2) he was still angry that his good friend Diệm had been killed. Furthermore, why on earth was he walking *away* from Dealey Plaza in that photograph, i.e., walking away from all the action?

Conclusion: Everyone was Linked

Horne and Jacob Hornberger meticulously describe the perpetual war between JFK and his national security state.[604] JFK's foreign-policy goals often collided with those of the establishment – during the height of the Cold War. In the eyes of the military and also of the CIA, his policies posed a grave threat to national security. This clique viewed JFK as a traitor. Here is what is particularly powerful: soon after JFK died, both Robert McNamara and General Maxwell Taylor overtly disagreed with JFK's plans to exit Vietnam. In fact, the war later became known as "McNamara's War."[605]

(Tatro, November 2023, p. 33).

603 By Dec. 3, 1963, a mere eleven days after 11/22/1963, Gen. Edward Lansdale had a job on the White House grounds in the Food for Peace program. His office was located in the Old Executive Office Building (EOB). This is the same building where LBJ had his office as Vice President (Important book by Max Boot, "The Road Not Taken" about life of General Edward Lansdale - JFK Assassination Debate - The Education Forum) (https://educationforum.ipbhost.com/topic/29545-important-book-by-max-boot-the-road-not-taken-about-life-of-general-edward-lansdale/).

Also read *The Road Not Taken: Edward Lansdale and the American Tragedy in Vietnam* (2019) by Max Boot. Then note that LBJ resurrected Lansdale's career and gave him a much-noted Vietnam portfolio (with the rank of minister) at the US embassy during 1965-1968. Was this LBJ's *quid pro quo*, i.e., LBJ showing his appreciation for 11/22/1963?

604 *JFK's War with the National Security Establishment: Why Kennedy Was Assassinated* (2014) by Douglas Horne and Jacob Hornberger.

605 Already in early 1965, McNamara urgently argued for enlarging US involvement in Vietnam. He was supported by McGeorge Bundy and the Joint Chiefs of Staff, so the

If possible, at seeing this U-turn by both advisors, JFK would have vomited in his grave.[606] McNamara seemed to have no doubts about the war until late in 1965. But even as late as May 19, 1967 (in a memo to LBJ), McNamara was optimistic about the military side of the war – after all, Americans were killing thousands of "Charlies" every month. Robert's scheme of "body counts" was winning the day. Especially after 11/22/1963, Taylor showed his true colors – he was not the intellectual heavyweight that JFK had expected. When I first recognized this betrayal by Taylor and McNamara, an analogous literary character promptly jumped into my head (as an all-time traitor); it was Iago from Shakespeare's *Othello*.[607] Clearly, JFK was totally fenced in by aliens who utterly opposed his ideals and goals.

---

war was properly named "McNamara's War" (Goodwin, p. 364). In fact, in early 1965, one of Bob's personal aides reported *"...his fear that he might not be able to talk the president into the bombing. He spent all night preparing arguments and lining up allies"* (Goodwin, p. 375).

606 *In Retrospect: The Tragedy and Lessons of Vietnam* (1995) by Robert S. McNamara. This is his perfunctory confessional for "McNamara's War;" his book was severely criticized in the media. At the time of publication, I also wrote a detailed, crushing critique, which I only placed into my personal files. I have never published it. See "How Robert McNamara Came to Regret the War He Escalated" | *Smithsonian* (https://www.smithsonianmag.com/smart-news/why-robert-mcnamara-came-regret-war-he-escalated-180961231/). McNamara said, *"we were wrong, terribly wrong,"* and expressed his sense of guilt for what had been done: Mac Bundy Said He Was 'All Wrong' | William Pfaff | *The New York Review of Books* (https://www.nybooks.com/articles/2010/06/10/mac-bundy-said-he-was-all-wrong/).

607 Due to Othello's unique trust in him, Iago is Shakespeare's most sinister villain; despite Othello's trust, Iago then betrayed Othello. According to Dante Alighieri, betrayal is the worst sin: traitors suffer in the 9th circle of hell – A Visitor's Guide to Dante's Nine Circles of Hell | Penguin Random House (https://www.penguinrandomhouse.com/articles/a-visitors-guide-to-dantes-nine-circles-of-hell/). But the betrayal of JFK by Taylor and McNamara should have been no surprise. At the end of 1961, Taylor returned from Vietnam and promptly proposed 8000 combat troops. McNamara enthusiastically supported this proposal. Of course, JFK rejected their opinion without delay – as he also did later when these two tried again. Richard Goodwin (who worked directly with LBJ for over two years) concludes: *"The decision to transform the war would be President Johnson's decision, and his alone"* (Goodwin, pp. 372-373, 380). Even General Matthew Ridgway (see his photograph in this book), way back in 1954, had claimed, *"even if two million men were sent to Vietnam, they would be swallowed up."* Of course, from his experience in Korea, Matthew well knew the risks of an Asian war. General David M. Shoup strongly supported Ridgway. The claim that Vietnam was *"vital"* to US interests was pure *"poppycock,"* he said. In fact, the whole of southeast Asia was not *"worth a single American life...."* (Tuchman, p. 341). By 1954, the French had suffered 50,000 killed and 100,000 wounded, but the US seemed not to notice (Tuchman, p. 269). In this *June 8, 1954,* cartoon (by Daniel Fitzpatrick – this won the 1955 Pulitzer Prize), note the caption at the bottom: HOW WOULD ANOTHER MISTAKE HELP? The American gunman is gazing into a swamp.

David Talbot has concluded that "The Big Event" was ensured by "***consensus***."[608] I concur. I also agree with Peter Dale Scott:[609]

> *"...the president was murdered by a coalition of forces inside and outside the government....far too much has been written about the roles of Texas oilmen, organized crime, the Dallas police, and army intelligence without looking at the ways* ***these superficially separate elements functioned together*** [emphasis added] ... [these] *relationships of long standing [are] immune to disclosure, and capable of great crimes including serial murder."*

Even Noel Twyman concurs with this conclusion:[610]

> *I began to see the Kennedy assassination as a phenomenon that* ***arose spontaneously*** [emphasis added], culminating in a few people *out of the legions of Kennedy haters, paranoid anti-Communists, criminals, and crazies....*

In this essay, although their roles are not always clear, the appearance of unusual names – e.g., Gelli, Lemnitzer, Sindona,[611] Mickey Cohen, Trafficante, Renzo Rocca, Borghese, Louis van Hooke, Stefano Delle Chiaie, General Carlo Ciglieri, Fassoulis, and Calvi – testifies to the transnational nature

608 Review Talbot's opening quote in this essay (and note "consensus"). This was clearly *not a public consensus* – after all, JFK's public approval rating was higher than any twentieth century (or subsequent) president – and it still is. On about 11/22/1963, his approval rating was 70% (Goodwin, p. 302). Rather, it was a consensus of the elite group that held the reins of power, i.e., banking, finance, defense, oil, steel, intelligence, the military, and the right (a pun) politicians. *"Like the rich in* The Great Gatsby, *elites are not like the rest of us:"* Re-Assessing Elite-Public Gaps in Political Behavior (https://jkertzer.sites.fas.harvard.edu/Research_files/Elite-Public-Gaps-Web.pdf). As usual, bullets proved more effective than ballots.

By contrast, after LBJ's visit to Austin on November 21 [the year is unstated], a special correspondent for the *Dallas Morning News* affirmed that *"he could not find a person – man, woman, or child – who was for Lyndon Johnson"* (Haley, p. 8).

609 *Deep Politics and the Death of JFK* (1993) by Peter Dale (1993), pp. 299-301.

610 Twyman, p. 578.

611 In 1960, Michele Sindona arranged to transfer funds (likely at least one million dollars) from the Vatican Bank to Nixon's presidential campaign (*The Essential Mae Brussell: Investigations of Fascism in America* (2014) edited by Alex Constantine, Kindle). Even though JFK was a Catholic, presumably with more links to the Vatican than the Quaker Nixon, it is likely that the Vatican bank did not inform JFK of this transfer. Also see Lernoux, pp. 180, 188. Sindona had been chosen by the Gambino family to manage their heroin profits. Sindona was the son of a bankrupt farmer; he became financial advisor to Pope Paul VI in 1969. Besides embezzlement, Sindona was later also charged with murder, after which the pope said much less about his financial advisor. On March 18, 1986, Sindona was sentenced to life imprisonment, so he finally stopped embezzling and murdering. His final drink (1986) was potassium cyanide-laced coffee.

of JFK's murder.[612] University of Pittsburgh sociology professor Donald Gibson has also concluded that the murder was an *"establishment crime."*[613]

Jacqueline Lancelot totally agrees with Gerry Hemming; based on her many CIA contacts in Haiti, she recalled:[614]

> ***Everyone was connected*** [emphasis added]: *George de Mohrenschildt and Howard Burris; Haiti and Martin Marietta; Delk Simpson*[615]

612 To add even more color to this international intrigue, there is surprising evidence that Yitzhak Rabin was in Dallas during November 1963: Why Israelis Assassinated John and Robert Kennedy - Page 8 - JFK Assassination Debate - The Education Forum (https://educationforum.ipbhost.com/topic/19206-why-israelis-assassinated-john-and-robert-kennedy/page/8/). Regarding Israel, also see "From Dallas to Gaza: How JFK's Assassination Was Good for Zionist Israel" - *LA Progressive* (https://www.laprogressive.com/foreign-policy/from-dallas-to-gaza). Finally, even LBJ agreed with the international flavor of the JFK assassination. He told Walter Cronkite that an *"international conspiracy"* was at play (Ganis, p. 298). So, in the end, LBJ got it right. Also see "LBJ: Oswald Wasn't Alone" - *The Atlantic* (https://www.theatlantic.com/magazine/archive/2013/08/lbj-oswald-wasnt-alone/309486/).

Permindex is another possible international connection; it was headquartered in Basel, Switzerland. Some students regard it as a front for the CIA. Clay Shaw, head of the International Trade Mart in New Orleans, represented the US on its board of directors. In 1979, Richard Helms testified under oath that Shaw (like many traveling businessmen) had been a part-time contact of the Domestic Contact Service (DCS) of the CIA, where Shaw volunteered information from his travels abroad, mostly to Latin America. Moreover, Paul Williams reports that Permindex, as arranged by Frank Wisner of the CIA, represented a branch of Gladio that supplied arms to rebel forces in communist Hungary (Paul Williams, p. 74). We should also note that Permindex was at least partly funded by Schroder's, the bank that was closely associated with Allen Dulles and the CIA (Fred Litwin, "On the Trail of Delusion - Part Three") (https://www.kennedysandking.com/john-f-kennedy-reviews/fred-litwin-on-the-trail-of-delusion-part-three).

According to Joan Mellen (who was quoting John Whitten of the CIA), the distinction between CIA "employee" and CIA "agent" was hypothetical. Joan concludes that, far from being a "mere asset," Clay Shaw was an "operative" (*A Farewell to Justice* (2013) by Joan Mellen, p. 143). There is more. Permindex was a subsidiary of Rome-based Centro Mondiale Commercial. In 1962, Italy kicked CMC out of the country; it was viewed as a CIA front. And the Swiss government dissolved Permindex when it proved to be a conduit from the OAS for de Gaulle's attempted assassination (Hinckle and Turner, p. 257). So, when Helms minimized Clay Shaw's contribution, he was likely (once again) deliberately misleading us.

613 Talbot 2015, p. 560. Regarding the role of white-collar crime in society, see "Elite Deviance and White Collar Crime – Subcultures and Sociology" (https://oldsite-copy.haenfler.sites.grinnell.edu/elite-deviance-and-white-collar-crime/). Also see *Elite Deviance* (2018) by David Simon, a sociologist. On Amazon, the hardcover sells for $240.

614 Mellen 2012, p. 140. The Baron and friends often visited Jacqueline Lancelot's Haitian restaurant. Her wealthy father owned one of the "essential oil" factories in Haiti. Ironically, the SS code name for JFK was Lancer.

615 Burris and Simpson had served together on LBJ's inauguration parade committee (Mellen 2012, p. 142). For more on Simpson, see "A Record from Mary's Database" (https://www.maryferrell.org/php/marysdb.php?id=8787). Jim DiEugenio has also commented on Simpson: "Who Is Gus Russo?" (https://www.kennedysandking.com/

> *and the Kennedy assassination. These associations do not rise to the level of either legal or historical evidence. Mere wisps, they collide in midair and are reflected in the italicized section: speculations, they bespeak the impossible, the illogical,* ***the real*** [emphasis added].

So, here is the chief objection that typically arises to this all-embracing conspiracy: secrets cannot be kept. I have previously addressed this common myth in some detail in my essay, "The Zapruder Film Controversy."[616] That notion is clearly false – secrets can be, and often have been, kept from the public. For example, on the morning of the uranium ("Little Boy") bomb (August 6, 1945) over Hiroshima, Mrs. Leslie Groves first learned of the Manhattan Project – but her husband had directed it! One can only wonder what these two talked about in their private moments. Even Truman himself did not learn of the project until shortly after he became president – and that was after Stalin knew about it! So, did FDR imagine that he was immortal?

A contemporary issue that perfectly illustrates how secrets can be kept is the Nord Steam pipeline explosion (September 26, 2022), which is still a mystery. My informal queries in Scandinavia during 2023 were consistent with this still-clandestine history. See "Who Blew Up the Nord Stream Pipeline? Suspects and Theories."[617]

In summary, the assassination was not executed by a single individual (e.g., Oswald) nor was it triggered by a single individual (e.g., LBJ – Nelson's choice, nor Dulles – Talbot's nominee, nor Hoover – Hemming's candidate), nor was it *merely* due to an isolated and secretive, small cadre (e.g., rogue CIA officers). In the JFK literature, the latter are commonly cited. On the contrary, the JFK assassination was the *inevitable conjunction* of critical individuals (and alliances) – domestic and foreign – sometimes with disparate goals.[618] Peter Dale Scott has labelled this as "deep politics." If a single cause can be cited, it is the Cold War. Without that war, JFK might have survived his presidency – but then there would have been no Vietnam War Memorial. But so long as JFK tried to reverse the Cold War, he was a

---

john-f-kennedy-articles/who-is-gus-russo-2).

616 Fetzer 2000, pp. 377 ff.

617 https://nymag.com/intelligencer/article/who-blew-up-the-nord-stream-pipeline-suspects-and-theories.html. And https://t.co/rHjH0MmVw1 "I'm the one who ended Nord Stream 2, going to a place called" / X.

618 Gerald Patrick Hemming: *"The thing is, when you had so many people planning the Kennedy thing, it was bound to come"* (Russell 2008, p. 63). The distinction between (1) an active, cognizant participant versus (2) an active *unwitting* participant versus (3) a passive observer is often obscure. As Noel Twyman cogently observed, *"The power elite simply stood by and* ***let it happen*** [emphasis added], *looking the other way in the aftermath"* (Twyman, p. 498). I concur. This may well describe many of the names associated with this crime.

dead man. Most likely, he understood this. JFK surely knew of prior plots (after all, the SS knew and some were in the news): Chicago,[619] Tampa, and Los Angeles.[620] A replay of history would almost certainly result in the same closing chapter (i.e., murder) – even without a William King Harvey or a David Sanchez Morales. Other conspirators would merely have subsumed their roles. Of course, the other plots against JFK (with different patsies) are mere corroboration for the persistence of the plotters.[621]

HISTORY ADORES SACRIFICIAL LAMBS

President Kennedy was a-ridin' high,
Being led to the slaughter like a sacrificial lamb.
He said, "Wait a minute boys, you know who I am?"
"Of course we do, we know who you are."
Shot down like a dog in broad daylight,
We've already got somebody to take your place.
The day they blew out the brains of the king,
Thousands were watchin', no one saw a thing...[622]

---

619 *The Plot to Kill President Kennedy in Chicago and the Other Traces of Conspiracy Leading to the Assassination of JFK* (late 2024) by Vince Palamara. Especially note his enlightening final chapter: "Conclusions."

620 That very morning, JFK had said, *"Anyone perched above the crowd with a rifle could do it"* (*The Day Kennedy was Shot: An Uncensored Minute-by-Minute Account of November 22, 1963* (1968) by Jim Bishop, p. 23). Also see *Who Really Killed Kennedy* (2013) by Jerome Corsi, pp. 193 ff. And here is a useful site: "The Three Failed Plots to Kill JFK: The Historians' Guide on how to Research his Assassination – with an addendum" (https://www.kennedysandking.com/john-f-kennedy-articles/the-three-failed-plots-to-kill-jfk-the-historians-guide-on-how-to-research-his-assassination).

621 "The Three Failed Plots to Kill JFK, Part 2" (https://www.kennedysandking.com/john-f-kennedy-articles/the-three-failed-plots-to-kill-jfk-part-2).

622 Excerpted from Bob Dylan © Universal Music Publishing Company. Incidentally, Bob Dylan (born Robert Allen Zimmerman), winner of the 2016 Nobel Prize in Literature, and Vincent Bugliosi were both born and raised in Hibbing, Minnesota. But they had quite opposite views of the JFK assassination. Vince believed that RFK, but not JFK, was a victim of a conspiracy. Vince published a door-stopper sized book, *Reclaiming History: The Assassination of President John F. Kennedy* (2007). It was essentially a prosecutor's long and tedious brief, which I severely critiqued, after which Vince kept me captive on the telephone for a long while. In memory of our conversations, he once sent me an album of Italian love songs.

But we have seen this drama before – sadly all too often.[623] Socrates was killed – by a public vote – in a democratic society.[624] Julius Caesar was killed by his friend Brutus. It was not a decision Brutus made lightly. He loved Caesar, but he loved the Roman Republic more; the Roman Senate used his loyalty to convince him that this one man had to die – in order to save the republic. Just so, the American power elite of 1963 was zealously patriotic – they fervidly longed to save the American republic from a perceived traitor. The Dallas plotters merely added JFK to a long pantheon of sacrificial lambs: Jesus[625] of Nazareth (convicted by the elite of his society – the Sanhedrin),[626]

623 *"Exclusion and shunning are part of behavior patterns that have occurred again and again in various cultures throughout all recorded history as a response to deviant or abnormal behavior"* (Exclusion and shunning as legal and social sanctions - ScienceDirect) (https://www.sciencedirect.com/science/article/abs/pii/0162309586900440). But I strongly object to this narrow-minded definition; sometimes such *"exclusion and shunning"* occurs in response to exceedingly healthy behavior. For example, was Jesus eliminated (by the Sanhedrin) because he had abnormal behavior? Well, on second thought, curing leprosy was indubitably abnormal.

624 Assuming a jury of 501, Socrates was convicted by a vote of 280-221. In the end, the sentence of death was passed by a greater majority than obtained for his original conviction. Because of the past war and the plagues, the Athenians were then living in fear. They did not want to trigger the anger of their gods again because of Socrates – so they voted to sacrifice one man in order to save their city (Trial of Socrates - Wikipedia). The JFK plotters would have understood this motive – they too believed that it was their duty to sacrifice one man in order to save their society. Well, actually they sacrificed two men – JFK and Oswald (assuming we don't count Tippit).

The word "ostracism" is derived from the pottery shards (called ostraka in Greek) used as voting tokens. Broken pottery was common and so served as a kind of scrap paper. Papyrus was much more expensive (origin of the word ostracism - Search). Each year the Athenians were asked whether they wanted an ostracism hearing. If so, the citizens offered their nominees to a scribe, as many of them (i.e., the citizens) were illiterate; then the name was inscribed on a pottery shard. The winner had to vacate within ten days. After ten years, a return – without stigma – was allowed. During 487-416 BC, thirteen men were ostracized. No women qualified. The winner had to receive at least 6000 votes. In retrospect, JFK never got that many. Ostracism - Wikipedia.

625 Jesus of Nazareth: *"You do not realize that it is better for you that* ***one man dies*** [emphasis added] *for the people than that the whole nation perishes"* –John 11:50. Allen Dulles, the son of a Presbyterian minister, had already placed a quotation from Jesus in the CIA lobby; this one should have been added after 11/22/1963. Of course, we would not have known if the sacrificed man was JFK or Oswald.

In plain view of the High Priest (Annas), Jesus is about to be struck (John 18:22)

626 Hyam Maccoby concludes that the trial did not take place before the official Sanhedrin, but *"...rather before a political tribunal in which the High Priest, as representative and henchman of the Romans, presided over a court of his own minions"* (*The Mythmaker: Paul and the Invention of Christianity*, 1986, p. 36). Maccoby emphasizes that the High Priest (Joseph ben Caiaphas) was a political appointee, specifically chosen by the Romans. (In addition, the Gospel of John describes an an-

Justin Martyr,[627] Giordano Bruno (burned at the stake in 1600 via a Catholic jury),[628] Galileo (lifetime house arrest – via a Roman inquisition[629]), and even a woman, Anne Hutchinson (outlawed in 1638 – 4 years before Galileo died) – by a posse of ignorant Puritan men.[630]

Lovers of democracy should meditate on the astonishing results of a 1970s survey. At the University of Hawaii-Manoa, a poll was taken among 570 students in evening psychology classes. After a fairly detailed presentation about the (presumably global) population explosion, 90% of participants agreed that some persons are more fit to survive than others. Of these participants, 91% agreed that *"under extreme circumstances, it is entirely just to* ***eliminate those*** *judged most dangerous to the general welfare."* Finally, 29% held onto this final solution – even if their own families fell

---

tecedent encounter that night with the former high priest, Annas, who was Caiaphas's father-in-law. See the painting here.) So, the public viewed Caiaphas as a quisling; in view of this, he fretted that Jesus might arouse the rabble and that, as a consequence, Pilate might fire him (for not preserving the peace), thus leaving him bereft of his position, power, and pension.

627 Justin was tried, together with six friends, by the urban prefect Junius Rusticus. Justin was then summarily beheaded (c.162-168). The court record of the trial has been preserved, but Justin's head was not.

628 Robert Bellarmine was one of the judges at Bruno's trial. For ordering Bruno's death by burning at the stake, he could justifiably be cited for murder. On the contrary, in 1930 the Catholic Church canonized him. He was also involved in the Galileo affair. Even today, you can visit the quite active St. Robert Bellarmine Church in Burbank, California, near my daughter's home.

629 ROME, Oct. 31, 1992. *"Moving formally to rectify a wrong, Pope John Paul II acknowledged in a speech today that the Roman Catholic Church had erred in condemning Galileo 359 years ago for asserting that the Earth revolves around the Sun"* (Galileo Galilei – https://baskent.edu.tr/~tkaracay/etudio/agora/news/Galileo.html). We can only hope that the US government will not require 3-4 centuries before it admits that Oswald was not the lone assassin.

Galileo on the hot seat

As a further irony (of multitudes in this JFK case), while in Rome Bill Harvey was quartered at a villa on Janiculum Hill, where Galileo had once gazed at the heavens through his telescope! (Talbot 2015, p. 474.) See the final image in this book to view the four moons of Jupiter that Galileo identified.

Before Harvey was sacked from his position in Rome, he had been quite busy. Besides his chronic alcoholism, he pursued sex recklessly – and endlessly. A story even circulated at the CIA station that he had successfully impregnated a young secretary. Unfortunately, we have no record of his wife's response to this (Talbot 2015, p. 474). But Bill's personal life was not the only issue – he *"played a role in the brusque and successful effort to intimidate Italian democracy"* (Talbot 2015, p. 476).

630 Although I would have found her theology a bit outrageous, I cannot but admire her persistent courage in the face of Puritan men with IQs several dozen points lower than her own. Like JFK she was far ahead of her time. Anne's well-deserved statue by Cyrus Edwin Dallin at the Massachusetts State House is displayed in this book.

victim to this verdict![631] So, if democracies can ethically defend such final decisions, what defense is needed for the American elite of the 1960s when they decided (by consensus) to protect the "general welfare" – and kill JFK? Were they truly worse than the Athenians who voted to kill Socrates? Incidentally, like the American elite, the Athenian voters were also a minority – after all, most Athenian residents were slaves, who could not vote. Athens was home to an estimated 60,000–80,000 slaves during the fifth and fourth centuries BC, with each household having 3-4 slaves.[632] Furthermore, who can argue against a huge majority of 91%? In view of this stunning American survey, we should recall that an American jury cannot sentence a person to death – unless the vote is *unanimous.* In other words, we Americans (wisely) have chosen to err on the side of caution.

Giordano Bruno

Anne Hutchinson

Socrates

Justin Martyr

Galileo Galilei

A Finale

So, who gave the order? Angleton claimed that he did not know: "*A mansion has many rooms; I'm not privy to who struck John.*"[633] Perhaps this time he was (finally) honest. With his persistent focus (for years) on the Soviets, he did seem disconnected. On the other hand, we can now speculate legitimately. We know who knew whom – and how most suspects were biased. However, given the lack of documents, we shall never know who kicked off this intrigue. In any case, though, the guilty chain must contain several critical individuals. And LBJ must bless this effort somewhere along the line, so if he is missing from the mainline, he must lurk closely along the sidelines. I should also emphasize that, although I placed LBJ at the end of each chain, that is not essential. Other options exist such as Dulles, Willoughby, Lansdale, J. Edgar Hoover, H. L. Hunt and perhaps even others. My point was solely to demonstrate the nefari-

631 Philip Zimbardo (*The Lucifer Effect*, p. 285) cites his reference as J. Carlson, "Extending the Final Solution to One's Family," unpublished report, University of Hawaii, Manoa, 1974.

632 "Slavery In Ancient Greece: What Was Life Like For Enslaved People?" | HistoryExtra (https://www.historyextra.com/period/ancient-greece/slavery-ancient-greece-life-society/).

633 CIA tradecraft & JFK's assassination: *'I'm not privy to who struck John'* – JFK Facts (https://jfkfacts.org/cia-tradecraft-jfks-assassination-im-not-privy-to-who-struck-john/).

ous networks among so many of these primary team members. We could even image a circle, or possibly even a spiral.[634] I leave that exercise to my readers. The devil is not in those details.

James Jesus Angleton

"A mansion has many rooms. I'm not privy to who struck John" – *New York Times,* December 25, 1974 (20,000+ employees in 2023).

Was J. Jesus A. subliminally recalling Jesus (Christ)?

Jesus (the original) said, "In my Father's house are many mansions" (John 14:2 – another John).

Note that his boss, Allen Dulles, also liked to quote the Bible.

Motto in the CIA lobby (chosen by Dulles): *"And ye shall know the truth, and the truth shall make you free"* (John 8:32).

I wonder: Did Dulles and Angleton kneel together for prayer meetings, as Nixon and Kissinger did in the Lincoln bedroom – around the table where Lincoln had signed the Emancipation Proclamation?[1]

1 https://www.onthetrailofdelusion.com/post/does-it-matter-where-allen-dulles-was-on-november-22-1963

634 As examples (other than LBJ and Allen Dulles and J. Edgar Hoover), Rob Reiner's podcast cited Willoughby as the overall tactician. Dick Russell also claimed (in a JFK Lancer speech) that Willoughby was the mastermind. In Part One, I emphasized that Dick Russell (in his 1992 book) had cited Willoughby on *48 pages*! Rob and Dick may very well be right about Willoughby. After all, the general was often in contact with Allen Dulles and H. L. Hunt; he also knew the anti-Castro Cubans and he was fluent in Spanish and he may well have been in Dallas at the right time. He had also met with Otto Skorzeny in Madrid; recall the headline, *"Mac's Aide in Spain."* Not much is missing from this resume. Ah, but we forgot one item. The American Friends of the Anti-Bolshevik Bloc of Nations (ABN) was supported heavily by Willoughby. Next recall that Spas T. Raikin was the first person to greet Oswald when he stepped ashore in Hoboken, NJ, on June 13, 1962. Raikin was *the secretary general of the ABN!* (Twyman, pp. 570-571). Willoughby was also secretly tied to Japanese militarists, including General Shirō Ishii (Twyman, p. 573). [Ishii is scheduled to appear in my next book, *Evil is Eternal*.] In Unit 731, Ishii had engaged in criminal bacteriological warfare – on a massive scale: Shirō Ishii - Wikipedia (https://en.wikipedia.org/wiki/Shir%25C5%258D_Ishii). Ishii's crimes are also extensively discussed here: *The Real Anthony Fauci: Bill Gates, Big Pharma, and the Global War on Democracy and Public Health* (2021) by RFK, Jr. This book is so dense with details that I had to read it twice.

But also recall this: in the 1950s, Willoughby had dispatched Edward Lansdale to the Philippines, where these two men plotted against the Hukbalahaps. While there, Lansdale revealed his skills at black magic; he used "vampires" to win a protracted war against these "communist" rebels ("How the CIA Used 'Vampires' to Fight Communism in the Philippines" |HowStuffWorks, https://history.howstuffworks.com/world-history/cia-vampires-communist-rebels-philippines.htm).

Furthermore, during World War II, MacArthur had declared, *"There have been three great intelligence officers in history. Mine* [Willoughby] *is not one of them"* (*MacArthur* (2007) by Richard B. Frank). On the other hand, Paul Linebarger was especially proud of Lansdale

Here then are some possible chains. Notice that none contain Angleton, but almost all contain Allen Dulles. (By the way, why was Dulles at the "Farm" that weekend?[635] After all, he was no longer employed by the CIA; in fact, he had been fired from the CIA. What other employee – of any firm – would have had such easy access to the grounds of his former employer? Beyond that, why on earth was he on the WC at all?[636]) So, you can play with the pieces almost endlessly – and reality may lie on more than one path. You can even incorporate other characters, e. g., Lemnitzer, E. H. Hunt, Delk Simpson, Gordon McLendon, WerBell, Frank Brandstetter, William C. Bishop, William Pawley, Helms, Shackley, Colby, George Brown, Bobby Baker, Fred Black, David Phillips, and perhaps even more.

E. Cabell → C. Cabell → Allen Dulles → Lansdale → Harvey

---

for his "black mind." So, perhaps Lansdale planted the black seeds (for the JFK assassination) into the fertile mind of Willoughby, where the plan sprouted. If so, who deserves the credit? And do recall that Lansdale was asked by Senator Howard Baker (of the Church Committee) about who originated the notion of assassination; Baker specifically wanted to know *"or did someone else suggest that?"* Lansdale replied: *"I did, as far as I recall."*

But Lansdale and Charles Cabell were also good friends, so maybe they hatched the plot together. Furthermore, Lansdale and Conein often worked together – and Conein actually boasted about his long and historic connection to the Corsicans. Then there is Nelson Rockefeller, also a friend of Lansdale. Edward seemed to know all the decisive people – but Nelson Rockefeller? Nelson was Ike's representative on the Operations Coordinating Board (OCB), a committee of the National Security Council (NSC). Other members were the Undersecretary of State, the Deputy Secretary of Defense, the director of the Foreign Operations Administration, and CIA director [**Allen Dulles**]. The OCB supervised the execution of security policy and plans, **including clandestine operations** (*The Life of Nelson A. Rockefeller: Worlds to Conquer*, 1908-1958 (1996) by Cary Reich, p. 558). William Farrell (of the *NY Times*): *"Nelson is a true democrat. He has contempt for everyone."* T. H. White called him *"simply the most ruthless man in politics"* (*The Rockefellers* (1976) by Peter Collier, p. 456). In turn, Rockefeller loathed Richard Nixon and believed he was mentally unstable (Collier, p. 452). Ironically, in November 1963, Nixon and Rockefeller lived in the same Fifth Avenue apartment building!

At the conclusion of his podcast Reiner was prudent to say: *"We can't say for a certainty who killed JFK. It's impossible. We'll never know for sure."* I agree with Rob. We simply cannot document conversations preceding the final hit. But that is typical in history, so this should surprise no one. In the end, several candidates exist, and Willoughby must lie near the top, but I clearly agree with Talbot that a *"consensus"* had arisen among the power brokers. And we can mostly agree on who was on that list.

Greg Burnham (e-mail to me of January 2, 2025): *"That was the 'consensus' reached by both Prouty and Hemming separately and from very different perspectives."*

635 According to Dulles's diary, he was at the "Farm" (i.e., the CIA's Camp Peary) that day. The image of his diary is here: "*Where Was CIA Spymaster Allen Dulles on Nov. 22?*" (https://jfkfacts.substack.com/p/where-was-cia-spymaster-allen-dulles). David Talbot also notes this in his 2015 book, pages 546-547.

636 "Does it Matter Where Allen Dulles was on November 22, 1963?" (https://www.onthetrailofdelusion.com/post/does-it-matter-where-allen-dulles-was-on-november-22-1963).

LBJ → Burris → Allen Dulles → Harvey

Willoughby → Lansdale → C. Cabell → Allen Dulles → Harvey

Murchison → Allen Dulles → C. Cabell → Lansdale → Harvey

Clark → H. L. Hunt → Willoughby → Lansdale → Harvey

Conein → Helliwell → Lansdale → C. Cabell → Allen Dulles→ Harvey

LeMay → Allen Dulles → Lansdale → Harvey

J. Edgar Hoover → Sullivan → Allen Dulles → Lansdale → Harvey

Ominous clues though are the visits to the LBJ ranch that summer by Howard Burris, Sr. and Allen Dulles. Allen, in particular, was out of office and had no excuse to visit. And Burris was a military aide – so what pressing war required a special visit to the ranch? And, did Ed Clark meet LBJ during those critical summer months? But perhaps Clark's daily logs are also full of gaps, just as those of Dulles were. In any case, someone might still look for Clark's schedule.

One final comment is required. By now I have surely given the impression that every member of the elite wanted JFK dead. But that can hardly be true. Even the verdict of Socrates was not unanimous. There are known exceptions (like L. Fletcher Prouty[637]) – but others are difficult to document. In any case, here is one more – a second Otto (besides Skorzeny).

Otto Otepka once told journalist Sarah McClendon that he knew who had killed JFK. But Otto was fired in 1963 by Cold War warrior and Secretary of State Dean Rusk. While still actively investigating Oswald's security credentials for the US Department of State, Otto was illegitimately fired *just 17 days before* the JFK assassination.[638] His State Department boss (John F.

637 In 1963, Lansdale was Fletcher Prouty's boss. Prouty insists that he was sent to the South Pole by Lansdale to get him out of the way so that he would not witness the events of 11/22/1963. See Quixotic Joust: "Excerpt from Manuscript by Richard Bartholomew" – https://quixoticjoust.blogspot.com/2011/10/excerpt-from-manuscript-by-richard.html. Also see *The Secret Team* (1973) by Fletcher Prouty, pp. 114-121. Here is just one more coincidence (of myriads) in this JFK case: Prouty had once been a neighbor of both Ed Lansdale and of Howard Burris! (Twyman, pp. 539-540.)

638 "What Did Otto Otepka Know About Oswald and the CIA?" (https://www.kennedysandking.com/john-f-kennedy-articles/what-did-otto-otepka-know-about-oswald-and-the-cia) and also see *Mr. President, Mr. President!* by Sarah McClendon (1996) p. 82.

Reilly) and Reilly's colleague *committed perjury* in their testimony against Otepka. Therefore both (Reilly and his colleague) had to resign. See *Despoilers of Democracy* (1965) by investigative journalist Clark Mollenhoff and *The Ordeal of Otto Otepka* (1969) by William J. Gill. Intriguingly, Rusk did not have a good relationship with JFK, but LBJ was quite fond of him. Hmm, maybe someone should take a closer look at Dean Rusk.[639]

In other cultures and times, an insubordinate character like Otepka would risk not only his career, but actually his life. Witness these two murders: Ernst Röhm was assassinated by Hitler in 1934, and the Jew, Leon Trotsky, was assassinated (in Mexico) by Stalin in 1940 (my birth year). A complete list would occupy several books.[640]

---

639 As he recalled in his autobiography (*As I Saw It*), Rusk did not have a good relationship with JFK, who was often irritated by Rusk's reticence in advisory sessions. JFK felt that the State Department was *"like a bowl of jelly"* and that it *"never comes up with any new ideas."* In *As I Saw It*, Rusk wrote that he had repeatedly offered to resign, but his offer was never accepted. Rumors of Rusk's dismissal before the 1964 election abounded prior 11/22/1963. Shortly after that, Rusk again offered to resign. However, LBJ liked Rusk and refused his offer, so Rusk was paid a salary throughout LBJ's term.

But Rusk stands guilty of not properly advising JFK about the Bay of Pigs. His undersecretary (Chester A. Bowles) had written a forceful memorandum that opposed the CIA's plans. Rusk simply ignored it and did not send it on to the White House (Goodwin, p. 177). Someone once said of Rusk (as Rusk was rushing to the White House):

> *If you told him right now of a sure-fire way to defeat the Viet Cong and get out of Vietnam, he would groan that he was too busy to worry about that now; he had to discuss next week's bombing targets* (Goodwin, p. 390).

Rusk cherished groupthink. He deported Averill Harriman (an expert on communist intentions) to Africa; he fired Roger Hilsman, who had served as secretary to the Far East – and replaced him with Bill Bundy, who would naturally be loyal to his brother. Readers should also recall that Rusk had managed to fire Otto Otepka during his diligent pursuit of Oswald's passport. It is likewise useful to recall that Rusk had been president of the Rockefeller Foundation.

I had long wondered why McGeorge Bundy kept signing the NSAMs, instead of the Secretary of State. After all, Dean's position was at the top of the cabinet – and it required Senate confirmation. On the other hand, National Security advisor (Bundy) was merely a presidential appointee. But Dick Goodman was able to resolve that anomaly. When he protested (to Bundy) about the plot to invade the Bay of Pigs, McGeorge suggested that he speak to Rusk, whose response was telling: *"You know, Dick, maybe we've been oversold on this thing."* Dick promptly wondered who could resist if the Secretary could not (Goodman, p. 177).

So Dick had finally understood why Rusk was a survivor; Dean just said little and went with the flow. Who could object to that? But JFK did! Dick also noted that Rusk tended simply to avoid meetings that might be heated or controversial (Goodwin, pp. 177, 187). In 1963, *Newsweek* ran a cover story on McGeorge Bundy under the title "Cool Head for the Cold War" which was cited in *Our Vietnam 1954–1975* (2000), by A. J. Langguth, p. 229. The article reported that Rusk *"was not known for his force and decisiveness"* and asserted that Bundy was *"the real Secretary of State."* So, I then finally understood why Rusk did not sign those NSAMs – but also why LBJ met with McGeorge so promptly and frequently after 11/22/1963, while Rusk was not to be seen.

640 *Assassinations: The Murders That Changed History* (1975) by Charlton Wind-

We began this long essay with an opening quotation from Richard Goodwin. We finish now with an acute observation by this same Dick Goodwin. After he investigated the quiz shows of the 1960s (for congress), where virtually everyone cheated, here is what he concluded (with my highlighting from many decades ago):[641]

A young, impoverished, poorly briefed Greenwich Village poet realized, in the middle of his appearance, that he was being asked

Investigating the Quiz Shows 59

the identical questions put to him during an earlier private session with a producer. On air, watched by millions of people, he felt compelled to answer, but immediately afterward he accused the production team of fraud and angrily refused to return for his next appearance. He wanted no part of their phony quiz show. The producers were stunned. And they had a right to be. For in my entire investigation, I found no other individual who refused to participate. A man of principle, or a fool, he alone sailed against the wind. I don't even remember his name, but I owe him a debt of gratitude, living proof that at least one man could cling to moral principle amid the wonderland of fantasy and greed.

Dick Goodwin had recognized that almost everyone (everywhere throughout history) conforms to the crowd. This had already been shown in 1951 psychological experiments, i.e., it was more important to agree with other folks than to trust one's own judgment.[642] Furthermore, obedience to authority makes it almost impossible to disagree with powerful figures, as Stanley Milgram had demonstrated in that fateful year of *1963*.[643] But none of this is new; two millennia ago, Jesus had already understood:

---

sor and *Assassination: Twenty Assassinations That Changed History* (1993) by Lee Davis. A useful reference manual is here: *The Handbook of Assassination* - PDFCOFFEE.COM (https://pdfcoffee.com/the-handbook-of-assassination-pdf-free.html).

641 "Investigating the Quiz Shows," *Remembering America: A Voice from the Sixties* (1988) by Richard Goodwin, pp. 58-59. Also see his chapter 21, "Descent," which describes his firsthand observations (with Bill Moyers) of LBJ's descent into *"paranoid disintegration."* Curiously, he does not tell us what he told his wife (Doris Kearns Goodwin) about LBJ's near reprise of *King Lear*. (They married in 1975, almost 3 years after LBJ had died; she published her biography of LBJ in 2015.)

642 "Solomon Asch Conformity Line Experiment Study" – https://www.simplypsychology.org/asch-conformity.html).

643 Milgram Shock Experiment | Summary | Results | Ethics (https://www.simplypsychology.org/milgram.html).

> *Enter ye in at the strait gate: for wide is the gate, and broad is the way that leadeth to destruction, for many blindly wander in through the wrong gate. The straightaway is narrow, and it leads to life, but few know how to use their* [ethical] *GPS.*
>
> –Matthew 7:13-14 [Mantik 2025 version].

Since Allen Dulles (superficially) enjoyed Bible verses, I shall (contemptuously) follow his "enlightened" example here. Even Michael Corleone would have agreed with this sentiment.

> *What has been will be again,*
> *What has been done will be done again;*
> *There is nothing new under the sun.*[644]
>
> –Ecclesiastes 1:9 (NIV).

644 Insofar as assassinations go, even extreme opposites (e.g., Donald Trump and Leon Trotsky) would concur with this ancient wise man (or woman or intergender person).

APPENDIX II-A

ZIONISM

In this essay, I have not focused on the possible role of Zionism in the JFK assassination; it lies well outside my domain of knowledge. But curiously, several Jews are notable in this JFK case: Jack Ruby,[645] Richard Goodwin, Abe Fortas, Sam Helpern, Reuben Efron,[646] Moe Dalitz, Mickey Cohen, Bernard Weissman,[647] Mickey Herskowitz[648] and Meyer Lansky.[649] Oddly, James Jesus Angleton (not a Jew, despite his name) held Israel's portfolio for decades.[650] There is even a memorial for him in Israel.[651] Some authors have tried to draw a Mossad connection to the JFK assassination, which I still find lacking.[652] In particular, I see no operation-

645 Ruby's first lawyer, Joe Tonahill, was an old friend of LBJ. Furthermore, Barr McClellan insisted that Ed Clark was Tonahill's brother-in-law. What are the odds (of each one) of these "coincidences"?

646 "New JFK documents reveal assassin's CIA monitor was Jewish spy Reuben Efron" | *The Times of Israel* (https://www.timesofisrael.com/new-jfk-documents-reveal-assassins-cia-monitor-was-jewish-spy-reuben-efron/).

647 "Bernard Weissman" (https://spartacus-educational.com/JFKweissmanB.htm)

648 D. H. Byrd, p. vii.

649 The most striking Jewish connection is the movie, *JFK* (1991); a Jew (Arnon Milchan) produced it. Milchan's father had laid the sprinklers that made Israel bloom, so he became wealthy. Arnon and Shimon Peres (1994 Nobel Peace Prize winner and prime minister of Israel during 1984-1986) were apparently best friends. Peres was the godfather of the Israeli nuclear program, which JFK had adamantly opposed. For decades, Milchan was Israel's primary weapons procurer. In 1985, he tried to obtain the critical nuclear triggers for solid fuel rockets. Mind-bogglingly, Peres was related to Lauren Bacall, but he was in the dark until she told him: Peres: Lauren Bacall was 'not an easy woman' | *The Times of Israel* (https://www.timesofisrael.com/peres-lauren-bacall-was-not-an-easy-woman/)

J. Gary Shaw reports that *"the* U.S. News and World Report *published a short news item that former WC lawyers had met in Washington, D.C. and accumulated a $4 million war chest to counter Stone's film"* ("The Assassination of John F. Kennedy" by J. Gary Shaw in *Garrison: The Journal of History and Deep Politics*, Issue #5, August 2020, pp. 152-165).

650 "Friend, ally, savior: Revealing LBJ's Jewish ties" (https://jweekly.com/2008/11/28/friend-ally-savior-revealing-lbj-s-jewish-ties/) by J. Correspondent | November 28, 2008. During the LBJ presidency, *"the US became Israel's chief diplomatic ally and primary arms supplier."* In 1964, 90% of Jews voted for LBJ. By contrast, JFK had received only 80% of their vote.

651 "In Honor of James Angleton, Founding Father of the CIA-Mossad Alliance" (https://www.deepstateblog.org/2019/03/09/in-honor-of-james-angelton-founding-father-of-the-cia-mossad-alliance/)

652 "Israel is behind serial assassinations of Kennedy brothers": Laurent Guyenot

al level at which Jews aided the assassination. But their possible motive is easy to appreciate; JFK was adamantly opposed to their creation of a nuclear bomb. Their incentive for a bomb is also easy to understand – surrounded by millions of Muslims, they just wanted to survive.

Ben-Gurion and JFK (i.e., David and Goliath). Their meeting in May 1961 helped to clear the air but did not remove lingering American doubts and suspicions about Israel's nuclear intentions. Credit: DPA / AFP

During the spring and summer of 1963, JFK and Ben-Gurion argued fiercely (via letters) about the Dimona nuclear reactor, but JFK would not budge. In 1968, the Mossad bought 200 tons of uranium ore from a Belgian company – by pretending it was for a Milanese chemical company. But the CIA believed that Israel's first bombs derived in the mid-1960s from stolen uranium (aided by careless material accounting) from a US navy plant operated by the Nuclear Materials and Equipment Corporation. After 11/22/1963, biannual Dimona inspections did not follow JFK's strict guidelines; LBJ had consented to these relaxed changes. (See *Israel and the Bomb* (1998) by Avner Cohen.)

- *Tehran Times* (https://www.tehrantimes.com/news/454926/Israel-is-behind-serial-assassinations-of-Kennedy-brothers-Laurent).

Appendix II-B

Excerpts (slightly paraphrased) from *JFK's War with the National Security Establishment: Why Kennedy Was Assassinated* (2014) by Douglas Horne and Jacob Hornberger.

As the first week of the Cuban Missile Crisis progressed, the Joint Chiefs of Staff gravitated quickly toward air strikes on all military targets in Cuba, followed by a massive US invasion as soon as possible. Even Maxwell Taylor, JFK's favorite general, supported this position.

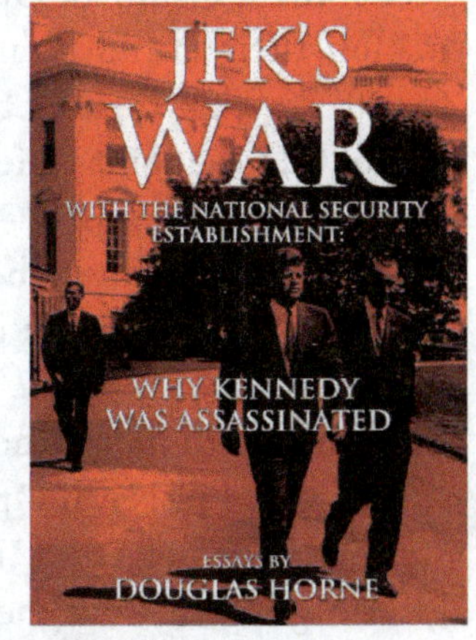

The Chiefs unanimously pressured JFK to bomb and then invade Cuba, and Air Force Chief of Staff LeMay's exchange with JFK was unusually blunt, rude, and provocative.

In his speech, JFK announced the blockade option. Just prior to his speech, he advanced DEFCON-5 to DEFCON-3.

On October 24, 1962, Thomas Powers (LeMay's hand-picked head of SAC)[653] *on his own authority,* placed all nuclear bombs and ICBMs at *DEFCON-2.* This was only one step from nuclear war. Powers *also* sent a follow-on, plain-English voice transmission (both surely monitored by the USSR) announcing the upgrade to DEFCON-2. His message began dramatically, *"This is General Powers...."* This placed 200 bombers in the air at all times.

Dino Brugioni's numbers are similar. In his book, *Eyeball to Eyeball,* Dino wrote that 1436 bombers and 134 ICBMs were placed on high alert by Thomas Powers, *on his own authority.* JFK was furious, because Powers's actions could have signaled that the US was about to launch a first strike.

653 Thomas Powers wrote Helms's biography: *The Man Who Kept the Secrets: Richard Helms and the CIA* (1979).

RFK stated that *"the President was in a grave situation and he was under strong pressure from the military to use force against Cuba. If the situation continues much longer, the President is not sure that the military will not overthrow him and seize power."*

CIA opinion, expressed to JFK, was that the warheads [in Cuba] were probably not yet present. The CIA was (again) wrong – as we now know.

When asked what he would do with Cuba, LeMay artlessly told his interlocutor, *"Fry it."*

In his book, *Eyeball to Eyeball* (1995), Dino Brugioni summarized the situation:

> *... the Joint Chiefs of Staff were unanimous during the crisis in calling for immediate military action, believing that a blockade of Cuba would be ineffective. A military attack was essential. The strike plan they advocated was a massive attack on all missile sites, all airfields, and all military camps, and invading the island.*

On the morning of October 18, 1962, as officials received new information, their attitudes hardened. McNamara called McCone (CIA director) to say that he now thought prompt and decisive action necessary. Taylor told the Joint Chiefs that the news tipped him toward supporting the maximum option[654] – a full invasion of Cuba. This then became the unanimous position of the JCS.

McNamara later said of LeMay that he [Curtis] was *"extraordinarily belligerent and even brutal."* That was a description of his relationships with his own subordinates – not with the enemy!

The Chief of Naval Operations (or "CNO"), Admiral George Anderson, had been picked by JFK's first Secretary of the Navy, John B. Connally. George was handsome and personable, with the nickname *"Gorgeous George."* Throughout his career he had bombarded his men with maxims on clean living, and had sermonized on the evils of prostitution, thus earning him a second nickname, *"Straight Arrow."*

AUTHOR'S NOTE: Ironically, Khrushchev was deposed less than a year after 11/22/1963. Like JFK's domestic opponents, the hardliners in the Kremlin also won their battle against their own peacemaker.

654 So, he was aptly named – "Max" Taylor!

Appendix II-C

Soviet Innocence on 11/22/1963[655]

According to J. Evetts Haley, at the direction of McGeorge Bundy, LBJ telephoned Khrushchev *that night* – to assure him that the US had only "*peaceful intentions*."[656] It was three hours later in Moscow. I have found no corroboration for this call, but if true, it is profoundly important. ***Help!*** That is, of course, what LBJ should have done.

The most damning evidence is the DEFCON history that weekend. According to the Joint Chiefs:[657]

> 2:50 PM EST, 11/22/1963. DEFCON: 5 → 4.
>
> 12:30 PM EST, 11/24/1963. DEFCON: 4→ 5.

Furthermore, during the flight from Dallas to Andrews that night, LBJ informed none of these:

> –National Command Center
>
> –White House Situation Room
>
> –the Joint Chiefs
>
> –Secretary of Defense.[658]

The Joint Chiefs were in a meeting when informed of the assassination. Instead of promptly dispersing to their operational or command centers, they merely stayed in their meeting for some time.[659]

> 6:20 PM EST, 11/22/1963: McNamara – on his own initiative (in the face of a potential nuclear holocaust, he was not asked to

---

655 See AARC Public Digital Library - LBJ Phone Calls - November 1963, pg (https://aarclibrary.org/publib/jfk/lbjlib/phone_calls/Nov_1963/html/LBJ-Nov-1963_0029a.htm).

656 Haley, p. 207.

657 Hancock 2006, p. 304. DEFCON 5 is the most relaxed level.

658 Ibid., p. 402.

659 Ibid., p. 304.

come!) – goes to the airport and meets LBJ, who asks: *"Any important matters pending?"*[660]

6:45 PM EST, 11/22/1963: LBJ meets with McGeorge Bundy in the Executive Office Building (EOB). The topic is not known, but this is the first of *many* prompt encounters with McGeorge.[661]

12:35 AM EST, 11/23/1963: Secretary of State Dean Rusk and the rest of the Cabinet arrive in DC.

10:30 AM EST, 11/23/1963: Hoover calls LBJ. They discuss Mexico City.[662] This is the infamous call with the 14-minute (deliberate) erasure. Rex Bradford's stimulating (and heroic) adventure is worth studying.[663]

Next LBJ meets with McNamara for 2 minutes. Then LBJ takes a call from McGeorge–for 3 minutes. After this he meets with McCone – for 4 minutes.

9:40 PM, 11/23/1963: LBJ takes his last call of the day–from the omnipresent McGeorge Bundy.[664]

10:09 AM, 11/24/1963. LBJ's first meeting of the day is with McGeorge (again!) and McCone – for up to one hour. This is an exceptionally long meeting for LBJ. And where is the Secretary of State, Dean Rusk? *"The highest-ranking cabinet member is the Secretary of State, but the most powerful member is the Secretary of Defense."*[665] So, while LBJ meets regularly – and often – with McGeorge, where is Rusk during these two critical days? Even McNamara, the Secretary of Defense, gets only *2 minutes* during this critical period – while we are (supposedly) at risk of a nuclear holocaust! Where are LBJ's priorities?

11/24/1963. According to Twyman (based on an HSCA official release), on this day John Scelso (a high-ranking CIA official) forwarded his report to Richard Helms, who then forwarded it to LBJ – Cuba and the USSR are innocent of the assassination!

660 Ibid., p. 402.
661 Ibid., p. 323.
662 Ibid., p. 324.
663 "The Fourteen Minute Gap" (https://history-matters.com/essays/frameup/FourteenMinuteGap/FourteenMinuteGap.htm).
664 Hancock 2006, p. 325.
665 whichcabinetmemberistop?-Search(https://www.bing.com/search?q=which+-cabinet+member+is+top?&qs=n&form=QBRE&sp=-1&lq=0&pq=which+cabinet+member+is+top?&sc=12-28&sk=&cvid=1E0331A216064D16BA598256AACDA00E&ghsh=0&ghacc=0&ghpl=).

> Scelso had also forwarded his report on Eugene Dinkin (see Part I in this book) to top CIA officials – *and to the ubiquitous McGeorge Bundy.*[666]

This only gets worse. On November 30, 1963, LBJ was informed by CIA director John McCone that the CIA investigation of Mexico City had shown *no evidence* of Cuban involvement.[667]

Twyman was very curious about the "crisis" atmosphere at the White House on 11/22/1963, so he interviewed Admiral Taswell Shepherd. Tas was the first military officer to meet with LBJ at the White House. *"Shepherd told me unequivocally that there was no such crisis that night.... One thing I can say for certain – when Johnson came back that night, there was no sense of an eminent* [sic] *nuclear war."* Tas knew because he had been with JFK during the Cuban Missile Crisis – which was totally different.[668]

One more LBJ-Hoover telephone call is worth noting. This is from September 18, 1964 (the Warren Report was released on September 24, 1964):[669]

> RUSSELL: *Well, it don't make much difference but they said, they believe ... the Commission believes that the same bullet that hit Kennedy hit Connally. Well, I DON'T BELIEVE IT.*
>
> *JOHNSON: I DON'T EITHER.* [Does the media report this every 11/22?]

The CIA's prior information on Oswald also rules out Soviet involvement. When George de Mohrenschildt asked about Oswald, J. Walton Moore (employed by CIA since its inception in 1947) assured the Baron that Oswald was *"safe."*[670] We can only wonder: Why didn't Angleton just ask Moore? Or maybe he should have asked his boss (John McCone),

666 Twyman, p. 810. Twyman displays the entire letter from Helms (p. 523).

667 Ibid., p. 810.

668 Twyman, pp. 499-500, 809. If Tas was correct, then LBJ's still-missing sense of a pending nuclear holocaust must have developed *after* that night, but shortly *before* he warned Earl Warren of this possible calamity. We can only wonder what new information LBJ had received about such a disaster – within an interval of just a few days. There is nothing in the record, so we can only wonder what LBJ had been smoking.

669 Lyndon Johnson, Richard Russell Phone Conversation Regarding The Warren Report : CSPAN : Free Download, Borrow, and Streaming : Internet Archive (https://archive.org/details/lyndon-johnson-richard-russell-phone-conversation-regarding-the-warren-report).

670 Russell 2008, p. 134. The Baron's services to the Haitian government had gone unrewarded and the CIA had abandoned him. So, on January 1, 1966, the Baron wrote to LBJ, reminding him that he had played along with the lone gunman scenario (Mellen 2012, pp. 255-256).

who believed in *two shooters* in Dealey Plaza. But McCone had seen the early briefing boards from the Zapruder film; we do not know if Angleton ever saw them.

The public surely did not swallow the myth of Soviet involvement. A Gallop poll in November 1963 reported that *only 1%* of Americans bought that story.[671]

Furthermore, within about a week after the fake Oswald telephone calls in Mexico City, that CIA station concluded, from its internal investigation, that these calls had not been faked by either Cuba or by the USSR. (This is the probably the same source where Twyman cites McCone, as noted just above.) But that left only a domestic source for the fakery. Did McGeorge, despite all of his face-to-face meetings with LBJ, simply forget to tell him that neither country had impersonated Oswald? Even worse, at almost the same time, LBJ had told Earl Warren that unless he agreed to chair the commission, 40 million humans would die. Did LBJ truly not remember that he had agreed to let JFK die? If so, he needed a psychiatrist then, not just before he died. Finally, if LBJ knew that it was a domestic conspiracy, why waste all this time, effort, misdirection, and money on the WC?[672] Perhaps another project would have been more productive – and less fabricated?

---

671 *Dallas Morning News*, December 6, 1963.

672 In an e-mail to me (January 9, 2025), Walt Brown advised me that the WC cost about \$6.5 million; multiply that by 32 for a current value = \$208 million.

The House Select Committee on Assassinations (HSCA) was the second major investigation of the JFK assassination, following the Warren Commission. The two-year inquiry cost \$5.8 million (https://en.wikipedia.org/wiki/United_States_House_Select_Committee_on_Assassinations).

Current value = \$5.8 x 4.8 = \$28 million.

The cost to kill one Viet Cong soldier was estimated to be \$400,000 (https://vn-agentorange.org/edmaterials/cost_of_vn_war.html). (Actually, it cost the same for *any* suspected "Charlie.") Current value (x8) = \$3.2 million per body. In other words (in comparable dollars), killing *nine* Vietnamese (of *any* color) cost as much as the entire HSCA budget! But Robert Blakey was an Uncle Scrooge – he returned some funds to congress. By contrast, Richard Sprague initially estimated the HSCA cost to be \$14 million (for that era) over two years (Tatro, November 2023, p. 93). That was more than twice as much as Blakey spent.

The US lost 5000 helicopters (and 5000 pilots) during the war: List of aircraft losses of the Vietnam War - WikipediaList of aircraft losses of the Vietnam War - Wikipedia (https://en.wikipedia.org/wiki/List_of_aircraft_losses_of_the_Vietnam_War).

During the Vietnam War, the cost of a helicopter, such as the Bell UH-1 Iroquois (Huey), varied depending on the model and purpose (https://www.civil-war.net/how-much-did-a-huey-helicopter-cost-in-1970/).

Using a modest estimate of \$300,000 each (at least \$2 million in contemporary dollars), Bell Helicopter would have made (for the entire war) \$10 billion in sales in contemporary dollars. For comparison, In the fiscal year of 2021, Bell Helicopter generated more than \$3.3 billion in revenue (https://www.statista.com/statistics/609707/reve-

As a disgraceful follow-up (to this so-called state of virginal ignorance), here is Richard Helms in congressional testimony that was declassified in 1998. Either Dick was speciously kept out of the JFK loop, or he was (once again) lying:

> QUESTION: *Can you be more specific?*
>
> ANSWER: *Yes, I can be specific. In other words,* ***the Soviet government ordered President Kennedy assassinated*** [emphasis added].[673]

---

nue-of-bell-helicopter/).

The Vietnam War cost $168 billion, or $1 trillion in today's dollars.

But that was a bargain – through fiscal year 2019: The cost of the war on terrorism is estimated to be $5.9 trillion (https://phys.org/news/2021-09-year-war-terror-trillion-dollars.html#google_vignette).

Among civilian projects, the Golden Gate Bridge cost $784 million in contemporary dollars: List of most expensive U.S. public works projects - Wikipedia. In other words, we could have traded our Vietnam War Memorial for about *214* Golden Gate Bridges.

In contemporary dollars, the Interstate Highway System would cost $642 billion. In other words, we could have traded our War on Terror for *nine* Interstate Highway Systems.

HHS's current estimate of the value per statistical (American) life is $13.1 million. With Vietnam lives valued (by Robert McNamara) at $3.2 million (in current dollars), that means that an American life (in comparable dollars) is now 4 times more valuable than a Vietnamese life was during the war: standard-ria-values.pdf (https://aspe.hhs.gov/sites/default/files/documents/cd2a1348ea0777b1aa918089e4965b8c/standard-ria-values.pdf).

673 *Legacy of Ashes* (2007) by Tim Weiner, p. 233. In direct opposition to this absurd claim by Helms, Victor Marchetti wrote, *"In the public hearings, the CIA will admit that* [E. Howard] *Hunt was involved in the conspiracy to kill Kennedy. The CIA may go so far as to admit that there were* ***three gunmen*** [emphasis added] *shooting at Kennedy"* (Talbot 2015, pp. 505-506). Marchetti had written an article for *Spotlight*, which claimed that CIA officials had decided that, if the HSCA got too close to reality, it would scapegoat Hunt and Sturgis. Unfortunately, Helms was never interrogated about this. Also see *The CIA and the Cult of Intelligence* (1974) by Victor Marchetti and John D. Marks.

The ultimate failure of the HSCA rested on the head of Robert Blakey. He had ingenuously accepted the claims of the federal agencies, a decision that later infuriated him. Of course, the HSCA was also beset by political and personal animosities. Furthermore, the relationship of its first HSCA chairman (Henry Gonzalez of Texas) to LBJ was highly suspect. In 1961, LBJ had stumped (*"without letup"*) in person for Henry in a tight race. In a remarkable *quid pro quo*, on Dember 28, 1961, Henry hunted, dined and slept overnight at the LBJ ranch. Investigative journalist, Robert Sherrill, wrote that Henry was *"as quick as any congressman to take LBJ handouts"* (*The Accidental President* (1967) by Robert Sherrill, pp. 93, 116). As for Henry, he described Richard Sprague as an *"arrogant self-serving power broker"* and *"a rattlesnake."* Based on Gaeton's family name, Henry also implied that Fonzi had *"underworld connections"* (Fonzi, pp. 184-185). Fonzi was not pleased.

Sprague had also to survive a spy who reported committee activities to Gonzalez. On September 5, 1977, the *New Orleans States-Item* published "I Was the Spy on JFK Probers." Edith Baish had made her confession in "The Sins of Robert Blakey" (https://www.kennedysandking.com/john-f-kennedy-articles/the-sins-of-robert-blakey). Gonzalez, in a solitary decision, fired Fonzi on February 10, 1977. And then all eleven committee members "countermanded" his decree. Henry waited for two weeks for congressional leadership to back him up. When they did not do so, he resigned.

Appendix II-D

Angleton's Terminal Confession[674]

Joseph Trento visited Angleton at his Arlington home in late 1985. (He died on May 11, 1987.)

> *I realize how I have wasted my entire life. I was always the skunk at the garden party, and even your friends tire of that.*

The last time I [Trento] saw James Angleton, his face, always thinner than thin, had changed little even though the cigarettes he would not give up had destroyed his lungs with cancer. The other cancer that was eating at him was the suspicion and fear that came with his job. He was a man estranged by his career from his wife and children and dying in total emotional isolation.

> *Do you know how I got to be in charge of counterintelligence? I agreed not to polygraph or require background checks on Allen Dulles and 60 of his closest friends.*[675]

Helms (who died in 2002) would have been deeply troubled by de Gaulle's polar opposite comments; they appeared in *C'était de Gaulle* (2002): C'était de Gaulle : Peyrefitte, Alain, 1925-1999 : Free Download, Borrow, and Streaming : Internet Archive (https://archive.org/details/cetaitdegaulle0000peyr): *"Better to assassinate an innocent man than to let civil war break out. Better an injustice than disorder.... They don't want to know. They don't want to find out. They won't allow themselves to find out."* Regrettably, de Gaulle's comments did not leak far from France.

674 *The Secret History of the CIA* (2001) by Joseph Trento, pp. 478-479. Notice that there is no corresponding confessional from Bill Harvey (even though he was a Lutheran by then). True to form, he kept the secrets – far better than Angleton did.

Angleton had a distinctly unconstitutional view of the CIA: *"It is inconceivable that a secret intelligence arm of the government has to comply with all the overt orders of the government."* He also stated, *"Sometimes a lie is more important than the truth"* (Mellen 2013, p. 391). One can only wonder if James Jesus had ever read Jesus' quotation in the CIA lobby (selected by Allen Dulles): *"And ye shall know the truth and the truth shall make you free"* – John 8:32. Even though Jim was liaison to the WC, he had also overlooked the motto of the WC – *Truth is the Only Client: The Official Investigation of the Murder of John F. Kennedy* (2019) - IMDb (https://www.imdb.com/title/tt12527548/).

675 Allen did not want to be asked about his collusion with Nazi party bankers during the 1930s – nor did his older brother, John Foster Dulles. Sadly, we do not know how their father (a Presbyterian minister) felt about their conviviality with Nazis. But we can predict Foster's response – after all, he was an elder in the Presbyterian church! (Kinzer 2013, Kindle, 168.) In view of that, here is the opinion of William O. Douglas: *"I'm*

His monologue would stop only for a sip of tea or a violent fit of coughing.

> *They were afraid that their own business dealings with Hitler's pals would come out. They were too arrogant to believe that the Russians would discover it all. The real problem was that there was no accountability. And without real accountability everything turned to shit. You know, the CIA got tens of thousands of brave people killed.... We played with lives as if we owned them. We gave false hope. We – I – so misjudged what happened.*
>
> *Fundamentally, the founding fathers of US intelligence were liars. The better you lied and the more you betrayed, the more likely you would be promoted. These people attracted and promoted each other. Outside of their duplicity, the only thing they had in common was a desire for absolute power.*
>
> *I did things that, in looking back on my life, I regret. But I was part of it and loved being in it. Allen Dulles, Richard Helms, Carmel Office, Frank Wisner were the grand masters. If you were in a room with them, you were in a room full of people that you had to believe would deservedly end up in hell. I guess I will be there soon. I am afraid that whatever sins I have committed in my life have now come home to roost.*
>
> *I am fundamentally a failure. I failed to protect the CIA, because there was no real desire to secure the place from the Soviets. I never understood the great advantage the Russians had over us.... As Americans we just hold no real value in secrecy. God, it was such a simple explanation."*[676]

---

not sure I want to go to heaven. I'm afraid I might meet John Foster Dulles" (Kinzer 2013, Kindle, 39). And here is what Winston Churchill thought about Foster: *"Dulles is a terrible handicap. Ten years ago I could have dealt with him. Even as it is I have not been defeated by this bastard"* (Kinzer 2013, Kindle, 152).

In 1945, a young Richard Nixon discovered documents that had been shipped to an old torpedo factory in Virginia. They confirmed that the Dulles brothers had actually *laundered Nazi funds during WW II!* (Talbot 2015, p. 162.) So, we now understand why these naughty Dulles boys preferred that Angleton not use his lie detector on them – or on their fellow Nazi aficionados.

676 During my irreverent moments I imagine the following dedicated (but now-departed) Catholics sequestered in a special corner of heaven – reserved just for Catholics. This elite (but rather motley) group includes the Diệm brothers, Madame Nhu, James Angleton, James Rowley (his brother was a priest), James Humes, JFK (and Jackie), RFK, Lawrence O'Brien, Kenny O'Donnell, Dave Powers. William Donovan, William Colby (a murder victim), Queen "Bloody" Mary, the Borgias, Charles de Gaulle, Galileo, Robert Bellarmine, Bruno, Gelli, Sindona, Calvi, William F. Buckley Jr., Joe McCarthy, Joe Kennedy, Silvio Berlusconi, Prince Borghese, Robert James McNamara (father of Robert Strange McNamara), William Casey, John McCone, Antonin Scalia, Frank Sinatra, Alfred Hitchcock, Robert Phillip Hanssen (an Opus Dei member), Doris Kearns Goodwin, Kobe Bryant, Vernon Walters, Otto Johann Anton Skorzeny, Juan Perón, Joseph Goebbels, Babe Ruth, Joe DiMaggio, Vince Lombardi, and Rocky Marciano. [The stated mission of

ANGLETON: THE FINAL SCORECARD

Indeed, he ruined his life. He never found even one mole, but he needlessly destroyed the lives of at least 14 CIA employees. According to John Newman, he was duped by two moles: Kim Philby and Bruce Solie. Helms was also likely duped, as he awarded Solie a medal for his (false) rehabilitation of Nosenko.

If Harvey had also duped him that would be #3.

Final Score: Moles 2 (or 3), Angleton 0.

Final Score: False Moles: 14, True Moles 0.

Opus Dei is to help its members seek holiness; Hanssen seems to have missed the target.]

David Morales may also be there; as a youth he had been a member of the St. Francis of Assisi choir. His funeral service was held in a Catholic church. Unfortunately, Bill Harvey will be absent. When Bill retired, he was still vastly overweight, hypertensive, with clots in his legs, more celibate than usual, and smoking three packs per day. Back home in Indiana though, he was baptized and joined a local Lutheran church. He even became a member of its governing board (*Flawed Patriot* (2006) by Bayard Stockton, p. 273). Ironically, a decade *before* that, while I was at Stanford, I had also been a Lutheran.

Meanwhile, the following, still-breathing Catholics must wait for their moment to contribute in heaven: J. D. Vance, Mike Gabbard (Tulsi's father), G. Robert Blakey, Gavin Newsom, John Boehner, Nancy Pelosi, Joe Biden, Hunter Biden (type into a search engine: *"Hunter's Chinese business associates"*), Jeb Bush, Paul Ryan, John Kerry, Marco Rubio, Melania Trump, Stephen Colbert, Mel Gibson, Martin Scorsese, Louis Freeh, Michael Moore, Brett Favre, Tom Brady, Newt Gingrich, Tim Kaine, Bobby Jindal, John Roberts, Samuel Alito, Anthony Kennedy (no JFK kin), Sonia Sotomayor and Clarence Thomas.

I would especially delight in eavesdropping as the group engages with Archbishop Carlo Maria Viganò and RFK, Jr.; both have approved of our book, *The Assassination of John F. Kennedy: THE FINAL ANALYSIS*. My co-author, Jerome Corsi, is also a Catholic. Meanwhile, I am no longer a Lutheran. After all, I could not possibly sit in the same pew as a man who almost – single handedly (actually via his private parts) – put the Roman sperm banks out of business. Or perhaps Bill had been listening for too long to LBJ, who said, *"When you have them by their private parts, their hearts and minds will follow:"* Lyndon B. Johnson's Strange Obsession With His Private Parts (https://rare.us/rare-news/lyndon-b-johnsons-weird-obsession/). But also see Source of a "hearts and minds" quote - Factual Questions - Straight Dope Message Board (https://boards.straightdope.com/t/source-of-a-hearts-and-minds-quote/412530/5). I finally discovered a second reason to leave the Lutheran church – Hitler's favorite author (another German) was Martin Luther! These two men are still among the world's foremost anti-Semites.

In any case, in their closeted corner, these everlasting Catholics can then endlessly dialogue about 11/22/1963 and other hidden histories of America – and even those of the entire world. As they survey global compartmentalized operations, they might even discover surprises among themselves. For example, William Colby might disclose how he wiretapped the Vatican; he could even expose the man who murdered him. And then Fr. Jorge Mario Bergoglio (aka Pope Francis I) can offer provocative tales about the two Jesuit priests who disappeared in Argentina (Paul Williams, p. 122).

Appendix II-E

The CIA Document on Souétre[677]

Here is the text of CIA document # 632-796:

8. Jean SOUETRE aka Michel ROUX aka Michel MERTZ—

On 5 March [1964], [Mr. Papich] of the FBI advised that the French had [hit] the Legal Attaché in Paris and also [the SDECE man] had queried the Bureau in New York City concerning subject stating that he had been expelled from the U.S. at Fort Worth or Dallas 48 hours after the assassination. He was in Fort Worth on the morning of 22 November and in Dallas in the afternoon. The French believe that he was expelled to either Mexico or Canada. In January he received mail from a dentist named Alderson living at 5803 Birmingham, Houston, Texas. Subject is believed to be identical with a Captain who is a deserter from the French Army and an activist in the OAS. The French are concerned because of de Gaulle's planned visit to Mexico. They would like to know the reason for his expulsion from the U.S. and his destination. Bureau files are negative and they are checking in Texas and with INS. They would like a check of our files with indications of what may be passed to the French. [The FBI's Mr. Papich] was given a copy of CSCI-3/776, 742 previously furnished the Bureau and CSD3-3/655, 207 together with a photograph of Captain SOUETRE.

677 This was copied from Ganis, p. 337.

Appendix II-F

Operation Northwoods

TOP SECRET SPECIAL HANDLING NOFORN

THE JOINT CHIEFS OF STAFF
WASHINGTON 25, D.C.

UNCLASSIFIED

13 March 1962

MEMORANDUM FOR THE SECRETARY OF DEFENSE

Subject: Justification for US Military Intervention in Cuba (TS)

1. The Joint Chiefs of Staff have considered the attached Memorandum for the Chief of Operations, Cuba Project, which responds to a request of that office for brief but precise description of pretexts which would provide justification for US military intervention in Cuba.

2. The Joint Chiefs of Staff recommend that the proposed memorandum be forwarded as a preliminary submission suitable for planning purposes. It is assumed that there will be similar submissions from other agencies and that these inputs will be used as a basis for developing a time-phased plan. Individual projects can then be considered on a case-by-case basis.

3. Further, it is assumed that a single agency will be given the primary responsibility for developing military and para-military aspects of the basic plan. It is recommended that this responsibility for both overt and covert military operations be assigned the Joint Chiefs of Staff.

For the Joint Chiefs of Staff:

SYSTEMATICALLY REVIEWED BY JCS ON 27 May 84 CLASSIFICATION CONTINUED

L. L. Lemnitzer

L. L. LEMNITZER
Chairman
Joint Chiefs of Staff

1 Enclosure
Memo for Chief of Operations, Cuba Project

EXCLUDED FROM GDS

EXCLUDED FROM AUTOMATIC REGRADING; DOD DIR 5200.10 DOES NOT APPLY

TOP SECRET SPECIAL HANDLING NOFORN

Here is related follow-up about the National Security Council. I have exerpted the entire comment from one site on the Education Forum.[678]

678 John Newman's commentary on Facebook - JFK Assassination Debate - The Education Forum (https://educationforum.ipbhost.com/topic/25739-john-new-

The Education Forum
John Newman's commentary on Facebook today

By Douglas Caddy. April 26, 2019 in JFK Assassination Debate
Top of Form
Posted April 26, 2019.

Note: Jim DiEugenio asked a question about this yesterday.
PART I: WHAT THE PRESIDENT DIDN'T SAY WHEN, AT THE 20 JULY 1961 NSC NET EVALUATION SUBCOMMITTE BRIEIFNG, LEMNITZER AND DULLES PRESENTED JFK WITH PLANS FOR A "SURPRISE NUCLEAR ATTACK [AGAINST THE USSR] IN LATE 1963":

According to Howard Burris' memo – the only surviving record of what happened at the meeting – *"The president directed that no member in attendance at the meeting disclose even the subject of the meeting...."* National Security Advisor McGeorge Bundy described the president's adverse reaction to the proposed surprise strike: *"He expressed his own reaction to Dean Rusk as they walked out of the cabinet room to the Oval Office for a private meeting on other subjects. "And we call ourselves the human race."*

The timing of the chiefs' proposal was not lost on the president. Kennedy was facing Soviet ultimatums on Berlin at a time when conventional U.S. military forces, by themselves, could not prevent the loss of West Berlin to East Germany. All present at the meeting understood that without the American nuclear deterrent, Berlin could not be saved.

But the crisis over Berlin wasn't all that Kennedy had on his mind during that bizarre Net Evaluation presentation. Twice, the president obliquely broached something that those present could not yet have been aware of. Burris' memo captured what else might have been on Kennedy's mind: The president asked for an appraisal of the trend in the effectiveness of the attack. General Lemnitzer replied that he would also discuss this [later personally] with the president. Because Kennedy had already been told that the best window of opportunity for such a nuclear attack against the USSR would occur in late 1963, his question about the predicted trend line betrays his interest about a time other than late 1963.

And Kennedy's next comment revealed what that period was: Since the basic assumption of this year's presentation was an attack in late 1963, the president asked about probable effects in the winter of 1962. Mr. Dulles observed that the attack would be much less

---

mans-commentary-on-facebook-today/).

effective since there would be considerably fewer missiles involved. Only the president knew what he was thinking about: how would the Cold War landscape look in late 1962? And, with the benefit of hindsight, we now know what the Kennedys had in mind. Their intention – after dealing with the flash points in Berlin, Laos, and Vietnam – was to reactivate the plan to overthrow Castro. The question was: what would Khrushchev be able to do about it?

[NEXT: WHY WAS THE ONLY RECORD OF THIS EXTRAORDINARY MEETING WRITTEN BY BURRIS? AND HOW DID HE GET ACCESS TO NSC DOCUMENT AND MEETINGS?]

–end of Newman's commentary–

Appendix II-G

Believers in a JFK Conspiracy

Lyndon Baines Johnson, President of the United States
Richard M. Nixon, President of the United States[679]
John B. Connally, Governor of Texas
J. Edgar Hoover, Director of the FBI
Clyde Tolson, Associate Director of the FBI
Cartha DeLoach, Assistant Director of the FBI
William Sullivan, FBI Domestic Intelligence Chief
John McCone, Director of CIA
David Atlee Phillips, CIA disinformation specialist, Chief of Covert Actions, Mexico City in 1963
Stanley Watson, CIA, Chief of Station
The family of JFK
Admiral George Burkley, MD, White House physician
James J. Rowley, Chief of the Secret Service

679 The following quotations are from Roger Stone (Stone, Kindle, 19-20). Nick Ruwe told me [Stone] that, on November 24, 1963, he [Ruwe] arrived at Nixon's Fifth Avenue apartment – an address he shared with Nelson Rockefeller…. It was 12:30 [PM]. Ruwe came into the room as Nixon turned the TV off. He had just witnessed Jack Ruby shoot Lee Harvey Oswald. Ruwe told me, "The Old Man [Nixon] was white as a ghost. I asked him if everything was all right." "I know that guy," Nixon muttered. Ruwe said that Nixon didn't elaborate. He [Ruwe] knew better than to ask questions. Incredibly, a US Justice Department document provided by the FBI regarding Jack Ruby's connection to Richard Nixon in the late 1940s proved Nixon's recollection was correct. [Covert History (https://coverthistory.blogspot.com/2006/12/many-researchers-believe-that-document.html). Note that the zip code was only added in 1978.]…. Ruby's service to the House Committee on Un-American Activities is not surprising. In 1950, Ruby would serve as an informant for the Kefauver Committee, a probe of organized crime. According to Luis Kutner, counsel to the committee, Ruby "briefed the Kefauver Committee about organized crime in Chicago," and his "staff learned" that Ruby was a "syndicate lieutenant." [The source for this is Lamar Waldron with Paul Heitsch, et al. *The Hidden History of the JFK Assassination: The Definitive Account of the Most Controversial Crime of the Twentieth Century* (2005), p. 486).] Stone also claims that Nixon once emphasized that although he had long sought the presidency, unlike Johnson, *"I wasn't willing to kill for it."* These matters (and others) are masterfully presented in a panoramic overview at this site: "American Pravda: JFK, LBJ, and Our Great National Shame," by Ron Unz - *The Unz Review* (https://www.unz.com/wp-content/uploads/2024/06/Ron_Unz_American_Pravda_JFK_LBJ_and_Our_Great_National_Shame.pdf).

Robert Knudsen, White House photographer (who saw autopsy photos)
Jesse Curry, Chief of Police, Dallas Police Department
Roy Kellerman (heard JFK speak after supposed magic bullet)
William Greer (the driver of the Lincoln limousine)
Abraham Bolden, Secret Service, White House detail & Chicago office
John Norris, Secret Service (worked for LBJ; researched case for decades)
Evelyn Lincoln, JFK's secretary
Richard Goodwin, speechwriter for JFK
Abraham Zapruder, famous home movie photographer
James Tague, struck by a bullet fragment in Dealey Plaza
Hugh Huggins, CIA operative, conducted private investigation for RFK
Sen. Richard Russell, member of the Warren Commission
John J. McCloy, member of the Warren Commission
Bertrand Russell, British mathematician and philosopher
Hugh Trevor-Roper, Regius Professor of Modern History at Oxford University
Michael Foot, British MP
Senator Richard Schweiker, assassinations subcommittee (Church Committee)
Tip O'Neill, Speaker of the House (he assumed JFK's congressional seat)
Rep. Henry Gonzalez (introduced bill to establish HSCA)
Rep. Don Edwards, chaired HSCA hearings (former FBI agent)
Frank Ragano, attorney for Trafficante, Marcello, Hoffa
Marty Underwood, advance man for Dallas trip[680]
Riders in follow-up car: JFK aides Kenny O'Donnell and Dave Powers
Sam Kinney, Secret Service driver of follow-up car
Paul Landis, passenger in Secret Service follow-up car
Maurice G. Marineau, Secret Service, Chicago office
John Marshall, Secret Service
John Norris, Secret Service
Bobby Hargis, Dealey Plaza motorcycle man
Mary Woodward, *Dallas Morning News* (and eyewitness in Dealey Plaza)
H. L. Hunt, right-wing oil baron
John Curington, H.L. Hunt's top aide
Bill Alexander, Assistant Dallas District Attorney
Robert Blakey, Chief Counsel for the HSCA
Robert Tanenbaum, Chief Counsel for the HSCA

680 Hancock, pp. 239-240. Also see "Vince Palamara: Secret Service-JFK Fact Sheet," and "V. Palamara: Mystery of JFK's motorcycle escort."

Richard A. Sprague, Chief Counsel for the HSCA
Gary Cornwell, Deputy Chief Counsel for the HSCA
Parkland doctors: McClelland, Crenshaw, Stewart, Seldin, Goldstrich, Zedlitz, Jones, Akin, et al.
Bethesda witnesses: virtually all the paramedical personnel[681]
All the jurors in Garrison's trial of Clay Shaw
Most of the American public
Most of the world's citizens

681 July 21, 2025. This new—and quite extraordinary—two-hour documentary confirms three casket entries into the Bethesda morgue: *The Three Casket Entries At Bethesda: Revisited*: https://youtu.be/iMl3zCOXk8s.

Appendix II-H

Howard Burris, Sr. (1918-2009)[682]

Burris had assisted in the 1953 coup in Iran against Mohammad Mosaddegh. (See *Our Man in Haiti* (2012) by Joan Mellen; view the center photograph section.) Since this coup was directed by Allen Dulles, there can be no doubt that – already *a decade before* 11/22/1963 – Allen Dulles and Burris were perennial close colleagues in covert action. Lest we forget though, we should recall that Harry Truman had *opposed* this coup; it was Ike who turned on the green light for the CIA.[683] Should the reader (mistakenly) believe that this ancient history is irrelevant to the nation of Iran today, read this: "A CIA-backed 1953 coup in Iran haunts the country with people still trying to make sense of it."[684]

The Bay of Pigs debacle was not the only Allen Dulles disgrace. As Allen later recalled, the US might have averted serious conflicts with the future USSR by complying with Vladimir Lenin's request. Lenin had telephoned, trying to meet with the American embassy on April 8, 1917, the day before he (Lenin) left Switzerland to trigger the Russian Revolution. (Dulles was too busy playing tennis that day.) On a German train (at German expense), Lenin then traveled via a locked compartment, bound for Saint Petersburg – and the world forever changed.[685]

682 "How Lyndon Johnson Expropriated Control Over the Pentagon and CIA Soon After the Inauguration of the Kennedy-Johnson Administration" (https://www.lewrockwell.com/2019/05/phillip-f-nelson/how-lyndon-johnson-expropriated-control-over-the-pentagon-and-cia-soon-after-the-inauguration-of-the-kennedy-johnson-administration/), "From My 1991 Interviews with Air Force Colonel Howard L. Burris" (https://jmnjmu.com/new-page-42/), "Newman on JFK v. Lemnitzer - The Burris Memo " (https://jfkcountercoup2.blogspot.com/2019/04/newman-on-jfk-v-lemnitzer-burris-memo.html).

683 *All the Shah's men : an American coup and the roots of Middle East terror* : Kinzer, Stephen : Free Download, Borrow, and Streaming : Internet Archive. (https://archive.org/details/allshahsmena00kinz).

684 https://apnews.com/article/iran-1953-coup-us-tensions-3d391c0255308a7c13d-32d3c88e5f54f.

685 *Gentleman Spy: The Life of Allen Dulles* (1994) by Peter Grose, p. 26.

Switzerland was special for Allen Dulles. From December 1942 until the end of WW II, he was head of US intelligence there. And there he began a long love affair and professional relationship with Mary Bancroft, who was a life-long friend of Michael Paine's parents. Michael's wife was Ruth Paine. Oswald and Roger Craig both claimed that the infamous Rambler in Dealey Plaza belonged to this forthright, fastidious Quaker (Ruth Paine), who persistently denied any connection to the CIA. Ruth Paine "forgot" to tell Oswald about another possible job; it was with Trans Texas Airways, as a cargo handler. It paid $310 per month, which was $100 more per month than his TSBD position. She also "forgot" to obtain an attorney for him after he had asked for her help. Ruth was friendly with the Baron, who clearly had CIA connections. In the 1980s, Ruth had assisted illegal anti-socialist activity in Nicaragua.[686] Furthermore, the FBI had no problem with attributing a spy camera (the Minox) to Michael Paine, who played along with this theatrical scheme.[687]

Given that Dulles already has two strikes against him for disastrous world events (the Bay of Pigs and his hapless tennis game – just when Lenin called for help), the current scene in Iran may yet become strike three for Allen. After all, he led the 1953 coup against Mosaddegh, and his covert colleague (Ted Shackley) had provided Iran with 98% bomb-grade plutonium.[688]

Of course, Allen often missed the target. After WW I, he helped to award the Sudetenland to Czechoslovakia[689] – which later served as a prelude to WW II. Then, despite his promise, he failed to support the Hungarian uprising (1956), which made Frank Wisner furious.[690] Besides his depressing efforts with Hungary and Lenin (1917) and Iran (1953) and Cuba (1961) – Allen also receives a failing grade for his dismal work in the Congo, Egypt, Indonesia, Vietnam, and Guatemala.

From Wikipedia: The Report on the Covert Activities of the Central Intelligence Agency ("The Doolittle Report") is a 69-page, formerly classified, comprehensive study of the personnel, security, adequacy, and efficacy of the CIA, written by Lieutenant General James H. Doolittle. Eisenhower had requested the report in July 1954 (shortly after he had visited

686 Salandria, p. 168.

687 For more on the culpability of the Paines, read *False Mystery* (2004) by Vincent Salandria, pp. 168-169. For even more "Painful Conclusions," read *The Other Oswald* (2019/2020) by Gary Hill, pp. 198-200.

688 See "Iran's Very Bad Year" (https://www.msn.com/en-us/news/world/irans-very-bad-year/ar-AA1vYypH?ocid=BingNewsSerp).

689 Kinzer 2013, Kindle, 30.

690 Kinzer 2013, Kindle, 274.

the Smoke Tree Ranch in Palm Springs). The report recommended that Allen Dulles be *fired,* but Ike merely ignored this sage advice.[691] In other words, after reading the Doolittle Report, Ike did little.

The Doolittle Report was right – Allen should have been fired. And Foster was little better – when Castro seized power, Foster was out of action, convalescing in Jamaica.[692] And during the Bay of Pigs, Allen was insouciantly lecturing in Puerto Rico![693] We should also recall that Allen had helped to initiate those profoundly unethical mind control experiments, whose core records were deliberately incinerated. Just read *Legacy of Ashes* by Tim Weiner.[694]

Quite poignantly, after his late 1958 global tour (while sick en route – and after visiting the World Council of Churches), Foster finally stopped at the Smoke Tree Ranch in Palm Springs,[695] just a few miles from my current home. In retrospect, Foster should have (permanently) enjoyed the delights of the desert even long before I arrived here – the world would have cheered for that. (Foster promptly died in 1959.) But an even bigger event had occurred four years earlier at the Smoke Tree Ranch. Frank Bogert, the cowboy mayor of Palm Springs, described the arrival of President Eisenhower in February 1954 as *"the biggest thing that ever happened"* in the valley. Furthermore, Ike (like Bob Hope and Frank Sinatra and Gerald Ford) did take my (belated) advice by moving to the desert, where for many years I served on the staff of the Eisenhower Medical Center. In fact, just today (March 26, 2025) I wore my Eisenhower white coat while in clinic (in Santa Fe).

Regarding Vietnam, the Dulles brothers campaign against Ho Chi Minh (1890-1969) began in 1954 in Geneva.[696] Had Foster accepted the Geneva Accords and persuaded Ike to do likewise, the US could have avoided its Vietnam debacle. Instead, Foster resisted it[697] and thereby in-

---

691 Kinzer 2013, Kindle, 187 and 214. Doolittle Report, 1954 - Wikipedia.

692 Kinzer 2013, Kindle, 286.

693 See "TIMELINE OF THE DULLES BROTHERS WHO WERE THE DEEP STATE PUPPETS OF THE BRITISH ROTHSCHILDS CRIME SYNDICATE THAT FAKED WARS & DID OVERTHROWS TO ROB HUMANITY" | Concise Politics -- Your Time should NOT be wasted (https://concisepolitics.com/2018/04/18/timeline-of-the-dulles-brothers-who-were-the-deep-state-puppets-of-the-british-rothschilds-crime-syndicate-that-faked-wars-did-overthrows-to-rob-humanity/).

694 Also see CIA activities by country - Wikipedia and cia assassinations list - Search and A SHORT HISTORY OF CIA INTERVENTION IN SIXTEEN FOREIGN COUNTRIES (https://www.cia.gov/readingroom/document/cia-rdp80-01601r000500130001-5).

695 Kinzer 2013, Kindle, 252.

696 Kinzer 2013, Kindle, 178.

697 Kinzer 2013, Kindle, 192.

vited the war to come. (Neither the US nor Hanoi nor Saigon signed.) Ho, via eight separate appeals, had written to US Secretary of State James Byrnes and also to Truman, but – of course – no one ever replied.[698] But Ho was acclimated

Ho Chi Minh (standing, third from left) and Vo Nguyen Giap (in a white suit) are shown with an OSS team in 1945.

to this – during the Versailles Conference (1919-1920), he tried to communicate with Woodrow Wilson, but he got the same silent treatment from Woodrow ("Trying to Win Wilson's Backing Against the French").[699] Ho is pictured here in 1945 – he was then working (against the Japanese) *with the OSS*, the forerunner of the CIA.

Serendipitously, Ho (like Malcolm X) had once worked in Boston at the Parker House Hotel, as a waiter (long before JFK got there). This was one of JFK's favorite restaurants (John Wilkes Booth and Charles Dickens liked it, too) – but even that did not prevent the Vietnam War. In 1953, JFK and Jackie announced their engagement at Table 40 in the Parker House; this should not be confused with Operation 40 – that came seven years later.

* * *

Burris (from Texas) had met LBJ way back in the 1930s. On May 9, 1961, LBJ was in New York when he learned that he would go to Vietnam the next day! Burris recalls: *"He heard it on the radio."* Burris reminisces:

> *I remember, I was sitting there against the wall in the NSC meeting listening to all this screaming taking place. Kennedy said he wanted Johnson to go and Johnson just refused. Kennedy said, "You're going tonight and the Foreign Service and* [McGeorge] *Bundy will brief you."* Burris recalls the next development. *"Johnson went out and just got stoned. He came back and went to sleep on his couch and finally let the Foreign Service guys in."*[700]

---

698 Kinzer 2013, 176-178; also *The March of Folly* by Barbara W. Tuchman, p. 242.
699 https://www.historynet.com/trying-to-win-wilsons-backing/.
700 This is from John Newman's interview with Burris on June 29, 1991. Newman cites this in *JFK and Vietnam* (1992), pp. 67-68.

Quite tragically, Burris also recalls, *"My feelings are that when Johnson said let's not get bogged down in that land war ... I don't think he had a really deep perception and comprehension of what the whole scene was about."* Arthur Schlesinger had also noted LBJ's lack of intellectual curiosity.[701] Dick Goodwin (in *Remembering America*) adds he rarely knew LBJ to read a book; on the other hand, JFK (like me) often devoured several books a day. LBJ's understanding of economics was also seriously questioned.[702] LBJ was clearly more interested in "private [anatomic] parts:" see an earlier footnote about this bizarre LBJ obsession. I had once protested a hit piece by Max Holland and sent a copy of my protest to Arthur Schlesinger, Jr.[703] Schlesinger – but not Holland – was kind enough to reply to me. He agreed that a personal reply from Holland would have been civilized. So, Holland – just like LBJ – suffered from a lack of intellectual curiosity.

February 25, 1961

Johnson Names Air Force Aide, Col. H. L. Burris

By the Associated Press

Vice President Johnson announced yesterday he will have a military staff.

He appointed Col. Howard L. Burris as his Air Force aide and said "aides from other services may be designated in the future."

* * *

Burris's insider status at the CIA is obvious – his close colleague, Lt. Colonel O'Wighton Delk Simpson, served on the board of the Association of Former Intelligence Officers (AFIO) – founded in 1975 by David Phillips and Gordon McLendon.[704] This creation was partly triggered by the negative publicity from movies like *The Day of the Condor* (1975) and the book, *Inside the Company: CIA Diary* (1975). Of course, Burris had also assisted Allen Dulles in the CIA plot to take out Iran's democratically elected Mosaddegh in 1953.

Incidentally, Howard A. "Skip" Burris, III, MD, is indeed the son of LBJ's military advisor: *"I was born on the Maryland side of the Potomac River and grew up on the Virginia side. My father was a career officer in the Navy...."* (ASCO President-Elect Howard A. Burris III, MD, FACP, FASCO, "Gained Leadership Skills From His Experience at West Point" - *The ASCO Post*).[705] In 1985, he graduated from the University of South Alabama College of Medicine. By the end of his military career, he had be-

701 Talbot 2015, p. 698.

702 Manchester, p. 360.

703 A copy of my protest letter appears in *Murder in Dealey Plaza* (2000), edited by James Fetzer, p. 400.

704 Mellen 2012, p. 142.

705 https://ascopost.com/issues/march-25-2019/asco-president-elect-howard-a-burris-iii-md-facp-fasco-gained-leadership-skills-from-his-experience-at-west-point/.

come a Lt. Colonel, just like his father. As a medical oncologist, he served (2019-2020) as president of the American Society of Clinical Oncology (ASCO). He said that he had gained his leadership skills from his experience at West Point, where he completed his undergraduate degree at the US Military Academy. I doubt that anyone has asked the good doctor what he knows about his father's career with LBJ. (He was only 13 on 11/22/1963.) He would surely rather discuss how he would have treated John Foster Dulles's colon cancer, which had spread to his bones.

The End is Here!

"Justice will not be served until those who are unaffected are as outraged as those who are."

Benjamin Franklin

Acknowledgments – Part Two

I am profoundly grateful for professional editors, critics, and contributors: Douglas Horne, Jeff Sundberg, Ed Tatro, Greg Burnham, Kris Millegan, and Beverly Sadowski. Roy Schaeffer is irreplaceable. His penetrating intellect, historic memory, and personal involvement are unmatched. For any residual errors, direct your arrows at me. I wear Kevlar.

And finally, as promised many pages ago, here are the four Galilean moons of Jupiter. They remind all of us to keep our minds open – the world (and even history) is never fully visible.

The four Galilean Moons of Jupiter

ACKNOWLEDGMENTS—PART TWO

POSTSCRIPT[1]

***Blind monks examining an elephant*, a ukiyo-e by the Japanese painter Hanabusa Itchō (1652–1724)**

This Japanese cartoon symbolizes the (necessarily) blinkered musings of previous pilgrims as they wandered through this convoluted JFK maze. This book has proposed a somewhat different vantage point – like a hologram it attempts a 3D reconstruction of persons and events. Another apt analogy would be the Bayeux Tapestry: just as this *English* embroidered cloth portrays (through 70 meters) the death of King (for just nine months) Harold II,[2] so my book is a memorial to the

1 *"...unmitigated arrogance is the physicist's curse"* (*The Physicists' Daughter: A Novel* (2022), by Mary Anna Evans, p. 200). Apropos, see my Ph. D. dissertation: "An X-ray scattering study of the hydration of proteins" | WorldCat.org (https://search.worldcat.org/title/An-X-ray-scattering-study-of-the-hydration-of-proteins/oclc/608736540).

2 Harold II was the ancestor (through 30+ generations) of QE II, but Harold had no royal English blood! And JFK (unlike King Arthur) had no English blood – he was only Irish. As for Jackie, she was neither royal nor English. Like William the Conqueror, she was a French import.

execution of John F. Kennedy. Or, perhaps to align with Jackie's classic taste, we should cite *Le Morte d'Arthur,* which venerated the death of King Arthur in Camelot. And just as Jackie subsequently opted for the Greek, so this book models JFK's tragedy after an earlier Greek, i.e., Socrates. However, this is still mostly an American calamity, with even Pocahontas (via the Cabell brothers) lurking in the background.

For a closing meditation, here is Noel Twyman's final (verbatim) summary, written in 1997, now almost 30 years ago. It could (almost) have been written yesterday (Twyman, p. 840):

> There is no evidence of a single arch fiend behind the plot. It was an evil idea that hatched at a lower level; then grew to where it was given the go-ahead by the ultimate sponsors at a high level. The weight of the evidence indicates that the concept of the plot was designed by the CIA's mentally unstable William Harvey, working with the fascist-racist-paranoid General Charles Willoughby. Both had experience with the Mafia in assassination plots of political leaders. And Willoughby was on the payroll of H. L. Hunt, who had a private telephone line direct to J. Edgar Hoover. Harvey could have coordinated his planning with Willoughby through Colonel William Bishop in Dallas, who was part of Harvey's ZR/RIFLE assassination program.

I must add a few comments to this. We truly do not know where the plot first appeared – or who conceived it. For example, rather than Harvey, it might have been Lansdale who first imagined "The Big Event." Recall that Lansdale (while before the Church Committee) admitted that killing Castro was *his* idea; this was apparently before anyone else had suggested it. But the plot might have arisen at a higher level than Noel had contemplated, e.g., with LBJ and Ed Clark. Or Noel could still be right, e.g., the anti-Castro Cubans might have lit the fuse. Like many schemes in history (and especially creative discoveries in science), the initial concept may well have emerged simultaneously in multiple minds. In any case, the interests of many powerful groups – and individuals – were remarkably aligned; it was a unique moment in American history. Moreover, the relevant personal relationships were long and ancient; for example, recall the Willoughby-William C. Bishop-Lansdale connection, which went way back to the WW II era. Even more suspect is the routine contact between Allen Dulles and Charles Willoughby. This specific detail gives Willoughby a resume for "The Big Event" that seems almost too perfect. But Willoughby was also connected to E. Howard Hunt, to William Pawley, and to military intelligence. Furthermore, H. L. Hunt was also very close to Willoughby; in fact, his son (Nelson Bunker Hunt) actually employed Willoughby. The general also knew the anti-Castro Cubans and he was fluent in Spanish – and he (like Lansdale) may have been in Dallas at that very moment. Furthermore, Willoughby (along with Lansdale – but few others) knew about the Golden Lily treasures.[3] Finally, he had also previously met with Otto Skorzeny[4] in Madrid; recall the headline, *"Mac's Aide in Spain."* Very little is missing from the general's resume. And then there are Hunt's billions; by himself, Hunt could have paid the entire bill.[5]

As these are likely to be my final words on this American execution, I shall indulge in a brief reverie. Although I remain in excellent health, I shall soon complete my 85th revolution around the sun, so those mythic pearly gates are now faintly visible. When I confront that Ancient of Days, I shall ask Him if any protagonists in this story have preceded me – or if, on the other hand, they punched their tickets for the wrong place. Like Rob Reiner and Dick Russell (and even Noel Twyman), I shall not be surprised to learn that Willoughby sat at the apex of this tragedy. Nor shall I be taken aback to learn that the on-site lieutenants (in Dealey Plaza) were Lansdale, Harvey and Morales – with likely assistance from Roselli and Robertson and Jenkins. If someone other than H. L. Hunt played Secretary of Treasury that day, I would be fairly astonished. On the other hand, should Dulles and Helms and Phillips and Angleton[6] prove to be

3 Recall that then-Captain Lansdale had flown to Tokyo to brief Generals MacArthur and Willoughby about this stunning (Golden Lily) discovery, and then Lansdale went on to DC to brief President Truman.

4 Twyman cites Skorzeny only once – on page 417 of his massive 909-page tome. And there it is only in a trivial fashion (i.e., Otto was a Nazi). Noel seems unaware that Bill Donovan (not the Florida basketball coach) had rescued Skorzeny from a prison camp; nor does he know about Otto's many subsequent contacts with American intelligence. From a current perspective, even more ill-omened is Noel's apparent ignorance of Operation Gladio – that name does not even appear in Noel's index. Even Talbot (2015) mentions Gladio only briefly in passing. As I persistently proclaim (as a believer in Darwin) – history just keeps evolving.

5 In 1963, H. L. Hunt's personal fortune was estimated at $16 billion; that was *four times* the visible wealth of all the Rockefellers! By comparison, in 1957 the Kennedys were only worth $¼ billion; that was only 1/64 of Hunt's wealth: https://www.bing.com/search?pglt=427&q=what+was+joe+kennedy+worth+in+1960?&cvid=3bc95c938b444f2cbeb183174f532ac8&gs_lcrp=EgRlZGdlKgYIABBFGDkyBggAEEUYOTIGCAEQABhAMgYIAhAAGEAyBggDEAAYQDIGCAQQABhAMgYIBRAAGEAyBggGEAAYQDIGCAcQABhAMgYICBAAGEDSAQkxMzI5MGowajGoAgCwAgA&FORM=ANNTA1&PC=U531.

6 April 1, 2025. After decades of research, Jefferson Morley has finally crashed into his tipping point – via three lying CIA men (with help from one woman): *"We now know that Helms, Angleton, and Joannides were responsible for, or complicit in, JFK's death,*

innocent, I shall apologize to them, but that seems most unlikely. Even if only as mostly passive (but cheering) bystanders, each one has much to account for. Then there are the complaisant members of the media and those compliant government employees – I would not be surprised to learn that most are still stuck in purgatory, silently trying to grasp their own culpability.[7]

So, it is now time for me to say farewell to the JFK assassination – and move on to my next book, *Evil is Eternal,* which has already left the starting blocks. I expect that some of these same villains will rematerialize in that book. However, they shall have new – but like-minded – accomplices from world history.

Meanwhile, everyday pleasures beckon, e.g., soaking in a hot jacuzzi under our starry desert sky (while cool breezes blow overhead), or assisting (even curing many) cancer patients, or dining with friends and family, or vacationing at Pacific Beach (or at the Oceanside Pier), but especially celebrating with our two children (Christopher, MD, and Meredith) as they mark the milestones of life. It is, after all, now time for the next generation to assume center stage for this singular event in American history.

---

either by criminal negligence or covert action" Morley-Written-Testimony.pdf (https://oversight.house.gov/wp-content/uploads/2025/04/Morley-Written-Testimony.pdf).

Also see: "Smoking Gun" Documents Point to CIA Machinations in JFK Assassination: Jefferson Morley Responds To Gerald Posner On The New CIA JFK Evidence (https://www.public.news/p/smoking-gun-documents-point-to-cia?utm_source=substack&utm_medium=email)

The following quotation is from George Joannides Personnel File (in chronological order): https://www.maryferrell.org/showDoc.html?docId=241315&utm_source=substack&utm_medium=email#relPageId=59. *"He continued in this assignment until June 1978, when he was selected to assist the Agency's senior coordinator for work with the House Select Committee on Assassinations. He was rated Outstanding for his handling of this unusual special assignment, in which he continued until his retirement on 12 January 1979."*

7 M. Scott Peck was a psychiatrist (and one of my favorite authors) who had worked with many troubled companies. He was so keenly aware of this "follow the leader" tendency of human beings that he made this claim: a survey of just a few company employees often provides major insight into the CEO himself. This Stanford business site concurs: "Follow the Leader: How a CEO's Personality Is Reflected in Their Company's Culture" | Stanford Graduate School of Business (https://www.gsb.stanford.edu/insights/follow-leader-how-ceos-personality-reflected-their-companys-culture). So, we might then ask: *Who was the CEO of the US government after 12:30 PM on 11/22/1963?*

Bibliography

NOTE: This list is strictly designed for this book. But also see my eccentric "An Uncommon Bibliography" in *THE FINAL ANALYSIS*. For a comprehensive list (through 2021), see *Honest Answers* by Vincent Palamara, pp. 389-444. Also see the sources listed by J. Gary Shaw, Danny Sheehan, George Michael Evica, Peter Kross, Stephen Kinzer, Noel Twyman, and Phillip F. Nelson. Most of these books do *not* contain bibliographies!

Abraham, Joseph N. *Kings, Conquerors, Psychopaths: From Alexander to Hitler to the Corporation,* 2020.

Adams, Don. *From an Office Building with a High-powered Rifle: A report to the public from an FBI agent involved in the official JFK assassination investigation,* 2012.

Agee, Philip. *Inside the Company: CIA Diary,* 1975.

Albarelli, H. P., Jr. *A Terrible Mistake: The Murder of Frank Olson and the CIA's Secret Cold War Experiments,* 2009.

Albarelli, H. P., Jr. *A Secret Order: Investigating the High Strangeness and Synchronicity in the JFK Assassination,* 2013.

Albarelli, H. P., Jr. with Dick Russell, Leslie Sharp, and Alan Kent. *Coup in Dallas: The Decisive Investigation into Who Killed JFK,* 2021.

Armstrong, John. *Harvey and Lee: How the CIA Framed Oswald,* 2003.

Bagley, Tennent H. *Spy Wars: Moles, Mysteries, and Deadly Games,* 2007.

Baker, Russ. *Family Secrets,* 2009.

Bamford, James. *Body of Secrets: Anatomy of the Ultra-Secret NSA,* 2001.

Barger, Robert. *The Washington pay-off: An insider's view of corruption in government,* 1972.

Bartholomew, Richard and Edgar Tatro. *The Deep State in the Heart of Texas,* 2018.

Bell, Bruce H. *My Father Killed President John F. Kennedy,* 2022.

Bird, Kai. *The Chairman: John J. McCloy and the Making of the American Establishment,* 1992.

Bird, Kai. *The Color of Truth: McGeorge Bundy and William Bundy: Brothers in Arms,* 2000.

Bishop, Jim. *The Day Kennedy was Shot: An Uncensored Minute-by-Minute Account of November 22, 1963,* 1968.

Blakey, G. Robert. *The Fatal Hour: The Assassination of President Kennedy by Organized Crime,* 1993.

Bobo, William (aka Roy Schaeffer). *The CIA Killed Camelot, Didn't They?*, 1997.

Boot, Max. *The Road Not Taken: Edward Lansdale and the American Tragedy in Vietnam*, 2019.

Brewton, Peter. *The Mafia, CIA & George Bush*, 1992.

Brown, Anthony Cave. *Treason in the Blood: H. St. John Philby, Kim Philby, and the Spy Case of the Century*, 1994.

Brown, Ray "Tex." *Broken Silence*, 1996.

Brown, Walt. *The Last Corpse*, 2023.

Brugioni, Dino. *Eyeball to Eyeball: The Inside Story of the Cuban Missile Crisis*, 1992.

Brugioni, Dino. *Photo Fakery: A History of Deception and Manipulation*, 1999.

Brussell, Mae, edited by Alex Constantine. *The Essential Mae Brussell: Investigations of Fascism in America*, 2014.

Bugliosi, Vincent. *Reclaiming History: The Assassination of President John F. Kennedy*, 2007.

Byrd, David H. *I'm an Endangered Species: The Autobiography of a Free Enterpriser*, 1978.

Caddy, Douglas. *Being There: Eyewitness to History*, 2018.

Calder, Michael. *JFK vs. CIA: The CIA's Assassination of the President*, 1998.

Caplan, Bryan. *How Evil are Politicians? Essays on Demagoguery*, 2022.

Carlisle, Rodney P. and Dominic J. Monetta. *Brandy, Our Man in Acapulco: The Life and Times of Colonel Frank M. Brandstetter*, 1999.

Caro, Robert. *The Years of Lyndon Johnson: Means of Ascent*, 1990.

Chivers, Tom. *Everything Is Predictable: How Bayesian Statistics Explain Our World*, 2024.

Cohen, Avery. *Israel and the Bomb*, 1999.

Collier, Peter and David Horowitz. *The Rockefellers: An American Dynasty*, 1976.

Colodny, Len and Robert Gettlin. *Silent Coup: The Removal of a President*, 1991.

Corn, David. *Blond Ghost: Ted Shackley and the CIA's Crusades*, 1994.

Cormier, D. Frank. *LBJ the Way He Was*, 1977.

Corsi, Jerome. *Who Really Killed Kennedy?*, 2013.

Crenshaw, Charles A. with Jens Hansen and J. Gary Shaw. *JFK: Conspiracy of Silence*, 1992.

Currey, Cecil B. *Ed Lansdale*, 1988.

Curry, Jesse. *Retired Police Chief Jesse Curry Reveals his Personal JFK Assassination File*, 1969.

Dale, Alan and Malcolm Blunt. *The Devil is in the Details*, 2020.

Dallek, Robert. *Flawed Giant: Lyndon Johnson and His Times, 1961–1973*, 1998.

Davis, Lee. *Assassination: Twenty Assassinations That Changed History*, 1993.

Denton, David. *Essays on the Assassination of President John F. Kennedy,* 2020.

De'Veritas, Raphael Luceri. *The Big Event: Kill Kennedy – Created Reality, Theater, and Puppet Mastery in the Killing of Kennedy, Tippit, and Oswald,* 2023.

DiEugenio, James and Lisa Pease. *The Assassinations: Probe Magazine on JFK, MLK, RFK, and Malcolm X,* 2002.

DiEugenio, James with Paul Bleau, Matt Crumpton, Andrew Iler, and Mark Adamczyk. *The JFK Assassination Chokeholds,* 2023.

Dobbs, Michael. *One Minute to Midnight,* 2008.

Douglas, James. *JFK and the Unspeakable: Why He Died and Why it Matters,* 2008.

DuBois, Brendan. *Resurrection Day,* 1999.

Dulles, Allen. *The Craft of Intelligence.* 1965.

Eddy, Paul. *Cocaine Wars,* 1988.

Escalante, Fabian with Mirta Muniz, et al. *The Secret War: CIA Covert Operations Against Cuba 1959-62,* 1995.

Estes, Billie Sol. *A Texas Legend: The Man Who Knows Who Shot JFK,* 2005.

Estes, Pam. *Billie Sol: King of Texas Wheeler-Dealers,* 1984.

Evica, George Michael. *A Certain Arrogance: The Sacrificing of Lee Harvey Oswald and the Cold War Manipulation of Religious Groups by US Intelligence,* 2006.

Fay, Paul B., Jr. *The Pleasure of his Company,* 1966.

Fetzer, James. *Assassination Science,* 1998.

Fetzer, James. *Murder in Dealey Plaza,* 2000.

Fetzer, James. *The Great Zapruder Film Hoax,* 2002.

Fetzer, James and Mike Palecek. *JFK: Who, How, and Why,* 2017.

Fonzi, Gaeton. *The Last Investigation,* 2013.

Ford, Gerald. *Portrait of the Assassin,* 1965.

Ford, Henry. *My Life and Work,* 1922.

Frank, Anthony. *Destroying America: The CIA's Quest to Control the Government,* 2019.

Frank, Richard B. *MacArthur,* 2009.

Freed, Donald and Mark Lane. *Executive Action,* 1973.

Furiati, Claudia and Maxine Shaw. *ZR Rifle: The Plot To Kill Kennedy and Castro, 1994.*

Ganis, Ralph and Dick Russell. *The Skorzeny Papers: Evidence for the Plot to Kill JFK,* 2018.

Ganser, Danielle. *NATO's Secret Armies: Operation Gladio and Terrorism in Western Europe,* 2005.

Garay, Ronald. *Gordon McLendon: The Maverick of Radio,* 1992.

Gelman, Joseph and Meir Doron. *CONFIDENTIAL: The Life of Secret Agent Turned Hollywood Tycoon Arnon Milchan*, 2011.

Gill, William J. The *Ordeal of Otto Otepka*, 1969.

Gladwell, Malcolm. *Revenge of the Tipping Point*, 2024.

Glennon, Michael J. *National Security and the Double Government*, 2015.

Griffith, Michael. *A Comforting Lie: The Myth that a Lone Gunman Killed President Kennedy*, 2023.

Goldstein, Gordon M. *Lessons in Disaster: McGeorge Bundy and the Path to War in Vietnam*, 2008.

Goldwater, Barry with Jack Casserly. *Goldwater*, 1988.

Goodwin, Richard N. *Remembering America: A Voice from the Sixties*, 1988.

Goodwin, Doris Kearns. *Lyndon Johnson and the American Dream*, 2015.

Goulden, Joseph & Raffio,Alexander. *The Death Merchant: The Rise and Fall of Edwin P. Wilson*, 1985.

Graff, Henry. *America: The Glorious Republic: Teacher's Annotated Edition*, 1988.

Grose, Peter. *Gentleman Spy: The Life of Allen Dulles*, 1994.

Gross, Bertram. *Friendly Fascism: The New Face of Power in America*, 1999.

Halberstam, David. *The Best and the Brightest*, 1972.

Haley, J. Evetts, *A Texan Looks at Lyndon*, 1964.

Hancock, Larry and Debra Conway. *Someone Would Have Talked*, 2006.

Hancock, Larry. *Tipping Point: The Conspiracy that Murdered President John F. Kennedy*, 2021.

Hancock, Larry and David Boylan. *The Oswald Puzzle: Reconsidering Lee Harvey Oswald*, 2025.

Hersh, Seymour. *The Dark Side of Camelot*, 1997.

Hershman, D. Jablow and Julian Lieb, MD. *Brotherhood of Tyrants: Manic Depression and Absolute Power*, 1994.

Hershman, D. Jablow. *Power Beyond Reason: The Mental Collapse of LBJ*, 2002.

Heyman, C. David. *RFK: A Candid Biography of RFK*, 1998.

Hill, Gary. *The Other Oswald: The Story of Lee Harvey Oswald and Robert E. Webster*, 2019/2020.

Hinckle, Warren and William Turner. *Deadly Secrets: The CIA-Mafia War Against Castro and the Assassination of JFK*, 1981 and 1992.

Hitchens, Christopher and Ariel Dorfman. *The Trial of Henry Kissinger*, 2012.

Hodgson, Godfrey. *JFK and LBJ: The Last Two Great Presidents*, 2015.

Holzman, Michael. *James Jesus Angleton, the CIA, and the Craft of Counterintelligence*, 2008.

Honegger, Barbara. *October Surprise*, 1989.

Hopsicker, Daniel. *Barry & 'the Boys': The CIA, the Mob, and America's Secret History*, 2016.

Hornberger, Jacob. *An Encounter with Evil: The Abraham Zapruder Story*, 2022.

Horne, Douglas. *Inside the Assassination Records Review Board: The U.S. Government's Final Attempt to Reconcile the Conflicting Medical Evidence in the Assassination of JFK* - Volumes 1-5, 2009.

Horne, Douglas and Jacob Hornberger. *JFK's War with the National Security Establishment: Why Kennedy Was Assassinated*, 2014.

Hunt, Saint John, with Eric Hamburg, et al. *Bond of Secrecy: My Life with CIA Spy and Watergate Conspirator E. Howard Hunt*, 2012.

Jackson, Gayle Nix. *Orville Nix: The Missing JFK Assassination Film*, 2014.

Jacobsen, Annie. *Surprise, Kill, Vanish: The Secret History of CIA Paramilitary Armies, Operators, and Assassins*, 2020.

Janney, Peter with Noah Michael Levine, et al. *Mary's Mosaic: The CIA Conspiracy to Murder John F. Kennedy, Mary Pinchot Meyer, and Their Vision for World Peace*, 2012.

Johnson, S. H. *My Brother Lyndon*, 1970.

Kaiser, David. *The Road to Dallas: The Assassination of John F. Kennedy*, 2008.

Kennedy, Robert F. Jr. *The Real Anthony Fauci: Bill Gates, Big Pharma, and the Global War on Democracy and Public Health*, 2021.

Kiel, R. Andrew. *J. Edgar Hoover: The Father of the Cold War*, 2000.

Kinzer, Stephen. *All the Shah's Men: An American Coup and the Roots of Middle East Terror*, 2008.

Kinzer, Stephen. *The Brothers: John Foster Dulles, Allen Dulles, and Their Secret World War*, 2013.

Knebel, Fletcher and Charles W. Bailey II. *Seven Days in May*, 1962.

Kross, Peter. *JFK: The French Connection*, 2012.

Kroth, Jerry, PhD. *The Kennedy Assassination: What Really Happened*, 2023.

Kruger, Henrik. *The Great Heroin Coup*, 1981/2016.

Krusch, Barry. *Impossible: The Case Against Lee Harvey Oswald*, 2012.

Kwitny, Jonathan. *The Crimes of Patriots: A True Tale of Dope, Dirty Money, and the CIA*, 1987.

Langguth, A. J. *Our Vietnam: the War 1954-1975*, 2000.

Lane, Mark with Mark Boyett, et al. *Last Word: My Indictment of the CIA in the Murder of JFK*, 2011.

Lavin, Gregory C. *Chasing Ed: Was Major General Edward G. Lansdale the Mastermind of the JFK Assassination?*, 2025.

Lernoux, Penny. *In Banks We Trust – Bankers and Their Close Associates: the CIA, the Mafia, Drug-Traders, Dictators, Politicians, and the Vatican*, 1984.

Levine, Michael. *The Big White Lie: The CIA and the Cocaine Crack Epidemic*, 1993.

Lifton, David S. *Best Evidence: Disguise and Deception in the Assassination of John F. Kennedy*, 1988.

Livingstone, Harrison. *The Hoax of the Century: Decoding the Forgery of the Zapruder Film*, 2004.

Maas, Peter. *Manhunt: The Dramatic Pursuit of a CIA Agent Turned Terrorist*, 1986.

Mahoney, Richard. *JFK: Ordeal in Africa*, 1983.

Manchester, William. *The Death of a President*, 1967.

Mangold, Tom. *Cold Warrior: James Jesus Angleton: The CIA's Master Spy Hunter*, 1991.

Mantik, David W. *The JFK Assassination Decoded: Criminal Forgery in the Autopsy Photographs and X-rays*, 2023.

Mantik, David W. and Jerome Corsi. *The Assassination of John F. Kennedy: THE FINAL ANALYSIS*, 2024.

Marchetti, Victor and John Marks. *The CIA and the Cult of Intelligence*, 1974.

Marshall, Jonathan with Peter Dale Scott, et al. *The Iran-Contra Connection: Secret Teams and Covert Operations in the Reagan Era*, 1987.

Martin, David C. *Wilderness of Mirrors: Intrigue, Deception, and the Secrets that Destroyed Two of the Cold War's Most Important Agents*, 1980.

Martin, David. *The Assassination of James Forrestal*, 2021.

McBride, Joe. *Into the Nightmare: My Search for the Killers of President John F. Kennedy and Officer J. D. Tippit*, 2013.

McClellan, Barr. *Blood, Money & Power: How LBJ Killed JFK*, 2003.

McCoy, Alfred. *The Politics of Heroin in Southeast Asia*, 1972.

McCoy, Alfred. *The Politics of Heroin: CIA Complicity in the Global Drug Trade*, 1991.

McKnight, Gerald. *Breach of Trust: How the Warren Commission Failed the Nation and Why*, 2005.

McNamara, Robert. *In Retrospect: The Tragedy and Lessons of Vietnam*, 1995.

Mellen, Joan. *Our Man in Haiti*, 2012.

Mellen, Joan. *A Farewell to Justice*, 2013.

Mellen, Joan. *Blood in the Water: How the US and Isreal Conspired to Ambush the USS* Liberty, 2018.

Menninger, *Bonar. Mortal Error: The Shot that Killed JFK*, 1992.

Metta, Michele. *On the Trail of Clay Shaw: The Italian Undercover CIA the Mossad Station and the Assassination of JFK*, 2018.

Milgram, Stanley. *Obedience to Authority*, 1974.

Miller, Nathan. *Stealing from America: A History of Corruption from Jamestown to Reagan,* 1992.

Mills, C. Wright. *The Power Elite,* 1956.

Mollenhoff, Clark. *Despoilers of Democracy,* 1965.

Morley, Jefferson. *Our Man in Mexico: Winston Scott and the Hidden History of the CIA,* 2008.

Morley, Jefferson. *The Ghost: The Secret Life of CIA Spymaster, James Jesus Angleton,* 2017.

Morley, Jefferson. *Scorpions' Dance: The President, the Spymaster, and Watergate,* 2022.

Morrow, Robert D. *The Senator Must Die,* 1988.

Morrow, Robert D. *First Hand Knowledge: How I Participated in the CIA-Mafia Murder of President Kennedy,* 1992.

Nelson, Phillip. *LBJ: The Mastermind of the JFK Assassination,* 2013.

Newman, John. *JFK and Vietnam: Deception, Intrigue, and the Struggle for Power,* 1992.

Newman, John. *Oswald and the CIA: The Documented Truth About the Unknown Relationship Between the U.S. Government and the Alleged Killer of JFK,* 2008.

Newman, John. *Uncovering Popov's Mole: The Assassination of President Kennedy,* 2022.

Noguchi, Thomas, MD. *Coroner,* 1983.

Noguchi, Thomas, MD. *Coroner at Large,* 1985.

North, Mark. *Betrayal in Dallas: LBJ, the Pearl Street Mafia, and the Murder of President Kennedy,* 2011.

O'Neill, Tom. *Chaos: Charles Manson, the CIA, and the Secret History of the Sixties,* 2019.

O'Sullivan, Shane. *Who Killed Bobby? The Unsolved Murder of RFK,* 2008.

Palamara, Vince. *The Plot to Kill President Kennedy in Chicago and the Other Traces of Conspiracy Leading to the Assassination of JFK,* 2024.

Paris, James L. and Robert G. Yetman, Jr. *Executive Order 11110: Did the Fed Kill JFK?,* 2013.

Peck, M. Scott. *People of the Lie: The Hope for Healing Human Evil,* 1983.

Peyrefitte, Alain. *C'était de Gaulle,* 2002.

Phillips, David Atlee. *The Night Watch,* 1977.

Phillips, David Atlee. *Secret Wars Diary: My Adventures in Combat, Espionage Operations and Covert Action,* 1989.

Polmar, Norman with John D. Gresham, et al. *DEFCON-2: Standing on the Brink of Nuclear War During the Cuban Missile Crisis,* 2006.

Poulgrain, Greg. *The Incubus of Intervention: Conflicting Indonesian Strategies of John F. Kennedy and Allen Dulles,* 2015. (Introduction by Oliver Stone. Afterword by James DiEugenio, 2020.)

Powers, Thomas. *The Man Who Kept the Secrets: Richard Helms and the CIA,* 1979.

Prouty, L. Fletcher. *JFK: The CIA, Vietnam, and the Plot to Assassinate John F. Kennedy*, 1992.

Prouty, L. Fletcher. *The Secret Team: The CIA and Its Allies in Control of the United States and the World*, 2011.

Rather, Dan. *The Camera Never Blinks: Adventures of a TV Journalist*, 1977.

Reed, Terry and John Cummings. *Compromised: Clinton, Bush and the CIA*, 1994.

Reeves, Richard. *President Kennedy: Profile of Power*, 1993.

Reich, Cary. *The Life of Nelson A. Rockefeller: Worlds to Conquer, 1908-1958*, 1996.

Rockefeller, John D. *The Autobiography of John D. Rockefeller: Random Reminiscences of Man and Events*, 2021.

Rodríguez, Félix & Weisman, John. *Shadow Warriors: The CIA Hero of a Hundred Battles*, 1989.

Rusk, Dean. *As I Saw It*, 1990.

Russell, Dick. *The Man Who Knew Too Much*, 1992.

Russell, Dick. *On the Trail of JFK Assassins*, 2008.

Russell, Dick. *The Real RFK, Jr.: Trials of a Truth Warrior*, 2023.

Salandria, Vincent. *False Mystery: Essays on the Assassination of JFK*, 2004.

Salinger, Pierre. *With Kennedy*, 1969.

Salla, Michael E. *Kennedy's Last Stand: Eisenhower, UFOs, MJ-12 & JFK's Assassination*, 2013.

Savage, Gary. *JFK: First Day Evidence*, 1993.

Schotz, E. Martin. *History Will Not Absolve Us*, 1996.

Schrecker, Ellen W. *No Ivory Tower: McCarthyism and the Universities*, 1986.

Schwimmer, George. *Doppelgänger: The Legend of Lee Harvey Oswald*, 2016.

Scott, Peter Dale and Jonathan Marshall. *Cocaine Politics: Drugs, Armies, and the CIA in Central America*, 1991.

Scott, Peter Dale. *Deep Politics and the Death of JFK*, 1993.

Scott, Peter Dale. *Oswald, Mexico, and Deep Politics: Revelations from the CIA Records on the Assassination of JFK*, 2013.

Scott, Peter Dale. *American War Machine: Deep Politics, the CIA Global Drug Connection, and the Road to Afghanistan*, 2014.

Scott, Peter Dale. *The American Deep State: Wall Street, Big Oil, and the Attack on US Democracy*, 2015.

Seagrave, Sterling and Peggy Seagrave. *Gold Warriors: America's Secret Recovery of Yamashita's Gold*, 2010.

Sheehan, Daniel. *The People's Advocate: The Life and Legal History of America's Most Fearless Public Interest Lawyer*, 2013.

Sherrill, Robert. *The Accidental President*, 1967.

Shesol, Jeff. *Mutual Contempt: LBJ, RFK, and the Feud That Defined a Decade*, 1998.

Simon, David R. *Elite Deviance*, 2008.

Simpich, Bill. *State Secret,* undated (online).

Simpson, Christopher. *Blowback: The First Full Account of America's Recruitment of Nazis and Its Disastrous Effect on The Cold War, Our Domestic and Foreign Policy,* 1989.

Smith, Joseph Burkholder. *Portrait of a Cold Warrior,* 1981.

Sneed, Larry. *No More Silence*, 1998.

Sorensen, Theodore C. *Kennedy,* 1965.

Stich, Rodney. *Defrauding America: Encyclopedia of Secret Operations by the CIA, DEA, and Other Covert Agencies,* 1992.

Stockton, Bayard. *Flawed Patriot: The Rise and Fall of CIA Legend Bill Harvey,* 2006.

Stone, Roger with Mike Colapietro. *The Man Who Killed Kennedy: The Case Against LBJ,* 2013.

Strober, Deborah H. *Let Us Begin Anew, An Oral History of the Kennedy Presidency,* 1993.

Swanson, Michael. *The War State: The Cold War Origins of the Military-Industrial Complex and the Power Elite, 1945-1963,* 2013.

Talbot, David. *Brothers: The Hidden History of the Kennedy Years,* 2007.

Talbot, David. *The Devil's Chessboard,* 2015.

Theoharis, Athan G. *A Culture of Secrecy: The Government Versus the People's Right to Know,* 1998.

Thomas, Evan. *The Very Best Men: Four Who Dared: The Early Years of the CIA,* 2006.

Thomas, Gordon. *Journey into Madness: The True Story of Secret CIA Mind Control and Medical Abuse,* 1989.

Titovets, Ernst and Paola Botan. *Oswald: Russian Episode,* 2010.

Tourney, Phillip. *What I Saw That Day: Israel's June 8, 1967, Holocaust of US Servicemen Aboard the USS* Liberty *and its Aftermath,* 2011. Buy used on Amazon at $2,995.00.

Trask, Richard B. *Pictures of the Pain: Photography and the Assassination of President Kennedy,* 1994.

Trask, Richard B. *National Nightmare on Six Feet of Film,* 2005.

Trento, Joseph John. *The Secret History of the CIA,* 1991.

Tuchman, Barbara W. *The March of Folly,* 1984.

Turner, Stansfield. *Secrecy and Democracy: the CIA in Transition,* 1985.

Twyman, Noel. *Bloody Treason: The Assassination of John F. Kennedy,* 1997.

Waldron, Lamar with Paul Heitsch, et al. *The Hidden History of the JFK Assassination: The Definitive Account of the Most Controversial Crime of the Twentieth Century,* 2005.

Wallechinsky, David and Irving Wallace. *The People's Almanac,* 1975-1981.

Weiner, Tim. *Legacy of Ashes,* 2007.

West, John. *Fry the Brain: The Art of Urban Sniping and Its Role in Modern Guerrilla Warfare,* 2008.

White, Ricky with Brian K. Edwards, et al. *Admitted Assassin: Roscoe White and the Murder of President Kennedy,* 2024.

White, Theodore. *The Making of the President 1964,* 1966.

Wiesak, Monica. *America's Last President: What the World Lost When it Lost JFK,* 2022.

Williams, Paul L. with Michael Prichard, et al. *Operation Gladio: The Unholy Alliance Between the Vatican, the CIA, and the Mafia,* 2018.

Windsor, Charlton. *Assassinations: The Murders That Changed History,* 1975.

Wise, David. *Molehunt: The Secret Search for Traitors that Shattered the CIA,* 1992.

Zelikow, Philip and Ernest May. *The Kennedy Tapes,* 2002.

Zimbardo, Philip. *The Lucifer Effect: Understanding How Good People Turn Evil,* 2007.

Zirbel, Craig I. *Texas Connection: The Assassination of President John F. Kennedy,* 1991.

About the Author

David W. Mantik, M.D., Ph.D.

In 1905, during Einstein's miraculous year, my maternal grandfather was drafted for a second time by the Russian Czar (to fight the Japanese). During his first tour of duty, he had become a decorated sharpshooter – even better than Oswald. But after this second draft, he ducked out – and so the Russians lost the war. During his escape from the Czar he and his brother-in-law, dressed as a married couple, illegally crossed the border on a train. But my grandmother, an illiterate and often barefooted peasant, did not worry about the Czar. These grandparents, like many other German-speaking Lutherans, later moved to Milwaukee. Then shortly after my mother was born (one month before JFK was born), they bought a dairy farm in the Wisconsin Northwoods. I arrived shortly before the Japanese visited Pearl Harbor, so my brother and I grew up milking cows beside a trout stream that meandered through the woods.

After attending a one-room country school, and then the local high school, I had seen enough of the farm. (See the 1953 photo above; the little girl is my sister Sharon Lewis – creator of the most widely used nursing textbook: *Lewis's Medical-Surgical Nursing.*[1]) I declined my mother's advice to attend medical school and instead opted for a PhD in physics at the University of Wisconsin-Madison. A postdoctoral fellowship in bio-

1 https://shop.elsevier.com/books/lewiss-medical-surgical-nursing/harding/978-0-323-78961-5

physics came next at Stanford University, and then a tenure-track physics post at the University of Michigan. While there I often pointed my best students to medical school, but then I finally took my own counsel – and thus met my future wife in medical school at Michigan.

After residency at the USC/Los Angeles County Medical Center I joined the faculty at Loma Linda University Medical School, and supervised the residency training program. I eventually used the newly available proton beam to treat cancers of the head & neck and prostate. I have also spent many years in private practice in Rancho Mirage/Palm Desert, CA, but then more recently (as old age arrived) I have become a peripatetic radiation oncologist. I am currently licensed in eight states and have also worked in Hawaii and New Zealand.

In my spare time I like to write about the JFK assassination. I have spent nine full days at the National Archives to view (and perform measurements on) the JFK autopsy X-rays, the autopsy photographs, JFK's clothing and the ballistic artifacts. So, we now know that the Warren Commission was not very interested in the truth, but that indifference still seems to afflict Washington, DC. (For my website: just type ***The Mantik View***.)

My hobbies are history, science, movies, sports, classical music, opera, and traveling. To further fend off old age, I now swim, or jog on the golf course (adjacent to our back deck), or visit the local gym. My wife maintains a busy medical practice (with many nonagenarians), while my daughter is an industrious film editor in Burbank. (Watch *The Burial* with Jamie Foxx and Tommy Lee Jones.) My son in Redlands is board certified in physical medicine and sees some of the most desperate patients in medicine.

Photographs

NOTE: Additional photographs are at the author's website.

Dealey Plaza – the killing field

From the movie, *JFK*

Muchmore film: with judiciously placed (and mysterious) splice

Morning – 11/22/1963 12:30 PM – 11/22/1963

When did Mary Moorman change her shoes – from black to white?

We did try to contact Mary to ask her, but were unable.

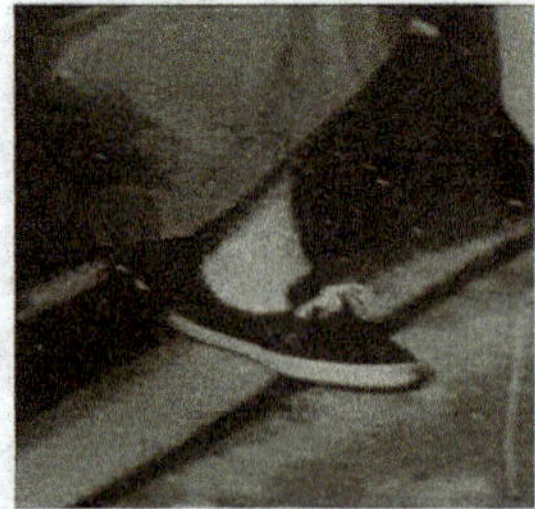

Tongue of shoe goes above instep to ankle. White laces contrast with black shoe upper. White sole. White sox.

Shoe, left foot, is same color as sox. No high tongue over instep. No shoelaces, no contrasting sole.

What Zapruder film show should look like.

Courtesy of Jack White: Moorman Revisited

(https://assassinationresearch.com/v5n2/v5n2-moorman-revisited.pdf)

Security Stripping in Dallas: no motorbikes beside the presidential limousine

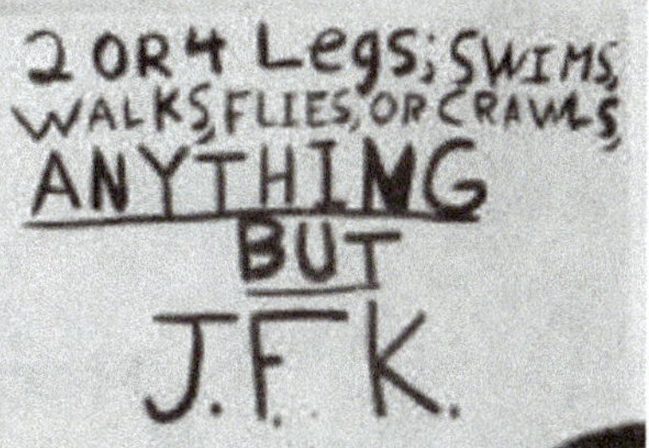

A warm Dallas welcome for JFK

Gerry Patrick Hemming and Roy M. Hargraves

The Goodwins: Dick and Doris

Edgar F. Tatro
Repository of Texas Shenanigans

Was Oswald on TIME? October 2, 1964

Pittsburgh 2023. L to R: Meredith Mantik, Mike Nurko, Mrs. Cyril Wecht, Glenda deVaney. Cyril Wecht is on the background screen, repeating his 1993 presentation.

Five Californians in Dallas + Douglas Horne

1998: Douglas Horne, David Mantik, David Lifton (seated)

Plaque at the Sixth Floor Museum

David W. Mantik's Books

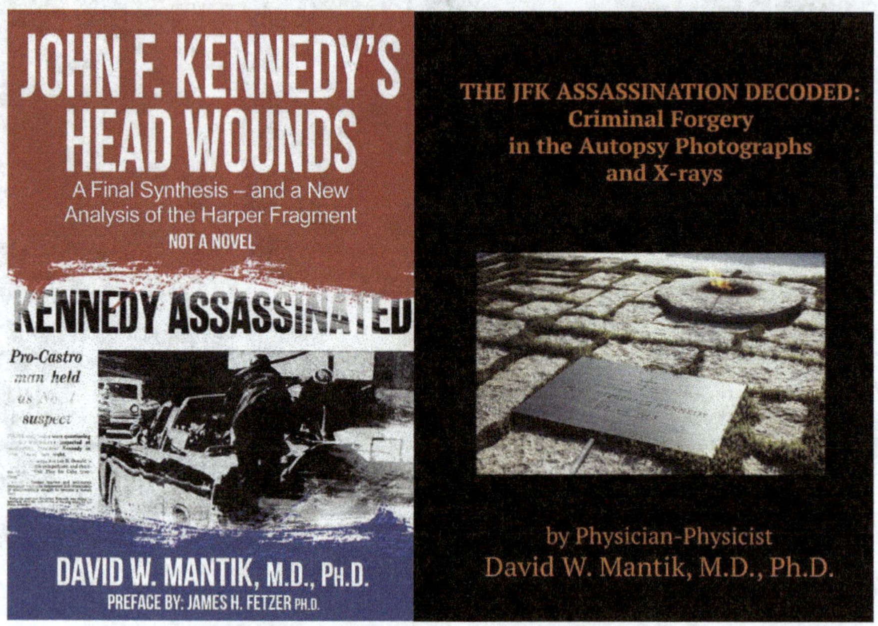

2015 2023

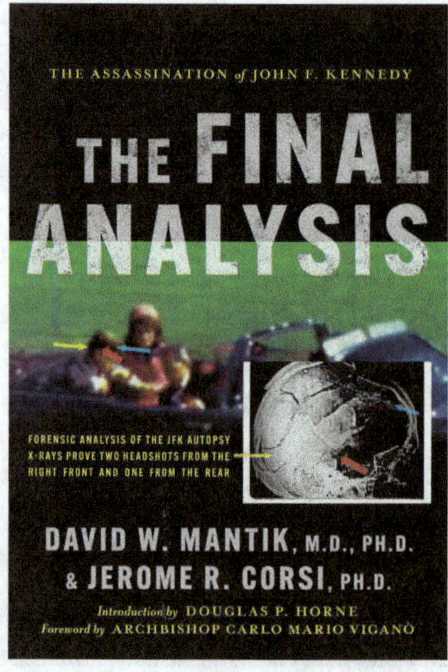

2024

David W. Mantik's Family

Our riverside farm in Wisconsin

Four generations of farmers

Brothers

Always with fish stories, my mother and her brother

Christopher at Arlington

Days of Innocence in Cabo San Lucas

A wedding for Meredith, February 22, 2025

Ever the patriot – July 4, 2024

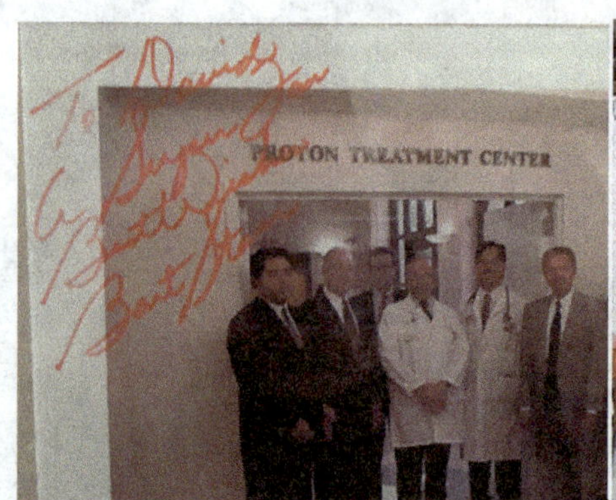

Always a Packer fan: Bart and me

In the Oval Office: a tête-à-tête

The CIA: ever-vigilant

Emil Siewert (maternal grandfather) – a sharp-shooter for the Czar

Afterword

Unique Understandings

There have been more books written about the murder of JFK than can be read in a lifetime. According to sources that keep records of these things, the number is around 1,400. This amazing figure shows the undying desire to find the truth about what happened on November 22, 1963. It shows the continued commitment that keeps many authors, scientists, investigators, researchers and regular citizens up in the wee hours searching for the answer.

After reading David Mantik's new book, I understood how important it is. If there is a fresh look at the assassination, *JFK WAS KILLED BY CONSENSUS* is that fresh look.

David Mantik has done something extraordinary. For the first time that I know of, the assassination has been explored by uncovering the many relationships of those persons that are the most likely to have been able to pull this crime off. Divided into the Mechanics and the Sponsors, Mantik deeply explores the relationships between those that are the most likely candidates to have carried out the actual shooting, and the sponsors; those that were able to put all the right people together to have JFK killed. Like a detective drama, Mantik uncovers the paper trails, the physical links, the military industrial old boy networks that ultimately brought down the 35th President of the United States. Through classified documents, personal memos, interviews and many other sources, David Mantik blows away the fog of time and offers a most incredible examination.

This is a fascinating exploration of the many persons that had the means, motive and opportunity to get the job done. Some names will be familiar and others will not. I have read many books on JFK's murder, but this book, and this book alone shows how each conspirator had a unique relationship with the different military, political and private groups that could pull off the killing of John F Kennedy.

St. John Hunt, 6/12/2025
Author of *Bond of Secrecy: My Life with CIA Spy and Watergate Conspirator E. Howard Hunt*

Index

D

F

G

H

M

S

Y

Z